D1237796

# Accounting and the Analysis of Financial Data

## McGRAW-HILL ACCOUNTING SERIES

Norton M. Bedford, *Consulting Editor*

---

*Blocker and Weltmer*—Cost Accounting

*Foulke*—Practical Financial Statement Analysis

*Henrici*—Standard Costs for Manufacturing

*Keller*—Management Accounting for Profit Control

*Jencks*—Auditing Principles

*Johnson*—Accounting Systems in Modern Business

*MacFarland, Ayars, and Stone*—Accounting Fundamentals

*March*—Cost Accounting

*Smith and Ashburne*—Financial and Administrative Accounting

*Taylor and Miller*—C.P.A. Problems and Questions in Theory and
Auditing

*Taylor and Miller*—Solutions to C.P.A. Problems

*Taylor and Miller*—Intermediate Accounting

*Walker and Davies*—Industrial Internal Auditing

Dean F. H. Elwell of the University of Wisconsin was Consulting Editor of the McGraw-Hill Accounting Series from its inception until his retirement in 1955.

# ACCOUNTING
## *and the Analysis of*
# FINANCIAL DATA

**EDISON E. EASTON** and **BYRON L. NEWTON**

*Department of Business Administration, Oregon State College*

McGRAW-HILL BOOK COMPANY, INC.

New York     Toronto     London

1958

ACCOUNTING AND THE ANALYSIS OF FINANCIAL DATA

*Library of Congress Catalog Card Number* 57-11850

III

18840

THE MAPLE PRESS COMPANY, YORK, PA.

# PREFACE

*Accounting and the Analysis of Financial Data* is intended to fill the need of nonaccountants for a comparatively brief coverage of the important principles of accounting and statement analysis. Many men in business, industry, and in the professions need a basic understanding of these principles but have limited time for such study, and many college students who have the same need are limited by their programs to a one-semester or one-term course in accounting. These individuals should have, within the limited time available, the opportunity to study more than the principles of general accounting and bookkeeping. They should also have the opportunity to become familiar with the more important principles of cost accounting, tax accounting, budgeting, and particularly the analysis and interpretation of financial statements.

The authors have attempted to include all of these principles and to emphasize the purpose of accounting and the meaning and limitations of financial statements. The text has been designed particularly for the use of students who can devote only one semester or one term to the study of accounting. It is not a condensation of the materials usually presented in a one-year text. Comparatively, it provides for the following:

1. A more rapid coverage of general accounting fundamentals
2. Less emphasis on bookkeeping procedures
3. Less emphasis on complex bookkeeping problems and the manipulation of figures (all problems and illustrations are in round numbers to simplify the arithmetic and place greater emphasis on the principles involved)
4. More emphasis on theories, principles, and conventions
5. More emphasis on cost accounting, income taxes, and budgeting, and especially
6. A great deal more emphasis on the analysis and interpretation of financial statements

The study of the accounting cycle, which is fundamental to an understanding of accounting itself, is completed in the first three chapters. Other basic fundamentals and procedures are discussed in Chapters 5, 6, and 7. Chapter 4, dealing with special journals, can be omitted if desired

v

since problem solutions in the chapters that follow are not dependent upon the use of these special recording devices. Any one of the chapters in Part II and Chapter 17 of Part III can be omitted or studied in a different sequence without impairing the continuity of the discussions. Chapters 13 to 16, on the interpretation of financial statements, should be studied in sequence. In a one-term course with lower-division students, most instructors will prefer to omit one or more chapters. In a one-semester course with upper-division students, it should be possible to cover all chapters, including a fairly wide variety of problems.

We extend thanks for the valuable suggestions and assistance of Profs. C. E. Maser, E. E. Goddard, and L. B. Strickler, who reviewed the manuscript and made many valuable suggestions for its improvement. We also wish to express our thanks to public accountants Harold C. Olsen, CPA, and C. Hoy Briggs, PA; to Mrs. L. B. Strickler for her able assistance in the preparation of the manuscript; and to Prof. A. N. Davidson, CPA, for his help in reviewing the manuscript and preparing the index. The final responsibility for the accuracy of the content and proofreading the text is accepted by the authors alone.

*Edison E. Easton*
*Byron L. Newton*

# CONTENTS

# PART 1

# FUNDAMENTALS OF ACCOUNTING

# CHAPTER 1

# BASIC CONCEPTS AND TERMINOLOGY

Business records are among the earliest known forms of writing. The histories of ancient civilizations in Asia, Africa, and Europe reveal that clay tablets were often used to record business transactions, and knotted strings were used for hundreds of years to record amounts owed by South American Indians. Most of these records, however, were used for contracts or as evidence of indebtedness and were not a part of an organized "accounting system."

The great merchant cities of Venice and Genoa probably saw the earliest development of a system of record keeping which closely resembles the methods of today. During the early part of the fifteenth century, many merchants and city governments began to feel a need for more adequate data in regard to properties owned, debts owed, sources of income, costs incurred, and profits arising out of their trading ventures. To meet these needs, various methods of record keeping were devised. By 1494 these procedures had developed into a fairly definite form, for in that year the monk Pacioli included in his *Suma de Arithmetica* a chapter describing a double-entry system of bookkeeping used in the cities of the Italian peninsula. Because of the ease with which the procedures could be learned and the checks provided by the system, it spread rapidly throughout Western civilization. A description of the system indicates that the basic principles were the same as today, but the earliest records were kept in Roman numerals; there was no formal closing of the books, and profits were determined only at irregular intervals, usually at the end of a venture, regardless of the date. No provision was made for financial statements as we know them today; however, lists of account balances were prepared, and profits for the ventures were determined before distributions were made to the participants.

Until the past few decades, accounting and the analysis of financial statements developed slowly, primarily because most businesses were small and owned by sole proprietors or small groups of partners. Owners were personally liable for the debts of the business, and accounting records were, therefore, not important as a basis for establishing credit. Commercial banks, mercantile credit agencies, public accountants, income taxes,

3

and corporations have assumed their present importance largely within the past one hundred years. During this period there has been a slow emergence of the many additional factors which are necessary for accounting and statement analysis to assume an important place in business thinking. Most important among these factors has been the development of generally accepted accounting principles and conventions. Without these principles and conventions it would be extremely difficult to determine the bases employed for the preparation of financial statements, and there would be so little comparability from period to period that the statements would lose much of their value.

Generally speaking, the need for accounting data grows with the size and complexity of a business. As business activities grow more varied and numerous, accounting descriptions and measurements also tend to increase, for managers, owners, and other interested parties find themselves more and more dependent upon accounting data to satisfy their need for information.

## FINANCIAL STATEMENTS

For each unit of business there is a need not only to describe but also to measure:

1. What comes in
2. What goes out
3. What properties remain
4. The equities of the owners and creditors in what remains

Accounting meets these needs by providing appropriate descriptions and by providing the means of accumulating the necessary measurements in terms of monetary values. Information so accumulated is then presented in the form of financial reports that are classified and arranged in a logical, systematic fashion. In brief, accounting describes and measures changes in values and summarizes the results of these changes in financial reports.

"Financial statements" are descriptive, monetary measurements of financial condition and operating results for a unit of enterprise. The phrase "financial reports" is often employed in the same sense but is normally considered a broader term which includes all types and forms of reports that are expressed in dollars. The term "statements" is most frequently used to include:

1. Statement of financial condition
2. Statement of changes in earned equity
3. Statement of income and expense

These statements are illustrated in Exhibits 1-1, 1-2, and 1-3.

EXHIBIT 1-1
JONES WHOLESALE CO.
Statement of Financial Condition as of December 31, 1957

| *Assets* | | *Equities* | | |
|---|---|---|---|---|
| | | Liabilities: | | |
| Cash........................ | $ 1,400 | Accounts payable.... | $3,000 | |
| Accounts receivable........... | 4,000 | Notes payable....... | 7,000 | $10,000 |
| Inventory................... | 16,000 | Owner's equity: | | |
| Equipment.................. | 18,000 | Invested equity...... | $6,000 | |
| Prepaid rent................. | 600 | Earned equity....... | 24,000 | 30,000 |
| Total assets............. | $40,000 | Total equities........... | | $40,000 |

This statement is a descriptive measurement of (1) the properties (assets) owned by the company, (2) the equity of the creditors, and (3) the equities of the owners in these assets. Equities, as the word is used here, means rights, equitable claims, or a financial interest in something of value. The money measure of equities and assets will always be equal but the two are not equal in themselves. *Assets are things of value; equities are claims* in these things of value.

EXHIBIT 1-2
JONES WHOLESALE CO.
Statement of Changes in Earned Equity for the Year Ended December 31, 1957

| | |
|---|---|
| Earned equity, Jan. 1, 1957.............. | $20,000 |
| Add net profit for the year.............. | 12,000 |
| Total................................ | $32,000 |
| Less withdrawals during the year.......... | 8,000 |
| Earned equity, Dec. 31, 1957............. | $24,000 |

This statement shows that the equity of the owners arising from retained earnings amounts to $24,000. At the beginning of the year the earned equity was $20,000. The valuation of the owner's equity in the business assets was increased by the "net profit" resulting from operations; i.e., the inward flow of values has exceeded the outward flow and the resulting asset increase belongs to the owner. However, his interest in the business was decreased by the value of the assets that were withdrawn during the period for his personal use. The difference between the profits earned ($12,000) and the amounts withdrawn ($8,000) accounts for the $4,000 increase in the owner's equity.

A statement of income and expense shows the amount of income created and the costs of creating that income. It is sometimes called a "profit and loss" statement and is often called an "operating" statement because it is a description and dollar measurement of the results of operations. This particular example shows that the owner has operated profitably, since the inward flow of values (income) exceeded the outward flow

EXHIBIT 1-3

JONES WHOLESALE CO.

Statement of Income and Expense for the Year Ended December 31, 1957

| | | |
|---|---:|---:|
| Income from sales........................ | | $86,000 |
| Cost of goods sold: | | |
|   Inventory, Jan. 1, 1957............ | $12,000 | |
|   Cost of purchases................ | 56,000 | |
|   Available for sale................. | $68,000 | |
|   Inventory, Dec. 31, 1957.......... | 16,000 | 52,000 |
| Gross margin.............................. | | $34,000 |
| Expenses: | | |
|   Wages expense.................... | $14,000 | |
|   Rent expense..................... | 3,600 | |
|   Utilities expense................. | 2,400 | |
|   Other expense.................... | 2,000 | 22,000 |
| Net profit................................ | | $12,000 |

of values (costs and expenses) and thereby resulted in an asset increment which is measured in dollars and described as "net profit."

The financial statements illustrated above are fairly typical, although oversimplified. These are practically the only types of statements that many persons ever see, and, although they are extremely valuable to an individual who wants to acquire an over-all picture of a business, one should realize that there are many other types of financial reports that are equally valuable for use in the day-by-day management of a business concern.

## BASIC TERMINOLOGY

The six statement headings that represent the major classifications of accounting data are:

1. Assets
2. Liabilities
3. Owner's equity
4. Income
5. Expenses
6. Costs of goods sold

The first three are major headings on the statement of financial condition, frequently called a "balance sheet." The latter three are typical headings on the statement of income and expense (or *profit and loss* statement) for a trading firm. A concern selling only a service would not, of course, include cost of goods sold.

### Assets

*Assets* are wealth provided by owners and creditors, plus such wealth as is accumulated through operations and retained for use in the business. In brief, they can be defined as *things of value owned*. They have value because of their ability to provide future services and thereby earn income, or because they can be exchanged for cash or goods even though they do not provide operating services. The asset Cash has value as a means of exchange for goods or services desired. Cash substitutes—accounts and notes receivable, for example—have value because they can be exchanged for cash.

Those things that *provide services* for operational purposes are often considered "costs." Equipment owned and used by a firm is recorded at cost, measured by the amount of cash exchanged for it (or to be paid later in order to liquidate the debt incurred if the equipment is purchased on credit). Salary expense is a cost, also measured by the amount paid, or to be paid, to employees for work that has been done. Both are costs required for operating the business. But the cost or value given up in exchange for services of the employees has no value at the end of an accounting period. This type of cost is therefore known as an "expired cost." Assets on the other hand are "unexpired costs," for, by definition, they continue to have value because of their ability to provide future services.

The assets included in the statement of financial condition shown in Exhibit 1-1 are typical of assets found on most such statements:

*Cash* indicates the sum of cash on hand and the checking account balance.

*Accounts receivable* consist of amounts receivable from customers, parties that have purchased merchandise or services from the firm. They do not represent written promises, but rather implied promises that are legal *rights* which can be sold or used as security for a loan.

*Inventory* is made up of merchandise (goods, stock in trade) held for *resale* to customers. An enterprise that sells only services may have a "supplies inventory" but not an "inventory" in the normally accepted meaning of the term.

*Equipment* is a broad term that may include a variety of items although it usually includes only operating devices and machines other than vehicles.

*Prepaid rent* indicates that future rental services valued at $600 have been paid in advance.

## Liabilities

*Liabilities* are debts due to outsiders, normally measured by the dollar amounts that must be paid out in order to liquidate the obligations. They represent creditors' equities in the assets of the firm until such time as the debts are satisfied by payment.

Two common forms of liabilities are shown on the statement of financial condition for the Jones Wholesale Co. (Exhibit 1-1):

*Accounts payable* are amounts due suppliers for merchandise purchased on open account. (In some businesses suppliers are known as vendors, manufacturers, wholesalers, or jobbers.) "Purchased on open account" indicates that the buyer has made an implied promise to pay on the due date.

*Notes payable* are amounts due creditors based on a written, signed promise of the debtor to make payment at a fixed or determinable future date.

## Owner's Equity

*Owner's equity* expresses the financial interest of the owner in the assets of the business. This interest or equity is secondary to that of the creditors, for, in the liquidation of a business, the claims of the creditors must be satisfied before any assets can be distributed to the owner or owners. The measure of the owner's equity will always be equal to the net assets: the excess of the money measure of the assets over the money measure of the liabilities (or assets minus liabilities) equals the owner's equity.

For informational purposes the owner's equity can be subdivided into two major parts:

*Invested equity* represents ownership claims equal to the valuation of assets invested by the owners.

*Earned equity* is a valuation of the ownership interest that has resulted from profitable operations. It is equal to the amount of assets acquired through operations, less the sum of costs expired and assets distributed to the owners. The earned equity is often called surplus, earned surplus, or retained earnings.

## Income

*Income* is a monetary measurement of valuation received in exchange for goods sold and/or services rendered. It is a valuation of the inward flow of assets arising from operations and a description of the source. Under no circumstances is income synonymous with the cash or accounts receivable that are received in exchange for assets sold or services furnished.

*Sales income*, as shown in Exhibit 1-3, is a monetary measurement of the total valuation received from customers in exchange for merchandise sold during a given period of time.

*Fee income* is a measurement of value received in exchange for services rendered.

## Expenses

*Expenses* are expired costs—costs of items or services that have been consumed or used.

*Wages expense* is a monetary measurement of the cost of employees' services that have been rendered and have no value to future periods. In other words, all the value of the services was consumed or absorbed during the current period.

*Rent expense* represents the cost of services already provided, normally being for the use of a building or equipment. If the cost of any rental service had been paid in advance, however, it should be classified as an unexpired cost under the title of *Prepaid rent* on the statement of financial condition.

*Utilities expense* normally includes such things as telephone, light, power, heat, and water costs for the period. Any one of these utility costs might be shown as a separate item of expense if it were significant and management needed the more detailed information.

### Cost of Goods Sold

The *cost of goods sold* represents the net cost of the merchandise that has been sold to customers during the period of time shown. The following computation was included on the statement of income and expenses shown in Exhibit 1-3:

| Cost of goods sold: | |
|---|---|
| Inventory, Jan. 1, 1957 | $12,000 |
| Cost of purchases | 56,000 |
| Available for sale | $68,000 |
| Inventory, Dec. 31, 1957 | 16,000 |
| Total cost of goods sold | $52,000 |

The ledger accounts normally do not show the cost of goods sold figure—$52,000 in this example—but serve as a means of accumulating the data for the computation. This computation starts with the cost of the merchandise on hand at the beginning of the period. The cost of the stock acquired during the period is then added, and the resulting total shows the cost of all stock that was available for sale to customers within the stated period. The cost of the merchandise *unsold* as of the last day of the period is then determined, usually by taking inventory, and is deducted to arrive at the cost of the goods that have been sold.

The cost of goods sold is an expired cost and, for this reason, is sometimes included under the classification *expenses*. Expenses, however, are services acquired in order to sell goods or merchandise. Merchandise does not, in the usual sense of the word, provide services; it actually passes from the business to the customer. For this reason, the cost of goods sold is considered a distinct type of expired cost and a separate, major classification of financial data.

## RECORDING FINANCIAL DATA

*Transactions and Journal Entries*

In accounting, any change in the amount or classification of financial data is a *transaction*. In order to provide a complete record of each financial change in one place, all transactions are *first* entered, chronologically, in books called "journals" or "books of original entry." Individual increases and decreases, as indicated by the journal entries, are later transferred to the appropriate general ledger accounts. This means that *all* transactions are recorded *twice:* first, when journalized in a book of original entry; and, second, when posted to the book of final entry, the general ledger. To facilitate the posting, journal entries must be made up of account titles, exactly as they appear in the general ledger.

To illustrate the procedure for recording and summarizing transactions, assume that on December 1, 1957, the Jones Wholesale Co. had a cash balance of $1,000, and that this represents cash in a bank checking account. During the month a $200 check was issued in payment of wages, $700 was received from the sale of merchandise, and a $100 check was issued in payment of merchandise purchased. (An active firm will issue many checks and make a number of deposits during any given month but the procedures used can be illustrated by this simple example.) The first step is to make journal entries in chronological order as the transactions occur. The entries required to reflect the changes described above are:

General Journal

| Date 1957 | | Accounts and explanations | Dr. | Cr. |
|---|---|---|---|---|
| Dec. | 6 | Wages Expense | 200 | |
| | |     Cash in Bank | | 200 |
| | | (Payment of wages) | | |
| | 14 | Cash in Bank | 700 | |
| | |     Sales Income | | 700 |
| | | (Current cash sales deposited) | | |
| | 23 | Merchandise Purchases | 100 | |
| | |     Cash in Bank | | 100 |
| | | (Cash purchase of merchandise) | | |

Notice that the increase in Cash in Bank has been indicated by positioning both the account title and the dollar amount to the left; the decreases have been indicated by positioning the account title and dollar amounts to the right.

*General Ledger Accounts*

After the changes have been recorded in the journal, their effect on each account must be summarized. To do this, a separate page is set up for each account and the transactions are transferred from the journal to the ledger accounts affected; e.g., each change in Cash is transferred to the Cash in Bank account in the general ledger as indicated by the positioning in the journal entry, i.e., to the left-hand or right-hand side. The ledger account for Cash in Bank, reflecting the effect of the transactions shown, is illustrated below.

Cash in Bank

| Date | Explanation | Left side | Right side | Balance* |
|---|---|---|---|---|
| 1957 | | | | |
| 11-30 | Balance forward | | | 1,000 |
| 12- 6 | (Check issued) | | 200 | 800 |
| 12-14 | (Deposit) | 700 | | 1,500 |
| 12-23 | (Check issued) | | 100 | 1,400 |

\* Balances after each transaction may be omitted and only month-end balances shown.

The explanations included in parentheses would not usually be included in the account and are actually unnecessary, since normally the only increases in Cash in the Bank are deposits and the only decreases are checks that have been issued. The explanation column is employed only for the description of irregular items where it is felt an explanation will provide useful information.

The source of each amount on the financial statements is a general ledger account just as in the case of Cash, where the balance of $1,400 was taken from the Cash in Bank account.

## ACCOUNTING—DEFINITIONS, CONCEPTS, AND USES

*Accounting* consists of principles and procedures which are primarily concerned with recording, presenting, and interpreting financial data for a unit of enterprise. The *principles* represent generally accepted theories and conventions that pertain to the measuring and classifying of financial data. The *procedures* are the methods, techniques, and work involved in the process of recording and presenting the financial data.

A *unit of enterprise* is, in general terms, a combination of services and properties for the accomplishment of certain purposes. Such a unit might be a business such as a grocery store, a chain of grocery stores, or a state government. This text is principally concerned with accounting for *business* units—that is, those units of enterprise which are operated with the intention of creating a profit—rather than for nonprofit, institutional, and governmental units.

Accounting is not an end in itself but a service function, responsible for supplying accurate, informative data to enterprise management in the form of reports that describe financial position and measure operating results. It is an important part of the language of business.

*Bookkeeping* differs from accounting in that it is concerned only with the recording of financial data on the forms selected by, and in accordance with procedures established by, the accountants. Bookkeeping is considered a part of accounting, since the field of accounting includes the procedures that deal with the recording of monetary data. Accounting, however, is a broader field that also involves problems of valuation and measurement, presentation, and interpretation.

An *accounting system* includes the personnel, procedures, forms, and devices for accumulating, recording, and summarizing financial data for use by management, owners, creditors, taxing authorities, and others. It must include *trained personnel*, capable of making the necessary decisions; *procedures*, to assure the expedient and satisfactory completion of the necessary work; *forms*, for both the original recording of data and the final summarization of these data; and, in many cases, *devices*, such as bookkeeping and data-processing machines, to mechanize the routine recording and summarizing functions. The personnel of an accounting system are constantly concerned with the preparation of various reports and with the proper application of generally accepted accounting principles and conventions in the preparation of these reports.

A bookkeeping system is a part of the accounting system—a system within a system. The term is normally employed to indicate only that part of the accounting system which deals with the recording functions for an accounting unit.

For purpose of illustration, it will usually be assumed that the accounting unit is a relatively simple business with only one location. Most discussions will be concerned with service and trading enterprises. A doctor's office, for example, is typical of the former, for a doctor sells his services. Trading enterprises sell tangible items and are more commonly known as retailing and wholesaling businesses. Even though accounting problems related to such specialized types of business as public utilities, banks, or the transportation and extractive industries are not discussed, most of the accounting practices, principles, and conventions are fundamental to all types of business.

## Basic Concepts in Accounting

Several concepts are basic to an understanding of accounting for a business. These concepts or theories, briefly described below, are assumed to be applicable to the discussions within this text unless something to the contrary is indicated.

1. The *entity concept* considers a business as a unit separate and apart from its owner or owners. Consequently, in order to measure accurately

the financial condition and activities of a business, the personal transactions of the owner or owners are not included in the business records or reports. The idea that a business is a separate entity is so commonly accepted that a business is often discussed as though it were an individual.

2. The *going-concern concept* is the assumption that a business will continue for an extended period of time, perhaps indefinitely. This assumption is normally accepted in accounting unless there is evidence that a business will be liquidated or sold in the near future, or that it will be necessary to reorganize a business with lower asset and equity valuations.

3. *Original cost* is usually the total amount paid and/or to be paid for a service, right, or tangible item. The *cost evaluation* or *book value* of an asset is the original cost less any portion of original cost that has been charged as an expense. The current market value of operating assets, such as buildings and equipment, is usually ignored under the going-concern concept, for it is assumed that the original cost will be recovered through future operations and not through sale of the assets in the current market.

4. The *doctrine of consistency* is the generally accepted belief that the methods of valuation and other accounting principles adopted by a business should be altered or changed as infrequently as possible. Such alterations or changes should be made only when it is certain that the advantages to be gained will be greater than the disadvantages arising from loss of comparability between the financial statements for different periods.

### How Does Accounting Serve Business Managers?

It is generally agreed that one of the principal purposes of the accounting department of a business enterprise is to provide the financial data necessary for the effective control and management of the business. These data are collected and recorded in a carefully planned group of books, registers, lists, and cards and are sorted and summarized in a general ledger.

Most of the values to be obtained from the records are not obtained from studying the records themselves but from analyzing and interpreting the reports prepared from these records. The following list will illustrate some of the principal ways in which the accounting department serves the business in the preparation of reports:

1. It provides data for use in improving management efficiency and in controlling costs.

2. It provides information needed to control the assets of the business. This includes records of cash, receivables, and all fixed properties owned.

3. It provides information needed by stockholders in judging the efficiency of the managers.

4. It provides information required by law. This includes records of

employee earnings and taxes paid, profits earned and subject to income tax, and reports required by the government regulatory agencies.

5. It provides information for banks which have been asked to extend credit.

6. It provides information required by investment banks and by prospective investors in bond issues.

7. It provides information required by manufacturers or wholesalers who have been asked to supply merchandise, equipment, or supplies on credit.

8. It provides information needed in arbitrating wage disputes and in arriving at labor contracts.

Though the list is not exhaustive, it is complete enough to indicate that the service rendered by the accounting department is usually in the form of a financial report or statement which is to be analyzed by the person receiving it and, in the light of existing economic conditions, market trends, imminent legislation, competition, and the ability and efficiency of management, used as a basis for a business decision. The accountant is normally in the best position to understand, analyze, and interpret financial data, but in questions involving management decisions he is no more responsible for interpreting the statements than are the other executives of the business. He should be ready to present his interpretations. But, since he does not make the final decisions, it is obvious that the other executives of the firm must also be in a position to analyze and make their own interpretations. It may safely be said that every business executive who takes part in policy-making decisions must have an understanding of the figure-facts upon which most decisions are based.

### How Does Accounting Serve Owners, Creditors, and Others?

Financial statements prepared by accountants provide owners with a variety of information. A statement of financial condition describes the assets owned and the values attached to these assets, the type and extent of debts due, and the valuation assigned to the ownership interest in the business. A statement of income and expense informs the owners of the sources and amounts of the incomes which serve to increase their equity, and also tells them of the nature and amount of the expired costs that decrease their equity. They can learn from the statements whether the net profit is adequate when compared with their investment or equity, and whether the net profit compares favorably with competitive businesses. Both statements may be used to advantage for comparison with industrial averages in order to find out if costs, debts, and income seem to be in line. Comparisons of current reports with those for preceding periods are extremely valuable to owners as a means of determining if their business is growing or declining, if the distribution of costs seems reasonable, if creditors' claims are becoming more or less important, etc.

Short-term creditors are primarily interested in the relationships of current assets (cash and assets that will be converted into cash in a relatively short time) to current liabilities (debts due within the coming year) as shown on the statement of financial condition. Funds for payment of debt due in 30 to 60 days usually come from the collection of receivables or the sale of inventory items. A firm may have difficulty obtaining additional short-term loans if the amount of current liabilities is already large in comparison with inventory, receivables, and other current assets. Long-term creditors are also interested in this ratio of current assets to current liabilities, for a firm that is unable to pay its current liabilities may be forced to liquidate. They are, however, more interested in the long-term economic outlook since they must determine from the statements (and other sources) if the debtor concern is likely to be relatively stable and profitable and if there are assets which might serve as suitable security for a loan.

Potential investors with an adequate knowledge of accounting and finance can make good use of financial reports in their attempts to judge rates of return on investments, growth possibilities of different firms, degree of risk involved, and so on. Lawyers frequently make use of financial statements when dealing with cases that involve businesses. Legislators often need an understanding of accounting fundamentals in order to judge the effect of certain proposed legislation. Plant supervisors can frequently benefit if their knowledge of accounting and financial reports is sufficient to provide an understanding of the nature of recorded costs, income earned, and the way the two are matched in computation of profit; and even salesmen who pass on the extension of credit to customers should be able to interpret statement data. Indeed, all persons expecting to make business decisions on the basis of figure-facts should have some knowledge of accounting and ways to analyze and evaluate financial data.

The purpose of this text is to give the nonaccountant an understanding of accounting principles and statements that will enable him to interpret the financial data that are essential to the formulation of business and investment decisions.

## THE ACCOUNTING PROFESSION

Those who are responsible for the accumulation and presentation of accounting data are known as "accountants." There are, however, many different classes of accountants since accounting work must be performed for a wide variety of units of business enterprise. Those who are responsible for the accounting functions of a single employer are generally referred to under the broad classification of "private" accountants. This inadequate adjective serves only to distinguish *private* accountants from *public* accountants. Many who work in private accounting are more specifically classified as specialists according to the particular industry in which they are employed. For example, an accountant employed by a power company is in private accounting but is generally known as a utility accountant. A man who has training and experience in accounting for department stores may be considered a retail accountant. An accountant working for a governing body may be classed as a governmental accountant.

Accountants are also distinguished by the type of work they perform, rather than by the type of enterprise that employs them. Those who specialize in the field of taxes may be classified as tax accountants; those who specialize in cost work are called cost accountants. The cost accountants are responsible for the development of detailed costs to aid in the control of various functions. Those employed in manufacturing industries are generally concerned with the development of unit product costs, departmental costs, operational costs, etc. Cost accountants may also specialize in distribution costs or administrative costs—or in costing for any other function where there is a need for more information than can be supplied by general accounting alone.

Accountants who specialize in the checking and verification of financial records and reports prepared by other accountants are called auditors. They are usually responsible for ascertaining whether all the required data have been properly recorded and reported and, subsequently, rendering an audit report to disclose their findings. If an auditor examines and reports only on the records of his employer, he is considered an internal auditor. If his services are sold to various clients, he is known as a public accountant.

## Public Accountants

Business units organized for the purpose of providing accounting services to others are generally known as public accounting firms; those who provide the services are called public accountants. They perform a variety of tasks—auditing, systems installations, preparation of tax returns, general accounting work, consulting on all phases of accounting, etc. The large, national partnerships of certified public accountants do a great deal of audit work. (All firms listed on the New York Stock Exchange are required to have annual audits performed by certified public accountants.) The smaller, local firms may have very little audit work and provide, instead, mostly general accounting and tax services to their clients.

In most states there are at least two classes of public accountants, certified and noncertified. The certified public accountant (CPA) must first have passed a 2½-day qualifying exam which consists of problems and questions on many phases of accounting practice and theory, auditing, and business law. Some states now require that all applicants have a degree from a recognized college before they are allowed to sit for the examination. In addition to the examination, it is usually required that the applicant serve an internship period with a CPA firm before his certificate is issued. Once an accountant has been granted his CPA certificate by the state, he must operate within a strict framework of ethical and work standards in order to retain his status as a CPA.

The professional organization for the certified public accountants is The American Institute of Certified Public Accountants. The AICPA's pronouncements on principles, practice, and terminology are generally accepted as standards for the accounting profession.

The term *noncertified* has been employed merely to distinguish the public accountant from the *certified* public accountant. In most states all public accountants must be licensed, but the requirements for obtaining the license or PA certificate vary greatly from state to state. Some require successful completion of comprehensive examinations, plus a certain amount of experience; other states allow accountants to operate as PAs without examination and with relatively little experience.

*Machine Accountants*

A vast new branch of record-keeping work is developing at the present time. As the cost of bookkeeping has grown, so has the determination to mechanize more of the record keeping. Bookkeeping machines that perform a number of related operations automatically have been in use for years; e.g., once credit sales data have been entered in the keyboard of a typical bookkeeping machine, the sales journal, sales invoice, customer's statement, and customer's ledger card can all be prepared automatically. Punched cards have also been in use for years as source data for processing in International Business Machines (IBM) and comparable equipment. After the basic data have been punched in the cards, the equipment can automatically perform sorting, computing, and printing operations at very high speeds. To obtain even greater speed and flexibility, and eventually lower economic cost, electronic data-processing equipment has been adapted to record-keeping work. Such equipment is currently too expensive for any but the larger businesses but undoubtedly will be available to smaller concerns before too many years have passed.

Those persons trained to supervise punched-card or electronic data-processing systems are sometimes referred to as machine accountants. This is often a misnomer, since these persons frequently are not accountants. They are, however, individuals whose background and training most certainly qualify them as professionals in their own special field. The vast new field of electronics offers a great challenge to the accountant, who must attempt to make use of this new potential. It also offers new problems to auditors and systems accountants, who must understand how the magnetic tapes and electronic tubes perform the record-keeping processes.

## SUMMARY

Accountants, whether public or private, assume that certain concepts or principles serve as the basis for their accounting procedures. The entity concept requires that the owner's personal records be kept separate from those of the firm; the valuation of assets is influenced by the going-concern concept; and the need for comparability is recognized in the doctrine of consistency. History shows that principles and concepts as well as the means and extent of recording transactions have changed with time.

Transaction data are now recorded originally in the form of journal entries and later posted to general ledger accounts. These accounts serve as devices for the accumulation of all changes and period-end balances in each classification of financial data. Financial statements are a summary of these general ledger balances, classified according to whether the balances measure financial position at the end of a period (the statement of financial condition), changes in ownership interest (the statement of changes in earned equity), or the results of operations for the period (the statement of income and expense). These processes can be expressed diagrammatically as follows:

$$(\text{Transactions}) \rightarrow (\text{journals}) \rightarrow (\text{ledger}) \rightarrow (\text{statements})$$

## QUESTIONS

**1.** Define accounting and bookkeeping. How does bookkeeping differ from accounting?

**2.** What is the primary difference between a service and trading enterprise?

**3.** Why did accounting and financial analysis develop so slowly for many years?

**4.** What are financial reports? Financial statements? What does the term statements normally include?

**5.** Describe a statement of financial condition, a statement of changes in earned equity, and a statement of income and expenses.

**6.** Why should most business executives have a knowledge of accounting principles and financial statements? How can other groups make use of such knowledge?

**7.** Name and define the six major classifications of accounting data. Which classification may not always appear on the statements? Why?

**8.** What other titles are often used in place of statement of financial condition, statement of income and expenses, and statement of changes in earned equity?

*expired - by def refers to
end of period ...would
seem only breakage etc.*

**9.** What are costs, expired costs, and unexpired costs? Can all or a portion of a cost that was originally recorded as unexpired be expired at the end of an accounting period? Give an example.

**10.** Can the amount of income or net profit for a period usually be determined by an analysis of changes in the cash account?

**11.** Expenses are sometimes referred to as period costs. Why would such a title be appropriate?

**12.** All increases in cash are recorded on which side of the accounts?

**13.** How do entries in general journal form indicate on which side of the account each amount is to be posted?

**14.** The words value, valued, and valuation, as used in accounting terminology, usually refer to original cost or original cost less the amount of original cost that has been expired as operating expenses (book value). When would original cost and current market value be the same? Why would the two be quite different at certain times?

**15.** What is a journal? A general ledger?

**16.** Why is an understanding of the "entity" and "going-concern" concepts important to the study of accounting?

**17.** What is the principal distinction between private accountants and public accountants?

**18.** What are the various classifications of private accountants? What is a CPA?

## CHAPTER 2

# ACCOUNTING FOR A SERVICE ENTERPRISE

In the preceding chapter typical financial statements were illustrated and the methods used to accumulate the data necessary for their preparation were very briefly described. No attempt was made to explain the basis for making the required journal entries or to explain the many problems involved in recording a firm's financial transactions and summarizing and presenting its operating results. This chapter presents a detailed description of these record-keeping procedures. Because of the problems involved in accounting for the purchase and sale of merchandise, the discussion will be confined to the procedures followed by a service enterprise. This is the type of accounting system used by doctors, lawyers, engineers, and other professional people, and by repair shops, laundries, transfer and storage companies, theaters, and other firms which do not sell a tangible product. Accounting problems of merchandising concerns will be discussed in Chapter 3.

## THE ACCOUNTING CYCLE FOR A SERVICE ENTERPRISE

The major function of an accounting system is to accumulate the data from business papers (checks, invoices, etc.), to summarize these data, and to present periodical reports of the firm's operations and financial condition. The procedures employed in this process are referred to as the "accounting cycle." The steps in this cycle can be outlined as follows:

1. Journalize the regular transactions—prepare journal entries for each financial change that takes place during the period.
2. Post—transfer debit and credit amounts from the journal entries to the indicated ledger accounts.
3. Compute account balances—to each beginning account balance add the increases for the period, deduct the decreases for the period, and note the final balance.
4. Journalize adjustments—prepare journal entries to correct balances already recorded and to record missing data.
5. Post adjustments and compute new balances.

6. Take a trial balance of the general ledger accounts to be certain that the total debits and credits are equal.

7. Prepare the financial statements from the general ledger trial balance.

8. Journalize and post the closing entry—"close" the income and expense accounts and enter the net profit in the Earned Equity account.

## ANALYZING AND RECORDING TRANSACTIONS

An amount that is to be or has been recorded on the left-hand side of an account is a debit amount; an amount that is to be or has been recorded on the right-hand side is a credit amount. To "debit" an account, then, simply means that the dollar amount is to be entered on the left-hand side of the appropriate account; to "credit" an account means that the amount is to be placed on the right-hand side. Persons working in accounting and finance almost always speak in terms of *debiting* and *crediting* accounts or of accounts having debit or credit balances. For this reason it is necessary to become familiar with this terminology, although in the beginning it may be advisable to think of changes in financial data as increases and decreases in the accounts.

Financial data are recorded twice: once in the original journal entry and for the second time when the amounts are posted to the general ledger accounts. The financial changes are first recorded in the form of journal entries for two reasons: (1) to provide a complete record of each transaction in one place, and (2) to furnish a chronological history of the business activities. Data from the journal entries are transferred to the general ledger in order to accumulate all the changes in each account classification for a period of time and, subsequently, to compute a final balance for each of these classifications. Once it is assumed that the original entries are correct, the posting becomes a somewhat routine process, for the bookkeeper must debit and credit the accounts exactly as indicated by the journal entries.

In each journal entry under a double-entry bookkeeping system,[1] the dollar amount of the debit (or debits) must be equal to the dollar amount of the credit (or credits). For example:

1. If an asset is invested by the owner, the asset account must be increased, and the increase in the owner's equity in the firm must also be shown.

2. If an asset is obtained from a creditor, the asset account is increased, and we must also show the increase in the firm's debts.

---

[1] Under a single-entry system, only one side of a transaction is recorded and no check is provided on the mathematical accuracy of the final balances.

3. If an asset is received from a customer, as when merchandise or services are sold for cash, we must show the increase in the asset, and we must also show the source of the income.

4. If an asset is decreased, such as cash when a debt is paid, we must show the decrease in the asset, and we must also show the decrease in the liability;

5. If an asset is decreased by the payment of expenses, we must show the decrease in the asset, and we must also show the amount of each expense incurred.

Each transaction has two "sides," and the recording entry must reflect both. If an account is to be debited, the journal entry has to show the appropriate title and amount to the left; the offsetting credit must be placed to the right. Each entry is actually an equation; i.e., debits equal credits. Since this equality is true of the parts (each transaction), it must also be true of the whole. That is, the sum of the debits must be equal to the sum of the credits after all dollar amounts have been transferred from the journal to the general ledger. If an amount is transferred incorrectly, the sums will not be equal. This is one of the major advantages of the equation form of entry—its capacity to disclose arithmetic error through lack of equality.

*Assets and Expenses*

All increases in anything acquired for the intended use or benefit of the business are to be recorded on the *left* (debit) side of the accounts, i.e., all increases in cash, cash substitutes, unexpired costs, and expired costs. Such increases are, therefore, recorded by placing the appropriate account titles and dollar amounts on the left side in the original journal entries to indicate that the dollar amounts are to be posted on the left side of the general ledger account named. Decreases in assets and expenses are indicated by placing the appropriate account titles and dollar amounts to the right in the original journal entries. These amounts will then be posted to the right-hand side of the accounts named. For example, if office equipment costing $350 is purchased for cash on January 2, 1958, the journal entry would appear as:

General Journal

| Date 1958 | | | Dr. | Cr. |
|---|---|---|---|---|
| Jan. | 2 | Office Equipment | 350 | |
| | | Cash | | 350 |
| | | (Purchased office equipment for cash) | | |

The placement of the account titles and amounts indicates that the Office Equipment account is to be increased $350 while the Cash account is to be decreased $350. Regardless of increases or decreases, the accounts to be *debited* are always listed first.

*Equities and Income*

Most assets—cash, cash substitutes, and unexpired costs—are acquired from three major sources:

1. From owners through their investments in the firm
2. From creditors through purchases on account or through loans
3. From customers through the sale of merchandise or services

Increases in the "sources" are entered to the *right*, or as credits, in order to distinguish them from increases in assets and expenses.

*Owner Investment.* If the owners invest land valued at $20,000, it is obvious that we must record the $20,000 increase in the asset Land. But in double-entry accounting we must also show that the equity of the owners in the assets of the firm has increased by an equal amount. The correct journal entry shows *both* sides of the picture, as follows:

General Journal

| Date 1958 | | | Dr. | Cr. |
|---|---|---|---|---|
| Jan. | 1 | Land | 20,000 | |
| | | Invested Equity | | 20,000 |
| | | (Land invested by owners) | | |

*Creditors.* Assets are also acquired in exchange for implied or written promises to make payment at a future date. Suppose, for instance, that the owners purchase a $3,000 truck and give a promissory note in exchange. The truck becomes the property of the business and its full value must be recorded but, at the same time, the creditors gain rights in the firm's assets to the extent of $3,000. The journal entry for the transaction would be:

General Journal

| Date 1958 | | | Dr. | Cr. |
|---|---|---|---|---|
| Jan. | 1 | Truck | 3,000 | |
| | | Notes Payable | | 3,000 |
| | | (Truck purchased from X Co.) | | |

All increases in the equities of both creditors and owners are recorded to the right. The owner's equity can be represented by two accounts, Invested Equity and Earned Equity. The equity of the creditors is normally represented by numerous account classifications such as Accounts Payable, Notes Payable, Wages Payable, Taxes Payable, etc.

Each significant liability should be entered under a specified account title that adequately describes the type of debt due.

*Customers.* In addition to owners and creditors, customers are also a source of assets. The value received from customers during a *period of time* is measured under the descriptive title Fee Income (or Sales Income if the firm sells merchandise). Increases in this source account, as in all other source accounts, are recorded on the right (or credit) side. But, there is a major difference in the sources: owners and creditors have equitable claims in the assets of the business; customers, conversely, have no such claims, for there has been an even exchange. Customers receive merchandise or services from the business; in exchange, the business usually receives cash or a promise for future payment of cash. At this point the transaction is complete and the customers have no claims against the assets of the business. Entries to record services rendered for cash and on credit would be made as follows:

General Journal

| Date 1958 | | | Dr. | Cr. |
|---|---|---|---|---|
| Jan. | 2 | Cash | 160 | |
| | | Fee Income | | 160 |
| | | (Service rendered for cash) | | |
| | 4 | Account Receivable—A. B. Dow | 230 | |
| | | Fee Income | | 230 |
| | | (Service rendered A. B. Dow on account) | | |

In both transactions the business unit received something of value: Cash, which can be exchanged for goods and services; or an Account Receivable, which gives a legal right to collect cash at a future date.

*Typical Transactions*

Presented below are a number of typical journal entries that illustrate the original recording of various types of entries (dates have been omitted):[1]

**1.** Acquisition of assets by owner's investment:

```
Cash in Bank                        3,000
    Invested Equity                         3,000
(Cash invested by A. B. Smith, owner)
```

**2.** Acquisition of assets by borrowing:

```
Furniture and Fixtures              1,200
    Notes Payable                           1,200
(Note payable to C. D. Green, due 6-1-58)
```

[1] Account titles are capitalized; cents are eliminated to simplify the illustrations and problems.

**3.** Expense item paid in cash:

| | | |
|---|---|---|
| Rent Expense | 150 | |
| Cash in Bank | | 150 |
| (Payment for January rent) | | |

**4.** Expense and liability incurred, to be paid later:

| | | |
|---|---|---|
| Taxes Expense | 430 | |
| Taxes Payable | | 430 |
| (Property taxes applicable to this period) | | |

**5.** Services rendered for cash:

| | | |
|---|---|---|
| Cash in Bank | 610 | |
| Fee Income | | 610 |
| (Cash collected for services rendered) | | |

**6.** Services rendered on account:

| | | |
|---|---|---|
| Account Receivable—E. F. Bilk | 170 | |
| Fee Income | | 170 |
| (Services to E. F. Bilk) | | |

**7.** Collection on account:

| | | |
|---|---|---|
| Cash in Bank | 100 | |
| Account Receivable—E. F. Bilk | | 100 |
| (Partial payment deposited 1-7-58) | | |

In transaction 1 the Cash in Bank account was debited to show the increase in the cash. The owner's invested equity account is credited to show that the equity of the owner was increased by his investment. At this point a statement of financial condition would show only one asset, cash, and since no liabilities have been incurred, the only equity in the assets would be that of the owner.

Transaction 2 shows an increase in the asset Furniture and Fixtures. Since a note was given to Green for these assets, a credit to Notes Payable was made to record this liability and show the equity of the creditor in the firm's assets.

Transaction 3 shows that the Cash account has been decreased to pay the rent for the first month. All expired costs are recorded in expense accounts as debits and, at the end of the period, are matched against the income produced to determine the net profit from operations.

Transaction 4 shows that an expense, taxes, has been incurred. Since this expense has not been paid, the firm has a liability to the tax levying agency and this liability must be recorded by a credit to Taxes Payable.

Transaction 5 records an increase in cash resulting from services rendered to a client. The source of the income is shown by the credit to Fee Income. This income will be matched against the expenses incurred to determine the profit and the resulting increase in the owner's equity.

Transaction 6 records the increase in the asset Accounts Receivable arising from services rendered. The income account is credited to show the source of the income, which has been earned but not yet collected.

Transaction 7 records the increase in the cash and the decrease in accounts receivable resulting from the collection of an account. The net effect of transactions 6 and 7 is the same as that of transaction 5.

## GENERAL LEDGER ACCOUNTS

For each account title used to record the financial transactions there is a separate page in the general ledger. Each page, with its respective title, is known as an account. Each journal entry must include exact account titles, for a journal entry says, in essence, debit this account, credit that account. Judgment has to be used in the preparation of journal entries, for the entry is the interpretation of the transaction. From this point forward the problem is simply how the information recorded by the original journal entries is to be summarized and presented.

Ledger accounts are constructed with two vertical columns that serve to accumulate changes in the dollar balances during a period. The amount column at the left is known as the debit side; the adjoining column to the right is the credit side. A third amount column, usually at the extreme right, is for account balances and is not included when reference is made to an amount being recorded on "the right side" of an account.

The Cash in Bank account, after the typical transactions from the preceding page have been posted, is shown in Exhibit 2-1. (The column marked F (folio) is used to show the journal page from which the entries were posted.)

EXHIBIT 2-1
Account: Cash in Bank                                             Page 1

| Date |  | Explanation | F | Debit | Credit | Balance |
|------|--|-------------|---|-------|--------|---------|
| Jan. | 1 | Investment |  | 3,000 |  | 3,000 |
|  | 3 | January Rent |  |  | 150 | 2,850 |
|  | 5 | Services Rendered |  | 610 |  | 3,460 |
|  | 7 | Collection on Account |  | 100 |  | 3,560 |
|  |  |  |  | (Left) | (Right) |  |

All other accounts named in the journal entries would be summarized in similar ledger accounts. To visualize the effect of transactions, accountants often set up "T accounts" showing only the name of the account and the debit and credit columns. The effect of the owner's investment of $10,000 cash and land worth $8,000, for example, would be shown as:

| Cash | Land | Invested Equity |
|---|---|---|
| 10,000 | 8,000 | 18,000 |
| (Dr.) | (Dr.) | (Cr.) |

The usual abbreviation for debit is dr.; for credit, cr.

### Account Classifications

The number and titles of the accounts used depend upon the type of business and the amount of detailed information desired. If few "breakdowns" are desired, there can be relatively few accounts. When more detailed information is wanted, more accounts are necessary to provide for the accumulation of additional data. The *titles* of accounts are primarily determined by the nature of the costs and debts incurred, the kind of income, etc., and consequently, there can be no specific formula for the selection of account titles for a particular business. Judgment must be employed in the selection of account titles and, when appropriate, the most commonly accepted titles should be used in order to make statements comparable. When there is no commonly accepted title that fits, the briefest possible description that is appropriate for an account title should be adopted.

A list of account titles used by a particular firm is a *chart of accounts*. This list represents the account classifications for that business only at a given time; new accounts may be necessary if the nature of the recorded data changes. Note, too, that the classification for identical items may be quite different from business to business. For example, in one business a pickup truck may be classified as Trucks; in another, as Vehicles. When the cost of stamps is significant, management may want a Postage Expense account maintained; but such cost is more often classified as Office Supplies and Expense or as Miscellaneous Expense, since it is often comparatively insignificant.

### Summary of Debit and Credit Conventions

Before proceeding to the illustration of succeeding steps in the cycle, let us summarize the debit and credit conventions of double-entry bookkeeping.

General Ledger Accounts

| *Debit side* | *Credit side* |
|---|---|
| *Increases* in anything obtained for the intended use or benefit of the business: | *Increases* in the "source" accounts: |
| 1. Cash<br>2. Cash substitutes (receivables and investments)<br>3. Unexpired costs (operating assets)<br>4. Expired costs (expenses)<br><br>Decreases in the above accounts are entered on the credit side. | 1. Liabilities (Creditors are sources for things used in the business; they continue to have claims until paid)<br>2. Owner's equity (Owners invest things in business or leave portion of asset increase arising from operations; have secondary claims)<br>3. Income (Operating source; even exchange, no claims against assets; represents a period measurement of inward flow of assets from customers, etc.)<br><br>Decreases in these "source" accounts are entered on the debit side. |

Using the common T-account form for the major account classifications, the same information may be summarized as:

| Asset Accounts | | Liability Accounts | | Owner Equity Accounts | |
|---|---|---|---|---|---|
| Debits | Credits | Debits | Credits | Debits | Credits |
| Normal Bal. | | | Normal Bal. | | Normal Bal. |
| Increases | Decreases | Decreases | Increases | Decreases | Increases |

| All Cost and Expenses | | All Income Accounts | |
|---|---|---|---|
| Debits | Credits | Debits | Credits |
| Normal Bal. | | | Normal Bal. |
| Increases | Decreases | Decreases | Increases |

A good general rule, subject to minor exceptions to be covered later, is: All asset and expense accounts have debit balances and are increased by debits; all equity and income accounts have credit balances and are increased by credits.

### "Cash" or "Accrual" Accounting

The method of accounting for income and expense employed in most business units is known as the *accrual* basis of accounting. However, many individuals and many small service enterprises use what is called the *cash* basis of accounting. If statements are to be prepared on the cash basis, income will be recorded only when cash or its equivalent is received and most costs will be recorded only when cash is paid out. Depreciation is often the only expense shown that does not represent a current out-of-pocket expenditure. There are two obvious, and frequently important, weaknesses in the cash basis of reporting. First, income may have been earned but not reported, simply because payment has not yet been received (and despite the fact that the business has gained an asset, a valuable legal right to future receipts). Secondly, costs may have been incurred but not reported because payment has not yet been made. In such instances, not only is the cost omitted from the reports but also the liability that has been incurred.

These omissions normally do not occur when the accrual basis of accounting is employed, since this method requires (1) that all income—and the resulting asset increases—be recorded as of the time earned, i.e., as soon as the transactions are complete; (2) that all costs and liabilities be recorded as of the time incurred. Because of these requirements, financial reports prepared on the accrual basis should be consistently more complete and accurate than statements prepared on the cash basis.

Some firms use a combination of the two bases: all significant changes are reported on the accrual basis but a number of items that are considered relatively insignificant are reported on the cash basis, thereby eliminating unimportant adjustments that would otherwise have to be made at the end of each period. For example, the telephone bill may be charged to expense in the period when it is paid, regardless of the time period covered by the billing.

### ILLUSTRATION OF THE COMPLETE ACCOUNTING CYCLE

To illustrate the procedures and principles described in the preceding paragraphs, and to complete the accounting cycle, assume that we wish to keep the financial records of a small engineering firm. The firm uses only two books of record: a general journal (the book of original entry) and a general ledger (the book of final entry). A description of the firm's organization and operations follows.

In March, 1958, Mr. A. B. Dow, a registered engineer, decided to open his own consulting firm under the name of A. B. Dow, Consulting Engineer. During the month he made arrangements to rent a completely furnished office to be ready for him on April 1, at which time he signed a one-year lease and paid the rent for the first and last month of the year. On April 1, he invested $400 cash and his personal car which had a current market value of $2,000. Double-entry bookkeeping and the accrual basis of accounting are to be employed and statements are to be prepared at the end of each month.

*Journalizing the Transactions*

Journal entries to reflect Dow's transactions during the first month of operations would be recorded in the general journal as follows:

General Journal　　　　　　　　　　　　　Page 1

| 1958 | Accounts and explanations | Dr. | Cr. |
|---|---|---|---|
| | (1) | | |
| 4-1 | Cash in Bank | 400 | |
| | Car | 2,000 | |
| |     Invested Equity | | 2,400 |
| | (Owner's original investment: $400 placed in checking account; car valued at market) | | |
| | (2) | | |
| 4-1 | Prepaid Rent | 100 | |
| | Rent Expense | 100 | |
| |     Cash in Bank | | 200 |
| | (One-year lease signed; rent paid for current month and last month) | | |
| | (3) | | |
| 4-3 | Supplies on Hand | 160 | |
| |     Accounts Payable—Todd Co. | | 160 |
| | (Supplies purchased from Todd Co. on open account) | | |
| | (4) | | |
| 4-16 | Cash in Bank | 140 | |
| |     Fee Income | | 140 |
| | (Payment received for consulting work) | | |
| | (5) | | |
| 4-30 | Account Receivable—W. W. Jones | 480 | |
| |     Fee Income | | 480 |
| | (Amount billed for consulting work through April 30) | | |
| | Adjustments | | |
| | (6) | | |
| 4-30 | Supplies Expense | 50 | |
| |     Supplies on Hand | | 50 |
| | (Mr. Dow estimates the month-end inventory of supplies at $110. Total of $160 available less $110 equals $50 used) | | |
| | (7) | | |
| 4-30 | Depreciation Expense | 40 | |
| |     Accumulated Depreciation | | 40 |
| | (Car has expected useful life of 40 months; estimated trade-in value of $400. Monthly depreciation is: $1,600 ($2,000 less $400) divided by 40 months or $40 per month) | | |

The journal entries which reflect explicit business transactions or events (entries 1 to 5) are customarily posted before the adjustments are made because it is often necessary to have all transactions to the end of the period recorded in certain accounts before adjustments can be computed. The two adjustments shown (entries 6 and 7) are examples of the expiration of costs originally recorded as assets. In the first adjustment the decrease in the unexpired cost is accomplished by a credit to the asset account, Supplies on Hand, for the dollar valuation of supplies consumed. In the second adjustment the decrease is not credited to the Car account but rather to Accumulated Depreciation, which is deducted from the asset balance on the statement of financial condition in order to show both the original cost and the expired cost that has been charged off as an operating expense. The telephone bill has not been received but an adjustment is not made. Dow believes that the cost of his telephone service will be relatively small and should be charged to expense in the month paid, rather than attempting to estimate the cost at the end of each month.

## The General Ledger Accounts

Each form shown in Exhibit 2-2 represents an account page in the general ledger of the firm. They are shown in their usual order: (1) asset accounts, (2) liability accounts, (3) owner's equity accounts, (4) income accounts, and (5) expense accounts. This order of arrangement expedites preparation of statements since this is the same sequence that is customarily employed for presentation on the statements.

Each debit and credit in the general journal is posted individually to the corresponding account in the general ledger.

EXHIBIT 2-2
General Ledger Accounts

(1) Cash in Bank

| 1958 | | Dr. | Cr. | Bal. |
|---|---|---|---|---|
| 4-1 | | 400 | | |
| 4-1 | | | 200 | |
| 4-16 | | 140 | | 340 dr. |

(2) Account Rec.—W. W. Jones

| 1958 | | Dr. | Cr. | Bal. |
|---|---|---|---|---|
| 4-30 | | 480 | | 480 dr. |

(3) Car

| 1958 | | Dr. | Cr. | Bal. |
|---|---|---|---|---|
| 4-1 | | 2,000 | | 2,000 dr. |

(4) Accumulated Depreciation—Car

| 1958 | | Dr. | Cr. | Bal. |
|---|---|---|---|---|
| 4-30 | | | 40 | 40 cr. |

(5) Supplies on Hand

| 1958 | | Dr. | Cr. | Bal. |
|---|---|---|---|---|
| 4-3 | | 160 | | 160 dr. |
| 4-30 | | | 50 | 110 dr. |

(6) Prepaid Rent

| 1958 | | Dr. | Cr. | Bal. |
|---|---|---|---|---|
| 4-1 | | 100 | | 100 dr. |

(7) Accounts Payable

| 1958 | | Dr. | Cr. | Bal. |
|---|---|---|---|---|
| 4-1 | | | 160 | 160 cr. |

(8) Invested Equity

| 1958 | | Dr. | Cr. | Bal. |
|---|---|---|---|---|
| 4-1 | | | 2,400 | 2,400 cr. |

EXHIBIT 2-2 (Continued)

| (9) | Fee Income | | | | | (11) | Supplies Expense | | | |
|-----|------|-----|-----|------|---|------|------|-----|-----|------|
| 1958 | | Dr. | Cr. | Bal. | | 1958 | | Dr. | Cr. | Bal. |
| 4-16 | | | 140 | | | 4-30 | | 50 | | 50 dr. |
| 4-30 | | | 480 | 620 cr. | | | | | | |

| (10) | Rent Expense | | | | | (12) | Depreciation Expense | | | |
|------|------|-----|-----|------|---|------|------|-----|-----|------|
| 1958 | | Dr. | Cr. | Bal. | | 1958 | | Dr. | Cr. | Bal. |
| 4-1 | | 100 | | 100 dr. | | 4-30 | | 40 | | 40 dr. |

## Taking a Trial Balance

A trial balance is taken after all general journal entries have been posted and the final account balances computed. The trial balance is simply a list of all accounts with their respective balances. It serves two purposes: (1) It shows whether the accounts are, or are not, "in balance," i.e., whether or not the sum of the debit balances equals the sum of the credit balances; (2) it provides a summary of the general ledger which can be used for the preparation of statements.

The adjusted trial balance of the general ledger accounts is shown in Exhibit 2-3.

## Preparing the Statements

A statement of income and expense, as illustrated in Exhibit 2-4, measures in dollars the inward and outward flow of values arising from operations. If, during a given period of time, the measure of the inward flow (income) exceeds the measure of the outward flow (expense), there has been a net increment in the valuation of the assets (measured as net profit); and subsequently, the measure of the owner's equity is increased by the same amount. The statement of income and expense should be constructed first in order to provide this net profit figure. The net profit is then used on the statement of changes in earned equity to determine the earned equity at that time, and this "present" earned equity is added to the invested equity on the statement of financial condition to show the total equity of the owners in the firm's assets at the end of the accounting period.

In this example the net profit represents the only change in earned equity for the period, and consequently, a statement of changes in earned equity is not needed. In future periods the statement should show the earned equity at the beginning of the period, the net profits for the period

should be added, and the owner's withdrawals during the period should
be deducted to determine the owner's equity resulting from retained
earnings.

Notice that the "earned equity" amount of $430 is the only figure
which does not appear on the trial balance. It is normally taken from the

EXHIBIT 2-3
A. B. Dow, CONSULTING ENGINEER
Trial Balance as of April 30, 1958

| Accounts | Dr. | Cr. |
|---|---|---|
| Cash in bank...................... | $  340 | |
| Account receivable................. | 480 | |
| Car.............................. | 2,000 | |
| Accumulated depreciation........... | | $   40 |
| Supplies on hand................... | 110 | |
| Prepaid rent...................... | 100 | |
| Accounts payable.................. | | 160 |
| Invested equity.................... | | 2,400 |
| Fee income....................... | | 620 |
| Rent expense...................... | 100 | |
| Supplies expense................... | 50 | |
| Depreciation expense............... | 40 | |
| Totals........................ | $3,220 | $3,220 |

EXHIBIT 2-4
A. B. Dow, CONSULTING ENGINEER
Statement of Income and Expense for the Month of April, 1958

| | | |
|---|---|---|
| Fee income........................... | | $620 |
| Expenses: | | |
| Rent expense.................... | $100 | |
| Supplies expense................ | 50 | |
| Depreciation expense............ | 40 | 190 |
| Net profit............................ | | $430 |

(Some persons are inclined to believe that net
profit is an increase in cash. This is not true.
Notice that in this illustration the net profit is
measured as $430 but that during the same
period there was a $60 decrease in the cash
balance.)

statement of changes in earned equity. In this instance the amount used
is the net profit for April, since there was no beginning balance in the
Earned Equity account and the owner did not withdraw cash or other
assets for his personal use. The ending balance of earned equity total will
be different in subsequent periods, however, because earned equity is a
measurement of retained earnings *to date*.

EXHIBIT 2-5
A. B. DOW, CONSULTING ENGINEER
Statement of Financial Condition as of April 30, 1958

*Assets*

| | | |
|---|---:|---:|
| Cash in bank.................................... | | $ 340 |
| Account receivable............................ | | 480 |
| Car.................................. | $2,000 | |
| Less accumulated depreciation............ | 40 | 1,960 |
| Supplies on hand............................... | | 110 |
| Prepaid rent...................................... | | 100 |
| Total assets................................ | | $2,990 |

*Equities*

| | | |
|---|---:|---:|
| Liabilities: | | |
| Account payable............................ | | $ 160 |
| Owner's equity: | | |
| Invested equity........................ | $2,400 | |
| Earned equity, April 30, 1958.......... ... | 430 | 2,830 |
| Total equities............................ | | $2,990 |

## *Closing the Temporary Accounts*

Income and expense are monetary measurements made within the framework of time limitations. The measurements can be made for any period of time but are usually for a month, a quarter, or a year. When the end of the period comes, the measurements are made and the resulting increase or decrease is reflected as a change in the earned equity. This is apparent on the statements, for expenses are deducted from income and the profit increment forwarded as an increase in the owner's equity.

What is done on the statements must also be accomplished in the general ledger at least once a year: expenses must be deducted from income and the increase in Earned Equity recorded. At the same time the "temporary" accounts—income and expense—must be cleared to allow for the accumulation of data that will measure the operating results for the following period. This is accomplished within the accounts by preparing and posting a "closing" journal entry. This entry, in effect, transfers all temporary balances to the Earned Equity account. Separate entries, such as the following, could be made to accomplish the purpose:

| | | |
|---|---:|---:|
| Fee Income | 620 | |
|     Earned Equity | | 620 |
| (To transfer fee income balance to earned equity) | | |
| Earned Equity | 100 | |
|     Rent Expense | | 100 |
| (To transfer rent expense balance to earned equity) | | |

Nothing is to be gained, however, by recording all of the income and expense balances in the Earned Equity account—except cluttering that account with unnecessary detail. The same net effect can be accomplished with one general journal entry:

General Journal                                         Page 3

| 1958 | Accounts and explanations | Dr. | Cr. |
|------|---------------------------|-----|-----|
| 4-30 | Fee Income | 620 | |
|      | Rent Expense | | 100 |
|      | Supplies Expense | | 50 |
|      | Depreciation Expense | | 40 |
|      | Earned Equity | | 430 |
|      | (To close the temporary accounts and record net profit in the Earned Equity account) | | |

Information for the above entry can be taken directly from the statement of income and expense (or trial balance): debit all income accounts listed; credit all expense accounts listed; deduct the latter from the former and enter the difference as an increase in Earned Equity. The difference is then compared with the net profit to be certain the two are the same. If there is a net loss, the difference will be a debit (decrease) to Earned Equity. After the closing entry is posted, balances for the temporary (income and expense) accounts are computed. The resulting balances should all be zero and, as a result, the accounts are ready for the accumulation of data pertaining to the next period; i.e., the income and expense accounts have been "closed."

In the general ledger of A. B. Dow, the Earned Equity and temporary accounts, after posting of the closing entry, would appear as shown in Exhibit 2-6.

EXHIBIT 2-6
General Ledger Accounts Affected by Closing Process

Fee Income

| 1958 | | Dr. | Cr. | Bal. |
|------|-----------|-----|-----|--------|
| 4-16 | | | 140 | |
| 4-30 | | | 480 | 620 cr. |
| 4-30 | To close | 620 | | 00 |

Rent Expense

| 1958 | | Dr. | Cr. | Bal. |
|------|-----------|-----|-----|--------|
| 4-1  | | 100 | | 100 dr. |
| 4-30 | To close | | 100 | 00 |

Supplies Expense

| 1958 | | Dr. | Cr. | Bal. |
|------|-----------|-----|-----|--------|
| 4-30 | | 50 | | 50 dr. |
| 4-30 | To close | | 50 | 00 |

Depreciation Expense

| 1958 | | Dr. | Cr. | Bal. |
|------|-----------|-----|-----|--------|
| 4-30 | | 40 | | 40 dr. |
| 4-30 | To close | | 40 | 00 |

Earned Equity

| 1958 | | Dr. | Cr. | Bal. |
|------|------------------|-----|-----|--------|
| 4-30 | Profit for April | | 430 | 430 cr. |

After posting of the closing entry, the Earned Equity account has been increased by the amount of the net profit and should have the same balance as already shown for that item on the statement of financial condition, and all income and expense accounts have zero balances. (Under another method of closing, net income is not carried directly to Earned Equity. Instead, income and expense balances are transferred to a Profit and Loss Summary account and the net difference is then transferred from the summary account to Earned Equity. This method will be discussed in Chapter 4.)

## SUMMARY

For accounting purposes all changes in the amount or classification of financial data are considered transactions. All transactions are first recorded in journals, which are also known as books of original entry. This original record of each transaction is known as a journal entry. When double-entry bookkeeping is employed, the dual nature of each transaction is recognized and, as a consequence, each entry is an equation; i.e., the debit side equals the credit side. Debits are recorded or entered on the left and credits on the right, and the debit portion of each entry is presented first.

Increases in anything acquired for the intended use or benefit of the business are recorded on the left-hand (debit) side; increases in sources are entered on the right-hand (credit) side. Assets and expenses, therefore, are increased by debits; liabilities, owners' equity, and income are increased by credits. Decreases in asset and expense accounts are placed on the opposite (credit) side in order to distinguish them from increases in the same class of accounts. For the same reason, decreases in equities and income are entered on the left-hand (debit) side.

If the records of a business unit include only a general journal and a general ledger, the accounting cycle can be summarized as follows:

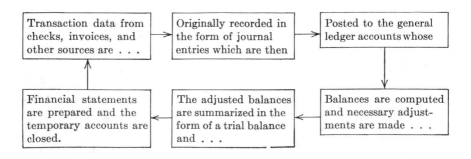

| Transaction data from checks, invoices, and other sources are . . . | Originally recorded in the form of journal entries which are then | Posted to the general ledger accounts whose |
|---|---|---|
| Financial statements are prepared and the temporary accounts are closed. | The adjusted balances are summarized in the form of a trial balance and . . . | Balances are computed and necessary adjustments are made . . . |

## QUESTIONS

**1.** Most general ledger accounts have five columns. What is included in each column? What is a T account and why is it used?

**2.** All increases in anything acquired for the intended use or benefit of an enterprise are recorded on what side of the accounts? Which is the debit side? The credit side?

**3.** How do entries in general journal form indicate where each amount is to be posted?

**4.** What is the meaning of double-entry bookkeeping? Why should the general ledger in a double-entry system always be "in balance"?

**5.** Why are financial statements that are prepared on the accrual basis of accounting supposedly more accurate than statements which report data on the cash basis?

**6.** What costs are not reported on a cash basis even when the cash basis of accounting is employed? What costs may be reported on a cash basis despite the fact that the statements are assumed to be accrual basis statements?

**7.** What determines the selection of account titles? What determines the number of accounts that are included?

**8.** One accounting book of record is sometimes referred to as a book of original entry, another as a book of final entry. Why? Why not omit the journal and record the data directly in the general ledger accounts? Or omit the ledger and prepare only journal entries?

**9.** Explain the meaning of "the accounting cycle."

**10.** Define the following: journalize, post, adjustments, and trial balance.

**11.** A. B. Dow's equity in his business was valued at $2,400 as of the first day of the month; at $2,830 on the last day of the month. What caused this increase? Did his cash balance increase by the same amount during the month? Did net assets (total assets less total liabilities), from the time of the original investment to the end of business on April 30, increase by the same amount as the owner's equity? Why?

**12.** When is a cost incurred? When is income earned? (Assume the accrual basis of reporting.)

**13.** Why should the trial balance of a general ledger maintained under the double-entry system always balance?

**14.** How are the three primary financial statements dated? Why?

**15.** In what order are the statements usually prepared? Why?

## CHAPTER 3

# ACCOUNTING FOR A TRADING ENTERPRISE

Trading enterprises sell, primarily, tangible items rather than services. Accounting for such firms must, therefore, include the recording and reporting of purchases and sales of merchandise, as well as the numerous other costs incident to buying and selling goods and the general operation of the business. In accounting for most retail and wholesale firms, the cost of merchandise sold is computed at the end of the period from data accumulated in the accounting records and a physical count of merchandise on hand at the end of the period; i.e., the beginning inventory plus purchases (which are separately recorded) equals the cost of merchandise available for sale, less the ending inventory (determined by a physical count of goods on hand) equals the cost of merchandise sold. Many other types of costs incurred by trading concerns are the same as those incurred by service and manufacturing enterprises, e.g., wages expense, rent expense, and the depreciation of fixed assets. Those aspects of accounting which are peculiar to manufacturing enterprises will be discussed in Chapter 11.

## THE ACCOUNTING CYCLE—TRADING ENTERPRISES

The accounting cycle of a trading enterprise follows the same pattern as that of a service enterprise. The steps in the procedure may be shortened somewhat and outlined as follows:

1. Journalize and post the regular transactions.
2. Compute account balances and take a preliminary trial balance (if desired).
3. Journalize and post the adjusting entries.
4. Take a trial balance.
5. Prepare statements.
6. Journalize and post the closing entry.

To provide a review of the procedures already described and to illustrate the new problems encountered in buying and selling merchandise

38

and computing the cost of goods sold, let us examine the records of a typical, small retail operation.

The Machinery Sales Company is a franchised dealer, selling machinery directly to a few large contractors. Machinery is purchased from one manufacturer, usually on open account. The company reports on a calendar year basis and, as of December 31, 1957, had completed ten years of operations. The owner-manager has just signed a fifteen-year renewal of the lease on the warehouse-office building.

The entries below record the transactions of the firm for the month of January, 1958. They have been numbered, as they frequently are under actual working conditions, to facilitate reference to particular transactions. Although each entry is explained in the usual manner, transactions 3, 4, 5, 7, 10, and 14 require additional discussion. These entries are fully explained at the end of the general journal. Study carefully each transaction and the related explanation.

The steps in the accounting cycle have been included as headings for the following discussions whenever appropriate.

*Journalize and Post the Regular Transactions*

Transactions for the Machinery Sales Company during January, 1958, are first entered in the general journal following the same rules for debits and credits as described in Chapter 2. (The explanations included with the entries are, in some instances, more detailed than might be necessary in actual practice.)

General Journal                                            Page 1

| 1958 | Accounts and explanations | Dr. | Cr. |
|------|---------------------------|-----|-----|
| | (1) | | |
| 1-2 | Account Receivable—C. D. Wall | 22,600 | |
| | Sales Income | | 22,600 |
| | (Credit sale) | | |
| | (2) | | |
| 1-3 | Prepaid Insurance | 720 | |
| | Cash in Bank | | 720 |
| | (Renewal of fire and liability insurance for three years; effective date 1-1-58) | | |
| | (3) | | |
| 1-8 | Cash in Bank | 5,940 | |
| | Sales Discounts Allowed | 60 | |
| | Account Receivable—Contractors, Inc. | | 6,000 |
| | (Collection on December sale; 1 per cent discount taken by customer) | | |
| | (4) | | |
| 1-10 | Purchases | 20,000 | |
| | Account Payable—XYZ Mfg. Co. | | 20,000 |
| | (Credit purchase from XYZ Mfg. Co.; terms 1/10, n/30) | | |

General Journal (*Continued*)                    Page 2

| 1958 | Accounts and explanations | Dr. | Cr. |
|------|---------------------------|-----|-----|
|      | (5) | | |
| 1-10 | Freight In | 200 | |
|      | Cash in Bank | | 200 |
|      | (Paid freight charges on above shipment) | | |
|      | (6) | | |
| 1-14 | Account Receivable—City Builders | 16,700 | |
|      | Sales Income | | 16,700 |
|      | (Credit sale) | | |
|      | (7) | | |
| 1-17 | Account Payable—XYZ Mfg. Co. | 20,000 | |
|      | Purchase Discounts Earned | | 200 |
|      | Cash in Bank | | 19,800 |
|      | (Paid XYZ Mfg. Co. within the ten-day discount period) | | |
|      | (8) | | |
| 1-20 | Purchases | 5,100 | |
|      | Account Payable—XYZ Mfg. Co. | | 5,100 |
|      | (Credit purchase from XYZ Mfg. Co. Terms 1/10, n/30) | | |
|      | (9) | | |
| 1-23 | Cash in Bank | 1,100 | |
|      | Sales Income | | 1,100 |
|      | (Cash sale) | | |
|      | (10) | | |
| 1-24 | Sales Returns and Allowances | 1,300 | |
|      | Account Receivable—City Builders | | 1,300 |
|      | (Credit allowed customer for return of defective machinery) | | |
|      | (11) | | |
| 1-27 | Advertising Expense | 140 | |
|      | Cash in Bank | | 140 |
|      | (Payment of January advertising) | | |
|      | (12) | | |
| 1-29 | Withdrawals | 600 | |
|      | Cash in Bank | | 600 |
|      | (Cash withdrawn by the owner for his personal use) | | |
|      | (13) | | |
| 1-30 | Vehicles | 3,000 | |
|      | Note Payable | | 2,600 |
|      | Cash in Bank | | 400 |
|      | (Purchased truck; $400 down and note for balance: $1,300 due 7-30-58, $1,300 due 1-30-59) | | |
|      | (14) | | |
| 1-31 | Sales Salaries Expense | 500 | |
|      | Office Salaries Expense | 300 | |
|      | FOASI Withheld | | 18 |
|      | Income Taxes Withheld | | 82 |
|      | Cash in Bank | | 700 |
|      | (Salaries for January) | | |

General Journal (*Continued*)  Page 3

| 1958 | Accounts and explanations | Dr. | Cr. |
|------|---------------------------|-----|-----|
| | (15) | | |
| 1-31 | Rent Expense | 330 | |
| | Cash in Bank | | 330 |
| | (January rent paid) | | |

Entry (3): Machinery Sales Company sells on credit terms of 1/10th, n/e.o.m. This means that the customers can deduct 1 per cent from the amount due if payment is made by the tenth of the month following the month of sale. If not paid by this time the full "net" amount is to be paid by the end of the month (e.o.m.). In this instance the company allows the debt of $6,000 to be paid by a check for $5,940. The $60 loss on the conversion of receivables to cash is an expense, generally called Sales Discounts or Sales Discounts Allowed.

Entry (4): The Purchases account is reserved for the accumulation of the cost of merchandise that is purchased for resale to customers.

Entry (5): The machinery purchased was forwarded f.o.b. shipping point by the manufacturer. This indicates that the purchase is free on board only at the shipping point and that the freight must be paid by the buyer. F.o.b. destination would indicate just the opposite; i.e., the shipment is free on board to the destination and the shipper, not the purchaser, would pay the freight charges.

Entry (7): Credit purchases are on terms of 1/10, n/30. If payment is made within ten days of the invoice date, 1 per cent can be deducted from the gross purchase price. This entry shows that a debt of $20,000 was satisfied by issuing a check for only $19,800. The gain of $200 is classified as Purchase Discounts Earned, an income account. If payment had not been made within ten days, the full amount would have been paid sometime between the tenth and the thirtieth day.

Entry (10): This entry reveals that City Builders, a customer, has returned machinery and that the company has allowed "credit" on their account receivable. (If a man charges a $5 shirt and a $2 necktie and later returns the $2 necktie, the store would give him credit for $2 and decrease his receivable to $5.) Returned merchandise actually represents a decrease in sales, but the amount is normally debited to Sales Returns and Allowances, often considered a negative income account. The balance of this account is shown separately on the income statement, where it is deducted from gross sales to arrive at net sales. Too many sales returns and allowances may indicate inefficiency and customer dissatisfaction and this information would not be available if the Sales Income account were debited for the returns and allowances.

Allowances are decreases in charges to customers for defects, etc. A TV shop, for example, might allow a credit of $10 to a customer because his new set was scratched at time of delivery.

A *Purchase* Returns and Allowances account is used for the accumulation of credits allowed the purchaser for goods returned or allowances granted. The balance of this account is deducted from Purchases in determining the cost of goods sold on the statement of income and expense.

Entry (14): As this entry shows, an employee rarely receives a check for the full amount of his salary. Most employers must withhold $2\frac{1}{4}$ per cent for FOASI (Federal Old-Age and Survivors Insurance, often known simply as social security or old-age benefits) on the first $4,200 paid each employee and a certain amount for Federal income taxes, determined by the amount of the salary and the number of personal exemptions claimed by the employee. Many employers withhold for a number of other items, e.g., state income tax, insurance, union dues, etc.

"Withheld" means that the cash is left in the bank rather than paid to the employees, that the employer must forward the amounts at a later date, and that a liability must be recognized for these amounts in the meantime. The employer is actually in the position of a trustee who is legally responsible for the safekeeping of the funds withheld and for the making of adequate and timely payments from these funds.[1]

*Compute Account Balances*

The general ledger accounts for the Machinery Sales Company are shown on pages 44 to 47. A new ledger has been "opened" by entering the final balances of the preceding year for assets and equities on new account pages. Each of these has been noted as the "balance" for the first day of the new period. Data from the journal entries for January, 1958 have been posted, added or deducted from the beginning balances, and the new balances noted. [A check ($\checkmark$) mark is usually entered after each dollar amount in a journal entry to show that the amount has been posted to the ledger.] A trial balance may be taken at this point, if desired.

*Journalize and Post the Adjusting Entries*

After the regular entries have been posted and new balances computed, the accountant will normally proceed with the preparation of adjustments. Explanations of the adjusting entries are presented immediately below each entry. More complete discussions are again given to make clear the reason for each entry.

Entry (16): The total original cost of the fixtures and equipment

---

[1] To simplify this example several common expenses have not been included.

General Journal (*Continued*)  Page 4

| 1958 | Accounts and explanations | Dr. | Cr. |
|------|---------------------------|-----|-----|
| | Adjustments | | |
| | (16) | | |
| 1-31 | Depreciation Expense | 140 | |
| | Accumulated Depreciation—Fixtures and Equipment | | 40 |
| | Accumulated Depreciation—Vehicles | | 100 |
| | (Fixtures and equipment: original cost of $4,800 divided by 120 months is $40. Vehicles: original cost of $6,000 divided by 60 months is $100) | | |
| | (17) | | |
| 1-31 | Insurance Expense | 20 | |
| | Prepaid Insurance | | 20 |
| | (Monthly expense equals total premium of $720 divided by 36 months, or $20) | | |
| | (18) | | |
| 1-31 | Bad Debt Expense | 202 | |
| | Allowance for Doubtful Accounts | | 202 |
| | (The amount estimated as doubtful is equal to ½ per cent of January sales) | | |

and the vehicles is divided by the *estimated useful life* to compute the monthly depreciation expense. Scrap or trade-in value has been ignored, as is often the case. This method absorbs the original cost over the expected useful life but may result in book values that are quite different from current market values. (Additional discussions of depreciation and other typical adjustments will be found in Chapter 4.)

Entry (17): The advance premium of $720 gives the firm insurance protection for three years; the premium cost should be expired ratably over the period; i.e., total cost of $720 divided by 36 months yields a charge of $20 per month.

Entry (18): A governing principle of accounting is that all costs related to the income earned should be reported in the same period in which the income is earned; i.e., related income and expenses should be matched. Past experience shows that this firm will be unable to collect approximately ½ per cent of its credit sales and that this amount should, therefore, be deducted as bad debt expense each period. The entry serves to record this expense and also to value the accounts receivable by deducting the doubtful amount from the gross amount due.

*General Ledger Accounts of the Machinery Sales Company.* Each of the following accounts would represent a page in the general ledger of the Machinery Sales Company. The accounts have been numbered to indicate their order in the ledger. Both the regular entries and the adjusting entries have been posted and the subsequent balances noted.

EXHIBIT 3-1

General Ledger Accounts

(1) Cash in Bank

| 1958 | | Dr. | Cr. | Bal. |
|---|---|---|---|---|
| 1-1 | Bal. | | | 18,900 dr. |
| 1-3 | | | 720 | |
| 1-8 | | 5,940 | | |
| 1-10 | | | 200 | |
| 1-17 | | | 19,800 | |
| 1-23 | | 1,100 | | |
| 1-27 | | | 140 | |
| 1-29 | | | 600 | |
| 1-30 | | | 400 | |
| 1-31 | | | 700 | |
| 1-31 | | | 330 | 3,050 dr. |

(2) Account Receivable—City Builders

| 1958 | | Dr. | Cr. | Bal. |
|---|---|---|---|---|
| 1-14 | | 16,700 | | |
| 1-24 | Cr. on returns | | 1,300 | 15,400 dr. |

(3) Account Rec.—Contractors, Inc.

| 1958 | | Dr. | Cr. | Bal. |
|---|---|---|---|---|
| 1-1 | Bal. | | | 6,000 dr. |
| 1-8 | | | 6,000 | 00 |

(4) Account Receivable—C. D. Wall

| 1958 | | Dr. | Cr. | Bal. |
|---|---|---|---|---|
| 1-2 | | 22,600 | | 22,600 dr. |

(5) Allowance for Doubtful Accounts

| 1958 | | Dr. | Cr. | Bal. |
|---|---|---|---|---|
| 1-1 | Bal. | | | 40 cr. |
| 1-31 | | | 202 | 242 cr. |

(6) Inventory

| 1958 | | Dr. | Cr. | Bal. |
|---|---|---|---|---|
| 1-1 | Bal. | | | 37,400 dr. |

(7) Fixtures and Equipment

| 1958 | | Dr. | Cr. | Bal. |
|---|---|---|---|---|
| 1-1 | Bal. | | | 4,800 dr. |

(8) Accumulated Depreciation (F&E)

| 1958 | | Dr. | Cr. | Bal. |
|---|---|---|---|---|
| 1-1 | Bal. | | | 2,600 cr. |
| 1-31 | | | 40 | 2,640 cr. |

(9) Vehicles

| 1958 | | Dr. | Cr. | Bal. |
|---|---|---|---|---|
| 1-1 | Bal. | | | 6,000 dr. |
| 1-30 | Truck | 3,000 | | 9,000 dr. |

(10) Accumulated Dep.—Vehicles

| 1958 | | Dr. | Cr. | Bal. |
|---|---|---|---|---|
| 1-1 | Bal. | | | 4,100 cr. |
| 1-31 | | | 100 | 4,200 cr. |

(11) Prepaid Insurance

| 1958 | | Dr. | Cr. | Bal. |
|---|---|---|---|---|
| 1-3 | | 720 | | |
| 1-31 | | | 20 | 700 dr. |

(12) Account Payable—XYZ Mfg. Co.

| 1958 | | Dr. | Cr. | Bal. |
|---|---|---|---|---|
| 1-10 | | | 20,000 | |
| 1-17 | | 20,000 | | |
| 1-20 | | | 5,100 | 5,100 cr. |

(13) FOASI Withheld

| 1958 | | Dr. | Cr. | Bal. |
|---|---|---|---|---|
| 1-31 | | | 18 | 18 cr. |

**Exhibit 3-1**
General Ledger Accounts (*Continued*)

(14)  Income Taxes Withheld

| 1958 | | Dr. | Cr. | Bal. |
|---|---|---|---|---|
| 1-31 | | | 82 | 82 cr. |

(15)  Note Payable

| 1958 | | Dr. | Cr. | Bal. |
|---|---|---|---|---|
| 1-30 | | | 2,600 | 2,600 cr. |

(16)  Invested Equity

| 1958 | | Dr. | Cr. | Bal. |
|---|---|---|---|---|
| 1-1 | Bal. | | | 30,000 cr. |

(17)  Earned Equity

| 1958 | | Dr. | Cr. | Bal. |
|---|---|---|---|---|
| 1-1 | Bal. | | | 36,360 cr. |

(18)  Withdrawals

| 1958 | | Dr. | Cr. | Bal. |
|---|---|---|---|---|
| 1-29 | | 600 | | 600 dr. |

(19)  Sales Income

| 1958 | | Dr. | Cr. | Bal. |
|---|---|---|---|---|
| 1-2 | | | 22,600 | |
| 1-14 | | | 16,700 | |
| 1-23 | | | 1,100 | 40,400 cr. |

(20)  Sales Returns and Allowances

| 1958 | | Dr. | Cr. | Bal. |
|---|---|---|---|---|
| 1-24 | | 1,300 | | 1,300 dr. |

(21)  Purchases

| 1958 | | Dr. | Cr. | Bal. |
|---|---|---|---|---|
| 1-10 | | 20,000 | | |
| 1-20 | | 5,100 | | 25,100 dr. |

(22)  Purchase Returns & Allowances

| 1958 | | Dr. | Cr. | Bal. |
|---|---|---|---|---|

(23)  Freight In

| 1958 | | Dr. | Cr. | Bal. |
|---|---|---|---|---|
| 1-10 | | 200 | | 200 dr. |

(24)  Sales Salaries Expense

| 1958 | | Dr. | Cr. | Bal. |
|---|---|---|---|---|
| 1-31 | | 500 | | 500 dr. |

(25)  Advertising Expense

| 1958 | | Dr. | Cr. | Bal. |
|---|---|---|---|---|
| 1-27 | | 140 | | 140 dr. |

(26)  Office Salaries Expense

| 1958 | | Dr. | Cr. | Bal. |
|---|---|---|---|---|
| 1-31 | | 300 | | 300 dr. |

(27)  Bad Debt Expense

| 1958 | | Dr. | Cr. | Bal. |
|---|---|---|---|---|
| 1-31 | | 202 | | 202 dr. |

(28)  Rent Expense

| 1958 | | Dr. | Cr. | Bal. |
|---|---|---|---|---|
| 1-31 | | 330 | | 330 dr. |

(29)  Insurance Expense

| 1958 | | Dr. | Cr. | Bal. |
|---|---|---|---|---|
| 1-31 | | 20 | | 20 dr. |

EXHIBIT 3-1
General Ledger Accounts (*Continued*)

(30)      Depreciation Expense

| 1958 | | Dr. | Cr. | Bal. |
|------|--|-----|-----|------|
| 1-31 | | 140 | | 140 dr. |

(32)      Sales Discounts Allowed

| 1958 | | Dr. | Cr. | Bal. |
|------|--|-----|-----|------|
| 1-8 | | 60 | | 60 dr. |

(31)   Purchase Discounts Earned

| 1958 | | Dr. | Cr. | Bal. |
|------|--|-----|-----|------|
| 1-17 | | | 200 | 200 cr. |

(33)      Sundry Expenses

| 1958 | | Dr. | Cr. | Bal. |
|------|--|-----|-----|------|
| | | | | |

## *Take a Trial Balance*

A list of the general ledger accounts with their respective balances as of January 31, 1958, appears as shown in Exhibit 3-2.

Two of the amounts in the Machinery Sales Company trial balance represent beginning balances as of January 1, 1958: Inventory, $37,400, and Earned Equity, $36,360. The final balance for Earned Equity cannot be computed until the statement of income and expense is finished and the amount of net profit is known, and this statement cannot be completed until the cost value of the ending inventory is known. Since it is sometimes costly to take monthly counts, inventory estimates may be used for the preparation of interim statements. A complete physical inventory should be taken at least once each year, however, in order to check the estimates and ensure the accuracy of the annual statements.

A physical count of machinery on hand was made by the owner of Machinery Sales Company as of January 31, 1958. After the compiling of quantities, the inventory items were priced in accordance with the latest purchase invoice prices. On this basis, the total value of the ending inventory was $26,192.

## *Prepare Financial Statements*

The financial statements shown in Exhibits 3-3, 3-4, and 3-5 have been prepared directly from the trial balance and appear in the order that they are usually prepared; they are often presented in the opposite sequence.

This statement has classified income and the various expenses by the use of appropriate descriptions, has measured in dollars the income earned and the costs expired during the month of January, and has measured the results of operations as a net profit of $1,100; i.e., value gained has exceeded value relinquished by $1,100.

EXHIBIT 3-2

MACHINERY SALES COMPANY

Trial Balance as of January 31, 1958

| Accounts | Dr. | Cr. |
|---|---|---|
| Cash in bank | $ 3,050 | |
| Account receivable—City Builders | 15,400 | |
| Account receivable—C. D. Wall | 22,600 | |
| Allowance for doubtful accounts | | $ 242 |
| Inventory | 37,400 | |
| Fixtures and equipment | 4,800 | |
| Accumulated depreciation (F & E) | | 2,640 |
| Vehicles | 9,000 | |
| Accumulated depreciation (Vehicles) | | 4,200 |
| Prepaid insurance | 700 | |
| Accounts payable—XYZ Mfg. Co | | 5,100 |
| FOASI withheld | | 18 |
| Income taxes withheld | | 82 |
| Note payable | | 2,600 |
| Invested equity | | 30,000 |
| Earned equity | | 36,360 |
| Withdrawals | 600 | |
| Sales income | | 40,400 |
| Sales returns and allowances | 1,300 | |
| Purchases | 25,100 | |
| Freight in | 200 | |
| Sales salaries expense | 500 | |
| Advertising expense | 140 | |
| Office salaries expense | 300 | |
| Bad debt expense | 202 | |
| Rent expense | 330 | |
| Insurance expense | 20 | |
| Depreciation expense | 140 | |
| Purchase discounts earned | | 200 |
| Sales discounts allowed | 60 | |
| Totals | $121,842 | $121,842 |

Three new statement classifications are introduced in Exhibit 3-3:

1. "Operating expenses" consists of those expired costs that are essential to the primary operation of the business.

2. "Net operating profit" is gross profit less operating expenses.

3. "Other income and expense" includes income and expense that are not directly necessary to the primary operation; e.g., Machinery Sales Company could have operated without sales and purchase discounts but not without salaries and rent expenses.

Although incidental to the major operation "other income and expense" may be significant in amount and importance. Interest expense, for example, may be important—and even necessary—but such financial expenses are

EXHIBIT 3-3
MACHINERY SALES COMPANY
Statement of Income and Expense for the Month Ended January 31, 1958

Income:
Sales income............................. $40,400
Less sales returns and allowances........... 1,300
Net sales............................. $39,100
Cost of goods sold:
Inventory, Jan. 1, 1958............ $37,400
Purchases............... $25,100
Freight-in................ 200
Cost of purchases................ 25,300
Available for sale................. $62,700
Inventory, Jan. 31, 1958.......... 26,192   36,508
Gross profit............................. $ 2,592
Operating expenses:
Sales salaries expense.............. $    500
Advertising expense.............. 140
Office salaries expense............. 300
Bad debt expense................. 202
Rent expense.................... 330
Insurance expense................. 20
Depreciation expense............ 140   1,632
Net operating profit........................ $    960
Other income and expense:
Purchase discounts earned.......... $    200
Sales discounts allowed............ 60
Net other income...................... 140
Net profit................................. $ 1,100

usually included as other expenses because operations are presumably unaffected by the source of funds.

The next statement to be prepared shows in detail the changes in the owner's earned equity.

EXHIBIT 3-4
MACHINERY SALES COMPANY
Statement of Changes in Earned Equity for the Month Ended January 31, 1958

Earned equity, Jan. 1, 1958........................ $36,360
Add net profit for the period........................ 1,100
Total........................................ $37,460
Less owner's withdrawals during the period.......... 600
Earned equity, Jan. 31, 1958....................... $36,860

The statement of changes in earned equity indicates that as of January 1, 1958, the ownership interest in the business assets resulting from ten years of operations was valued at $36,360 and that the net profit represents an increment of $1,100 in this interest during the current period. Owner's withdrawals indicate that property valued at $600 has been drawn from the business for personal use and that the valuation of the owner's rights has, therefore, been decreased by that amount.

Invested equity is *not* reduced by withdrawals. Owners usually want the amount they have invested in the business shown as a separate item on the statements, and, in addition, they assume that they are withdrawing profits or earnings, not amounts invested. As a consequence, the amount of the withdrawals is considered a reduction of earned equity rather than invested equity, for earned equity is the measure of ownership interest arising from profits or earnings retained in the business.

After the ending balance for Earned Equity has been developed, the statement which presents a listing of assets owned and the equity interests therein can be completed.

EXHIBIT 3-5

MACHINERY SALES COMPANY

Statement of Financial Condition as of January 31, 1958

*Assets*

| | | |
|---|---:|---:|
| Cash in bank | | $ 3,050 |
| Accounts receivable | $38,000 | |
| Less allowance for doubtful accounts | 242 | 37,758 |
| Inventory | | 26,192 |
| Fixtures and equipment | $ 4,800 | |
| Less accumulated depreciation | 2,640 | 2,160 |
| Vehicles | $ 9,000 | |
| Less accumulated depreciation | 4,200 | 4,800 |
| Prepaid insurance | | 700 |
| Total assets | | $74,660 |

*Equities*

| | | |
|---|---:|---:|
| Liabilities: | | |
| Account payable | $ 5,100 | |
| FOASI withheld | 18 | |
| Income taxes withheld | 82 | |
| Note payable | 2,600 | |
| Total liabilities | | $ 7,800 |
| Owner's equity: | | |
| Invested equity | $30,000 | |
| Earned equity | 36,860 | |
| Total owner's equity | | 66,860 |
| Total equities | | $74,660 |

Total assets per the statement will not agree with total debits per the trial balance because there are several credit balances that are listed among, and deducted from, the asset values on the statement. Allowance for Doubtful Accounts and Accumulated Depreciation are examples of valuation accounts (or "negative-asset" accounts) that are regularly deducted from their related asset balances.

The amounts due from *each* customer are not considered sufficiently important to be presented separately on the statement. For that reason, only the total of all accounts receivable is customarily shown, as in the statement presented above. This is particularly true if the receivables are more numerous than they are in this illustrative problem. Even small firms usually have dozens of accounts receivable; large firms often have thousands.

### *Journalize and Post the Closing Entry*

If the books are to be closed, the closing entry must remove the old inventory balance, set up the new inventory as an asset (debit), and reduce the balances in all expired cost and all income accounts to zero. When these debits and credits are entered in the journal, it will be found that the difference between their totals measures the change in the owner's equity. The closing entry for the Machinery Sales Company, taken from the Income and Expense columns of the working trial balance, Exhibit 3-6, would be as shown below.

General Journal (*Continued*)                     Page 5

| 1958 | Accounts and explanations | Dr. | Cr. |
|---|---|---|---|
| | (19)<br>Closing Entry | | |
| | Inventory | 26,192 | |
| | Sales | 40,400 | |
| | Purchase Discounts Earned | 200 | |
| |     Inventory | | 37,400 |
| |     Sales Returns and Allowances | | 1,300 |
| |     Purchases | | 25,100 |
| |     Freight In | | 200 |
| |     Sales Salaries Expense | | 500 |
| |     Advertising Expense | | 140 |
| |     Offiice Salaries Expense | | 300 |
| |     Bad Debt Expense | | 202 |
| |     Rent Expense | | 330 |
| |     Depreciation Expense | | 140 |
| |     Insurance Expense | | 20 |
| |     Sales Discounts Allowed | | 60 |
| |     Earned Equity | | 1,100 |
| | (To record the new inventory, close the old inventory, close all cost, income, and expense accounts, and transfer the net profit to the owner's Earned Equity account) | | |

When this entry has been made, it is posted to the general ledger and the books are then said to be closed. A more detailed discussion of closing procedures appears in Chapter 5.

In all probability the accountant or bookkeeper for the Machinery Sales Company would not prepare a closing entry at the end of an interim period, because the income and expense accounts should be allowed to accumulate data for the entire year in order to expedite preparation of the annual statements and because formal closing of the temporary accounts is not necessary for the preparation of statements. When the temporary accounts are not closed, income and expenses for a particular month can be computed by deducting cumulative balances at the beginning of the month from cumulative balances at the end of the month. If sales from the first of the year to the end of May were $60,000 and at the end of June were $70,000, sales for June would be $10,000.

### WORKING TRIAL BALANCE

A working trial balance is a summarizing device which consists of a preliminary trial balance plus columns for adjustments and for the classification of each item according to the statement on which it appears. This device is particularly useful under certain circumstances: (1) in auditing it serves as a permanent summary of the financial data and as a central index to the many schedules that support the various account balances; (2) when the accounts for a firm are very numerous and there are many adjustments to be made, the working papers give the accountant a concentrated, over-all view of the account balances, which normally expedites preparation of statements and often increases accuracy, since the statement information does not have to be transcribed from a great number of account pages and perhaps from several different books; (3) in the preparation of *interim* statements it is usually better to enter the adjustments only on the working trial balance rather than actually to journalize and post the adjusting entries at the end of each interim period. At the end of the year, however, the annual adjustments are journalized and posted in the usual manner.

The working trial balance is also a useful learning device. It provides, in one place, a complete picture of the preliminary balances, the adjustments to these balances, and the subsequent classification of each balance according to the statement on which it appears. (Statement columns are usually provided for each statement that is to be prepared, as illustrated on the working trial balance for the Machinery Sales Company in Exhibit 3-6.)

Comments on certain features of the working trial balance follow:

**Preliminary Trial Balance.** This is a trial balance of the general ledger accounts before adjustments are made. The trial balances presented earlier in this chapter are frequently called "adjusted trial balances" because they are prepared after adjustments have been recorded in the accounts.

## EXHIBIT 3-6
### MACHINERY SALES COMPANY
### Working Trial Balance as of January 31, 1958

| Accounts | Preliminary trial balance | | Adjustments | | Statement of income and expenses | | Statement of changes in earned equity | | Statement of financial condition | |
|---|---|---|---|---|---|---|---|---|---|---|
| | Dr. | Cr. | Dr. | Cr. | Dr. | Cr. | Dr. | Cr. | Dr. | Cr. |
| Cash in bank | 3,050 | | | | | | | | 3,050 | |
| Account receivable—City Builders | 15,400 | | | | | | | | 15,400 | |
| Account receivable—C. D. Wall | 22,600 | | | | | | | | 22,600 | |
| Allowance for doubtful accounts | | 40 | | (c)202 | | | | | | 242 |
| Inventory | 37,400 | | | | 37,400 | 26,192 | | | 26,192 | |
| Fixtures and equipment | 4,800 | | | | | | | | 4,800 | |
| Accumulated depreciation—F & E | | 2,600 | | (b) 40 | | | | | | 2,640 |
| Vehicles | 9,000 | | | | | | | | 9,000 | |
| Accumulated depreciation—vehicles | | 4,100 | | (b)100 | | | | | | 4,200 |
| Prepaid insurance | 720 | | | (a) 20 | | | | | 700 | |
| Accounts payable—XYZ Mfg. Co. | | 5,100 | | | | | | | | 5,100 |
| FOASI withheld | | 18 | | | | | | | | 18 |
| Income taxes withheld | | 82 | | | | | | | | 82 |
| Note payable | | 2,600 | | | | | | | | 2,600 |
| Invested equity | | 30,000 | | | | | | | | 30,000 |
| Earned equity | | 36,360 | | | | | | 36,360 | | |
| Withdrawals | 600 | | | | | | 600 | | | |
| Sales income | | 40,400 | | | | 40,400 | | | | |
| Sales returns and allowances | 1,300 | | | | 1,300 | | | | | |
| Purchases | 25,100 | | | | 25,100 | | | | | |
| Freight in | 200 | | | | 200 | | | | | |

52

Exhibit 3-6 (Continued)

| Accounts | Preliminary trial balance | | Adjustments | | Statement of income and expenses | | Statement of changes in earned equity | | Statement of financial condition | |
| --- | --- | --- | --- | --- | --- | --- | --- | --- | --- | --- |
| | Dr. | Cr. | Dr. | Cr. | Dr. | Cr. | Dr. | Cr. | Dr. | Cr. |
| Sales salaries expense | 500 | | | | 500 | | | | | |
| Advertising expense | 140 | | | | 140 | | | | | |
| Office salaries expense | 300 | | | | 300 | | | | | |
| Bad debt expense | | | (c)202 | | 202 | | | | | |
| Rent expense | 330 | | | | 330 | | | | | |
| Insurance expense | | | (a) 20 | | 20 | | | | | |
| Depreciation expense | | | (b)140 | | 140 | | | | | |
| Purchase discounts earned | | 200 | | | | 200 | | | | |
| Sales discounts allowed | 60 | | | | 60 | | | | | |
| | 121,500 | 121,500 | 362 | 362 | 65,692 | 66,792 | | | | |
| Net profit to earned equity | | | | | 1,100 | | | 1,100 | | |
| | | | | | 66,792 | 66,792 | 600 | 37,460 | | |
| | | | | | | | 36,860 | | | 36,860 |
| Earned equity Jan. 31, 1958 | | | | | | | 37,460 | 37,460 | 81,742 | 81,742 |

**Adjustments.** Since this is a working trial balance for an interim period, the adjustment need not be entered in the books of record. If this work sheet were as of the end of the fiscal year, the adjustments would have to be journalized and posted after the statements were prepared in order to provide a complete financial history in the permanent books of record.

**Classification of Account Balances.** After the preliminary trial balance and adjustments are entered on the working trial balance, the next problem is one of classification according to statement. The items are normally extended one by one in the order they are presented on the trial balance. All asset and liability balances and the Invested Equity balance are extended to the Statement of Financial Condition columns; earned equity and withdrawals balances to the Statement of Changes in Earned Equity columns; and the income and expense balances to the Statement of Income and Expense columns. Where an adjusting amount appears on the same line with a preliminary balance, it is added or deducted as indicated, and the adjusted balance extended to the proper statement column. A preliminary debit balance would be increased by a debit adjustment and decreased by a credit adjustment; the opposite would be true for a preliminary credit balance.

**Inventories.** Reference to the statements of the Machinery Sales Company will show that in the computation of cost of goods sold the opening inventory is added, and the closing inventory is deducted, and that the closing inventory also appears among the assets. The same results are accomplished on the working trial balance by extending the beginning inventory balance to the Statement of Income and Expense columns as a debit (increase) in the costs for the period, by entering the final inventory balance as a credit (decrease) in the same columns, and by recording this latter amount as a debit (increase) among the assets in the Statement of Financial Condition columns.

**Net Profit.** In the Statement of Income and Expense columns a total of the credits and a total of the debits are taken. The difference is the net profit; this amount is transferred to Earned Equity, just as it is on the statements or in the closing of the books.

**Earned Equity.** The Earned Equity columns on the working trial balance accumulate the same data that are presented on a statement of changes in earned equity: opening balance for earned equity, plus net profit, less withdrawals. The net result represents the balance of earned equity at the end of the period and is transferred to the Statement of Financial Condition columns, just as the ending balance for earned equity is transferred from the Statement of Changes in Earned Equity to the Statement of Financial Condition.

In concluding this particular discussion, one point should be emphasized: a working trial balance is not a statement or report; it is a means of accumulating, adjusting, and classifying accounting data for use in the preparation of statements.

## SUMMARY

Financial transactions are recorded in journals as of the date of their occurrence. At the end of each accounting period, however, it is usually necessary to prepare entries to adjust data already recorded and to accrue certain data that have not yet been recorded. After all necessary adjustments, including accruals, have been journalized and posted, the account balances are assumed to be reasonably correct. If a working trial balance is not prepared, the adjustments may be recorded and posted before a trial balance is taken. When a working trial balance is to be included, a trial balance of the general ledger accounts is prepared *before* the adjustments are recorded. Statements are then prepared from the completed working trial balance, and if year end, the adjustments are entered in the books *after* completion of the statements. If a working trial balance is not employed, the financial statements are prepared directly from the "adjusted" trial balance.

Recording transactions in the form of general journal entries is a slow, laborious process. As a consequence, most transactions are usually recorded in special journals that make it possible to eliminate the writing of many account titles and to post periodic totals, rather than each and every dollar amount included in the individual entries. A knowledge of these special journals, which are discussed in the next chapter, is not necessary for an understanding of accounting principles, but is necessary for an understanding of the record-keeping processes that are employed by most businesses.

## QUESTIONS

**1.** The dollar measures of earned equity and net profit will be equal at the end of the first reporting period but not thereafter. Why?

**2.** Costs should be absorbed as expenses during the periods in which they provide services. On what basis are the costs of operating assets usually allocated as expenses?

**3.** All financial changes, including closing entries, must be recorded in both permanent books of record (the journal and the general ledger). What is accomplished by a closing entry? Is a closing entry necessary at the end of an interim period? Why?

**4.** In accounting, what is meant by "purchases"?

**5.** On June 25 a customer is billed for $200 on terms of 2/10, n/30. If payment is received on July 7, what amount should the customer have paid? What amount could have been paid if the terms were 2/10th, n/e.o.m.?

**6.** A purchases merchandise from B. Freight charges are f.o.b. shipping point. Who should pay the freight bill?

**7.** B allows A credit for defective merchandise that was returned. What accounts should each of them debit and credit?

**8.** An employer "withholds" from an employee. What does this mean?

**9.** Why should an adjusting entry for estimated bad debts be made by a firm that has a significant amount of credit sales?

**10.** What two amounts on a trial balance usually represent opening balances rather than closing balances? Why?

**11.** Describe a working trial balance. Why is it useful in the preparation of interim statements?

**12.** How are inventories, net profit, and ending earned equity entered on a working trial balance?

**13.** Why should the cost of a fixed asset be charged as expense during the useful life of the asset? Why not charge the entire cost as expense in the year of purchase?

## CHAPTER 4

# SPECIAL JOURNALS AND SUBSIDIARY LEDGERS

An accounting entry, which is the record of a transaction, is recorded twice, once in a journal and again in the general ledger. A journal entry is the original record of a transaction expressed in the form of account titles and dollar amounts. If the entries are recorded in the general journal form previously discussed and illustrated, each account title that is affected must always be entered and each dollar change must be posted individually to the general ledger. This method proves slow and costly, and accountants, therefore, make use of various other journal forms which eliminate the entering of many account titles and make it possible to post fewer amounts.

## COMBINED COLUMNAR JOURNAL

A combined columnar journal, as illustrated on page 59, affords one means of reducing the time and effort required for journalizing and posting the transactions of a small firm. To illustrate the procedure, the following list of typical transactions has been entered:

Jan.  1.  Cash received for merchandise sold, $140
      3.  Sale of $230 to C. B. Endres on account
      8.  Purchase of merchandise, Alaskan Co., $680 on account
   10.  Collection on account, Brown Inc., $200 less 2 per cent discount
   10.  Paid on account, Abbey Co., $300 less 1 per cent discount
   14.  Collection on account, Wilson Co., $310, no discount
   15.  Purchase of merchandise, Wm. Penn Co., $213 on account
   17.  Cash purchase of merchandise, $60
   20.  Paid on account, Jay Wholesale, $400, no discount
   22.  Sale of $460 to Elkton & Co. on account
   23.  Collected $30 for rent on office above store
   24.  Purchase of merchandise, Torrance Co., $310 on account
   28.  Sale of $176 to Fog Corp. on account
   31.  Paid wages $600 less $86 income tax withheld
   31.  Cash purchase of merchandise $180, Thomas Corp.

Inspection of the columnar journal form shows that "special" columns accumulate either increases or decreases in the accounts that are used most frequently by the XYZ Company; that is, Cash in Bank, Accounts Receivable, Accounts Payable, Purchases, and Sales. All increases and/or decreases in these accounts are entered in the columns which are already headed with the appropriate account title; it is, therefore, unnecessary to enter these account titles and the work of the bookkeeper is reduced. For example, only the name C. B. Endres had to be entered to record the second transaction shown in the columnar journal; it was unnecessary to write "accounts receivable" and "sales." In the average business there would be many more credit sales than the number shown here for the XYZ Company; consequently, the advantage gained would be even more impressive than in this hypothetical example.

The combined journal also illustrates the advantage of fewer postings. For instance, only two postings need be made to Cash in Bank at the end of the month, one for the total amount received during the month and one for the total of all checks issued during the month. The general ledger account for Cash in Bank would appear as follows after the postings at month end had been completed:

Cash in Bank

| 1958 | Explanation | Dr. | Cr. | Bal. |
|------|-------------|-----|-----|------|
| 1-1 | Balance (assumed) | | | 1,842 dr. |
| 1-31 | | 676 | | |
| 1-31 | | | 1,451 | 1,067 dr. |

If the entries had been recorded in general journal form there would have been four debit postings and five credit postings. Most firms will have many more cash transactions than were included here, and there would also be comparatively fewer entries affecting the Other Accounts columns and a much larger proportion of entries affecting the *special* columns. Thus, the advantages gained by employing this type of journal would again be much greater than indicated by the illustration.

An important by-product of this type of journal is a reduction in the number of errors. There are, for instance, fewer chances for errors if only two postings to cash are necessary rather than nine, or if only two are necessary rather than fifty or several hundred, as might be the case in even a fairly small business. This would be true, not only for Cash, but for all accounts that are represented by special columns in the journal. Another factor that decreases the chances for errors is that the journals are "self-balancing." Since the debits and credits for each individual entry must be equal, the sum of the debit column totals must be equal to the sum of the credit column totals. By comparing these two sums the

Exhibit 4-1
XYZ Company
Columnar Journal

| | Debits | | | | | | Credits | | | | |
| --- | --- | --- | --- | --- | --- | --- | --- | --- | --- | --- | --- |
| Cash in bank | Accounts receivable | Accounts payable | Purchases | Other accounts | Date 1958 | Names of customers, creditors, and other accounts | Cash in bank | Accounts receivable | Accounts payable | Sales | Other accounts |
| 140 | | | | | 1-2 | C. B. Endres | | | | 140 | |
| | 230 | | | | 1-3 | Alaskan Co. | | | | 230 | |
| | | | 680 | | 1-8 | Brown, Inc. | | | 680 | | |
| 196 | | | | 4✓ | 1-10 | Discounts Allowed | | | | | |
| | | | | | 1-10 | Abbey Co. | | 200 | | | |
| | | 300 | | | 1-14 | Discounts Earned | 297 | | | | 3✓ |
| | | | 213 | | 1-15 | Wilson Co. | | | 213 | | |
| | | | 60 | | 1-17 | Wm. Penn Co. | 60 | | | | |
| | | 400 | | | 1-20 | Jay Wholesale | 400 | | | | |
| | 460 | | | | 1-22 | Elkton & Co. | | | | 460 | |
| 30 | | | | | 1-23 | Rental Income | | | | | 30✓ |
| | | | 310 | | 1-24 | Torrance Co. | | | 310 | | |
| 310 | 176 | | | | 1-28 | Fog Corp. | | 310 | | 176 | |
| | | | | 600✓ | 1-31 | Wages Expense | 514 | | | | |
| | | | | | | Income Tax Withheld | | | | | 86✓ |
| | | | 180 | | 1-31 | Thomas Corp. | 180 | | | | |
| 676 ✓ | 866 ✓ | 700 ✓ | 1,443 ✓ | 604 X | | | 1,451 ✓ | 510 ✓ | 1,203 ✓ | 1,006 ✓ | 119 X |

Preposting proof:
Sum of debit columns—$4,289
Sum of credit columns—$4,289

Note: Check (√) marks indicate amounts that have been posted to the general ledger accounts: "special" column totals and individual items from the "other accounts" columns. "X" indicates that a column total is not posted but that the corresponding detail has been posted.

mathematical accuracy of all the entries for the period can be easily proved *before* any postings to the general ledger are made.

Despite its advantages, this type of columnar journal is seldom used in a large business since many additional advantages can be gained with the use of a variety of special journals.

## SPECIAL JOURNALS

A single combined columnar journal would not only become extremely large and unwieldy if there were many transactions, but it must also be recognized that there is a physical limit to the number of special columns that can be conveniently included in one book. To extend this limit, more special columns can be introduced by the use of several journals rather than one. Because many transactions continually affect the same classification of financial data, it is customary to establish separate books of record for these classes of transactions. Cash, for instance, is received by a business unit from many sources and, for that reason, a separate record is usually maintained for recording the various increases in cash and the origins thereof. Many checks are issued and, as a consequence, a separate journal is normally employed for all entries that result in a decrease in cash. If a large number of credit sales are transacted, a special book is often employed to maintain a chronological record of these sales and the resulting accounts receivable. Credit purchases of merchandise may also be numerous and, if so, an individual journal can be maintained solely for these purchases and the resulting accounts payable.

The records discussed above are considered *special* journals as contrasted with the *general* journal, which includes a wide variety of current, correcting, adjusting, and closing entries. These books are also *special* in that all entries of a certain type must be entered in a specific journal, assuming that a special journal for that type of entry is maintained. If the five journals described above are in use, it would be required that *all* increases in cash be recorded in the cash receipts journal; that *all* checks issued be entered in the cash disbursements journal; that *all* credit sales of merchandise be entered in the sales journal; that *all* purchases of merchandise for resale which are not paid for immediately be recorded in the purchases journal. Should a firm have other transactions that continually affect the same one or two accounts, special journals can be established to expedite their recording.

Despite the many advantages afforded, it is not feasible to have a special journal to take care of all different classes of transactions. Hence, all accounting systems must still have a general journal. This book of original entry is for all financial data that cannot be recorded in the special journals, which frequently means that it is for all entries other than those that affect cash, accounts receivable, or accounts payable. If an entry will "fit" in a special journal, it must be entered there. If an entry will not fit in a special journal, then it is recorded in the general journal.

The special journals also make possible a subdivision of the bookkeeping work that could not be achieved if only a combined columnar journal were in use. For example, one or many persons are able to concentrate on cash disbursements, or one individual or a department may be concerned only with the recording of credit purchases and accounts payable.

The special journals that follow include the same entries that were introduced in the columnar journal for the XYZ Company. These journals would customarily contain more special columns than have been introduced in these illustrations. All of them are self-balancing in that the sum of the debit totals should equal the sum of the credit totals.

*Cash Receipts Journal*

As already mentioned, *all* incoming cash, regardless of source, must be recorded in a cash receipts journal. Exhibit 4-2 shows a page from a cash receipts journal (cents have been omitted as usual).

EXHIBIT 4-2
XYZ COMPANY
Cash Receipts Journal

| Date received 1958 | Received from | Dr. Cash | Cr. Sales | Cr. Accts. Rec. | Sundry | | |
|---|---|---|---|---|---|---|---|
| | | | | | Dr. | Cr. | Account |
| 1-2 | W. W. Green | 140 | 140 | | | | |
| 1-10 | Brown, Inc. | 196 | | 200 | 4 | | Disc'ts Allowed |
| 1-14 | Wilson Co. | 310 | | 310 | | | |
| 1-23 | Tally-Ho Co. | 30 | | | | 30 | Rental Income |
| | | 676 | 140 | 510 | 4 | 30 | |

Those columns headed with a specific account title are identified as *special columns* (as contrasted with the sundry or miscellaneous columns). Special columns eliminate the entering of many account titles and make it possible to total all like changes in one account during a period, thereby simplifying the posting. Space limits the number of special columns that can be used and there should always be sundry columns for the other accounts that cannot be represented by special columns. The most active account classifications are selected for special columns.

The entries in the journal exhibited above can be explained as follows: (1) sale to a customer, payment received immediately; (2) collection of

$196 in satisfaction of an account receivable for $200—the loss of $4 on the exchange is recorded as an expense under the title of Discounts Allowed; (3) collection from a customer for a credit sale made at an earlier date, no discount taken; and (4) a $30 check received for rental services provided.

## Cash Disbursements Journal

A cash disbursements journal could be called a check disbursement journal or check register, since *all checks* issued must be entered in this record. Even petty cash expenditures paid with currency or coin are finally recorded in the cash disbursements journal when the check is drawn to reimburse the petty cash fund. One form of journal sheet for cash disbursements is shown in Exhibit 4-3.

EXHIBIT 4-3
XYZ COMPANY
Cash Disbursements Journal

| Date issued 1958 | Payable to | Check no. | Cr. Cash | Dr. Pur-chases | Dr. Accts. Payable | Sundry | | |
|---|---|---|---|---|---|---|---|---|
| | | | | | | Dr. | Cr. | Account |
| 1-10 | Abbey Co. | 826 | 297 | | 300 | | 3 | Disc'ts Earned |
| 1-17 | ABC Suppliers | 827 | 60 | 60 | | | | |
| 1-20 | Jay Wholesale | 828 | 400 | | 400 | | | |
| 1-31 | E. E. Smith | 829 | 514 | | | 600 | | Wages Expense |
| | | | | | | | 86 | Income Tax Withheld |
| 1-31 | Thomas Corp. | 830 | 180 | 180 | | | | |
| | | | 1,451 | 240 | 700 | 600 | 89 | |

The transactions recorded in the cash disbursements journal can be described as (1) payment of $297 that satisfies a $300 debt which was incurred for the purchase of merchandise—the gain of $3 is classified as income under the title of Discounts Earned; (2) payment for merchandise at time acquired; (3) payment on account for merchandise purchased on credit at an earlier date, no discount; (4) a check for $514 was issued to an employee for the net amount due—the $86 withheld represents a liability for the employee's Federal income tax that must be paid the government at a later date; (5) another cash purchase.

## Sales Journal

The cash journals, in one form or another, will always be included as a part of an accounting system. Another journal frequently included is the sales journal. This book of original entry is employed for recording *credit sales of merchandise* to customers and could just as well be entitled a "credit sales journal." Since all cash received must be entered in the cash receipts journal, cash sales are *not* recorded in the sales journal.

Credit sales on open account cause identical increases in Accounts Receivable and Sales. For that reason, the dollar amount is recorded only once but is considered both a debit to Accounts Receivable and a credit to Sales. For purposes of cross reference the sales journal contains columns for the customers' names and the invoice numbers.

EXHIBIT 4-4
XYZ COMPANY
Sales Journal

| Invoice number | Invoice date, 1958 | Customer's name | Amount |
|---|---|---|---|
| 619 | 1-3 | C. B. Endres | 230 |
| 620 | 1-22 | Elkton & Co. | 460 |
| 621 | 1-28 | Fog Corp. | 176 |
| | | | 866 |

The total of $866 represents a debit to Accounts Receivable for that amount and a credit to Sales for the same amount. A separate card or ledger sheet is usually maintained apart from the general ledger for *each* account receivable, i.e., for each customer. The charges (debits) to this subsidiary detail can be transcribed directly from the credit sales invoices† or from the detail provided in the sales journal. If monthly statements are prepared, the business unit has to maintain subsidiary ledger cards to provide the information needed for billing. (A detailed discussion of subsidiary ledgers is introduced later in this chapter.)

## Purchases Journal

Purchases journals are not used as frequently as sales journals because many smaller business units prefer to record purchase invoices when paid, and at the end of a period prepare a general journal entry for those that remain unpaid. If credit purchases become numerous, it is usually preferable, however, to establish a purchases journal. This helps assure entry of all merchandise invoices as of the time the costs are incurred and assists in the control of payments.

A purchases journal is for *credit purchases of merchandise for resale* to customers. Those purchases which are paid at the same time the merchandise is acquired are entered in the cash disbursements journal. The purchases journal, consequently, is a credit journal—for credit purchases only. Each entry represents both a debit to Purchases and a credit to Accounts Payable. For this reason, the dollar amount is listed only once.

† invoice – itemized statement of merchandise shipped or sent to a purchaser etc. w. the quantity, value or prices & charges annexed.

When posting as of the end of January, Purchases should be debited and Accounts Payable should be credited for $1,203. Payments on the accounts would be in the cash disbursements journal. If merchandise purchases are sufficiently numerous to require a purchases journal for better control, the firm may also maintain subsidiary detail for each account payable. Subsidiary accounts payable detail consists of a card

EXHIBIT 4-5
XYZ COMPANY
Purchases Journal

| 1958 | Vendor | Amount |
|------|--------|--------|
| 1-8  | Alaskan Co.  | 680 |
| 1-15 | Wm. Penn Co. | 213 |
| 1-24 | Torrance Co. | 310 |
|      |              | 1,203 |

or ledger sheet for each vendor that sells to the firm on credit. The credits to the individual accounts payable can be taken directly from the purchase invoices or from the purchases journal. The payments, or debit decreases, are transcribed from the cash disbursements journal. Balances in these subsidiary accounts can be used as a basis for payments and/or as a check against the amounts due shown on the suppliers' monthly statements.

*General Journal*

If the accounting system for a business unit included the four special journals described above, the following transactions would be entered in these journals: (1) all transactions which included a debit to cash; (2) all transactions which included a credit to cash; (3) credit sales of merchandise to customers; and (4) credit purchases of merchandise from vendors. All other entries would be entered in a general journal.

The general journal shown in Exhibit 4-6 is a simple two-column record such as was employed in the illustrative examples presented in Chapter 2. To shorten the original illustration, the entries in Exhibit 4-6 were not included in the combined columnar journal of the XYZ Company.

Notice in the general journal that, as mentioned before, debits and credits are indicated by position as well as by columnar headings. Debit account titles are to the left; credit account titles are indented to the right. Debit amounts are to the left, credit amounts to the right. For the sake of consistency debits are always listed first in a general journal entry. Unless entirely self-explanatory, the entries are followed by an explanation which is set off in parentheses. To expedite and simplify problem solutions it is usually requested that transactions be prepared in general journal form, even though many of the transactions would be entered in special journals under actual working conditions.

EXHIBIT 4-6

General Journal

| Date 1958 | Accounts and explanations | Dr. | Cr. |
|---|---|---|---|
| 1-8 | Sales Returns and Allowances | 40 | |
| |     Accounts Receivable—C. B. Endres | | 40 |
| | (Merchandise returned for credit) | | |
| 1-15 | Sales Returns and Allowances | 165 | |
| |     Accounts Receivable—Elkton & Co. | | 165 |
| | (Credit allowed for defective merchandise sold but not returned) | | |
| 1-20 | Accounts Payable—Wm. Penn Co. | 16 | |
| |     Purchase Returns and Allowances | | 16 |
| | (Merchandise returned for credit) | | |
| 1-28 | Accounts Payable—Torrance Co. | 154 | |
| |     Purchase Returns and Allowances | | 154 |
| | (Credit allowed for damaged purchases) | | |
| 1-31 | Equipment | 90 | |
| |     Supplies on Hand | | 90 |
| | (To reclassify cost of tools charged to supplies account in error) | | |
| 1-31 | Supplies Expense | 320 | |
| |     Supplies on Hand | | 320 |
| | (To transfer cost of supplies used to an expense account) | | |
| 1-31 | Depreciation Expense | 32 | |
| |     Accumulated Depreciation—Equipment | | 32 |
| | (Equipment depreciation for the month of January, 1958. Total equipment cost of $3,840 divided by estimated life of 120 months equals $32 per month) | | |
| 1-31 | Wages Expense | 140 | |
| |     Wages Payable | | 140 |
| | (To record wages due but unpaid as of 1-31-58) | | |

The first four general journal entries presented above serve as corrections based on credits allowed to customers or as corrections based on credits allowed the firm by vendors. A customer may return or retain unsatisfactory or defective merchandise. In either case the customer is entitled to a credit or reduction of the amount due (credit Accounts Receivable). At the same time, sales should be reduced by the amount of the credit allowed. But the Sales account is not credited directly. Management should know the amount and extent of credits allowed, for this may indicate dissatisfaction on the part of the customers. Managers are likewise benefited by a knowledge of the extent of purchase returns and allowances. A large amount of purchase returns and allowances is indicative of time lost in handling and may also warn of inefficiency in purchasing policies and methods.

Because of this need for information, the reductions in sales and purchases due to returns or allowances are made in separate accounts and the deductions are shown on the operating statement as separate items. For example:

| | |
|---|---:|
| Sales income | $4,906 |
| Less sales returns and allowances | 205 |
| Net sales | $4,701 |

and

| | |
|---|---:|
| Purchases | $3,785 |
| Less purchase returns and allowances | 170 |
| Net purchases | $3,615 |

## *Voucher System*

A small service-type business which reports on the cash basis may have only three books of original entry: a cash receipts journal, a cash disbursements journal, and a general journal. Moderate-size firms buying and selling merchandise on credit will very likely have at least one additional journal—the sales journal—and perhaps a purchases journal. As companies grow larger and there is a greater volume of paper work, management may desire an accounting system that affords better control over the recording of costs and cash disbursements. They want to be reasonably sure that *all* invoices and bills are recorded as soon as received, a process providing greater assurance that all costs for the period are reported. They also want to be reasonably certain that checks are not issued unless bills and invoices have been properly recorded, checked, and approved for payment by responsible parties. To accomplish these objectives a so-called "voucher system" is often introduced.

A voucher system is actually a system within a system. It is that part of an accounting system which deals with the authorization, recording, and payment of all items requiring the expenditure of cash. Certain employees are made responsible for verifying that the service or merchandise was received as ordered, that the charges are proper, and that the extensions and additions are accurate. One executive is usually responsible for the final approval which indicates that payment is authorized) Following the final approval, each item that requires the expenditure of cash must be recorded in the voucher register as of the date the cost was incurred. All payments are then entered in a check register.)("Register" is another word for journal.) The items entered in the voucher register are credited to a Vouchers Payable account and the payments in the check register, therefore, must be debited to Vouchers Payable.

The voucher system employed by most business units is composed of a voucher register, a check register, and procedures for systematically verifying, recording, approving, and paying all costs incurred. These records are used in addition to the cash receipts journal, sales journal, and general journal previously described. When a so-called voucher system is employed, the voucher register and check register replace the purchases journal and cash disbursements journal, and all charges that would otherwise be made through a purchases and cash disbursements journal are entered in a voucher register. (The term "voucher" is also used to mean a document, business paper, or group of business papers that serves to support or verify a transaction.)

### Business Papers

Business papers are usually printed forms that contain information pertaining to a business transaction. Many of them serve as the basis for accounting entries and all of them are normally retained as verification for the recorded transactions. Common examples are sales invoices, purchase invoices, and bank checks. Exhibit 4-7 shows these particular business papers and the changes in financial data that would be recorded from the information provided on them. (The business and accounting unit is assumed to be the XYZ Company.)

There are a number of other business papers which indicate that a cost has been incurred, an income earned, etc. There are also a number of business forms that do not, in themselves, initiate accounting entries but do serve as a part of a complete voucher that supports the transaction. Typical of these are the following three:

(1) Purchase requisitions are requests for the purchasing agent to acquire certain items or services. (2) Purchase orders are issued to vendors, suppliers, etc., as formal notice that the company is ordering the specified goods or services. (3) Receiving reports, like purchase requisitions, are purely internal business forms. They serve as written notice that materials, merchandise, or supplies have been received.

### SUBSIDIARY RECORDS AND CONTROLLING ACCOUNTS

### Subsidiary Records

A subsidiary record represents detail which supports summary data in a general ledger account. If the detail is in account form, it is called a subsidiary ledger. If it is in nonaccount form, it is usually identified as some type of subsidiary record or simply as "subsidiary detail."

Exhibit 4-7

*a. Sales invoice issued:*

*The resulting financial changes reflected as general journal entries:*

| January 22, 1958 |
| --- |
| Invoice from:                  To: |
| XYZ Company                    Elkton & Co. |
| Sheridan, Ohio                 Pasco, Calif. |
|  |
| ☑ Charge or ☐ Cash sale |
|  |
| Description                    Charge |
| 100 men's hats                 $460 |

Accounts Receivable    460
    Sales Income              460

*b. Purchase invoice received:*

| Invoice |
| --- |
| Wm. Penn Co.                   Tampa, Mich. |
|                                1-15-58 |
|  |
| To: XYZ company               ☐ Cash |
|      Sheridan, Ohio           ☑ Credit |
|  |
| Items                          Amount |
| 400 hat bands                  $213 |

Purchases                  213
    Accounts Payable      213

*c. Check received for cash sale:*

| The Fourth National Bank |
| --- |
| Mohawk, Alabama          No. 213  Date 1-2-58 |
|  |
| Pay to    XYZ Company              $140.00 |
|  |
| One hundred forty & no/100....dollars |
|  |
| Signed    W. W. Green |

Cash in Bank               140
    Sales Income              140

*d. Check issued for cash purchases:*

| Ohio State Bank |
| --- |
| Sheridan, Ohio        No. 827       Date 1-17-58 |
|  |
| Pay to    ABC Suppliers            $ 60.00 |
|  |
| Sixty & no/100....................dollars |
|  |
| Signed   A. B. Zee, XYZ Company |

Purchases                   60
    Cash in Bank              60

Some of the more important reasons for maintaining subsidiary records are discussed in the following paragraphs.

In order to subdivide the bookkeeping work it may be necessary to place a group of accounts in a separate book or file. This is often true of accounts receivable for the reason that an individual account is usually maintained for transactions with each customer. If there are relatively few of these, the accounts can be retained in the general ledger. If, on the other hand, there are several dozen—or several hundred—or several thousand—accounts with customers, it becomes necessary to maintain these accounts apart from the others. Customers' accounts have to be available for billing (preparation of invoices), for credit analyses, and for the posting of numerous charges and collections. It would be literally impossible for the general ledger to be efficiently employed for all these purposes.

Individual accounts payable accounts with vendors are likely to be established if a business customarily makes payments only once a month, since these accounts provide information as to the amounts due and payable to each supplier. If there are only a few such accounts, they are likely to be retained in the general ledger. If there are many, the accounts are likely to be segregated into a separate accounts payable subsidiary ledger.

The inventory accounts, particularly in a manufacturing business, often need to be supported by subsidiary detail. Quantities of materials on hand need to be known and, in many cases, the material withdrawn from stock must be "costed" as of the time it is used. Since it is not practical to maintain this necessary detail in the general ledger, *perpetual inventory* cards are set up for each type of material used. These cards contain a record of the quantity received, the number used, and the quantity on hand. If dollar costs are also recorded, the total of all the dollar balances on the inventory cards should equal the dollar balance in the general ledger Inventory account, since all purchases and withdrawals are entered in summary form in this control account when the perpetual inventory method is employed.

In very large businesses certain subgroups of accounts can become so numerous that the accountant may have them removed from the general ledger and placed in another binder to make up a subsidiary ledger or ledgers. This may be done to keep the general ledger at a workable size or to aid in subdividing the office work. Selling expense accounts, for instance, might be established as a subsidiary ledger.

*Controlling Accounts*

Accounts Receivable, with supporting detail in an accounts receivable subsidiary ledger, is a controlling account; an Inventory account is a controlling account when a perpetual inventory with costs is maintained;

etc. A *controlling account* can be defined as a general ledger account that summarizes financial data which are maintained elsewhere in detail. It is the same in appearance as any other general ledger accounts where only the summary totals of debits and credits from special columns in the journals are regularly recorded. The individual amounts that make up these totals are, however, recorded in detail in a subsidiary record. Consequently, the balance in a controlling account after all postings are completed should be equal to the sum of the balances in the corresponding detail. Detail maintained in a subsidiary must always be represented in the general ledger by a summary controlling account, otherwise the completeness of the general ledger would be destroyed. To illustrate these conditions with a simple example, assume the following:

1. Balances in customers' accounts as of October 1, 1957, were:

$$
\begin{array}{ll}
\text{A. B. Jones}\dots\dots\dots\dots & \$1,200 \\
\text{B. C. Smith}\dots\dots\dots\dots & 800 \\
\text{C. D. Brown}\dots\dots\dots\dots & \underline{2,000} \\
& \underline{\$4,000}
\end{array}
$$

2. The sales journal for October includes:

Sales Journal

| Invoice no. | Date, 1957 | Customer's names | Amount |
|---|---|---|---|
| 284 | 10-7 | A. B. Jones | 2,600 |
| 285 | 10-18 | C. D. Brown | 900 |
| 286 | 10-29 | E. F. Caruso | 1,500 |
| | | | 5,000 |

3. The cash receipts journal shows that during October the following has been collected on account:

$$
\begin{array}{ll}
\text{B. C. Smith}\dots\dots\dots\dots & \$\ \ 400 \\
\text{A. B. Jones}\dots\dots\dots\dots & 1,200 \\
\text{C. D. Brown}\dots\dots\dots\dots & \underline{1,900} \\
& \underline{\$3,500}
\end{array}
$$

4. The general journal contains one entry affecting the accounts receivable:

| 10-6-57 | Sales Returns and Allowances | 100 | |
|---|---|---|---|
| | Accounts Receivable—C. D. Brown | | 100 |
| | (Defective merchandise returned) | | |

After the above data were posted, the general ledger controlling account would appear as follows:

Accounts Receivable

| Date 1957 | Explanation | Debit | Credit | Balance |
|---|---|---|---|---|
| 10-1 | | | | 4,000 dr. |
| 10-31 | (Sales on account) | 5,000 | | |
| 10-31 | (Collections on account) | | 3,500 | |
| 10-31 | (Merchandise returned) | | 100 | 5,400 dr. |

Accounts in the subsidiary accounts receivable ledger would be as shown below (the subsidiary ledger cards are usually arranged in alphabetical sequence). It is assumed that debits arising from sales are posted directly from invoice copies or from the detail in the sales journal, and that credits representing payments received are posted from detail included in the cash receipts journal.

Customer's ledger cards:

C. D. Brown, Boise, Idaho

| Invoice No. | Date 1957 | | Dr. | Cr. | Balance |
|---|---|---|---|---|---|
| | 10-1 | | | | 2,000 |
| | 10-6 | Merchandise returned | | 100 | 1,900 |
| | 10-11 | | | 1,900 | 00 |
| 285 | 10-18 | | 900 | | 900 |

E. F. Caruso, Phoenix, Arizona

| Invoice No. | Date 1957 | | Dr. | Cr. | Balance |
|---|---|---|---|---|---|
| 286 | 10-29 | | 1,500 | | 1,500 |

A. B. Jones, Canon City, Colorado

| Invoice No. | Date 1957 | | Dr. | Cr. | Balance |
|---|---|---|---|---|---|
| | 10-1 | | | | 1,200 |
| 284 | 10-7 | | 2,600 | | 3,800 |
| | 10-9 | | | 1,200 | 2,600 |

## B. C. Smith, Omaha, Nebraska

| Invoice No. | Date 1957 | | Dr. | Cr. | Balance |
|---|---|---|---|---|---|
| | 10-1 | | | | 800 |
| | 10-8 | | | 400 | 400 |

At the end of the month an adding machine may be used to take a total of all the period-end balances, or a list can be prepared that includes both customers' names and amounts receivable:

Schedule of Customers' Accounts as of October 31, 1957
C. D. Brown................... $  900
E. F. Caruso................... 1,500
A. B. Jones................... 2,600
B. C. Smith...................   400
$5,400

Balance of Accounts Receivable
account in general ledger
October 31, 1957.............. $5,400

Under normal circumstances there would be a large number of customers' accounts and many postings to these accounts during each month and, consequently, many chances for errors. There would be comparatively few postings to the controlling account and proportionately fewer chances for error. If the schedule of customers' balances does not agree with the controlling account balance, the error is much more likely to be in the subsidiary accounts than in the general ledger account. The balance of Accounts Receivable in the general ledger should, therefore, serve as a "control" or check on the subsidiary detail.

### SUMMARY

Recording all transactions in general journal form is slow and costly. Use of a combined columnar journal expedites the recording process by the inclusion of special columns, but special journals are used more often in order to provide space for additional special columns and to allow more persons to work on the records. Subsidiary ledgers also make it possible to subdivide the work load by segregating certain accounts or detail. A controlling account summarizes the detail that is kept in the subsidiary records and, at the same time, maintains the completeness of the general ledger.

## QUESTIONS

**1.** Are postings from a general journal likely to be more or less accurate than postings from a combined columnar journal? Why?

**2.** What are the advantages of a combined columnar journal as compared with a general journal? Of special journals as compared with a combined columnar journal?

**3.** What are special columns in a journal? What advantages do they provide?

**4.** Why is a general journal always used in conjunction with special journals?

**5.** How should an accountant determine the type and number of special journals that can be used effectively by a particular firm?

**6.** Two of the special journals described in Chapter 4 can be termed "cash" journals; two can be termed "credit" journals. Why?

**7.** Regardless of the accounts included, any and all entries involving the receipt of cash can be entered in a cash receipts journal such as the one illustrated in the chapter. Why is this true?

**8.** What is the account title for cash discounts taken by customers? For cash discounts deducted from amounts due suppliers? For amounts that are to be paid the Federal government as prepayments on employees' income tax obligations?

**9.** What is a controlling account? A subsidiary ledger? A perpetual inventory?

**10.** Why should the balance of a controlling account be equal to the sum of the balances in the corresponding subsidiary accounts?

**11.** A schedule of customers' balances does not agree with the balance of the Accounts Receivable controlling account. Is the error more likely to be in the subsidiary ledger or in the controlling account? Why?

**12.** All of the individual accounts representing balances due suppliers are removed from a general ledger, but they are not replaced with a summary controlling account. What will happen to the general ledger trial balance?

**13.** Why are entries in general journal form frequently used for the solution of problems, even though many of the entries involved would normally be recorded in special journals?

**14.** Why are "returns and allowances" usually maintained in separate accounts rather than being recorded as decreases in the Sales and Purchases accounts?

**15.** In a voucher system all costs that will require the expenditure of cash must be recorded in a voucher register, and all checks issued will be recorded as debits to the Vouchers Payable account. Why?

**16.** What business papers serve as the direct source of data for many journal entries? Which ones do not initiate accounting entries but do become part of a voucher that serves to verify or support a transaction?

**17.** An "entry" is the record of a business transaction. In what two places is an entry recorded?

# CHAPTER 5

# ADJUSTING AND CLOSING ENTRIES

Smaller business units that sell only services often record income and expenses on a cash basis. "Cash basis accounting" means that income is recorded only when payment is received and that most expenses are recorded only when payment is made. A statement of financial condition prepared on a cash basis will not include receivables for income earned but not yet collected and will not include payables for costs incurred but not yet paid. Such a statement might very well exclude significant valuations of legal rights and obligations and, as a result, could be very misleading. This is also true of a statement of income and expenses which does not include all income earned and all expenses incurred.

Income statements for doctors and dentists, though customarily prepared on a cash basis, are normally reasonable, however, because (1) the expenses incurred but not reported are often comparable to expenses for the prior period that have been paid in the current period, and (2) even though some of the income earned in the current year will not be reported until the subsequent year when it is collected, it must be remembered that some of the income reported in the current year was earned in the prior year. These two factors often offset each other to such an extent that the net income reported is usually very close to the amount actually earned; but service enterprises that have comparatively few, but large, sales definitely should not employ the cash basis of accounting, since the collections from prior year sales are not likely to offset uncollected but earned income of the current year.

"Accrual basis accounting" requires that income be recorded when earned and that costs be recorded when incurred. Income is considered earned as soon as a transaction is completed. Costs are considered incurred as soon as an obligation to make payment has arisen. Statements prepared on the accrual basis should be reasonably accurate, for all income earned and all costs expired in earning that income are included on the operating statement and all amounts receivable and payable are shown on the statement of financial condition. (Use of the accrual basis of accounting is assumed throughout this text, unless there is a specific statement to the contrary.)

Federal tax regulations that apply to firms selling merchandise are similar to the accrual basis principles in many respects. Federal income tax regulations, for example, require that trading and manufacturing concerns report both sales and purchases on an accrual basis and that inventories be recognized in the computation of cost of goods sold. If they were allowed to report on a cash basis, collections could be deferred until the next year in order to lower taxable income for the current year. If the ending inventory were not deducted in the computation of the cost of goods sold, the costs for a period could be increased or decreased and the net profits juggled to yield a tax advantage by simply increasing or decreasing purchases. For this reason, both tax regulations and accounting principles require that the cost of goods sold be determined by adding purchases and the beginning inventory and deducting the cost of goods on hand. This means that only the cost of the goods actually sold (or stolen) can be deducted from the sales income in computing a firm's gross profit.

*Need for Adjustments*

At the time certain costs are incurred it is not possible to determine the amount that will expire during the period or remain unexpired at the end of the period, and either an asset account or an expense account may be charged at the time the cost is incurred. Supplies are an example. When purchased, the bookkeeper could charge the cost of supplies to an asset account, Supplies on Hand, or to an expense account, Supplies Expense. If all supplies were charged originally to an asset account, at the end of the period the amount used would have to be withdrawn from the asset account with a credit and charged as expired cost by a debit to an expense account. The general journal entry to make this and similar corrections is known as an adjustment or an adjusting entry. Had the bookkeeper charged all supply costs to an expense account, an adjusting general journal entry would be made to transfer the unexpired cost from the Supplies Expense account to the asset account, Supplies on Hand.

Costs which will lose value over a relatively long period of time should be charged originally to an asset account. Certain examples of such assets are classified as fixed assets, which can be defined as tangible assets, necessary for operations, with a life greater than one year. No one knows exactly how long each fixed asset, such as equipment, will have value to the business, but someone must make an estimate as to its total useful life. The total original cost can then be expired or written off as expense during this estimated life. Advance payments for insurance protection are normally handled in the same way; i.e., the total premium cost is charged to the Prepaid Insurance asset account and adjustments to the Insurance Expense account are made at the end of each period for that portion of the premium cost that has expired since statements were last prepared.

If, on the other hand, it is known that a cost will expire during the current period, it can be charged originally to the appropriate expense account to avoid the necessity for an adjustment later. The same logic applies to income received in advance: if all of the income will not be earned in the current period, the original credit is to a liability account, which must then be adjusted at the end of the period for the amount that has been earned; if all of the income will be earned during the current period, the original credit is to an appropriate income account and no adjustment would be required at the end of the period.

### Need for Accruals

The adjustments discussed above typify corrections of data that *have been recorded*. Other financial data necessary for the preparation of accurate financial statements may not be recorded at all. Adjustments which serve to enter these unrecorded data are known as accruals or accruing entries. These entries accrue or accumulate financial data regarding costs incurred or incomes earned which *have not been entered* in any of the firm's system of journals as of the time statements are prepared. Wages, for instance, often have to be accrued, for it is usually impossible to compute and pay all wage expense incurred before the period ends. Even though unpaid, the business unit has incurred a cost and, as of the end of the period, is liable for any unpaid amounts. Both the wages expense and the liability for wages due employees must be recorded if accurate financial statements are to be prepared.

### PREPARING AND RECORDING ADJUSTMENTS

A firm's accountant will enter the period-end adjustments in the general journal as soon as it is determined what entries are necessary. If a working trial balance is not used, the adjustments can be journalized before a trial balance is prepared. If a working trial balance is used, a preliminary trial balance is taken and the adjustments are first entered on the work sheet. The adjusting journal entries are later prepared from the work sheet.

Adjustments can be divided into six groups if it is assumed (*a*) that costs which apply to more than one period are charged originally to asset accounts, and (*b*) that income amounts which will be earned during more than one period are credited to liability accounts at time of receipt.

1. Adjustments for the allocation of fixed asset costs to expense
2. Adjustments for the estimated amount of bad debt losses

3. Adjustments to charge the expired or used portion of temporary assets to expense accounts

4. Adjustments to transfer earned amounts from the unearned income (liability) accounts to the appropriate income accounts

5. Accruals of unrecorded costs and liabilities

6. Accruals of unrecorded income and receivables

(All adjustments are in a sense corrections. General journal entries to correct *errors* in recording are not, however, generally considered adjustments. Most accountants would probably classify them as "correcting" entries.)

### Adjustments for the Allocation of Fixed Asset Costs to Expense

Adjustments for depreciation are based on original cost, an estimate of the asset's useful life, and the probable scrap or trade-in value (the latter is often assumed to be zero). If a concern reporting on a calendar year pays $3,000 for an automobile that will probably be used for four years and then traded at an estimated trade-in value of $600, the following adjusting entry would be made at the end of the year in which the car was purchased (car received July 1):

| | | |
|---|---|---|
| Depreciation Expense | 300 | |
|     Accumulated Depreciation—Vehicles | | 300 |
| (Cost of car, $3,000 less estimated trade-in | | |
| value of $600 divided by four years equals | | |
| annual depreciation of $600. Depreciation | | |
| for six months is $300) | | |

This method of calculating depreciation is known as the *straight-line method* because depreciable cost divided by the number of periods in the useful life yields the amount of original cost that is to be expired each period as depreciation expense, and since this amount is the same for each full period, the depreciation expense for a number of periods would appear as a straight line if plotted on a graph. There are several other methods for prorating the total depreciable cost (total cost less estimated scrap or trade-in value) over the estimated useful life. Some methods are preferred because they may provide a book value (cost less accumulated depreciation) which is fairly close to market value. Some are preferred because they yield a tax advantage by providing for comparatively larger expense deductions during the early years of asset life.

### Adjustments for the Estimated Amount of Bad Debt Losses

Some firms do *not* estimate the amount of bad debt loss but simply write off accounts at the time they are proved uncollectible. For example, in 1957 a concern makes a $400 credit sale to the Nopay Company. In

1958 the Nopay Company fails and its owner hurriedly departs for South America. When this is discovered by the credit manager or accountant, the following entry would be made:

Bad Debts Expense                                    400
    Accounts Receivable—Nopay Company        400
(To write off uncollectible amount)

The preceding example illustrates what is known as the *direct write-off method* for bad debts. This method violates a generally accepted accounting principle: all expense related to income earned during the period should be reported in the same period. In the example above, the income of $400 was reported in 1957 but the related expense was not recorded until 1958. To avoid this, most accountants prefer to estimate the amount of bad debts that will arise from the current year's credit sales and to record this estimated expense in the same period that the sales were earned. This is particularly true if the firm has a comparatively large volume of credit sales and significant bad debt losses.

The estimate is most frequently expressed as a percentage which has been derived from prior experience. It can be a percentage of net sales, credit sales, or accounts receivable. A percentage of net sales is used frequently, particularly for monthly statements, since the net sales figure is easily computed. An estimate based on a percentage of credit sales should be more accurate, however, for bad debts can arise only from credit sales. Some accountants feel that an estimate based on accounts receivable as of the end of the period is preferable, for the accounts receivable represent only amounts uncollected and, therefore, the only amounts that can be lost through noncollection.

Let us assume that a company employing the *estimated basis* for bad debts has accounts receivable at the year end in the amount of $60,000. Experience in prior years has shown that on the average ¾ per cent of the customers' receivables is never collected. The credit manager believes that the percentage uncollectible will be the same this year. An adjusting entry would then be made to record this estimate:

Bad Debts Expense                    *asset*        450
    Allowance for Doubtful Accounts              450
(¾ per cent of accounts receivable, $60,000)

If the Allowance for Doubtful Accounts already had a credit balance of $60, the entry would be for $390. That is, the entry would increase the balance to the required $450. The $60 balance would, in theory at least, represent amounts estimated as uncollectible at the end of the prior year. But, since these amounts had not yet proved uncollectible, they are still included in the current accounts receivable and should not be charged as bad debts again. This is automatically what happens when only $390, instead of $450, is credited to the Allowance for Doubtful Accounts.

The Allowance for Doubtful Accounts is often known as the Reserve for Bad Debts. This title should be avoided, however, since nothing has been "reserved" or set aside. The balance of the account simply expresses an estimate of the amount that will not be collected and is, consequently, deducted from Accounts Receivable to provide for an estimated valuation of the true worth of this asset. When the direct write-off method is employed, there is no deduction made for estimated uncollectible accounts and, as a result, the accounts receivable are frequently overvalued on the statement of financial condition.

Notice that the estimated decrease in accounts receivable is entered in a separate account and deducted on the face of the statement. A person reading the balance sheet is thereby informed of the gross amount due from customers and also of the amount that is estimated as uncollectible. If only the net figure is shown, the reader cannot determine if the allowance for bad debts seems reasonable. This is sometimes important, for the amount may be overestimated in order to increase expenses and thereby decrease taxable income; or it may be underestimated in order to present larger asset and profit figures to potential investors or creditors. A responsible accountant, however, should always be certain that the estimate provides a reasonable valuation of both accounts receivable and bad debt expense.

As noted above, the entry to record bad debt expense under the estimated basis is an *adjusting* entry, made at the end of the period and based on a percentage of sales or receivables. The only entry needed when a specific account proves uncollectible is the entry which removes the account from Accounts Receivable and reduces the balance in the Allowance for Bad Debts. Assume for example that A. W. Toms' account for $60 proves to be uncollectible. The entry is:

| | | |
|---|---|---|
| Allowance for Doubtful Accounts | 60 | |
|    Accounts Receivable—A. W. Toms | | 60 |
| (To write off uncollectible account) | | |

After the above entry has been posted, the net receivables will be the same, since both the Allowance and Accounts Receivable have been decreased by the same amount. For example:

| | Before | Write-off of bad account | After |
|---|---|---|---|
| Accounts receivable ................... | $60,000 Dr. | $60 Cr. | $59,940 Dr. |
| Deduct allowance for doubtful accounts.. | 450 Cr. | 60 Dr. | 390 Cr. |
| | $59,550 Dr. | | $59,550 Dr. |

Occasionally an account that has been written off as uncollectible will be collected at a later date. At this point some firms would simply make the following entry (assume that A. W. Toms' bad account was collected):

| | | |
|---|---|---|
| Cash in Bank | 60 | |
|     Other Income | | 60 |
| (Collection of an account | | |
| that had been written off) | | |

This entry, however, would *not* provide a record of payment in A. W. Toms' account. Most concerns want all changes in receivables to be entered on each customer's account in order to furnish a complete credit history on the one record. To accomplish this the original write-off is reversed, thereby returning the original charge to the receivable account, and the payment is then recorded as a credit to the account.

| | | |
|---|---|---|
| Accounts Receivable—A. W. Toms | 60 | |
|     Allowance for Doubtful Accounts | | 60 |
| (To reverse write-off of account that has been collected) | | |
| Cash in Bank | 60 | |
|     Accounts Receivable—A. W. Toms | | 60 |
| (Payment of account previously written off as uncollectible) | | |

*Adjustments to Charge the Expired or Used Portion of Temporary Assets to Expense Accounts*

It is assumed that prepaid expenses are usually charged to an asset account when the cost is incurred. Common examples of costs paid in advance are insurance, rent, and interest. For instance, a firm on October 1 borrows $10,000 for six months at 6 per cent interest, payable in advance. The original entry in the cash receipts journal would be:

| | | |
|---|---|---|
| Cash in Bank | 9,700 | |
| Prepaid Interest | 300 | |
|     Notes Payable | | 10,000 |
| (Loan from 2d National Bank) | | |

When interest is payable in advance, it is sometimes withheld from the principal amount, as shown above. The borrower could issue a check for the prepayment but having the amount withheld makes this unnecessary. (An interest rate, such as 6 per cent, is always an *annual rate*, unless a statement to the contrary is made. The prepaid interest amount in this example can be computed as $10,000 \times 0.06 \times \frac{6}{12} = \$300$.) At the end of the calendar year the firm would have had the use of the borrowed funds for three of the six months loan period and one-half of the prepayment should be recorded as expense:

Interest Expense 150
    Prepaid Interest 150
(One-half of $300 paid for 6 months
or $10,000 \times 0.06 \times \frac{3}{12}$)

Adjusting entries for supplies used, expired insurance, and expired rent have been illustrated in preceding chapters.

*Adjustments to Transfer Earned Amounts from the Unearned Income (Liability) Accounts to the Appropriate Income Accounts*

Income collected in advance must usually be adjusted at the end of the period for the amount earned. Assume that a firm with a fiscal year ending June 30 had received a prepayment for one year on property rented at $100 per month. Payment was received on May 1.

Cash in Bank 1,200
    Unearned Rental Income 1,200
(One year's rent received in advance)

The Unearned Rental Income account is listed under the heading of deferred income on the statement of financial condition. It is a liability that would have to be repaid at any time the business was unable to continue providing the rental services. As of June 30 an adjustment would be necessary to record the amount of rental that had been earned.

Unearned Rental Income 200
    Rental Income 200
(To record rental earned—$\frac{2}{12}$ of
$1,200 prepayment for one year)

*Accruals of Unrecorded Costs and Liabilities*

When the bookkeeping system does not include the use of a voucher register, there may be a number of current invoices unpaid and unrecorded at the end of the period. Assume that as of the year end, December 31, a firm had the following unpaid December invoices not yet recorded: telephone bill, $124; water bill, $43; invoice for supplies already consumed, $86; and an invoice for the purchase of merchandise that was received after the purchases journal had been posted, $210. All current invoices must be recorded, even though received in January, as long as they are received before statements are prepared. Even costs incurred but not yet billed should be accrued if it is at all possible to estimate the amount.

A general journal entry to accrue the above data would be as follows:

| | | |
|---|---|---|
| Telephone and Telegraph Expense | 124 | |
| Utilities Expense | 43 | |
| Supplies Used Expense | 86 | |
| Purchases | 210 | |
|     Accounts Payable—X Co. | | 210 |
|     Accounts Payable—Other | | 253 |
| (To accrue unrecorded December invoices) | | |

In the above entry it has been assumed that the firm's chart of accounts shows that all costs incurred for heat, lights, and water are to be charged to a Utilities Expense account; that supplies are charged directly to an expense account when purchased; and that accounts payable for merchandise are segregated in a separate controlling account to provide a balance that can be compared with the sum of the balances in the accounts payable subsidiary ledger.

Interest and rent expenses must often be accrued by an adjusting general journal entry. If a concern borrows $10,000 on October 1 and is to repay this amount plus 6 per cent interest at the end of six months, an accrual would have to be made to record the expense incurred for the use of the funds from October 1 until the end of the fiscal period, December 31.

| | | |
|---|---|---|
| Interest Expense | 150 | |
|     Interest Payable | | 150 |
| (To accrue interest on $10,000 | | |
| at 6 per cent for three months) | | |

If, on the first day of each month, a firm paid $100 for rent for the preceding month, an accrual would have to be made at the end of each period for the unpaid rent.

| | | |
|---|---|---|
| Rent Expense | 100 | |
|     Rent Payable | | 100 |
| (To accrue current month's rent | | |
| which is not due and payable | | |
| until the first day of the next month) | | |

Should the chart of accounts not include an account for rent payable, the credit could be to "Accounts Payable–Other."

When the payroll period does not coincide with the fiscal period, any unpaid and unrecorded wages must be accrued. In addition, all employers of one or more persons, except in certain excluded classes of employment, are required to withhold a $2\frac{1}{4}$ per cent tax on the first $4,200 of each employee's gross pay for Federal Old-Age and Survivors Insurance; and the employer must then contribute an equal amount, which he enters as a payroll tax expense. For example, assume that the total accrued payroll at the end of the fiscal period is $2,000. Assume also that the total amount is subject to payroll tax, and that $240 is to be withheld for Federal income taxes. The adjusting entries to set up the unrecorded costs and liabilities are:

```
Wages Expense                                2,000
        Wages Payable                                1,715
        Income Tax Withheld                            240
        FOASI Tax Payable (or withheld)                 45
    (To record accrued payroll and taxes withheld)

Payroll Tax Expense                            45
        FOASI Tax Payable                               45
    (To record employer's liability for FOASI)
```

The Federal Old-Age and Survivors Insurance tax is, unfortunately, known by several other titles—social security, old-age benefits, Federal Insurance Contributions Act. In the example above, the employer's contribution might be charged to Taxes Expense and credited to Taxes Payable, but when there are a number of different taxes, all comparatively large in amount, it is preferable to segregate the amounts in separate accounts.

*Accruals of Unrecorded Income and Receivables*

In some instances a business unit will have earned income that has not yet been collected or invoiced. Income from credit sales will be recorded as the sales invoices are entered in the sales journal, but only credit sales can be included in the sales journal. Other income is ordinarily recorded in the cash receipts journal when received or in the general journal by a period-end accrual.

Assume, for example, that a firm subleases a portion of its warehouse at $200 per month, payable on the first day of the following month. Should the fiscal year end March 31, the March rent would have been earned but not yet paid. If the firm has sent a bill to the lessee for this amount, a copy of the bill can serve as a voucher to substantiate the adjusting entry; but regardless of whether or not a bill has been prepared for the rent, the following entry would be made as of March 31:

```
Rent Receivable                              200
        Rental Income                                  200
    (To accrue Mar. rent earned but not due until Apr. 1)
```

Assume that as of June 30, the last day of a firm's fiscal year, a loan to an officer for $4,000 at 3 per cent has been outstanding for four months. Interest is payable at the time the principal amount of $4,000 is to be repaid. A general journal entry, dated June 30, would be prepared to reflect the interest earned as of that date.

Interest Receivable                              40
    Interest Income                                    40
    (To record interest earned on $4,000,
    3 per cent note from Mar. 1 to June 30)

The word "accrued" is frequently included in the account title for receivables and payables that arise from accruing entries. Common examples would be: Accrued Interest Receivable, Accrued Wages Payable, Accrued Rent Payable, etc. "Accrued" should never be included as a part of the title for income and expense accounts, however.

## FINAL STEPS IN THE ACCOUNTING CYCLE

*Closing the Temporary Accounts*

A statement of income and expense is a means of measuring the amount received from the sale of goods and services and the costs of producing those goods and services. It is a measure for a period of time. When the period is finished, the increase or decrease in the owner's earned equity resulting from operations is depicted on the statements as an addition of net profit to the beginning earned equity (or as a deduction of net loss). Net assets have been increased or decreased by the same amount *during* the period, for the various asset and liability accounts have been increased and decreased as the income and expense transactions were recorded.

All changes reflected on the statements must also be recorded in the general ledger accounts. The excess of the inward flow (income) over the outward flow (expense), assuming a net profit, must be reflected in the earned equity account. This shows that the owners have full equity in this increase which resulted from the operations of their business. On the operating statement the expenses are deducted from the income in order to compute this amount. In the general ledger an account is established to accomplish the same purpose. All income and expense balances are transferred to this one account and the excess of one over the other computed. This excess is then transferred to the Earned Equity account and added to or subtracted from the beginning balance of earned equity (just as it is on the face of the statement). Closing entries not using a Profit and Loss Summary account have already been explained in Chapters 2 and 3. The entries described here should be considered an alternative, and possibly more common, closing procedure.

General journal entries to transfer the balances of the income and expense accounts to the summary account and the balance of the summary account to Earned Equity are known as closing entries, because the accounts have a zero balance—are "closed"—after the balances are transferred out. To illustrate this, assume that a company has the following balances in its Earned Equity and temporary accounts at the end of a period. (The company does not prepare a statement of changes in earned equity.)

| Earned Equity | | P & L Summary | |
|---|---|---|---|
| | 16,000 | | |

| Fee Income | | Wages | | Other Expense | |
|---|---|---|---|---|---|
| | 60,000 | 40,000 | | 10,000 | |

The statement of income and expense would summarize these data as follows:

```
Fee income.................... $60,000
Expenses:
    Wages............... $40,000
    Other...............  10,000  50,000
    Net profit..................... $10,000
```

On the statement of financial condition the equity section would appear as shown below:

```
Earned equity—Jan. 1, 19—............ $16,000
Add net profit........................  10,000
Earned equity—Dec. 31, 19—................. $26,000
```

To accomplish the same changes within the general ledger, the bookkeeper would turn to the temporary accounts after they were adjusted (or a detailed statement of income and expense) and begin preparation of the closing entries in the general journal. The first closing entry would consist of a debit to each income account for the amount of its credit balance. The offsetting credit to the P & L Summary account would be the sum of all the debits.

The second closing entry would consist of a credit to each expense account for the amount of its debit balance. The offsetting debit would be to the summary account, the P & L account, as it is usually called. (P & L is the commonly accepted abbreviation for profit and loss.) As an illustration, the following closing entry is presented to show how the temporary account balances above are closed and transferred to the summary account:

```
Fee Income                      60,000
    P & L Summary                       60,000
    (To close income account)

P & L Summary                   50,000
    Wages                               40,000
    Other Expenses                      10,000
    (To close expense accounts)
```

After these general journal entries were posted, the accounts would appear as below:

| Earned Equity | | P & L Summary | |
|---|---|---|---|
| | 16,000 | 50,000 | 60,000 |

| Fee Income | | Wages | | Other Expenses | |
|---|---|---|---|---|---|
| 60,000 | 60,000 | 40,000 | 40,000 | 10,000 | 10,000 |

The P & L account now contains, in summary form, the same information as the statement of income and expense. The net credit balance of $10,000 represents the net profit for the period which should now be transferred to Earned Equity, just as it was transferred from the operating statement to the "owner's equity" section on the balance sheet. To achieve this, the following general journal entry would be made and then posted:

| | | |
|---|---|---|
| P & L Summary | 10,000 | |
| Earned Equity | | 10,000 |
| (To close net profit for period to Earned Equity) | | |

Subsequently, the two accounts would display the following data:

| Earned Equity | | P & L Summary | |
|---|---|---|---|
| | 16,000 | 50,000 | 60,000 |
| | 10,000 | 10,000 | |

Earned Equity now has an ending balance of $26,000, just as shown on the statement of financial condition.

In many firms there would be one additional closing entry to reflect a reduction in the owner's equity equal to the amount of assets withdrawn by the owner. Properties, usually cash, taken from the business by the owners are debited to an account entitled "withdrawals" or "dividends." These decreases in the owner's equity are usually summarized in a separate account until the end of the year and at that time the balance can be transferred to Earned Equity to reflect the total decrease in the ownership interest for the period. In a business where the owner had drawn out $5,000 during the year, the entry would be as follows:

| | | |
|---|---|---|
| Earned Equity | 5,000 | |
| Withdrawals | | 5,000 |
| (To close owner's drawing account) | | |

*Inventory Balances in the Closing Process*

The majority of trading enterprises do not maintain perpetual inventory records. That is, they do not charge the cost of merchandise to the Inventory account and then credit this account with the cost of the merchandise as it is withdrawn from stock. Instead they choose to compute the total cost of goods sold for a period by accumulating total purchases, adding opening inventory to arrive at the total amount available for sale, and deducting ending inventory from this total. This procedure, known as the *periodical inventory method,* requires that a physical inventory be taken at least once each year but, at the same time, avoids the keeping of detailed inventory records. The periodical inventory method, however, does not provide certain detailed information, and some firms are compelled to adopt the perpetual inventory method in order to obtain necessary cost data.

The computation of cost of goods sold is one of the major groupings on the statement of income and expense for a concern that sells tangible items. It can be illustrated as follows:

```
Cost of goods sold:
    Inventory, Jan. 1, 19—........................ $ 4,000
    Cost of purchases:
        Purchases.......................... $25,000
        Less returns & allowances............   1,000
        Net purchases...................... $24,000
        Freight in.........................   2,000   26,000
    Available for sale.............................. $30,000
    Inventory, Dec. 31, 19—........................    6,000
    Cost of goods sold.............................. $24,000
```

*All* data that appear on a statement of income and expense are transferred or closed to the P & L Summary account. Purchases, Purchase Returns and Allowances, and Freight In balances (as illustrated above) would be closed with the two entries that transfer all temporary account balances—debit and credit—to the P & L Summary account. Two additional entries are required for inventories: one to add the opening amount to the P & L account, just as it is added in the computation of cost of goods sold on the statement; another to deduct the ending inventory amount from the P & L account and classify this unsold portion as an asset, as it is on the statement of financial condition. Closing entries for the two inventories in the illustration above would be:

```
(1) P & L Summary                       4,000
        Inventory                                 4,000
    (To close out the opening inventory balance)

(2) Inventory                           6,000
        P & L Summary                             6,000
    (To set up the ending inventory balances)
```

These entries are actually more in the nature of adjustments than closings, except that it can be said the opening inventory is "closed to P & L." It is usually assumed that the entries are prepared at the same time as the entries for transferring the temporary account balances to the P & L account and, therefore, they are considered as closing entries.

Although the closing procedures described above are commonly followed, the direct method explained in Chapters 2 and 3 may still be used. The books of any merchandising concern may be closed by a single journal entry:

| | |
|---|---|
| Inventory | Dr. for amount of new inventory |
| Income Accounts | Dr. *each* account individually |
| Earned Equity | Dr. if a net loss |
|     Cost and Expense Accounts | Cr. *each* account individually |
|     Inventory | Cr. for amount of old inventory |
|     Earned Equity | Cr. if a net profit |

Data for this entry can be found in the accounts, on an adjusted trial balance, in the income and expense columns of the working trial balance, or on a detailed income statement, whichever is most convenient. After the entry is made, the bookkeeper has only to transfer the withdrawals to the Earned Equity account and the cycle is completed.

### SUMMARY

A firm reporting on the cash basis frequently has only one adjustment at the end of a fiscal period, an adjustment for depreciation. Firms reporting on the accrual basis usually have a number of adjustments, for income and related expenses must be matched and all income earned and all costs incurred must be recorded. Fixed asset costs must be expired, a portion of receivables written off to expense, certain other recorded costs and credits adjusted, and all unrecorded data accumulated and entered (accrued). The statement of financial condition will usually indicate the method employed for reporting. If the accrual basis has been used, some of the following will probably be included: accounts receivable, accounts payable, and various other accrued receivables and payables. If the cash basis has been employed, receivables, payables, and accrued items will usually not appear on the statement of financial condition.

Closing general journal entries are necessary for a number of reasons: to "close" out the balances of the temporary accounts and ready them for the accumulation of data during the next period; to record net profit in the general ledger; to increase the Earned Equity account by the amount of the net profit; and to decrease Earned Equity by the amount of the withdrawals.

### QUESTIONS

**1.** What basis of accounting is always assumed in this text, unless there is a notation to the contrary?

**2.** Under what conditions may cash basis statements be reasonably accurate?

**3.** Assume that income tax regulations allowed a deduction for purchases and that opening and ending inventory amounts could be ignored. In November, 1957, it is announced that tax rates will be lower in 1958. Assuming a calendar year for tax purposes, what would you do during the last two months of 1957? Why?

**4.** Supplies with a total cost of $720 have been charged to Supplies on Hand during the year. Supplies with a cost of $80 are still on hand at the end of the year. What adjustment should be made? What adjustment should be made if the $720 had been charged to Supplies Expense?

**5.** Why is there a need for adjusting and accruing entries? In what journal are these entries recorded?

**6.** Joe College pays $300 cash for a car that he expects to drive for three years and then junk. What is the amount of his expenditure? What is his annual depreciation cost on a straight-line basis?

**7.** Mr. X borrows $12,500 at 3 per cent for two years, interest payable at maturity. What amount should be accrued at the end of five months? Give the required entry.

**8.** A depreciable asset (a fixed asset other than land) with depreciable cost of $10,000 and a life of ten years is acquired on the first day of the year. No depreciation is recorded. What three figures on the year-end statements are incorrect and by what amount are they over or short?

**9.** Explain the direct write-off basis for handling bad debts; the estimated basis. Under what conditions can the former be used? When should the estimated basis be used?

**10.** Credit sales for the year are $400,000; accounts receivable at the year end are $100,000. Experience has shown that $\frac{1}{2}$ per cent of the unpaid balances is not collected. What would be the adjusting entry at the year end? What entry would be required if the Allowance for Bad Debts already has a balance of $800?

**11.** What $2\frac{1}{4}\%$ excise tax must be paid by most employers?

**12.** On the financial statements, expenses are deducted from income, net profit is added to owner's equity, and withdrawals are deducted from owner's equity. How are the same changes reflected in the permanent books of record?

**13.** Inventory figures are added and deducted on the face of the operating statement. How are the same mathematical results accomplished in the general ledger?

**14.** Why does the estimated basis for recording bad debts meet the prerequisites for accrual accounting?

**15.** Does the entering of depreciation on the records provide assurance that funds will be available for replacements? Why?

**16.** Why is Unearned Rental Income classified as a liability?

CHAPTER 6

# THE PREPARATION OF FINANCIAL STATEMENTS

The accounting cycle described in the preceding chapters includes (1) recording the transactions of the firm in the journals or other books of original entry; (2) posting these transactions to the appropriate ledger accounts; (3) taking a preliminary trial balance, if desired, as a partial check on the accuracy of the work already done; (4) making the adjustments necessary to record estimated depreciation and estimated losses from bad debts and to cause the expense and income accounts to show the expenses actually incurred and the income actually earned during the period; (5) preparing financial reports to be used by management; and (6) closing the temporary income and expense accounts to prepare the ledger for the following period and to reflect the effect of operations on the owner's equity. From this description of the work of the accounting department, it is clear that the contact of a typical businessman with a firm's financial records is largely through the financial statements which are prepared by the accountant from the adjusted trial balance of his general ledger or through other special reports or analyses which the accounting department may be asked to make.

The statements which are most commonly used and which are prepared at the end of each fiscal period have been illustrated in their simplest form in Chapters 1, 2, and 3. Their importance as evidence of a firm's financial position and operating efficiency and as one indication of the quality of its operating policies and general management makes necessary a more detailed study of their form and content. The preparation of the usual financial reports is explained in this chapter. Methods used in their analysis and interpretation are described and illustrated in Chapters 13, 14, 15, and 16.

## STATEMENT OF INCOME AND EXPENSE

Probably the most important statement prepared by the accounting department is the statement which shows the sources of the firm's income and the reasons for or kinds of costs incurred in producing this income. The statement is usually called an income statement, a statement of income and expense, a profit and loss statement, or a statement of operations. Regardless of the name by which it is called, its purpose is to provide management with descriptions and amounts of each source of income and of each item of cost incurred in producing this income. The difference between the total of the income produced and the total cost of producing it is, of course, the net income or net profit for the period.

*The Fiscal Period*

The financial data accumulated by the accounting department are summarized and reported at the end of each "fiscal" period. The total time elapsed between operating reports cannot exceed one year because of income tax law requirements that profits and losses be reported annually, but the period covered need not coincide with the calendar year and reports can be made for any period of time which the management may require. As a general rule, businesses which have a fiscal year ending at a time other than December 31 select a date (month end) which comes at the "natural" ending point for the annual cycle. The selection of a *natural* business year has the following advantages over the usual calendar year period:

1. The inventories will be at their lowest and will be easier to take. Errors in valuation will be less important than if made at any other time since quantities will be smallest. This means that profits will be more accurately stated.

2. There will be less interference with other operations since all operations will be at their annual low points. More help will be available for taking inventories.

3. The work involved in closing the books will be more easily handled since other transactions to be recorded will be at a minimum.

4. Management will be best able to evaluate policies and to make procedural or policy changes since each cycle of operations will stand out as a unit.

5. Current liabilities will have reached their annual low points as inventories have been sold and temporary loans repaid. Ratios showing current financial position will be at their most favorable point and reports to banks or mercantile creditors will look best.

*Interim Reports*

Statements may be prepared monthly or quarterly even though the books are not formally closed, but the preparation of statements always requires that inventories be taken (or estimated) unless perpetual inventories are maintained. (Where perpetual inventories are kept, the amounts should be checked by a physical count at least once a year.) In addition to finding the inventory, adjustments for depreciation, estimated bad debt losses, and accrued and deferred expenses and income must be computed to the date of the statement. If the books are not to be formally closed, however, these adjustments may appear only on the work sheet. Only annual adjustments need be journalized and posted to the ledger accounts.

Most businesses prepare monthly and quarterly statements for use by management in business policy formulation, but some firms are reluctant to issue these reports because of the relatively poor financial position which they seem to present. For example, packers or canning firms which have a great seasonal fluctuation have large inventories and large receivable balances which are financed by increased current liabilities at the peak of their seasons. Since equal increases in current assets and current liabilities will lower the current ratio (ratio of current assets to current liabilities), the liquid condition of the business appears to be much worse than would a competitor's condition where the competitor's position is judged by statements prepared at the end of his cycle. For this reason, the student is warned of the extreme importance of considering the *time* when a statement was prepared when he attempts to evaluate a firm from an analysis of the firm's statements.

### The One-step Income Statement

In its simplest form, the income statement shows the following facts:

NAME OF FIRM
Income Statement (or other suitable name)
*Period* Covered

| Income earned: | | |
|---|---|---|
| Income | xx | |
| Income | xx | |
| Total income | | xxx |
| Costs and expenses: | | |
| Expense | xx | |
| Expense | xx | |
| Total expenses | | xx |
| Net income | | xx |

It should be noted that the income statement is not simply dated; it shows the *period* in which the income was earned. If the statement were dated December 31, 1957, it would be impossible to tell whether income was earned in December, 1957, during the last quarter of 1957, or during the entire year. The period covered is indicated by phrases such as For the Month of December, 1957; For the Year Ended December 31, 1957; For the Fiscal Year Ending December 31, 1957; etc.

The report prepared by a service enterprise such as the John Doe Transfer and Storage Co. (Exhibit 6-1) is typical of this simple, one-step statement.

EXHIBIT 6-1
JOHN DOE TRANSFER AND STORAGE CO.
Income Statement for the Month of January, 1958

Income earned:

| | | |
|---|---|---|
| Transfer income | $600 | |
| Storage income | 300 | |
| Total income | | $900 |

Costs and expenses:

| | | |
|---|---|---|
| Rent expense | $200 | |
| Wages expense | 200 | |
| Gas and oil | 50 | |
| Supplies used | 10 | |
| Depreciation of truck | 15 | |
| Total costs and expenses | | 475 |
| Net income for January, 1958 | | $425 |

The income statement prepared by doctors, lawyers, and other professional persons and by all service enterprises, such as dry cleaners, laundries, theatres, transfer and storage companies, etc., would, or could, follow this simple pattern.

The income statements of manufacturing or trading concerns may follow this pattern and there has been a noticeable trend toward this type of report. This trend has been particularly evident in published annual reports where details are of little importance to the typical reader. The "Consolidated Statement of Earnings" of California Packing Corporation is typical of this type of report.

EXHIBIT 6-2
CALIFORNIA PACKING CORPORATION
Consolidated Statement of Earnings
Year Ended February 28, 1955

Sales and revenues:

| | | |
|---|---|---|
| Sales and operating revenues | $233,849,668 | |
| Dividends, interest, and other income | 226,130 | |
| Total | | $234,075,798 |

Costs and expenses:

| | | |
|---|---|---|
| Cost of products sold and operating expense | $188,369,863 | |
| Selling, general, and administrative expense | 31,172,737 | |
| Interest on indebtedness | 1,599,212 | |
| Sundry charges (credits) | (42,204) | |
| Minority interest in net earnings of subsidiary company | 10,015 | |
| Estimated Federal and foreign taxes on income | 6,380,000 | |
| Total | | 227,489,623 |
| Earnings for year before special credits | | $ 6,586,175 |

In its published form this statement was immediately followed by a section showing special credits arising from a refund of Federal taxes on income of prior years and from the sale of their investment in the stock of another corporation. The final earnings figure was then added to the unappropriated earnings at the beginning of the period, dividends paid during the year were deducted, and the final unappropriated earnings figure was shown. This method of combining the income statement with a statement showing extraordinary gains and losses and a statement of retained earnings is quite common.

It must be evident that firms using this simple form to present their operating results to stockholders do not wish to make public all the details of their operations. Many of these reports, for example, hide the cost of sales in a single total for "cost of goods sold, selling, advertising, and general administrative expenses." There may then follow a much more elaborate breakdown of minor and relatively insignificant expense amounts. While these statements are adequate for the purposes for which they are prepared—that is, to provide the owners and the prospective owners with the principal sources of income, the principal costs incurred, and the net earnings for the period—they obviously do not provide management with sufficient data for operating decisions. For management purposes, itemized lists of expenses with per cent of increase or decrease and the per cent each item is of total sales or of total expenses, and careful analyses of cost items and differences or variance from established standards, both in price and quantity, are needed. These details, of course, are not given to the general public or even to the stockholders.

A survey of recent annual reports of a number of major American corporations shows the increasing popularity of the one-step statement of earnings and a trend toward combining the statement of current earnings with a statement of earned surplus (retained earnings).

## Multiple-step Income Statements

The traditional form of the income statement is illustrated in the "Statement of Income and Expense" of the Machinery Sales Company in the example in Chapter 3. The "Statement of Profit and Loss" of the Apex Company (Exhibit 6-3) shows a slightly more detailed presentation but follows the same basic pattern as that of the Machinery Sales Company. Minor differences which may be noted are: The sales discounts and purchases discounts are considered adjustments of the sales and purchases amounts rather than as other income and expenses; the operating expenses have been divided into two categories with totals for each; "other" income and expense has been arranged in a slightly different manner; and a provision for Federal income taxes has been made. Because

EXHIBIT 6-3

APEX COMPANY

Statement of Profit and Loss for the Year Ending December 31, 1957

Income from sales:

| | | |
|---|---|---|
| Gross sales | | $462,000 |
| Less returned sales and allowances | $ 4,060 | |
| Discounts on sales | 6,140 | 10,200 |
| Net sales | | $451,800 |

Cost of goods sold:

| | | | |
|---|---|---|---|
| Merchandise inventory, Jan. 1, 1957 | | $ 68,500 | |
| Purchases | $332,800 | | |
| Returned purchases. *PR+a* | $2,600 | | |
| Purchase discounts | 5,800 | 8,400 | |
| Net purchases | $324,400 | | |
| Transportation in | 6,200 | 330,600 | |
| Cost of merchandise available for sale | | $399,100 | |
| Less merchandise inventory, Dec. 31, 1957 | | 72,300 | 326,800 |

*Net delivered cost of purchases*

| | | |
|---|---|---|
| Gross profit on sales | | $125,000 |

Operating expenses:

Selling expenses:

| | | |
|---|---|---|
| Sales salaries | $ 40,000 | |
| Salesmen's travel expense | 3,000 | |
| Advertising | 6,000 | |
| Delivery expense | 4,500 | |
| Depreciation on delivery equipment | 1,200 | |
| Store rent | 9,000 | |
| Total selling expense | | $ 63,700 |

General and administrative expenses:

| | | |
|---|---|---|
| Office salaries | $ 6,000 | |
| Officer's salaries | 18,000 | |
| Taxes (property) | 800 | |
| Insurance | 760 | |
| Depreciation of office equipment | 340 | |
| Rent (office building) | 1,200 | |
| Total general and adm. expense | | 27,100 |
| Total operating expense | | 90,800 |
| Net income from operations | | $ 34,200 |

Other income:

| | | |
|---|---|---|
| Interest income | $ 3,200 | |
| Income from rental of delivery equipment | 600 $ | 3,800 |

Other expenses:

| | | |
|---|---|---|
| Interest expense | 2,200 | |
| Net other income and expense | | 1,600 |
| Net income before provision for income tax | | $ 35,800 |
| Provision for estimated income taxes | | 14,000 |
| Net income for 1957 | | $ 21,800 |

of the various categories used to classify income and expense, this type
of statement is frequently referred to as a "classified" income statement.

### Preparation of Traditional Income Statements

**Income from Sales.** The first section of the traditional income statement shows the income from sales. In many published statements this
is shown as simply net sales since details about returns, allowances, and
discounts are of no real importance to persons outside the firm. Where
details are shown, the Sales account shows the gross sales for the period.
This account is sometimes divided into charge sales and cash sales but
this division is generally not considered of sufficient importance to
warrant its being made. If the total of charge sales is needed in setting
up the estimated bad debts expense or in figuring the turnover of receivables, the figure can be obtained from the total of the sales journal.

It would be possible to enter sales returns and allowances as debits
directly to the Sales account but these figures are of significance in
evaluating merchandise quality and merchandise adjustment policies and
are, therefore, kept separate. Corrections in invoice amounts due to errors
in extensions or in addition are entered directly in the Sales account since
they do not represent returns or allowances for defective merchandise.

The discounts on sales are sometimes deducted from gross sales as
shown in the Apex Company statement but may be included in the "other
expense" section. Accountants are not in perfect agreement as to whether
a cash discount represents an expense due to the financial policy of the
business or a reduction in the selling price of the goods. Because the
amount allowed is much greater than interest on the amount collected
and the granting of discounts is largely determined by competition and
trade practice, it is probably more logically considered a price adjustment
and should thus be shown as a deduction in determining the net sales.

**Cost of Goods Sold.** Firms which keep perpetual inventories may obtain
the cost of goods sold from the ledger account by that name. This account
is debited and the Inventory account credited for the cost of the goods
sold at the time the sale is made. Where perpetual inventories are not
kept, it is necessary to compute the cost of goods sold as illustrated in
the Apex Company statement. If the Apex Company had been a manufacturing company and had used simple manufacturing accounts, the
cost of goods sold section on the statement would have shown:

```
Cost of goods sold
    Finished goods inventory, Jan. 1, 1957..............  $ 68,500
    Cost of goods manufactured (see A)................   330,600
                                                        ─────────
    Total available for sale.........................   $399,100
    Less finished goods inventory, Dec. 31, 1957........    72,300
                                                        ─────────
    Cost of goods sold...............................   $326,800
```

The "cost of goods manufactured" amount should be supported by a schedule which shows the details of the cost of manufacturing the product of the Apex Company. This schedule shows the materials used, the direct labor, and the manufacturing expenses incurred in producing the finished goods. The actual supporting schedules would be arranged as shown in Exhibits 6-4 and 6-5.

EXHIBIT 6-4

APEX COMPANY—SCHEDULE A

Cost of Goods Manufactured for the Year Ending December 31, 1957

| | | |
|---|---:|---:|
| Materials used (see B)........................ | | $226,000 |
| Direct labor................................. | | 63,800 |
| Manufacturing expenses: | | |
| Factory rent............................. | $ 8,000 | |
| Taxes.................................... | 120 | |
| Indirect labor........................... | 13,000 | |
| Superintendence.......................... | 5,000 | |
| Depreciation of factory equipment........ | 2,000 | |
| Factory insurance........................ | 125 | |
| Supplies used............................ | 375 | |
| Miscellaneous factory expenses........... | 900 | 29,520 |
| Total placed in process...................... | | $319,320 |
| Add goods in process at Jan. 1, 1957......... | | 18,280 |
| Total in process.......................... | | $337,600 |
| Less goods in process at Dec. 31, 1957....... | | 7,000 |
| Cost of goods manufactured................... | | $330,600 |

EXHIBIT 6-5

APEX COMPANY—SCHEDULE B

Cost of Materials Used Year Ending December 31, 1957

| | | |
|---|---:|---:|
| Raw materials inventory, Jan. 1, 1957........ | | $ 23,000 |
| Raw materials purchased...................... | $232,800 | |
| Returned purchases............... $ 2,600 | | |
| Purchase discounts............... 5,800 | 8,400 | |
| Net purchases................................ | $224,400 | |
| Transportation in............................ | 6,200 | 230,600 |
| Total available.............................. | | $253,600 |
| Less raw materials on hand, Dec. 31, 1957.... | | 27,600 |
| Cost of materials used....................... | | $226,000 |

**Operating Expenses.** After the cost of goods sold is subtracted from the net sales income to obtain the gross profit (or gross margin) on sales, the operating expenses are listed and deducted to obtain the net profit from operations. These expenses may be divided into as many classes and subclasses as seem desirable but "selling" expenses and "general" or "administrative" expenses are the classes most often used. There is no perfect agreement on expense classifications but, as a general rule, expenses incurred in advertising, selling, and delivering the product are *selling* expenses; and expenses of running the office (buying, collecting, accounting, etc.) and expenses of administration are considered *general* expenses. Building occupancy costs are often shown entirely in the *general* section but may be divided between the two classes on the basis of floor space occupied or some other reasonable basis. Property taxes are usually shown as general expenses. Insurance and depreciation expenses should be classified on the basis of where the particular assets are used. Bad debt losses, estimated or actual, are sometimes shown as selling expenses and sometimes as general expenses, depending upon who authorizes the credit and who is responsible for collection.

**Other Expenses and Income.** Expenses due to the financial policies of the business, such as interest expense (and possibly sales discounts) and income earned through investments, as interest on loans, or from other sources clearly not a part of the firm's basic operations, are shown in the other expense and other income sections. In addition, gains and losses due to the sale of fixed assets or investments, or to other extraordinary occurrences, such as fire or theft, etc., are sometimes shown in this section. It would seem preferable, however, to show these extraordinary items in a section headed "extraordinary gains and losses" or to include them with the surplus items on a combined profit and loss and surplus statement.

**Footnotes.** The student should be aware of the importance of considering all footnotes an essential part of the statements which they accompany since they have an important effect upon the meaning of the values shown. Footnotes to profit and loss statements may explain:

1. The methods used in valuing inventories
2. That certain contracts of the firm are subject to renegotiation, which may have a considerable effect on the profits shown
3. That the company has "necessity certificates" which authorize it to amortize certain recent purchases of plant facilities over a five-year period, which may have an important effect on depreciation charges, net profits, and asset valuation on the balance sheet
4. That Federal income tax returns have (or have not) been examined by the Treasury Department and settlements have (or have not) been made
5. The company's financial accounting policy respecting depletion of mineral deposits, or
6. That the company began using a certain method of depreciation as of a certain date

## STATEMENTS OF RETAINED EARNINGS

*Capital Statement of a Proprietorship or Partnership*

It is customary for the accountant for a sole proprietorship to prepare a statement explaining the increase or decrease in the owner's equity for the fiscal period. The statement of changes in earned equity has already been described. If the statement describes changes in the total equity, it may be called a statement of capital. The statement of capital of a proprietorship begins with the owner's equity at the beginning of the period, adds the items which have increased his equity (additional investments and earnings) and deducts the items which have decreased his equity (withdrawals and losses from operating the business). A partnership prepares a similar statement with separate columns for each of the partners. Exhibit 6-6 shows a typical statement of this type. (The more commonly used term "Net Worth" has been used to replace the heading "Owner's Equity.")

EXHIBIT 6-6

JONES & SMITH

Statement of Partners' Capital for the Year Ended December 31, 1957

|  | Jones | Smith |
|---|---|---|
| Total net worth, Jan. 1, 1957.............. | $31,000 | $23,500 |
| Add: |  |  |
| Additional investment................... |  | 3,500 |
| Share of net earnings for year............ | 8,000 | 7,200 |
|  | $39,000 | $34,200 |
| Less: |  |  |
| Withdrawals of capital.................. | 4,000 |  |
| Withdrawals of current earnings......... | 3,000 | 3,000 |
| Net worth, Dec. 31, 1957................. | $32,000 | $31,200 |

In the example, no distinction was made between earned equity and invested equity since the partners may withdraw either earnings or investments and are personally liable for the firm's debts. An example showing how earned and invested equities may be kept separate is given under the discussion of partnership accounting in Chapter 8. A distinction was made between a major withdrawal of invested capital (made because the firm had excess capital, to equalize investments, or because the partner wished to invest in some other venture) and withdrawals of current earnings, which are made in lieu of or in addition to salaries.

*Corporate Statements of Retained Earnings*

In a corporation, the stockholders are not liable for the firm's debts and, as a result, are prevented by law from withdrawing funds in excess of earnings. (The amounts which may be withdrawn as dividends depend upon the laws of the individual states. Investments may be withdrawn if the firm is being liquidated, and surplus arising from sources other than profits may be withdrawn under certain conditions.) Creditors would have no security if the investment of the owners could be withdrawn since they cannot sue the individual stockholders. For this reason and because there are few changes in the invested equity of a corporation, the corporation is principally interested in the earned equity (earned surplus) amounts and the usual statement shows only the changes in the earned surplus. Exhibit 6-7 shows a typical arrangement.

EXHIBIT 6-7
JONES CORPORATION
Statement of Earned Surplus for the Year Ended December 31, 1957

| | | | |
|---|---|---|---|
| Earned surplus, Jan. 1, 1957 | | | $162,000 |
| Add: | | | |
| Net income for 1957 | | | 64,000 |
| Total | | | $226,000 |
| Less: | | | |
| Dividends paid on preferred stock, 6% on $150,000 | $ 9,000 | | |
| Dividends on no-par common stock, $12 per share | 24,000 | $33,000 | |
| Appropriated for sinking fund reserve | | 20,000 | 53,000 |
| Earned surplus, Dec. 31, 1957 | | | $173,000 |

This statement does not show the total owner equity but only the equity which is available for dividends. Since there were no extraordinary gains or losses shown, it is called a "clean" surplus statement; and it may be assumed that, if there were extraordinary gains or losses, they have been shown on the income statement.

The term "extraordinary gains and losses" would include such non-recurring items as gains on sales of investments, gains (or losses) on sales of major fixed assets, adjustments for tax refunds, adjustments for prior years' depreciation allowances, etc. Accountants have not been able to reach any agreement as to the best place to show such extraor-dinary, nonrecurring items. If they are included on the profit and loss statement, the reported income may not be comparable from period to period. On the other hand, if they are not presented on the profit and loss statement, there is the possibility that they may be overlooked and the reader given the wrong impression about the actual amount earned. The user of financial statements must always determine whether extraordinary gains and losses are included on the profit and loss state-ment, and must correct his impression of profitability if they are reported on the surplus statement.

## Combined Statement of Income and Retained Earnings

The "Consolidated Statement of Profit and Loss and Earnings Retained in the Business" of the Wesson Oil and Snowdrift Co., Inc. (Exhibit 6-8), is typical of the combined, multiple-step income statement and statement of earned surplus found in many annual reports. It will be noticed that the form is somewhat simplified and that gains and losses on the sales of fixed assets have been included in the other income section.

EXHIBIT 6-8

WESSON OIL AND SNOWDRIFT CO., INC., AND SUBSIDIARY COMPANIES

Consolidated Statement of Profit and Loss and Earnings Retained in the Business for the Fiscal Year Ended August 31, 1955

| | | |
|---|---:|---:|
| Net sales..................................................... | | $166,712,469 |
| Cost of goods sold (see note), including depreciation (on manufacturing equipment) of $1,823,891.................................... | | 141,967,808 |
| Gross profit................................................ | | $ 24,744,661 |
| Selling, administrative and general expense, including depreciation (on selling, office, etc., equipment) of $153,795...................... | | 16,461,319 |
| | | $ 8,283,342 |
| Other income: | | |
| Interest revenue................................. | $ 506,637 | |
| Interest expense.................................. | (321,962) | |
| Rents, dividends, commissions, gains and losses from dispositions of capital assets, and other misc. income, net......................................... | 1,088,704 | 1,273,379 |
| Profit before taxes on income................................. | | $ 9,556,721 |
| Federal income taxes............................. | $4,500,000 | |
| State income taxes............................... | 350,000 | 4,850,000 |
| Net profit........................................ | | $ 4,706,721 |
| Earned surplus at beginning of year............................ | | 56,211,734 |
| | | $ 60,918,455 |
| Cash dividends declared on: | | |
| Preferred stock, per share $4.00..................... | $1,167,600 | |
| Common stock, per share $1.40..................... | 1,632,400 | 2,800,000 |
| Earned surplus at end of year................................. | | $ 58,118,455 |

The income statement is completed after determining the net profit to be $4,706,721. The effects of profits and dividends on the owner's equity could have been shown on a separate statement of earned surplus. The note mentioned in the cost of goods sold section of the Wesson Oil Company emphasizes again the importance of considering all footnotes to financial statements as an essential part of the statement. In this case the note explains the procedures used in valuing inventories:

The vegetable oils and their by-products included in the inventories were valued on the last-in, first-out basis at cost established originally at August 31,

1941, except that the carrying value of one of the oils on a "lifo" basis was reduced to state such oil at market value at August 31, 1955. For all of the other oils in the inventory at August 31, 1955, costs were below market values as at that date. The other finished goods and other raw materials were valued at the lower of cost (computed on the first-in, first-out basis) or market. Market prices of the commodities and products therefrom used for comparison with costs were based on current published quotations where available; otherwise latest purchase costs were considered to represent current market. Inventories of packaging materials and supplies were valued at cost or less.

The method used in valuing inventories has an important effect on the cost of goods sold as well as upon the asset values shown on the balance sheet. For example, during a period of rising prices, the use of the last-in first-out method of inventory valuation will result in charging most recent and higher costs to the cost of sales, will "understate" inventory values, "overstate" costs, and "understate" current profits. (The terms *overstate* and *understate* are relative to other procedures possible.)

Where the profit and loss and the surplus statements are made separately, the analyst must not end his study with the analysis of the profit and loss statement—he *must* check the surplus statement for extraordinary gains or losses.

### THE BALANCE SHEET

Since double-entry bookkeeping is based on the principle that the assets owned must equal the equities in them, it is logical that one of the statements prepared at the end of each fiscal period would show what assets are owned and what are the equities of creditors and owners who have provided these assets. In its simplest form, a balance sheet shows only the following facts:

NAME OF FIRM
Balance Sheet
Date of Statement

| Assets | | Liabilities and Proprietorship | |
|---|---|---|---|
| List of properties | xx | List of debts owed................ | xx |
| owned by the firm | xx | Equity of owners................. | xx |
| Total assets owned | xxx | Total creditor and owner equity | xxx |

The balance sheet of Machinery Sales Company, which was illustrated in Chapter 3, follows this simple plan. Although the statement is still most often called a balance sheet, other names, such as statement of financial position, statement of financial condition, etc., are more descriptive and are commonly used. It is never called a trial balance. It should also be noted that the statement shows the financial position on a *particular date* rather than for a period of time. Though the arrangement illustrated is satisfactory for very small firms, most larger firms find that statements in which the items are classified or grouped are much more valuable. This type of statement is described and illustrated in the following paragraphs.

## Asset Classifications

While there is no standard way of presenting the assets owned by a firm, it is obviously desirable to group them in ways which will provide those who must use the statements with the maximum information about the properties owned. Since many analysts are interested in whether the firm will be able to meet its current debts as they come due, one desirable classification includes all the properties which are either in the form of cash or can reasonably be expected to be turned into cash in the near future and in the regular operation of the business. Assets of this type are called "Current Assets." Another classification (called Fixed Assets) includes all the fixed properties, such as land, equipment, machinery, and buildings, used in producing the goods or services which the business has to sell. A third often used group (called Prepaid Expenses) includes all properties of a temporary nature which will be used up (and thus turned into expenses) in subsequent periods. A fourth classification (called Intangible Assets) includes properties and rights of an intangible nature, such as patent rights, copyrights, trademarks, franchises, and good will. A fifth classification (called Investments) includes investments which the firm holds in subsidiary firms, or other long-term investments in securities or real estate not used in operating the business. (Temporary investments in readily marketable securities should be included under the current assets.) A miscellaneous or "Other Assets" group may be used if some properties owned cannot logically be included in any of the groups suggested.

A survey of a representative group of large American corporations shows that all of the classifications suggested are used by some of the firms, yet few firms used exactly the groupings suggested. All of the firms grouped cash and the assets which were expected to be turned into cash in the near future under the heading "Current Assets." The fixed properties were listed under such headings as "Fixed Assets," "Capital Assets," "Property," or "Plant and Equipment," or "Property, Plant, and Equipment." The prepaid expenses were included with the current assets by many firms but were shown under "Prepaid Expenses and Deferred Charges," or "Prepaid Expenses" on a number of statements. It is now considered better practice to include the prepaid expenses under "Current Assets" and to use the term "Deferred Charges" as a caption

*Current Assets - An item which is normally converted into cash or consumed during a 12 mo. period.*

for a special type of asset, such as organization expense or bond discount. These items are more fully discussed later.

Intangible assets are sometimes shown under such headings as "Goodwill," "Trademarks, Good will, and Patent Rights," etc., or may be included under "Other Assets." The term "Other Assets and Investments" is often used as a group heading to include both suggested groups. Among other headings used in practice are "Long-term Receivables" and "Noncurrent Investments and Receivables."

Regulation S-X of the Securities and Exchange Commission, which applies to most commercial and industrial firms submitting reports to this government regulatory agency, sets up the following asset classification system:

1. Current assets
   *a.* Cash and cash items
   *b.* Marketable securities
   *c.* Trade notes and accounts receivable (less reserves for bad debt losses)
   *d.* Inventories
   *e.* Other current assets (such as nontrade receivables meeting certain tests)
2. Investments
   *a.* Securities and noncurrent indebtedness of affiliates
   *b.* Other security investments
   *c.* Other investments (such as land held for possible future use)
3. Fixed assets (used in producing the firm's income)
   *a.* Property, plant, and equipment (less appropriate reserves for depreciation, depletion, or amortization)
4. Intangible assets
   *a.* Patents, trademarks, franchises, good will, and other intangibles (less appropriate reserves for depreciation or amortization)
5. Deferred charges
   *a.* Prepaid expenses (which may also be included under "Other Current Assets")
   *b.* Organization expenses (such as incorporation fees and costs)
   *c.* Debt discount and expense (at sale of a bond issue)
   *d.* Commission and expense on sale of capital stock (which may also be deducted from surplus)
6. Other assets
   *a.* Including amounts due from officers
   *b.* Special funds (such as pension funds) and other items not classified elsewhere

From this discussion it can be seen that there is a considerable degree of uniformity in reporting the properties owned, as far as grouping of the properties is concerned. However, when the statements being studied do not have the groupings which the analyst prefers, he should regroup the assets as a first step in his analysis. And since it is obvious that different grouping systems may be used, comparisons based on group totals are not valid unless the items are uniformly included under the same group headings. Ratios computed for different businesses cannot be considered comparable unless comparable groupings are used.

## Liability Classifications

The liabilities of a firm may be logically divided into three principal groups. First, there are those creditors who must be paid within a relatively short time (usually one year); these are called "Current Liabilities." Second are those debts which must be paid but which are not due within the next year, called "Fixed Liabilities," "Long-term Debt," or "Funded Debt." And third, there are debts owed by the firm because income has been collected, but has not yet been earned, as rental income collected in advance. Liabilities of this type are called "Deferred Credits." In the case of rental income which has been collected but not earned, it is obvious that something is owed the renter. But, since he will be paid by the use of a fixed asset instead of cash, it is also clear that the debt is different from wages, taxes, or trade accounts payable which will require the use of the firm's current assets in their settlement.

The corporations surveyed in regard to asset classifications were also checked for liability groupings used. It was found that all of them used the heading "Current Liabilities" although some included the words "and Accrued Liabilities." Since accrued liabilities (such as accrued wages, accrued taxes, and accrued interest payable) are always current liabilities, there is no real need for specifically including *accrued* in the heading. (In a similar way, accrued receivables, such as accrued interest on notes receivable or accrued rents receivable, are current assets and need not be specifically mentioned in the heading.)

The term "Fixed Liabilities" is commonly found in accounting texts but seems to be less often used in actual practice. "Long-term Debt" and "Long-term Liabilities" are more descriptive and are more commonly used.

The classification "Deferred Credits" is of minor importance. The term arises from the fact that the balance in the liability account will be credited to an income account as the income is earned. Many firms have no deferred credits and many others feel that in any case where current assets must be used to earn the income, the liability is not essentially different from one which is paid in cash and may, therefore, be included in the current liabilities.

Many balance sheets have a section for reserves. In the opinion of most writers, valuation reserves should be deducted from the fixed assets, liability reserves should be classified as liabilities, and surplus reserves should be shown in the surplus section. This subject will be more fully discussed in Chapter 13.

Regulation S-X of the Securities and Exchange Commission prescribes the following liability classifications:

1. Current liabilities
   a. Notes payable to banks
   b. Trade notes payable
   c. Trade accounts payable
   d. Accrued liabilities, such as wages, taxes, and interest
   e. Other current liabilities, such as dividends (cash) payable, bonds maturing within one year, and amounts owed officers, directors, parent companies, etc.
2. Deferred income (representing liability for income collected by firm but not yet earned)
3. Long-term debt
   a. Bonds, mortgages, long-term notes
   b. Notes to affiliates
   c. Long-term notes to officers, directors, etc.
4. Other liabilities, including contingent liabilities
5. Reserves, not shown elsewhere
   (These would include such reserves as Reserve for Contingencies, Reserve for Inventory Decline, etc. There is some question as to just what these reserves represent.)

Accounting convention requires that liabilities be measured by the amount of cash due or the agreed value of services received and that they be estimated as accurately as possible when such measures are impossible. Convention also requires that bond premium or discount arising from the sale of bonds at more or less than face value be amortized systematically over the life of the obligation. For this reason premium on bonds payable and discount on bonds payable are generally treated as deferred items and written off over the life of the bond issue.

## The Equity of the Owners

The owner's equity in a firm arises from two principal sources: (1) investments by the owners, and (2) earnings of the company which have been left in the business. In a proprietorship or partnership these two sources of equity are often shown in Capital and Surplus accounts which are set up for each of the owners. But there is no legal requirement that a distinction be made between the owner's invested and earned equities and they are often combined in a single capital account for each owner.

As a general rule the owners' equity in a corporation is shown under two major headings, capital stock and surplus. The capital stock is further subdivided into each of the types of stock outstanding (preferred, common, and possibly various types of each) and the amount of each type authorized, issued and outstanding, or subscribed is shown. The surplus may be divided into a number of classifications depending upon the source of its origin. Surplus may arise from earnings which have been retained in the business (earned surplus), from the sale of stock at amounts greater than par or stated value (paid-in or capital surplus), from donations of stock, land, or franchises to the company (donated surplus), and from the appraisal of fixed properties at values greater than their book value (appraisal surplus). Earned surplus and paid-in or capital surplus are the two most common classifications. Donated and appraisal surplus are often included under the capital surplus heading.

It may be seen that the owner's equity arising from investment may be found by adding the capital stock to the paid-in surplus balance and that the equity arising from earnings is shown in the earned surplus balance. It would seem logical, therefore, that capital stock and paid-in surplus should be grouped together and earned surplus should be presented separately. This is often done. However, since stock dividends reduce earned surplus and increase capital stock outstanding, it is not always possible to determine the actual amount of earnings retained. Thus, it is not possible to say just what part of the owner's equity was invested and what part was earned, though it is desirable that this be done, and accountants believe that it should be made possible.

One of the most common mistakes made by the beginner in financial analysis is the assumption that Earned Surplus or other surplus accounts represent surplus *funds* the firm has available to pay dividends. The balance in the Surplus account (unless there is a deficit) is always on the credit side. It cannot, therefore, be an asset, for assets have debit balances. The cash on hand is shown in the Cash account and both cash and fund accounts (such as an insurance fund) are wholly unrelated to the balance in earned surplus. Remember that this balance simply represents the equity arising out of earnings; it does not show what was done with the cash received.

Dividends are not paid in "Surplus"—they are paid in cash, in stock, or in some asset other than cash. It is true that, except for liquidating dividends, they cannot legally be paid unless a surplus exists, for to pay dividends when there have been no earnings would result in returning the investment of the stockholders. This could be disastrous to both stockholders and creditors.

**Footnotes to the Balance Sheet.** No balance sheet may be considered complete without considering the footnotes which accompany it. Foot-

notes are often necessary to explain or clarify the meaning of some figure
in the statement, and the analyst must consider the footnotes as important
as any other part of the statement. They should not be considered
improper—they are essential and often actually the only way of presenting the facts. However, when they are used to hide bad news, the analyst
should take this fact into account in appraising the character and depend-
ability of the management.

## *The Form of the Balance Sheet*

**The Account Form.** One of the most common forms of balance sheet
arrangement is called the "account" form because it resembles the traditional T account. Totals are shown for each subdivision of the statement
and the total assets and the total of liabilities, reserves, and capital are
shown to be equal. The report of the Polax Company shown in Exhibit
6-9 is in "Account" form and uses the subheadings suggested by the
Securities and Exchange Commission.

**The Report Form.** In the "report" or "vertical" form of the balance
sheet, the assets are listed first with totals for each subdivision and a
grand total; the liabilities are listed next with the usual subdivisions and
totals; and the net worth (capital or proprietorship) section is listed last.
This arrangement makes it clear that total liabilities are subtracted
from total assets to arrive at the owner's equity. The General Electric
Company, for example, lists and totals all assets and then deducts total
liabilities, which are also itemized. The difference is called "Excess of
assets over liabilities—ownership." This net asset figure is followed by a
section headed "Ownership evidenced by" which shows the owner's
invested and earned equities. The total ownership equity is, of course,
equal to the net assets (total assets less total liabilities).

**The Financial Position Form.** A variation of the report form of balance
sheet which is becoming increasingly popular is the report of financial
position. In this form the current liabilities are deducted from the
current assets to obtain the working capital. The other assets are then
added, a total is taken, and the noncurrent liabilities are deducted. The
resulting figure, called the net assets, is equal to the ownership interest,
which is presented in detail immediately following the net asset figure.
The statement of General Foods Corporation (Exhibit 6-10) follows this
form.

A notation at the bottom of the statement calls the reader's attention
to a series of footnotes which form an integral part of the statement.
These footnotes must be carefully studied before any attempt is made to
interpret the financial position of the company.

**Other Forms.** The annual reports of our major corporations show a
number of new arrangements which are believed to make the financial

position clearer to the average stockholder. For example, Westinghouse calls the statement a "Statement of Ownership." On the left-hand side the principal heading reads "The Companies Own." There are no subheadings of the usual type but a total is given for the current assets

EXHIBIT 6-9

THE POLAX COMPANY, INC.

Balance Sheet

December 31, 1958

| Assets | | | | Liabilities | | |
|---|---|---|---|---|---|---|
| Current assets: | | | | Current liabilities: | | |
| Cash on hand and in banks | | $ 10,600 | | Accounts payable | | $ 12,600 |
| Accounts receivable | $ 22,800 | | | Notes payable (trade) | | 3,000 |
| Less allowance for bad debts | 1,300 | 21,500 | | Wages payable | | 2,600 |
| | | | | Estimated income tax payable | | 14,000 |
| Notes receivable | | 1,640 | | Total current liabilities | | $ 32,200 |
| Merchandise inventory | | 54,300 | | Deferred income: | | |
| Prepaid insurance | | 200 | | Rent collected in advance | | 860 |
| Accrued interest receivable | | 60 | | Long-term debt: | | |
| Total current assets | | | $ 88,300 | Mortgage payable, 6% | $ 10,600 | |
| Investments: | | | | First mortgage bonds payable | 130,000 | |
| Investment in stock of subsidiary | $ 84,000 | | | Total long-term debt | | 140,600 |
| Ace Corporation bonds | 25,000 | | | Total liabilities | | $173,660 |
| Bond sinking fund | 28,000 | | | | | |
| Cash surrender value of life insurance | 14,000 | | | | | |
| Total investments | | 151,000 | | | | |
| Fixed assets: | | | | Net worth | | |
| Land | $ 12,000 | | | Capital stock: | | |
| Buildings | $156,000 | | | Preferred stock, 1,000 shares, $100 par, 6%, cumulative preferred | $100,000 | |
| Allowance for depr | 16,000 | 140,000 | | Common stock, 14,000 shares, no-par, $10 stated value | 140,000 | |
| Furniture & fixtures | $ 18,000 | | | Total capital stock | | $240,000 |
| Allowance for depr | 8,000 | 10,000 | | Surplus: | | |
| Total fixed assets | | 162,000 | | Earnings retained in the the business | $ 26,000 | |
| Intangible assets: | | | | Capital surplus, excess of amount paid in overstated value | 6,140 | |
| Patents | $ 17,000 | | | Total surplus | | 32,140 |
| Franchises | 22,000 | | | Total net worth | | $272,140 |
| Total intangible assets | | 39,000 | | Total liabilities and net worth | | $445,800 |
| Deferred charges: | | | | | | |
| Discount on bonds payable | $ 3,000 | | | | | |
| Organization expense | 2,500 | | | | | |
| Total deferred charges | | 5,500 | | | | |
| Total assets | | $445,800 | | | | |

(which include cash; United States government securities; amounts owed the company by customers, by the United States government as tax refunds, and by wholly owned companies not consolidated; materials, supplies, and inventories; and other amounts recoverable); and amounts shown for investments; land, buildings, and machinery; patents, charters, and franchises; insurance prepaid; noncurrent receivables; and property not used in operations. The main heading on the right side is "The Companies Owe." This is followed by a list of the various creditors, without headings, but with a total for the current debt and a total for all liabilities. This final total is subtracted from the total assets to get the "Stockholders' Equity." Below the double rules the stockholders' equity is broken down into the standard capital stock and surplus sections.

EXHIBIT 6-10
GENERAL FOODS CORPORATION AND CONSOLIDATED SUBSIDIARIES
Statement of Financial Position at March 31, 1956

| | |
|---|---:|
| Cash | $ 32,346,638 |
| Government securities (at cost, which approximates market) | 30,899,901 |
| Receivables (less estimated uncollectibles of $1,351,000) | 75,320,625 |
| Inventories | 139,320,133 |
| Expenses paid in advance (advertising, insurance, taxes, and others) | 6,758,039 |
| Current assets | $284,645,336 |
| Less current liabilities: | |
|     Notes and accounts payable | $ 29,596,266 |
|     Accrued liabilities | 14,425,925 |
|     Income and excess profits taxes | 52,273,475 |
| Current liabilities | $ 96,295,666 |
| Working capital (current assets less current liabilities) | $188,349,670 |
| Investments and sundry assets, less reserves | 2,487,642 |
| Land, buildings, and equipment (at cost, less accumulated depreciation) | 95,511,140 |
| Intangibles: | |
|     Patents and trademarks | 1 |
|     Good will | 1,283,869 |
| Working capital and other assets | $287,632,322 |
| Less long-term debt: | |
|     Notes payable | $ 18,000,000 |
|     3⅜% Debentures, due July 1, 1976 | 35,000,000 |
| | $ 53,000,000 |
| Excess of assets over liabilities | $234,632,322 |
| Represented by stockholders' interest: | |
|     Common stock (5,877,610 shares) | $120,909,492 |
|     Earnings retained in the business | 113,722,830 |
| | $234,632,322 |

The Johns-Manville Corporation uses the same form as General Foods but calls its statement "Investment." The Briggs Manufacturing Company and Burroughs call their report a "Statement of Financial Condition," list the stockholders' equity first, and then describe how the investment was used, i.e., how much was in Working Capital, Land, Buildings, etc. Most companies experiment with various arrangements of their financial data and change the form from year to year, but whatever the form, they always show the properties owned and the equities of the creditors and the owners in these properties.

## SUMMARY

A majority of firms still prepare financial statements on a calendar year basis, although an increasing number favor the natural business year. One-step income statements are popular in annual published reports, but detailed multiple-step statements are usually prepared for management purposes. If the income statement is for a trading concern, the cost of goods sold section will include cost of purchases and inventories; if the statement is for a manufacturing concern, "cost of goods manufactured" will replace "cost of purchases." The statement of income and expenses can be presented as a separate statement or combined with earned surplus and dividends data to form a combined statement of income and retained earnings.

Balance sheets contain three major classifications of financial data: assets, liabilities, and owner's equity. Numerous subheadings also appear in order to provide additional information. The order of presentation of the different items and groupings depends upon the form of the balance sheet, i.e., whether it is prepared in account form, report form, or financial-position form.

## QUESTIONS

**1.** What names are given the statement which shows the properties owned and the equities in them? The statement which matches costs incurred against the income earned during the period? The statement which explains changes in the owner's equity?

**2.** Why does an income statement always show the period covered while a balance sheet always shows a particular date?

**3.** What is a "fiscal period"? What is meant by a "natural" business year?

**4.** What are the advantages of using a natural business year rather than the calendar year?

**5.** What is an "interim" report? What must be done before any financial statements can be prepared?

**6.** "If a highly seasonal business prepares statements at the peak of its annual cycle, its current position will appear to be better than it really is." Why is this statement false?

**7.** What does a one-step income statement really show? What additional information is provided by a multiple-step or classified income statement?

**8.** What two methods of showing sales discounts are commonly followed in the preparation of a classified income statement? Which method do you prefer? Why?

**9.** How is the "gross profit on sales" figure determined?

**10.** What expenses are generally classified as operating expenses? Which of these are considered "selling" expenses and which are "general" expenses?

**11.** Explain why sales returns are not debited to the Sales account. Why are corrections in invoice amounts entered in the Sales account? What is the difference between a sales return, an allowance, and a correction?

**12.** How does a retail store determine the cost of goods sold? How does this differ from a manufacturing concern?

**13.** What expenses and income are included under "Other expenses and income"? What is the difference between "extraordinary gain" and "other income"?

**14.** What are the two possible places (statements) for showing extraordinary gains and losses? What are the arguments for and against each?

**15.** "The method used in valuing the inventory affects the asset inventory but has no effect on the income statement." Why is this statement false?

**16.** Compare the effect of LIFO and FIFO on profits and inventory balances during periods of rising prices. During periods of falling prices.

**17.** What effect does the method of valuing inventories have on profits earned over the entire life of a business?

**18.** What is the difference between a trial balance and a balance sheet? What are the three principal sections of a balance sheet?

**19.** What are the most commonly used asset classifications?

**20.** Define each of the following terms: current assets, fixed assets, intangible assets, investments, deferred charges.

**21.** What two possible classifications are used for prepaid expenses?

**22.** "All assets which may be quickly turned into cash are current assets." Why is this statement false?

**23.** What are the three principal types of liabilities?

**24.** Define each of the following: current liabilities, fixed liabilities, deferred credits.

**25.** How are accrued payables classified? Accrued receivables?

**26.** What justification is there for classifying some deferred income as current liabilities?

**27.** What are the two principal types of owner's equity in a corporation called?

**28.** What kind of balance does the Surplus account normally have? What kind of balance does Cash normally have? Does the Surplus account show the amount of cash on hand? What does it show?

**29.** Using the headings shown in the balance sheet of the Polax Company, classify each of the following accounts: Investment in Government Bonds, Prepaid Rent, Good will, Bond Sinking Fund, Accounts Receivable, Allowance for Bad Debts, Employees Withholding Taxes Payable, Mortgage Payable, Premium on Common Stock, Discount on Bonds Payable.

**30.** What is the "net working capital" and how is it determined?

## CHAPTER 7

# PRINCIPLES AND PROCEDURES

The profitability of a business enterprise is determined by its ability to sell the goods or services which it produces for more than the total cost of producing them. The owners of a firm cannot expect to benefit from their operations if it costs more to produce their service than their customers are willing to pay. Thus, those who are inefficient producers and those who are not sensitive to customer demands must improve their business management or fall by the wayside. The successful businessman must constantly analyze his operations, and accounting records can provide factual data which are essential to such analysis. They record and measure the flow of funds and match the operating costs (expense) against the revenues (income) which they produce. The preceding chapters have explained the basic procedures used to record and summarize this flow of funds. This chapter will present a graphic summary of the accounting process and explain some of the basic principles of the profession.

*How Accounting Records and Measures the Flow of Funds*

The chart shown in Exhibit 7-1 summarizes the flow of funds in a business enterprise. It shows how the cash received is used to produce the service which the firm provides, how the sale of goods replenishes the cash, and how the costs incurred are matched against the revenues produced to determine the increase in the owner's equity. The boxes used for each item are set up as T accounts in order to give a visual impression of the effects of the various transactions on the general ledger accounts. A careful study of the chart will be of help in understanding the purpose of the adjusting and closing entries and also in understanding the real meaning of the Earned Equity account, usually called the "surplus" account. For convenience of discussion, numbers have been assigned to various sections of the chart. These numbers indicate roughly the sequence of the events.

1. The business is organized and the owner invests his money in the venture. Cash flows into the firm. It is recorded by a debit to the Cash account and a credit to the Invested Equity account.

113

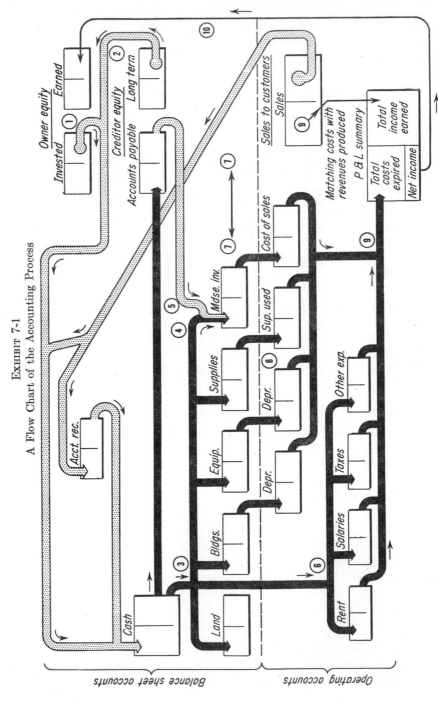

Eхнвіт 7-1
A Flow Chart of the Accounting Process

2. In some cases additional funds may be obtained from long-term creditors. This will also result in an increase in Cash, but since the long-term creditors are not owners, the firm's debt to them will be shown in a liability account.

3. The cash which the firm has received is used to purchase the land, buildings, equipment, and supplies which the firm needs to carry on its activities. The outflow of cash is recorded as a credit to Cash and debits are made to the various assets acquired.

4. Merchandise is purchased for cash. The outflow of cash is recorded and the increase in Inventory is shown.

5. Merchandise is purchased on account. The liability is recorded as a credit to Accounts Payable and the increase in Inventory is shown by the offsetting debit. When the payment is made, cash flows out and the liability is canceled.

6. In addition to the assets purchased in (3) and (4), other costs are incurred for labor, rent, taxes, etc. Since these items are immediately consumed and normally have no value at the end of the period, they are recorded directly in expense accounts.

7. When merchandise is sold, its cost is removed from the Inventory account and transferred to a special account which shows the cost of the goods sold (the perpetual inventory method). At the same time the sale to the customer is recorded at the agreed selling price. The income is shown in a Sales account, so that it may later be matched against the costs incurred, and the inflow of cash is recorded by a debit to Cash. If the sale is made on account, the value of the receivable will be shown and the actual inflow of cash will be delayed until the account is collected.

8. At the end of the period, adjustments are made to record the supplies used and the estimated expense of using the fixed assets (depreciation) and such other adjustments as may be necessary for a proper recording of costs and income for the period.

9. All of the expired costs are transferred to a summary account where they are matched against the income earned (sales) during the period. The inflow of cash from sales has already been recorded in (7). The outflow of asset value, or expired costs, were shown in (6) and (8). The excess of income over expired costs results in an increase in the net assets. This increase has *already* been reflected in the asset accounts but has *not* been reflected in the owner's equity accounts.

10. An entry is made to transfer the net income earned to the Earned Equity account of the owners. This will bring the permanent ledger accounts into balance.

Accounts above the dotted line show the assets owned and the equities of the creditors and the owners in them. These assets are largely unexpired costs. A balance sheet is prepared to summarize these data.

Below the dotted line are the temporary accounts which were used to measure the costs expired and income earned during the period. They are summarized on the income statement or profit and loss statement for the period. The balances in these temporary accounts were transferred to the summary account by entry (9) and, after the books are closed, these accounts can be used to record the costs and income of the next period.

Note that the owners and long-term creditors supply most of the original cash, that the mercantile creditors (Accounts Payable) supply a large part of the inventory, and that once the business is in operation, the inflow of cash is largely from the customers. The outflow is to pay for the goods necessary to fill customers' orders and to pay for operating costs. Some of the costs incurred are not immediately expired and are shown in asset accounts, such as Equipment, Buildings, or Supplies. As these assets are used, the expired portion flows into an appropriately named expense account. Other costs, such as rent or salaries, are incurred for services which are immediately consumed. These costs are entered directly in expense accounts.

If the revenues are greater than the expired costs, there has been an increase in the net assets. This increase, which belongs to the owner, has already entered the asset accounts, but no record has been made of its effect on the owner's equity until the net income is transferred from the Profit and Loss Summary to the account which shows the owner's equity from retained earnings.

It should also be noted that all amounts flowing into asset and expense accounts enter the left side and flow out the right side as they are used up or have their balances transferred to the summary account. On the other hand, all *sources* of assets are credited as the assets are brought on the books as debits.

## INTERNAL CONTROL PROCEDURES

The chief accounting officer for a business is the individual normally responsible for the financial reports being "in conformance with generally accepted accounting principles." This individual and his coworkers are also usually responsible for the maintenance of records and procedures that will serve to control, or assist in controlling, the properties of the business. To accomplish this, the work must be so arranged that the work of one employee serves as a check on the work of another. When possible, no single employee should be allowed to handle all or several phases of a transaction. There would, for instance, be many opportunities for theft or embezzlement if one individual were permitted to order, receive, and issue materials from stock; or if one employee were allowed to select, purchase, and authorize payment for equipment and also to dispose of equipment in any manner that he saw fit. There are also many possibilities for defalcations when only one person does both the purchasing and the writing of checks, the billing and collecting of payments, or the recording of receipts and the actual depositing of cash in the bank.

To decrease the possibilities of theft and misappropriation, the business must establish "internal control" procedures that will provide adequate records and division of work. Since cash is particularly subject to theft and misappropriation, a discussion of control procedures and techniques to provide for its protection is presented below. A detailed discussion of other procedures may be found in advanced accounting books, particularly auditing texts.

### Procedures for the Protection of Cash

To control cash several general rules should be followed:

1. A separate checking account should be maintained in the name of the business; i.e., an owner should not maintain a single bank account for both his personal and business expenditures.

2. As many payments as possible ought to be made by check; the canceled checks provide verification for disbursements and also serve as receipts for payment.

3. Expenditures should *not* be made from cash receipts, so that receipts can always be traced directly into the bank.

4. When possible, *all* cash receipts should be deposited daily. Large amounts of cash on hand increase the possibilities of theft, and combining the receipts for many days in one deposit makes it difficult to compare the journal debits for amounts received with the deposit totals.

5. If it is considered necessary or more convenient to make comparatively small expenditures by currency and coin, an "imprest" petty cash fund should be maintained.

6. All employees who handle any significant amounts of cash should be covered by a surety bond.

**Imprest Petty Cash Funds.** An imprest petty cash fund is maintained at one amount in order to make it easier to check the fund and control reimbursements to the fund. If, for example, a firm decided to establish an imprest fund for $80, a check for that amount would be drawn in favor of cash. The check would be cashed and the $80 in currency and coin placed in a safe or box. The entry in general journal form to record this transaction would be:

| | | |
|---|---|---|
| Petty Cash | 80 | |
|     Cash in Bank | | 80 |
| (To set up new petty cash fund) | | |

There will be no further entries in the Petty Cash asset account unless it is decided to increase or decrease the fund; as a consequence, the one debit for $80 is normally the only entry in this general ledger asset account. Expenditures and reimbursements do not affect the asset account. Assume, for instance, that at the time it was decided to reimburse the fund, it consisted of the following: coin and currency, $19; paid freight bills, $40; receipts for stamps, $20. The journal entry for reimbursement would appear as shown below:

| | | |
|---|---|---|
| Freight in | 40 | |
| Office Supplies | 20 | |
| Cash Short and Over | 1 | |
|     Cash in Bank | | 61 |
| (Check drawn and cashed | | |
| to reimburse imprest fund) | | |

The receipts, bills, memos, coin, and currency should always total $80, thereby making it comparatively easy to check out the fund at any time. Differences caused by errors in making payments are debited or credited to Cash Short and Over. If this account has a debit balance it represents an expense; a credit balance would represent an income. In either case, the balance is usually so small that it is included on the operating statement as a part of miscellaneous expense. Petty cash funds, when significant, should be reimbursed as of the date statements are prepared, for the expenses arising from petty cash expenditures are normally recorded only at the time of reimbursement; and, if reimbursement is not made, the asset Petty Cash will be overstated and expenses understated (unless corrected by an adjusting entry).

**Cash in Bank.** To protect cash receipts, one person should list amounts received, another should make deposits, and a third should prepare the journal entry to record the deposit. To protect disbursements by check, there should also be a separation of duties: one employee to be responsible for purchasing, another for authorizing payment of invoices, a third to draw checks, and a fourth to record the checks in the cash disbursements record. Under ideal circumstances there should be still another employee, independent of those mentioned above, who reconciles the bank account *each month.* In a small business where there are insufficient employees to subdivide the work to this degree, the owner-manager should at least make or supervise the making of deposits, authorize payments, sign the checks, and have someone who does not handle or record cash prepare the monthly bank reconciliation.

In reconciling the general ledger cash balance with the balance shown on the bank statement, there are several adjustments that must usually be made: (1) Receipts for the last day of the bank's statement period are often deposited late in the afternoon of that day or early the next morning—too late to be recorded by the bank as deposits for the current period. (2) Almost invariably there will be a number of checks that have been issued but have not yet cleared through the bank and, therefore, have not been deducted from the bank balance. (3) The bank frequently imposes a service charge and deducts this amount from the bank statement balance; the business does not know the amount of this charge until the statement and canceled checks are received. A simple bank reconciliation that illustrates these adjustments is presented in Exhibit 7-2 (cents have been omitted as usual).

EXHIBIT 7-2

BANK RECONCILIATION XYZ COMPANY

| | | |
|---|---:|---:|
| Balance per bank statement, Apr. 30.......... | | $2,600 |
| Add deposit in transit....................... | | 400 |
| Total.................................... | | $3,000 |
| Deduct outstanding checks: | | |
| Check number 641.................... | $ 69 | |
| 689.................... | 140 | |
| 703................... | 287 | 496 |
| Adjusted bank balance....................... | | $2,504 |
| | | |
| Balance per general ledger, Apr. 30............. | | $2,510 |
| Deduct bank service charge.................. | | 6 |
| Adjusted book balance....................... | | $2,504 |

## ACCOUNTING CONCEPTS, PRINCIPLES, AND CONVENTIONS

### Generally Accepted Principles

"In conformance with generally accepted accounting principles" is a phrase frequently quoted in relation to financial reports. Unfortunately this quotation does not carry the certainty that might seem to be implied, for principles change with time and there may well be considerable disagreement about some of the principles that are currently considered as generally accepted. Nevertheless, most of the "generally accepted" principles are approved as guides or standards and reputable accountants will plainly note any deviations from these norms. The principles have great value in this respect; i.e., a person who makes use of financial statements that have been prepared by professional accountants can assume that the data have been presented according to the commonly accepted conventions or, if not, that pertinent notes have been included to explain any other standards that may have been adopted. For instance, it is normally assumed that statements report financial data on the accrual basis if nothing is mentioned in regard to the method of reporting. If the cash basis has been employed there should be a notation to inform the reader of this fact.

### A Review of Principles and Concepts Already Discussed

A number of accounting principles that have already been mentioned in the preceding chapters are:

1. The cash basis of accounting should be employed only for service-type enterprises where sales or fees are sufficiently numerous and regular that the uncollected and unrecorded income is likely to be offset by collections on receivables earned in the prior period, and where expenses reported as of the time paid are likely to be approximately the same from year to year.

2. If income and expenses are irregular, or if the firm sells tangible items rather than services, the accrual method of reporting should be employed in order to assure reasonably accurate statements.

3. If accounts receivable and bad debt losses are significant, the amount of bad debts should be estimated to accomplish the proper valuation of the receivables and to match the related income and expense.

4. Depreciation, for accounting purposes, is recognized as the periodic allocation of fixed asset cost. It does not necessarily reflect the loss in market value during the period.

5. Assets are usually reported on the basis of original cost less accumulated depreciation, if any, and these book values may be quite different from current market values. The book value of the owner's equity may also be quite different from the actual present value of the business to the owners since the valuation of the ownership interest is directly dependent upon the values established for the assets.

6. If certain items on the statements need clarification, they must be accompanied by appropriate footnotes; e.g., methods used in costing inventory or in estimating depreciation frequently need to be explained.

A number of these principles, along with others, will be considered in greater detail in this chapter. More detailed discussions of certain basic concepts which were briefly explained in Chapter 1 are also included.

### Entity Concept

Accounting for businesses is based on the theory that business properties and activities form a unit or entity entirely separate and distinct from the owner or owners, regardless of the legal form of organization. This means that transactions of the owners that are not related to a particular business unit should have no effect on the accounting records for that unit. Since only transactions that are related to a particular business unit are recorded and reported for that unit, it is possible to provide financial reports that can be used to judge the operating efficiency of that business, the ownership interest in it, and the return to the owners on their investment in that business. These judgments would not be possible if non-related transactions were included.

Should an individual desire information as to his total wealth or total income for a period, it is possible and practicable to draw financial statements that will provide the desired information. Mr. X, for example, may be sole owner of a business with proprietorship valued at $60,000; a partner in another business with an equity valued at $40,000; and a shareholder in a third business where his proportion of the stockholders' equity is valued at $50,000. All three of these investments would appear as assets in a personal balance sheet for Mr. X, along with all other properties that he owns. His liabilities would also be listed, totaled, and deducted from his total assets to compute an estimate of his total net worth as an individual. If his personal income statement were prepared on the accrual basis, it would include his proportionate share in the profits of the three firms plus all other income earned. If such a statement were prepared on a cash basis, it would contain only amounts actually received as drawings or dividends, plus cash income from other sources. Only business expenses not reimbursed by the firms might be included on a personal income statement, or these and all personal expenditures could be included in order to determine whether or not there had been an actual net gain or loss in personal wealth during the period.

## Going-concern Concept

Accounting for most business entities is based on the "going-concern" or "continuity" concept. This concept or theory encompasses the assumptions that a business will continue indefinitely and that management is customarily not concerned with liquidation values. Managers and owners, in other words, think of costs as being applied to and recovered through operations; they are not, under normal circumstances, concerned about the amount that would be recovered if their concern were to be dissolved and the assets sold.

The going-concern concept is particularly evident in the accountants' approach to the problems of depreciation and fixed asset valuation. They readily admit that some book values may be quite different from the respective market or economic values; but to obtain current market values would require annual appraisals, an extremely costly and time-consuming process—and a process that could result in highly fluctuating values from year to year. If the appraisal value for the current year were higher than the appraisal value for the prior year, accounting would be faced with the question of whether or not to recognize an unrealized gain. In addition, the majority of accountants feel that such valuation procedures are unnecessary and that current values are not overly important, since the assumption is made that the enterprise has no intention of selling its operating assets and is primarily interested in apportioning costs according to services rendered. When operating assets are originally obtained, the question is not what the asset could be sold for tomorrow or next year, but rather, can the asset render sufficient service to the business to recover its cost through sales.

### Period Accounting

An accurate picture of the earnings of a business entity can, theoretically, be obtained only when the concern is liquidated—and even this theory presents serious problems, for the value of the dollar over an extended period may fluctuate radically. However, income tax regulations require an annual measurement of earnings, and financial reports for management purposes are generally needed even more frequently.

A fiscal year is an accounting period of twelve months that ends, customarily, on the last day of a given month. If a fiscal year ends December 31, it is known as a calendar year; if it ends on a month end that represents the low point in business activity, it is referred to as a natural business year. The Federal Internal Revenue Code, however, defines a fiscal year as any twelve-month period that ends on the last day of some month *other than* December. Many persons accept this usage, although "fiscal" is normally defined simply as "pertaining to financial matters"—which indicates that a calendar year is just as much a fiscal year as any other twelve-month period. An interim period is a period within a fiscal year, e.g. a month, a quarter, six months, etc.

The establishment of accounting periods, though necessary, creates many problems in accounting. At the end of each period it must be determined how much cost should be absorbed, how much cost is to be deferred to future periods, how much income has been earned, and how much has been collected in advance but is not yet earned. Some costs, such as sales salaries and advertising expense, are knowingly charged off as current expenses, despite the fact that portions of these costs will undoubtedly result in the creation of future income. Estimates of such future income are so unreliable that it is considered better to charge all of these costs as current "period costs" rather than attempt to prorate portions of them over a number of periods. Most expired costs for service and trading enterprises are considered *period costs*, for most of them are accumulated and allocated on time bases. Material, labor, and factory overhead costs of manufacturing concerns should be charged as product costs (cost of goods manufactured), but selling, administrative, and "other" costs for such concerns are normally charged as period costs in order to simplify the problems involved in cost allocation.

If errors are made in recording current income and expired costs, the reported profits for both the current and succeeding periods will be incorrect. Several examples, each assuming that the accounting period coincides with the calendar year, follow:

1. Income of $10,000 recorded early in 1958 was actually earned in 1957. The net profit for 1957 was understated by $10,000; the net profit for 1958 was overstated by $10,000.

2. Expenses of $6,000 incurred in 1957 were not recorded until 1958. The net profit for 1957 was overstated by $6,000 and the net profit for 1958 was understated by the same amount.

3. Errors in counting and pricing caused the inventory taken December 31, 1957, to be valued at $60,000 rather than $68,000 as it should have been. This means that $8,000 was charged as an expired cost in 1957 instead of 1958, and that the net profit was therefore understated by $8,000 in 1957 and overstated by $8,000 in 1958. The overstatement of the net profit in 1958 arises because the opening inventory for that year was the same as the ending inventory for the preceding year; i.e., only $60,000 is added to the cost of goods sold whereas the amount should have been $68,000.

4. Errors in taking and compiling the 1957 year-end inventory result in a valuation of $90,000 rather than the correct amount of $80,000. This means that $10,000 too much was included as unexpired cost in 1957, thereby understating cost of goods sold and overstating profit by that amount. In 1958 the opening inventory of $90,000 is charged to cost of goods sold, thereby overstating cost of goods sold by $10,000 and understating profits by $10,000. The effect of this error* on the cost of goods sold is illustrated below:

|  | 1957 | | 1958 | |
| --- | --- | --- | --- | --- |
|  | As reported | Should have been | As reported | Should have been |
| Inventory, Jan. 1 | $ 70,000 | $ 70,000 | $ 90,000* | $ 80,000 |
| Purchases (net) | 210,000 | 210,000 | 300,000 | 300,000 |
| Available | $280,000 | $280,000 | $390,000 | $380,000 |
| Inventory, Dec. 31 | 90,000* | 80,000 | 120,000 | 120,000 |
| Cost of goods sold | $190,000 | $200,000 | $270,000 | $260,000 |
| Effect on net profit | +$10,000 | | −$10,000 | |

*Matching Income and Expenses for a Period*

When the accrual basis of accounting is used for financial reporting, good accounting principles require that all income must be reported as of the period when it is earned, and that all expenses incurred in the creation of that income must be reported in the same period. If credit sales transactions are completed during the latter part of the period, the income has to be reported in that period—not in the next period when the accounts are collected. All merchandise purchased during the period must be recorded and the total cost of all goods sold during the period has to be reported. If wages and salaries have been earned by the employees but not yet paid, the expense thus incurred should be included as a part of the total expense for wages and salaries. Any bad debts expected to arise from current sales are to be recorded. The amounts of fixed asset costs that are estimated as having expired during the period are also to be reported. In other words, all income earned and *all* costs expired must be reported, unless they are too insignificant to justify an adjustment.

### Capital and Revenue Expenditures

Although this terminology is not employed in the text, one should be acquainted with the meaning of "capital" and "revenue" expenditures. Expenditure indicates that a certain cost has been incurred, which may or may not have been paid. If supplies priced at $100 have been purchased and a check for $100 issued in exchange, there has been an expenditure. If more supplies are purchased on credit and a liability thereby incurred, there has also been an expenditure, even though a payment has not yet been made.

A capital expenditure indicates that an operating asset has been purchased. A revenue expenditure indicates that a cost has been incurred that benefits only the current period, viz., an expense. Purchase of equipment, for example, is a capital expenditure because it benefits not only the current period but will also benefit the following periods. The cost of office salaries incurred represents a revenue expenditure, since it benefits only the current period; it is a charge against current revenue (income).

### Cost Valuation

Accountants are sometimes criticized for their continued adherence to cost as a basis of valuation, for recorded cost is usually equal to current value only at the time of acquisition. Many persons feel that assets should be consistently shown at current market value. A few also believe that net income ought to be reported on a basis which would take into account changing price levels and the subsequent changes in the purchasing power of the dollar. They are justifiably troubled by the fact that the value of a dollar changes from year to year and that, as a consequence, accounting reports combine data that are not expressed in measuring units of the same value.

Many of these changes may be desirable, and some of them will undoubtedly be adopted when a majority of those concerned feel that cost alone will no longer suffice, but a great deal of work remains to be done before satisfactory bases are determined for incorporating the desired changes. In the meantime, most accountants will continue to provide statements based on original cost, i.e., cost measured by cash outlay, past or future. They will continue to follow the principle that any deviation from cost must be clearly described; and, in the meantime, those who are dependent upon accounting statements for financial information will at least have knowledge that these statements have been prepared on a consistent basis of original cost. But they must also be aware of the fact that in some cases the current market valuation may be quite different from the book value displayed on the statements. Those who are responsible for the financial aspects of a business must be aware of the fact that asset replacement costs may be drastically more than original costs; and, as financial managers, they must attempt to make adequate provision for funding these replacements.

It should be noted that the apportionment of costs is often a matter of judgment—and that the apportionment can be no better than the judgment employed. The accountant is continually faced with the problem of how much cost should be reported as expired and how much cost should be considered as unexpired. Typically, he is faced with questions such as these: How much depreciation should be taken on fixed assets? What will our bad debt losses be for this period? How should we value our merchandise inventories? Are our investments overvalued? Etc., etc. Reasonable decisions—as to how much cost, if any, should be apportioned to each period—can be determined only by experienced judgment based on adequate information.

*Fluctuating Price Levels*

Accounting reports based primarily on original cost are sometimes criticized because they contain asset dollars of different value, and because the dollars used to report profit and owner's equity do not always have the same value. The dollar is not, as one might suppose, a stable, unfluctuating standard for valuation or measurement. Equipment valued at $60,000 on the balance sheet may include several lathes purchased at a cost of $5,000 each in 1950 and several comparable lathes purchased in 1957 at $6,000 each. A profit measured as $8,000 in 1940 might be equal in purchasing power to a profit of $14,000 in 1957; as a result, the measure of earned equity would include dollars having two radically different values.

Economists and others have argued that some sort of price index should be applied to equalize these changes in the value of the dollar. To date, however, there is no general agreement as to the best method, and the majority of accountants agree that there can be little change in this direction until a satisfactory basis has been established as an acceptable standard; and, before any changes are made, they want to be certain that the advantages to be gained outweigh the disadvantages involved. Attempts to absorb fixed asset valuations would, for example, become extremely complex if these valuations fluctuated continually.

### Fixed Asset Valuations and Depreciation Methods

It is generally agreed that the balance sheet valuation of an asset should include *all costs* incurred in obtaining the asset and preparing it for use, less accrued depreciation to date. Assume, for example, that a business firm purchases a piece of equipment with an invoice cost of $60,000. Freight and in-transit insurance on the equipment total $2,000. Employees' wages for installation work amount to $4,000. The total cost of this equipment is, therefore, $66,000. Suppose that the same business buys a tract of land for the erection of a warehouse. Before construction can begin, an old building on the land is demolished at a net cost of $7,000. Property taxes for prior years in the amount of $1,000 are paid. The price of the property was $24,000, but the total cost of the land to the company should be recorded as $32,000—the total cost of obtaining the land and preparing it for its intended use.

Land is not considered a depreciable asset—since it generally does not lose value through use alone—and gain or loss on land used in operations is usually recognized only when it is disposed of. Other classes of fixed assets, however, are depreciable; eventually they will have to be discarded. Many fixed assets are not discarded until they are worn out while others are scrapped, sold, or traded at a time when they are still operating with little mechanical trouble. Why? Probably because they are obsolete. Something may have been developed that will provide a more economical operating cost, or perhaps competition requires a change in product design that cannot be handled by existing equipment. Obsolescence may, consequently, become a major factor in the computation of depreciation. The physical life of a fixed asset may be estimated as 20 years, but due to factors of obsolescence, its useful life may be judged to be only ten years—and ten years should, consequently, be the basis employed for depreciating the original cost.

"Useful life" of machinery or equipment can be expressed in several different ways: (1) as a period of time, (2) as so many working hours, or (3) as a number of units to be produced. In the first instance, which has already been discussed, the total cost is divided by the number of periods in the expected life. For example, a machine that cost $6,600 has an estimated trade-in value of $600 and an estimated useful life of 60 months; the monthly depreciation charge on this machine would be $100 regardless of the amount of production. The useful life could, on the other hand, be established as 60,000 working hours and depreciation charged at the rate of 10 cents per hour for each hour the machine operates. Or it might be estimated that 600,000 units of product will pass through the machine before its useful life expires. In this case depreciation would be charged at one cent for each unit produced. The latter two methods have the advantage of charging depreciation in proportion to the amount of production or service rendered, whereas the straight-line method creates periodic charges which may bear little relationship to use or production. Straight-line depreciation will, as a consequence, often overstate expenses and understate profits during periods of comparatively little activity and understate expenses and overstate profits during periods of high activity.

Some accountants and businessmen believe that neither time nor use should be the sole factor in determining the rate for apportioning fixed asset cost to expense. They feel that the book values shown on the balance sheet should be decreased faster during the early years of asset life in order better to reflect obsolescence. Others want larger depreciation charges in the early years to keep the total charges for the use of fixed assets, depreciation plus maintenance, more constant from period to period. (The latter is based on the assumption that maintenance costs are usually higher in the later years of useful life, so that larger charges in the early years for depreciation will somewhat level the periodic charges.) An automobile, for example, may have a market value of $3,000 when new, a market value of $2,000 one year later, and a market value of $1,500 two years after purchase. Those accountants who are particularly concerned about reflecting decreases due to obsolescence would prefer the application, in such instances, of a depreciation method that would provide for larger charges in the early years as compared with the later years. Accountants who desire the sum of depreciation and maintenance charges to be more constant from year to year would also favor a depreciation method that yields more expense in the early years and less in later years when maintenance costs are higher.

"Accelerated" depreciation during the early years of asset life is now permitted for computation of income taxes. (See Chapter 12 for a detailed discussion of accelerated depreciation methods.) This is another reason for the adoption of depreciation methods that yield higher expense charges during the early years. Less income tax is paid and the business, in effect, gains an interest-free loan. There will have to be less depreciation charged in later years and, consequently, more income taxes; but in the meantime a business will have funds available that would otherwise have been paid out. If such a method is adopted for income tax reporting, it is likely to be adopted for all financial reporting in order to avoid maintenance of two sets of records for depreciation under two different methods. This is proper and in accord with generally accepted accounting principles, *if* the depreciation charges for a period appear reasonable when compared with *the maximum* decrease in valuation that might result from both use and obsolescence during that period.

Subsidiary records of fixed assets contain a description of each asset, its location, the date purchased, its total cost, and the estimated useful life. Such records are always valuable in the control of properties, but the additional record keeping would not be considered economical by some firms, particularly if their fixed assets are neither numerous nor varied. A small retail establishment, as an example, might have only two fixed asset accounts in the general ledger, one for store fixtures and one for office furniture and equipment. The expected useful lives of the store fixtures are often about the same; this may also be true of the office furniture and equipment. All acquisitions of fixed assets can then be charged to the appropriate general ledger accounts and the depreciation rates applied to the account balances in total. This is known as the *composite* method of depreciation and represents the method most commonly employed in reporting for small businesses—and many larger ones. The total cost of the fixed asset groupings can be apportioned on the basis of the straight-line method or on the basis of one of the methods that provides for comparatively larger charges during the early years. An illustration of the composite method with the use of straight-line rates is shown below. It has been assumed that furniture and fixtures have an estimated useful life of ten years (no scrap or trade-in value) and that, for depreciation purposes, each change takes effect as of the first day of the month following the transaction, i.e., as of July 1 and October 1.

| Furniture and fixtures | | | Computation of annual depreciation |
|---|---|---|---|
| 1-1  Bal. | $14,000 | 9-19 Files sold  $1,000 | $14,000 \times 10\% \times \frac{6}{12} = \$\ \ 700$ |
| 6-10  Desks | 2,000 | | $16,000 \times 10\% \times \frac{3}{12} = \ \ \ \ 400$ |
| | | | $15,000 \times 10\% \times \frac{3}{12} = \ \ \ \ 375$ |
| | | | Total depreciation          $1,475 |

### Meaning of Accounting Depreciation

What does a depreciation entry accomplish? First, it decreases the valuation of fixed assets and records an expense. This is as it should be, since the original cost must be absorbed during the periods of useful existence. Secondly, the loss in asset valuation is reflected as a loss in the owner's equity, as it should be, for certainly the loss in valuation does not decrease the equities of the creditors. Assume, for instance, that a firm has equipment with a cost of $10,000 that is expected to have a useful life of ten years. At the end of the first year after the equipment was purchased, statements are prepared that do not include an allowance for depreciation.

The operating statement:

| | |
|---|---:|
| Income | $20,000 |
| Expenses | 14,000 |
| Net income | $ 6,000 |

The balance sheet:

| | | |
|---|---:|---:|
| Cash | | $ 8,000 |
| Equipment | | 10,000 |
| Total assets | | $18,000 |
| Accounts payable | | $ 2,000 |
| Invested equity | | 3,000 |
| Earned equity | $7,000 | |
| Add profit | 6,000 | 13,000 |
| Total equities | | $18,000 |

These statements are not reasonably accurate: net income, equipment, and equity are all overstated. When properly prepared, the statements would be as follows:

The operating statement:

| | | |
|---|---:|---:|
| Income | | $20,000 |
| Expenses | $14,000 | |
| Depreciation | 1,000 | 15,000 |
| Net income | | $ 5,000 |

The balance sheet:

| | | |
|---|---:|---:|
| Cash | | $ 8,000 |
| Equipment | $10,000 | |
| Accumulated depreciation | 1,000 | 9,000 |
| Total assets | | $17,000 |
| Accounts payable | | $ 2,000 |
| Invested equity | | 3,000 |
| Earned equity | $ 7,000 | |
| Add profit | 5,000 | 12,000 |
| Total equities | | $17,000 |

Funds have *not* been set aside, but the owners have been shown that their ownership interest is actually valued at $15,000 ($3,000 plus $12,000) rather than $16,000 ($3,000 plus $13,000). As a result, a sole proprietor or partner is less likely to withdraw an extra $1,000 for his personal use; and, in the case of a corporation, the amount that can be legally distributed to the owners has been reduced by $1,000. (The laws of the different states generally state that the amount to be distributed to stockholders cannot exceed the amount of earned equity.) The recording of depreciation has also resulted in a decrease of $1,000 in the book value of the equipment. This decrease is the result of an estimate, but the results are more reasonable than if no depreciation were taken into account. It is better to show the estimated book value as $9,000 than to continue to value the asset at its full original cost of $10,000. But at the same time it must be remembered that the Earned Equity account overstates the amount that can be permanently withdrawn by the owners if the replacement cost of the asset will be more than the original cost of $10,000.

## Other Forms of Amortization

Amortization is a generic term for write-offs of limited-life assets. The amortization of fixed asset cost over the estimated useful life is referred to as depreciation. If, however, a fixed asset is a nonremovable part of a building which is leased for a period shorter than the asset's useful life, the write-off of cost is generally known as "amortization of leasehold improvements." Assume, for purposes of illustration, that a firm spends $500 to construct permanent partitions in a building that will last for 50 years, but that the firm's lease on the building runs for only ten more years. The total cost should then be amortized over ten years by an annual entry such as the following:

| | | |
|---|---|---|
| Amortization of Leasehold Improvements | 50 | |
| Leasehold Improvements | | 50 |
| (Annual write-off of lease improvements; | | |
| $500 divided by 10 years is $50) | | |

The amortization of the cost of natural resources is called "depletion." An estimated reserve of one million tons of ore purchased for $5,000,000 would be depleted at the rate of $5 per ton mined. At the end of a year in which 50,000 tons had been mined and sold, the following entry would be necessary to reflect expired cost:

| | | |
|---|---|---|
| Depletion Costs | 250,000 | |
| Ore Deposit | | 250,000 |
| (50,000 tons at $5 per ton) | | |

Assume, in another instance, that a logging company purchases five million board feet of standing timber at $40 per thousand, a total cost of $200,000. If during the year 250,000 board feet were cut and 50,000 were still on hand, the following journal entry would be made:

| | | |
|---|---|---|
| Log Inventory | 2,000 | |
| Depletion Costs | 8,000 | |
| Standing Timber | | 10,000 |
| (50,000 feet on hand; 200,000 feet sold; | | |
| at cost of $40/M) | | |

The above discussions present an oversimplification of several involved procedures and are intended only to illustrate major points. Those readers who are interested in these subjects can find detailed explanations in any standard text covering the field of advanced accounting.

## Lower of Cost or Market

The lower of cost or market principle for the valuation of assets is most frequently applied to marketable securities, other investments, and inventory. Assume that a firm has securities, with a market value of $12,000, recorded at their original cost of $16,000. An adjustment should be made to write off $4,000 of the asset cost to expense in order to reflect the loss of value. The same procedure should be followed in the case of unimproved land held as an investment which, as of the end of the fiscal period, has decreased significantly in value.

A majority of firms value inventory on the basis of "lower of cost or market." Market, as used in this sense, means "replacement" market, or the price that would have to be paid on the balance sheet date for a particular item if it were purchased in the usual quantities. An inventory item that was purchased in quantities of 1,000 at $6 each and is currently selling for $5 each in the same quantities, should be reduced to the lower figure. Application of this principle to each and every individual item in a large inventory is normally impractical. In such cases the *lower of cost or market* may be applied to only those items that constitute a major portion of the inventory on a dollar basis; or the principle may be applied to gross totals by use of an index number or on the basis of an educated estimate.

Firms can value inventory on the basis of "cost" or on the basis of the *lower of cost or market*. In either case it must be realized that *cost* for inventory purposes has several different meanings. The cost of a fixed asset and the fixed asset itself remain closely associated; i.e., both the cost and the asset can usually be identified and related to each other, but the identification of specific inventory items with specific cost prices is impractical under most circumstances. As a result, certain methods are used for the expiration of inventory costs that are based on assumptions as to the order in which costs should be applied. These assumptions may or may not bear any relationship to the actual flow or use of the goods or materials, since a unit of material and the price paid for it are frequently considered as two distinct things, unrelated and independent of each other.

## Valuation of Cost of Goods Sold and Inventory

The dollar valuations of cost of goods sold and inventory are frequently determined upon the basis of first-in first-out (FIFO) costing. This means that the first or earliest *costs* are applied as cost of goods sold and that the later costs left over are applied to the valuation of ending inventory. (Notice, however, that some of the "earliest" merchandise may still be on hand and that some of the "later" merchandise may have been sold.)

If subsidiary records are maintained for each item that is purchased for resale, the earliest cost not yet applied would be charged to the Cost of Goods Sold account as each item is sold. Where subsidiary perpetual inventories are not used, the same effect is obtained in the computation of cost of goods sold by valuing the ending inventory on the basis of the latest prices paid. For example:

| | |
|---|---:|
| Inventory, beginning................................... | $ 4,000 |
| Cost of purchases...................................... | 56,000 |
| Cost of goods available for sale (all prices included)........ | $60,000 |
| Inventory, ending (latest prices)........................ | 2,000 |
| Cost of goods sold (earlier prices)....................... | $58,000 |

The flow of costs on the FIFO basis frequently corresponds with the physical flow of the goods; that is, the "older" costs are applied first and the older merchandise is often sold first, particularly if the items are perishable or subject to style changes or obsolescence. Another method, which has quite the opposite results, is the last-in first-out method, better known as LIFO. Under this method the *latest* prices are charged to Cost of Goods Sold *first* and, consequently, the earlier prices are left for the valuation of the ending inventory. In many business units this means that the older items are being sold first, but that costs are actually being charged to Cost of Goods Sold on the basis of the latest prices. Assume, for instance, the following data for one item of merchandise:

| | Purchased | | | | Sold | | | | Balance | | |
|---|---|---|---|---|---|---|---|---|---|---|---|
| Date | Quantity | Unit | Total | Date | Quantity | Unit | Total | Quantity | Unit | Total |
| 2-4 | 100 | $0.90 | $ 90 | | | | | 100 | $0.90 | $ 90 |
| 6-7 | 400 | 1.00 | 400 | | | | | { 100 | 0.90 | 90 |
| | | | | | | | | { 400 | 1.00 | 400 |
| | | | | 7-20 | 200 | $1.00 | $200 | { 100 | 0.90 | 90 |
| | | | | | | | | { 200 | 1.00 | 200 |
| 9-24 | 300 | 1.05 | 315 | | | | | { 100 | 0.90 | 90 |
| | | | | | | | | { 200 | 1.00 | 200 |
| | | | | | | | | { 300 | 1.05 | 315 |
| | | | | 10-16 | { 300 | 1.05 | 315 | | | |
| | | | | | { 200 | 1.00 | 200 | 100 | 0.90 | 90 |

Note that all of the unit costs of $1.05 and $1 have been charged to Cost of Goods Sold and that only the earliest unit cost of 90 cents remains for valuation of the 100 items remaining at the end of the period. Actually, most of the 100 units purchased at 90 cents each in February have probably been sold. In other words, the flow of costs under the LIFO method very frequently does not follow the flow of merchandise or materials.

Those persons who support the LIFO method maintain that the latest costs *should be* matched with selling prices, and that only in this way can it be determined if sufficient funds are being obtained to replace inventory that was sold. If the first item sold on July 20 (referring to the example above) were sold for $2, they would insist that it is better to charge the latest purchase price of $1 to Cost of Goods Sold and report a gross profit of $1 rather than a gross profit of $1.10. They contend, with logic, that in a period of rising prices the replacement cost will be $1 per unit or more and that the profit should not include an amount that will almost immediately be needed to provide for replacements at higher prices.

LIFO may be adopted primarily as a means of reducing taxable income during a period of inflation. Since the latest and higher costs can be charged as Cost of Goods Sold, the net profit is lowered and, subsequently, the tax liability. During periods of deflation the opposite would be true, for the latest cost would be the lower cost and, as a result, cost of goods sold would be less and taxable income, more. This provides not only a tax advantage but also serves to stabilize profits to some extent: in periods of prosperity reported profits will be lower; in periods of recession reported profits will be higher. From many points of view this stabilization or leveling of reported profits is desirable.

The *average cost* method of valuing cost of goods sold and inventory combines some of the features of both the FIFO and LIFO methods. Each time a new purchase is made the total purchase cost is added to the total cost already on hand; the quantity received is added to the quantity on hand; and the total quantity then available is divided into the total cost to arrive at the new average cost. The resulting averages, a combination of older prices and the most recent prices, become the basis for charges to Cost of Goods Sold and the basis for valuation of the ending inventory. The illustration employed above with LIFO costs is repeated below with average costs:

| Purchased | | | | Sold | | | | Balance | | |
|---|---|---|---|---|---|---|---|---|---|---|
| Date | Quantity | Unit | Total | Date | Quantity | Unit | Total | Quantity | Avg. | Total |
| 2-4 | 100 | $0.90 | $ 90.00 | | | | | 100 | 0.90 | $ 90.00 |
| 6-7 | 400 | 1.00 | 400.00 | | | | | 500 | 0.98 | 490.00 |
| | | | | 7-20 | 200 | $ .98 | $196.00 | 300 | 0.98 | 294.00 |
| 9-24 | 300 | 1.05 | 315.00 | | | | | 600 | 1.015 | 609.00 |
| | | | | 10-16 | 500 | 1.015 | 507.50 | 100 | 1.015 | 101.50 |

If FIFO had been employed as a basis for the application of costs under the above conditions, the latest price of $1.05 would have been left for the valuation of ending inventory. When costs were applied on the basis of LIFO, the unit cost of 90 cents would have been the basis for valuation of ending inventory. In the example immediately above, the last average cost of $1.015 serves as the basis for valuation. It is a combination of the earlier costs and the latest costs and, consequently, falls between these two extremes.

The *lower of cost or market* reflects the conservative approach of the accountant; LIFO does so to an even greater degree. Under the LIFO method in a period of inflation the latest and highest costs are expired, thereby resulting in lower and more conservative figures for net profit, owner's equity, and inventory valuation.

### Conservatism

Many accountants, consciously or subconsciously, adopt the "theory" of conservatism. If there is a question of how much cost is to be expired in the current period, they are inclined to overestimate rather than underestimate. Should there be any doubt as to whether or not income has been earned, they are likely to defer reporting it as income until such time as there is no doubt whatever that it has been earned. If there is any question as to the possible overvaluation of an asset, they may consider it wise to expire a portion of the asset cost as expense. But, at the same time, most accountants normally refuse to recognize any "unrealized" gain. A building, for example, which has a market value of $80,000 may be carried on the books at a depreciated value of $60,000 because there is no intention of selling it. Any such increment in value would therefore be unrealized and would not be recorded until the building was sold and a gain actually realized.

This conservative approach is normally good, for it is better to reveal—when doubts or questions arise—a slightly pessimistic picture, rather than one that may be overly optimistic. The danger in this approach is that the accountant may occasionally be too conservative and, as a result, present understatements of asset, profit, and ownership equity valuations.

### Consistency

Comparison of current financial data with data for prior periods is a common and valuable means of interpreting accounting reports. Such comparisons can be misleading if the bases or principles employed are changed; e.g., if cost of goods sold and inventory are valued on the basis of FIFO one year and LIFO the next, or if operating assets are depreciated on a straight-line basis for a number of years and are later depreciated on an accelerated basis. Such changes may in themselves be valid, but they should be made as infrequently as possible; and when they are made, the statements should clearly indicate both what constitutes the change and the results thereof measured in dollars. If LIFO replaces FIFO as a method of inventory costing, the change in methods should be indicated and also the fact that the net profit and inventory valuation are so many dollars less (or more) as a result of the change.

The "doctrine of consistency" is a commonly accepted principle of accounting for the reasons stated above; i.e., to ensure comparability from year to year to as great a degree as possible; and whenever a change in a basic method or principle is contemplated, the advantage to be gained by the change must be weighed against the disadvantages that may arise from loss of comparability between periods.

## Imputed Costs

Accounting statements generally do not include deductions for salaries of sole proprietors or partners, for interest on the owner's equity, nor for rent on land owned and used in the business. This may hinder comparisons between similar businesses: for one may be incorporated and therefore deduct owners' salaries, while the other is a partnership and does not; or one business may own its land, while another does not and consequently must pay rent for land use. The exclusion of these imputed costs also fails to provide a complete picture of the profitability of a business in relation to its owner or owners.

Imputed or implicit costs would, however, be difficult to measure in many cases, and historically accounting has been responsible only for the measurement of costs actually incurred. However, many factors other than reported financial data are required for decision making and the exclusion of imputed costs from the statements does not preclude their use as supplementary information. Assume, as a hypothetical case, that Mr. Brown, who works full time in his own drug store, could sell his business for $60,000, retain the parking lot next door, and rent this lot to the new company for $100 per month. He could invest the $60,000 at 5 per cent or $3,000 annually, and work as a manager for one of the drug chains at $9,000 per year, doing the same work and working approximately the same number of hours each week. Before Mr. Brown decides whether or not to sell he should adjust his reported net profit for the imputed costs mentioned above:

| | | |
|---|---:|---:|
| Net profit per P & L statement | | $12,000 |
| Less imputed costs for: | | |
| Land rental | $1,200 | |
| Interest on present value of investment | 3,000 | |
| Managerial services, salary | 9,000 | 13,200 |
| Imputed loss | | $ 1,200 |

This type of computation would, of course, be only one of many things that Brown would consider. He would, for instance, undoubtedly consider the future growth possibilities of his business, the intangible value attached to being his own boss, the stability and future offered by a new job, whether or not he might be required to move to another city, and so on.

## SUMMARY

For accounting purposes a business is normally considered a "going concern" that will continue indefinitely, and each business is treated as a unit separate from its owner or owners. To provide data for these owners and many others, accounting reports are prepared at least once each year. This creates problems of matching amounts earned during the period with costs incurred in earning that income. So-called "period" accounting also calls for the regular amortization of certain fixed asset costs, which are established initially on the basis of original cost (only at the time of purchase are the book value and market value the same). Costs for inventories and investments are often based on the *lower of cost or market* theory, which is a reflection of the doctrine of conservatism adopted by most accountants. Whatever doctrines or principles are adopted, accountants believe in following them consistently in order to protect comparability.

## QUESTIONS

**1.** In a business unit, what are the three usual sources of cash? Who ordinarily supplies cash at the time the business is organized? What should be the major source of cash when a business is operating successfully?

**2.** The increase in net assets arising from operations has been recorded in the accounts by the end of each period, but the increase in the owner's equity is not recorded until the closing entry for net profit has been posted to the Earned Equity account. Why?

**3.** What are internal control procedures? Why are the procedures that apply to cash particularly important?

**4.** What is an imprest petty cash fund? When is an entry made for the expenses incurred through petty cash expenditures?

**5.** There are a number of adjustments that must usually be made in reconciling the bank account. What are they?

**6.** Why are financial statements prepared by professional accountants usually based on the same standards?

**7.** The going-concern concept assumes that costs should be absorbed on what basis?

**8.** Why does adherence to the entity theory make it possible to judge the efficiency and profitability of a business unit?

**9.** Why are periodic statements prepared? What problems are caused by the creation of accounting periods?

**10.** What is a fiscal period? What are period costs?

**11.** Is the purchase of a cash register a capital expenditure or a revenue expenditure?

**12.** Why do accountants adhere to cost valuation as a basis of measurement for reporting purposes?

**13.** A building is constructed, at a cost of $60,000, on land that cost $10,000. If the building is expected to last 40 years, what will be the annual charge for depreciation?

**14.** Machinery can be depreciated in three different ways. Explain.

**15.** What is the meaning of accelerated depreciation? Why is accelerated depreciation frequently preferred for income tax returns?

**16.** Depreciation of $4,000 is not recorded and, as a result, the owner's equity is overstated by this amount. Why? Will the failure to record depreciation decrease the amount available for the replacement of assets?

**17.** What is the meaning of amortization? Of depletion?

**18.** What three methods can be used for the allocation of merchandise costs to cost of goods sold? Which method will produce lower income taxes during a period of inflation?

**19.** Inventory costs as of year end are usually compared with what other figures before a final valuation is established?

**20.** Under which inventory method does the flow of costs most nearly correspond with the flow of goods?

**21.** What are the dangers inherent in the doctrine of conservatism?

**22.** Why is consistency very important in financial statements?

**23.** Describe several imputed costs. Why are they customarily omitted in the preparation of statements?

PART 2

# SPECIAL AREAS OF ACCOUNTING

CHAPTER 8

# PROPRIETORSHIPS AND PARTNERSHIPS

In the United States almost all business enterprises may be classified into three groups: (1) individual enterprises, owned entirely by one person and commonly called sole proprietorships; (2) partnerships, created by a voluntary association of two or more persons who carry on the activities of a firm as co-owners; and (3) corporations, legal entities, created by the state, in which the owners have a transferable interest represented by shares of capital stock. Chapters 8 and 9 briefly describe the advantages of each type of organization, the problems involved in accounting for each form, and the terminology used in describing and presenting their financial data.

## *Importance of Organization Form*

The form of organization used by a business firm is important in many ways. It determines whether it will have to obtain approval of state agencies before it is organized, whether the owners will be personally liable for the firm's debts, and whether the owners are legal agents for the firm. It affects the stability of the firm, the amount of money which can be obtained from the owners, and possibly the maximum size of the business. But, it has very little effect on the type of accounting records kept by the firm. The records of a wholesale grocery company, for example, will be quite similar to those of another wholesale grocery even though one firm is a partnership and the other is a corporation. On the other hand, records of a wholesale grocer will be quite different from those of a furniture manufacturer even though both firms are corporations. In other words, the problems involved in accounting for assets and liabilities, for costs, and for revenues are not affected by the form of organization. The only essential differences in the financial records of sole proprietorships, partnerships, and corporations arise from the problems involved in accounting for the equity of the owners.

### THE INDIVIDUAL ENTERPRISE OR SOLE PROPRIETORSHIP

When a single individual supplies the investment and is the only owner of the business, the firm is called a sole proprietorship. The invested

141

equity of the owner may be recorded in an account called Invested Equity but is usually shown under a heading which gives the name of the owner followed by the word *capital*. While the periodic changes in his earned equity may be entered in an Earned Equity account as previously described, an account showing the owner's name followed by the word "surplus" is often used and will be illustrated in the entries explained in this chapter. If property is withdrawn from the business, either in the form of cash or merchandise, a Drawings account should be used to show the amounts withdrawn during the period. When cash is withdrawn in anticipation of earnings, the owner's Drawings account is debited and Cash is credited. If merchandise is withdrawn, as when a furniture dealer takes out furniture for his own use, the entry made will be a debit to his Drawings account and a credit to Merchandise Inventory (if perpetual inventories are kept) or to the Purchases account. At the end of the period, the balance in the Drawings account is transferred to the Surplus account since drawings are considered a withdrawal of the profits earned. Partnerships and corporations use similar accounts to show the invested equity, the earned equity, and the withdrawals of earnings, but there are differences in the number of accounts needed, the titles of the accounts used, and the subsidiary details necessary for an adequate record. There is, however, no basic difference in the purpose of the accounts and the records kept.

## Owner's Equity Accounts

As an example of the account titles which are needed to record the equity of a sole proprietor, assume that John Ford invested $40,000 in cash to start a small sawmill business. He is the sole owner. During the period his income exceeded the costs and expenses incurred in producing the income by $6,000, and he withdrew $5,000 from the firm in anticipation of the profits being earned. After the expense and income accounts are closed to the Profit and Loss Summary and the net profit is transferred to his Surplus account, the general ledger account balances will appear as follows:

| John Ford, Capital | John Ford, Surplus (Earned Equity) |
|---|---|
| Jan. 1        40,000 | Dec. 31        6,000 |
| (Investment) | (Net income) |

| John Ford, Drawings | |
|---|---|
| Jan. 1 to | (To be transferred |
| Dec. 31        5,000 | to surplus) |

The balance in the Drawings account is then transferred to the Surplus account, leaving no balance in Drawings and a $1,000 credit balance in Surplus. After the final closing entry:

John Ford, Capital, $40,000, shows the invested equity.

John Ford, Surplus, $1,000, shows the equity remaining from earnings after $5,000 of the $6,000 earned is withdrawn.

John Ford, Drawings, a temporary account used to record the amounts withdrawn during a given accounting period, has no balance.

The owner's Surplus account, which shows his equity arising from retained earnings, is quite commonly eliminated and his total equity shown in a single Capital account. If this procedure had been followed for John Ford in the preceding example, the accounts would have shown:

| John Ford, Capital | | | John Ford, Drawings | | |
|---|---|---|---|---|---|
| | Jan. 1 | 40,000 | Jan. 1 to | | (To be transferred |
| | Dec. 31 | 6,000 | Dec. 31 | 5,000 | to Capital) |

When the balance in the Drawings account is closed to Capital, the balance in the Capital account will be $41,000. Details in regard to the invested and earned equities may be obtained by an examination of the items entered in the Capital account.

## Recording the Owner's Investment

The investment of the owner may be entirely in cash or it may be in the form of cash, land, buildings, equipment, or other assets. If the investment is in cash, the entry is made in the cash receipts journal where Cash is debited and the owner's Capital account is credited. If cash and other assets are received, they all may be entered in a cash receipts journal which includes a sundry debit column; or the other assets may be entered in the general journal, with debits to the individual asset accounts and a credit to the owner's Capital account for the total of the other assets. The latter procedure results in two credits to the owner's Capital account—one for the cash and the second for the total of the other assets.

Occasionally the owner has been in business before and transfers both assets and liabilities to his new firm, or, he may begin keeping double-entry books for the first time and have both assets and liabilities to record. In either case, the accountant will debit all the assets received, credit all the liabilities accepted, and credit the owner's Capital account for the difference between the total assets and total liabilities which is, of course, the net worth.

## Statement of Capital

Withdrawals of earnings are usually entered in the owner's Drawings account. Major withdrawals intended to decrease the permanent investment are, however, entered directly in the Capital account. If additional investments are made during the period, they are also entered in the Capital account. At the end of the period a statement of capital is prepared to show the effect of additional investments, major withdrawals, profits, losses, and drawings on the total owner's equity. This statement may be prepared as shown in Exhibit 8-1.

EXHIBIT 8-1

JOHN FORD

Statement of Capital for the Year Ended December 31, 1957

| | | |
|---|---:|---:|
| John Ford, capital, Jan. 1, 1957............................ | | $40,000 |
| Add capital investment of Mar. 15, 1957................. | | 10,000 |
| Total invested equity.................................. | | $50,000 |
| John Ford, surplus, Jan. 1, 1957.................. | $ 1,000 | |
| Add net profit for 1957....................... | 12,000 | |
| Total...................................... | $13,000 | |
| Less personal withdrawals, 1957................. | 4,500 | |
| Earned equity, Dec. 31, 1957.......................... | | 8,500 |
| Total equity of John Ford, Dec. 31, 1957.................. | | $58,500 |

## PARTNERSHIPS

### *What Is a Partnership?*

According to the Uniform Partnership Act, which has been adopted in a majority of the states, the essential features of a partnership are (1) there must be a voluntary association of two or more persons, (2) they must carry on a business as co-owners, and (3) the business must be operated for profit.

**A Contractual Association.** The association of the partners must rest upon a voluntary contract between the partners. But, while the contract may be written, it may also be an oral agreement, or even simply implied from their actions. This means that many persons enter into a partnership arrangement without fully realizing the duties and responsibilities which they have accepted, and without the benefit of a carefully prepared agreement covering such vital matters as the sphere of authority of each partner, the share which each shall have in the profits, the distribution of losses, or what shall be done in the event of the death of one of the partners.

**Partners are Co-owners.** The assets of a partnership are not owned by specific individuals but are the property of the group. For this reason, a person who is contemplating an investment of land, cash, or some other valuable property should realize that in case the firm dissolves and is liquidated, he has no right to reclaim his particular investment. For example, assume that A, B, and C form a partnership with the following investments:

A—Land and buildings valued at $20,000
B—Equipment valued at $20,000
C—$10,000 in cash

Assume that in the following week the partners disagree and dissolve the partnership. The land, buildings, and equipment are sold for only $10,000. The $30,000 loss on the sale is distributed equally (in the absence of an agreement to the contrary), leaving A and B with capital balances of $10,000 each and C with no capital balance. A and B may legally take $10,000 cash in settlement of their balances leaving C wiser but poorer by $10,000.

**Business for Profit.** The association of two or more persons is not a partnership unless the participants are in a business for profit. However, it is not necessary that an actual profit be earned; it is only required that they attempt to earn a profit. Profits, if earned, belong to all the partners. They may be distributed in any agreed manner, regardless of the investment, skill, or other contribution of the individual partners. However, in the absence of any agreement to the contrary, the courts will, if need be, assume that the partners intended to divide profits and losses equally.

## *Advantages and Disadvantages of Partnerships*

Advantages:

1. Not subject to Federal income tax as is a corporation.
2. Not required to pay state fees or to submit reports required of a corporation.
3. Usually better than a sole proprietorship for raising funds—but not as good as a corporation.
4. Can combine skills of various owners who could not be "hired."
5. Owners are usually the managers and have a direct interest in the firm's success.

Disadvantages:

1. Has a limited life.
2. Must be reorganized each time there is a change in the partners.
3. Each general partner has an unlimited liability for the firm's debts.
4. The firm is bound by acts of each partner (because each is an agent of the firm) even when the partner is acting outside his agreed sphere.
5. Where earnings are large, much of the cash arising from profits must be withdrawn in order for partners to pay their personal income taxes, thus often preventing expansion through retained earnings.

The advantages listed are obvious and self-explanatory. Some of the disadvantages are more fully treated below.

**Limited Life.** A partnership is automatically dissolved at the death or personal bankruptcy of any partner, if the objective of the firm is made illegal, or if war is declared between the countries of the partners. It may be dissolved if one of the partners becomes insane, if the partners cannot work together, or if one of the partners is guilty of fraud or misconduct which makes the successful operation of the firm impossible. The partners may dissolve the firm at any time they please. If the partnership is a "partnership at will," any partner may withdraw at any time he pleases; in other cases, a partner may withdraw without the consent of his copartners but he may be liable to them for any damages that result from his withdrawal.

The fact that a partnership is dissolved does not mean that the firm's business is discontinued. For example, if A, B, and C are partners and C withdraws, his place may be taken by a new partner or A and B may continue the business by themselves. In either case the old partnership is "dissolved" and a new partnership must be formed. An outsider may not be able to see any evidence of the dissolution or the formation of the new firm but a new contract is entered and a new partnership agreement should be drawn.

**Unlimited Liability.** It is extremely important to note that each partner in a *general partnership* has an unlimited liability for the debts of the partnership. The possible loss which a partner may suffer is not limited to the amount of his investment as in a corporation. Unpaid creditors may bring suit against *any* partner for settlement of their claims. While this is generally considered a disadvantage, it sometimes works to the advantage of the firm in that it may be easier for a partnership to obtain a bank loan or other credit than it would be for a similar firm organized as a corporation, where the personal resources of the owners are not generally available to the creditors.

In order to escape the unlimited liability of a general partnership, some firms organize as *limited partnerships*. In this way some partners limit their liability to the amount of their investment in the business. However, there must always be at least one general partner in a firm and "limited partners" can take no active part in company management without losing their status as limited partners.

**Mutual Agency of Partners.** Each general partner is the agent for the firm in all acts which are within the scope of the business, and he may bind the company on contracts which may prove disastrous to the firm even though these actions are outside the field of authority granted him in the partnership agreement. This means, for example, that a partner in a sawmill firm may buy timber for the company, and his acts will be binding on the firm in spite of the fact that the partnership agreement specifically limits his authority to the supervision of the mill. On the other hand, the firm would not be bound by acts of partners that are clearly outside the province of a sawmill, such as the purchase of livestock or jewelry.

## The Partnership Agreement

Individuals planning to start a partnership should make the preparation of a carefully drawn agreement or articles of copartnership the first step in the organization of the firm. There are certain to be many problems and points of disagreement among the partners. If these problems can be anticipated and solved before the business is started, the firm's chances for a long and dissension-free life will be greatly increased. The following points should be covered in the agreement:

1. The name of the firm.
2. The location, purpose, and agreed life of the firm.
3. The method of distributing the profits and the losses.
4. The duties of each partner and limitations of his authority.
5. The hours to be worked by each if some may not be able to devote all their time to the business.
6. Any limitations on engaging in other businesses.
7. Any agreement about investments, additional investments, loans, etc.
8. Limitations on withdrawals, if any.
9. What is to be done in case of the prolonged illness of a partner?
10. What is to be done in case of the death of a partner? When will books be closed? How are profits to be computed? Do heirs have permission to become partners? How are heirs to be paid and how is their equity to be computed?

## Journal Entries for Investment

The journal entries to record the investment of the individual partners are made in the same way as are the entries to record the investment of a sole proprietor. Capital, surplus, and drawings accounts are set up for each of the partners and are used to show the invested equity, the equity from earnings, and the earnings withdrawn during the period. Again, as for the sole proprietorship, the surplus accounts may be eliminated and the invested and earned equities may be combined in a single Capital account for each partner.

Because the partners are co-owners of the assets, it is extremely important that assets be properly valued at the time of a partner's admission. If a partner's contribution is overvalued, his capital balance will be overstated and, in the event of final dissolution, he will receive more than his fair share of the assets distributed in liquidation.

To illustrate the entries required, assume that A and B form a partnership to operate a retail drug store. A invests $25,000 in cash and B invests $10,000 in cash and land and buildings worth $12,000 and $20,000, respectively.

| | | | | |
|---|---|---|---|---|
| Cash | 25,000 | | Cash | 10,000 | |
|     A, Capital | | 25,000 | Land | 12,000 | |
| (To record A's investment) | | | Buildings | 20,000 | |
| | | |     B, Capital | | 42,000 |
| | | | (To record B's investment) | | |

If the land and buildings are not properly valued, B's equity in the firm will be misstated. If the land is overstated, A will lose in the event of liquidation because he will share in the loss at the time the land is sold. When depreciable fixed assets, such as the building, are overvalued, the profits will be understated because of excessive depreciation charges and A's share of the total profits will be reduced.

Where the new firm is formed by a combination of existing firms, many of the assets may have to be revalued before they are brought on the partnership books. The following entry shows how an investment of cash, land, buildings, accounts receivable (with allowance for bad debts), and merchandise would be recorded, assuming that the partnership agrees to accept responsibility for paying the outstanding trade creditors of the new partner.

| | | |
|---|---|---|
| Cash | $10,000 | (amount received) |
| Land | 4,000 | (fair market value) |
| Buildings | 20,000 | (present depreciated value) |
| Accounts Receivable | 6,000 | (total due from customers) |
| Merchandise Inventory | 2,000 | (cost to replace or agreed value) |
|     Allowance for Bad Debts | $    800 | (estimated losses on accounts) |
|     Accounts Payable | 2,800 | (amounts due suppliers) |
|     John Ford, Capital | 38,400 | (excess of assets over liabilities |
| (To record John Ford's original | | and bad debt allowance) |
| investment) | | |

### Distribution of Partnership Profits

The partners may make any agreement they wish in regard to the distribution of their profits. However, if no agreement is made, it is generally assumed and courts will hold that profits are to be divided equally. If an agreement is reached as to the distribution of profits but nothing is said about losses, the losses will be distributed in the same proportion as profits.

As a general rule, the partnership agreement tries to recognize any significant difference in the amounts invested and in the value of the work done by the partners. Typical agreements are:

1. Profits divided equally where the contribution of each partner is approximately the same.

2. In an arbitrary ratio, such as 50, 30, and 20 per cent to A, B, and C, respectively, where the total contribution of each partner is evaluated and rewarded in a single rate.

3. Interest on the investment, as 6 per cent, and balance divided equally—when the partners wish to recognize differences in investment.

4. Salaries of agreed amounts, as $8,000, $5,000, and $3,000 to A, B, and C, and the balance divided equally—when the partners wish to recognize differences in work done.

5. Interest on the capital invested, salaries of agreed amounts, and the balance to be divided equally—when recognition is given to differences in investment and differences in the value of the time contributed.

The journal entries to close the net profit under each of the five conditions may be illustrated as shown below. Assume that A, B, and C show total invested and earned equities in a single account for each and have capital balances of $20,000, $18,000, and $12,000, respectively; profits of $15,000 are to be distributed.

1. Profits distributed equally:

| | | |
|---|---|---|
| Profit and Loss Summary | 15,000 | |
| A, Capital | | 5,000 |
| B, Capital | | 5,000 |
| C, Capital | | 5,000 |

2. Profits distributed in the ratio of 5, 3, and 2 or 50 per cent, 30 per cent, and 20 per cent to A, B, and C:

| | | |
|---|---|---|
| Profit and Loss Summary | 15,000 | |
| A, Capital | | 7,500 |
| B, Capital | | 4,500 |
| C, Capital | | 3,000 |

3. Profits distributed to allow 6 per cent on beginning capital balances, and balance divided equally:

| | | |
|---|---|---|
| Profit and Loss Summary | 15,000 | |
| A, Capital | | 5,200 |
| B, Capital | | 5,080 |
| C, Capital | | 4,720 |

Computation:

|  | A | B | C | Total |
|---|---|---|---|---|
| Capital balances*............. | $20,000 | $18,000 | $12,000 | $50,000 |
| 6 % interest................... | $ 1,200 | $ 1,080 | $ 720 | $ 3,000 |
| Balance of $12,000 equally..... | 4,000 | 4,000 | 4,000 | 12,000 |
| Total share of profits........ | $ 5,200 | $ 5,080 | $ 4,720 | $15,000 |

\* This beginning balance should include both invested and earned equities unless otherwise agreed.

4. Salaries of $8,000, $5,000 and $3,000 to A, B, and C, and balance divided equally:

| Profit and Loss Summary | 15,000 |  |
|---|---|---|
| A, Capital | | 7,666 |
| B, Capital | | 4,667 |
| C, Capital | | 2,667 |

Computation:

|  | A | B | C | Total |
|---|---|---|---|---|
| Salaries........................ | $8,000 | $5,000 | $3,000 | $16,000 |
| Balance equally*................ | −334 | −333 | −333 | −1,000 |
|  | $7,666 | $4,667 | $2,667 | $15,000 |

\* Since the salaries allowed exceeded the total profits earned, the resulting balance to be divided equally is a negative amount. Where the agreement states that interest, salaries, or both are to be allowed, *they are allowed even if no profits are earned.*

5. Interest on the beginning capital balances, 6 per cent; salaries of $8,000, $5,000, and $3,000, respectively; and the balance divided equally:

| Profit and Loss Summary | 15,000 |  |
|---|---|---|
| A, Capital | | 7,866 |
| B, Capital | | 4,747 |
| C, Capital | | 2,387 |

Computation:

|  | A | B | C | Total |
|---|---|---|---|---|
| 6 % interest (as above)......... | $ 1,200 | $ 1,080 | $ 720 | $ 3,000 |
| Salaries as agreed.............. | 8,000 | 5,000 | 3,000 | 16,000 |
|  |  |  |  | $19,000 |
| Balance equally................ | −1,334 | −1,333 | −1,333 | −4,000 |
|  | $ 7,866 | $ 4,747 | $ 2,387 | $15,000 |

If the same situation as in example 5 had existed but profits to be divided had been $22,000 instead of $15,000, the entry would have been:

| | | |
|---|---|---|
| Profit and Loss Summary | 22,000 | |
| A, Capital | | 10,200 |
| B, Capital | | 7,080 |
| C, Capital | | 4,720 |

Computation:

| | A | B | C | Total |
|---|---|---|---|---|
| 6% interest.................... | $ 1,200 | $1,080 | $ 720 | $ 3,000 |
| Salaries....................... | 8,000 | 5,000 | 3,000 | 16,000 |
| Balance equally................ | 1,000 | 1,000 | 1,000 | 3,000 |
| | $10,200 | $7,080 | $4,720 | $22,000 |

Occasionally an agreement is made to allow interest on the average capital investment. When this is done, the total ownership equity of each partner is converted to "month-dollars" or "day-dollars" and interest is allowed on this amount. For example, if A, who had a beginning balance of $20,000, made an additional investment of $10,000 on March 1 and withdrew $6,000 of his investment on September 1, his interest would be computed as follows:

$$Month\text{-}dollars$$

$20,000 (Jan. 1 to Mar. 1) or 2 months = $ 40,000
$30,000 (Mar. 1 to Sept. 1) or 6 months = 180,000
$24,000 (Sept. 1 to Dec. 31) or 4 months = 96,000
$$\overline{\qquad 12 \qquad} \qquad \$316,000$$

Average investment, $316,000/12 = $26,333
Interest on $26,333 at 6% = $1,580

## Admission of New Partners

Any change in the persons who are engaged in a partnership means that the old partnership is dissolved and a new firm, with a new partnership agreement, must be formed. New partners are usually admitted under two basic circumstances:

1. One of the old partners sells his equity to a person who is not a partner.

2. A new partner is admitted by making an investment in the firm.

**Admission by Purchase.** If A, B, and C are members of a firm and C wishes to retire, he may sell his equity to D and D may become a member of the firm of A, B, and D, but *only* if A and B both agree to his admission. If A and B do agree, C's net equity is determined by transferring any balances in his Surplus or Drawings accounts to his Capital account.

D then pays C the agreed amount and the balance in C's Capital is transferred to the Capital account of D. The amount paid to C by D is not entered on the books since this is a personal transaction between D and C. As an example, assume that C's Capital and C's Surplus show credit balances of $20,000 and $6,000, respectively. Assume also that C agrees to sell D his total equity for $25,000 cash. The entries are:

| | | | |
|---|---|---|---|
| (1) | C, Surplus | 6,000 | |
| | C, Capital | | 6,000 |
| | (To transfer C's surplus to C's capital) | | |
| (2) | C, Capital | 26,000 | |
| | D, Capital | | 26,000 |
| | (To transfer the total equity of C to D) | | |

The $25,000 in cash passes directly from D to C and is not entered on the firm's books.

**Admission by Investment.** The admission of new partners by investment requires a great deal of bargaining between the old and new partners, and the final agreement reached depends upon how badly the new man wishes to be admitted to the firm, or how much the firm needs the funds or the services of the prospective partner. If the new partner is eager to be admitted, he may be willing to invest more than the amount to be credited to his Capital account and to have the excess credited as a bonus to the old partners' Capital accounts. Or, he may be willing to allow the old partners to record goodwill as an asset of the firm and to increase their capital accounts in proportion. On the other hand, the old partners may be willing to give the new partner credit for more than he actually invests by reducing their own capital accounts and giving a bonus credit to the new partner or by assuming that the new partner brings goodwill to the firm and recording both cash and goodwill as assets invested by him. The two most probable agreements, then, mean either that goodwill comes onto the books or that no goodwill is recorded and any adjustment required is effected through "bonuses," or transferals of capital balances from one partner to another.

To simplify the following illustrations, let us assume that the earned equity of each partner is included in his Capital account along with his invested equity instead of in a separate surplus account as it is sometimes shown.

**The Bonus Method.** If the bonus method is used, the bonus may go (1) from the new partner to the old or (2) from the old partners to the new. In either case, however, the *total in all their capital accounts will be the total actual investment* and no goodwill will appear on the books.

*Bonus to Old Partners.* Assume that A and B are partners with capital balances of $30,000 and $20,000 and share profits and losses in the ratio of 60 per cent and 40 per cent. C is to be admitted to the partnership. He agrees to invest $25,000 for a $20,000 equity in the firm. The entry:

| | | |
|---|---|---|
| Cash | 25,000 | |
|     A, Capital | | 3,000 |
|     B, Capital | | 2,000 |
|     C, Capital | | 20,000 |

(To admit C with a bonus to A and B of $5,000, shared in the P & L ratio)

*Bonus to New Partner.* Assume the same conditions as above except that C agrees to invest $22,000 for a one-third interest in the firm's total capital of $72,000. One-third of $72,000 is $24,000. The $2,000 bonus to the new partner is to be shared by A and B in their P & L ratio.

| | | |
|---|---|---|
| Cash | 22,000 | |
| A, Capital | 1,200 | |
| B, Capital | 800 | |
|     C, Capital | | 24,000 |

(To admit C with a bonus of $2,000 allowed by A and B)

**The Goodwill Method.** If the partners are not willing to have their capital balances reduced, the "goodwill method" may be used. Since this method results in writing goodwill into the records, it causes the *total of all the capital accounts to exceed the total assets actually invested,* and accountants generally consider it inferior to the bonus method. As in the case of the bonus method, the additional capital credit resulting from the addition of goodwill may be (1) granted to the old partners or (2) allowed the incoming partner.

*Goodwill Granted Old Partners.* Assume that A and B have Capital balances of $30,000 and $20,000 and share profits in a ratio of 6 to 4. C is to be admitted to the partnership upon making an investment of $30,000. If a credit for goodwill is to be granted the old partners, we must also know the total capital or the share of the total which C will have. If C is to have a one-third interest, then $30,000 is one-third and the total will have to be $90,000. The total actual investment of the three partners is $30,000 + $20,000 + $30,000 or $80,000 and the goodwill allowed the old partners is $10,000. The entry is:

| | | |
|---|---|---|
| Cash | 30,000 | |
| Goodwill | 10,000 | |
|     A, Capital | | 6,000 |
|     B, Capital | | 4,000 |
|     C, Capital | | 30,000 |

(To admit C, with goodwill of $10,000 to A and B in their P & L ratio)

*Goodwill Granted to New Partner.* Assume A and B have Capital balances of $30,000 and $20,000, and a P & L ratio of 6 to 4. C is to be admitted upon his investing $20,000. He is to receive an allowance for goodwill. We must also know either the total capital after C's admission or the share of the total which the *old* partners will have. If the old partners are to have a two-thirds interest, then their $50,000 total equity is two-thirds of the total, which must be $75,000. (It could be stated that the new partner is to have a one-third interest, but we *must know the interest of the old partners.*) This would mean that the new partner would get credit for $25,000 upon an investment of $20,000, or that he is allowed goodwill of $5,000. The entry is:

| | | |
|---|---|---|
| Cash | 20,000 | |
| Goodwill | 5,000 | |
|     C, Capital | | 25,000 |

(To admit C with an allowance of $5,000 for goodwill upon his investing $20,000)

As a summary of the possible agreements, assume that X and Y have capital balances of $60,000 and $20,000 and share profits in the ratio of 3 to 1. Z is to be admitted upon investing $50,000.

1. If no bonus or goodwill is granted:

| | | |
|---|---|---|
| Cash | 50,000 | |
|     Z, Capital | | 50,000 |

2. If the old partners are to receive a bonus of $10,000:

| | | |
|---|---|---|
| Cash | 50,000 | |
|     X, Capital | | 7,500 |
|     Y, Capital | | 2,500 |
|     Z, Capital | | 40,000 |

3. If the new partner is to get a bonus of $10,000:

| | | |
|---|---|---|
| Cash | 50,000 | |
| X, Capital | 7,500 | |
| Y, Capital | 2,500 | |
|     Z, Capital | | 60,000 |

4. If goodwill is to be granted the old partners, total capital is to be $150,000, and Z is to have a one-third interest:

| | | |
|---|---|---|
| Cash | 50,000 | |
| Goodwill | 20,000 | |
|     X, Capital | | 15,000 |
|     Y, Capital | | 5,000 |
|     Z, Capital | | 50,000 |

($150,000 − 50,000 = $100,000, total capital for old partners)

5. If goodwill is to go to the new partner, and the total capital is to be $140,000:

| | | |
|---|---|---|
| Cash | 50,000 | |
| Goodwill | 10,000 | |
| Z, Capital | | 60,000 |

($140,000 − 80,000 = $60,000, total capital
for new partner)

## Importance of Capital Balance

The total equity of a partner is of importance in that a profit-and-loss-sharing agreement may be in some way based on the capital balances, as when interest is allowed on the capital balances or when the profits are distributed in the ratio of the partner's investment. If the distribution of profits is in no way related to the investment of each partner, then the amount actually credited to a partner may be of little importance until he wishes to withdraw or the business is to be discontinued.

When a partner wishes to withdraw from a firm, and the other partners agree to his withdrawal, it is customary to close the books to determine the equity of the withdrawing partner. But, this does not mean that he must settle for his equity as shown by the books. If the business has met with little success, he may be willing to take far less than the book value of his equity. On the other hand, there may be many reasons why he can ask for far more than the books show his equity to be worth. It will be remembered that all fixed assets have been brought on the books at cost. It is quite likely, during a period of inflation, that the present market value of the land, buildings, and equipment is far above their net book value. In addition, the merchandise inventory almost never reveals the true value of the goods on hand since market prices are usually employed in inventory valuation only when they are *lower* than cost. Depreciation reserves may be too large, investments may be undervalued and dozens of other factors affecting the real worth of the assets may need to be corrected to determine the real value of a partner's equity. In addition, if the firm has been enjoying a high rate of return, the retiring partner may place a higher value on his equity. In summary: the real value of a retiring partner's equity determines the amount for which he will sell; the book value provides a basis for negotiations.

However, if the firm is to be dissolved and liquidated, it is the balance in a partner's capital account after all realization losses have been distributed which determines the amount he will receive in final settlement. For this reason, a new partner who is making an investment in a firm should determine whether the goodwill method or the bonus method will be to his long-run advantage. One example will serve to illustrate how this type of problem may be solved.

Assume that A and B are partners, having investments of $60,000 and $40,000, respectively, and sharing profits equally. C is to be admitted to the partnership upon his investment of $40,000. He is to have a one-third interest in the firm. Profits of the new firm are to be divided in the ratio of 3, 3, and 4. Should C prefer the goodwill or the bonus method? The entries are:

| *Goodwill method* | | | *Bonus method* | | |
|---|---|---|---|---|---|
| Cash | 40,000 | | Cash | 40,000 | |
| Goodwill | 10,000 | | A, Capital | 3,334 | |
| C, Capital | | 50,000 | B, Capital | 3,333 | |
| (To give C one-third interest in total | | | C, Capital | | 46,667 |
| capital of $150,000. If C has ⅓, the old | | | (To give C one-third interest in a total | | |
| partners have ⅔. Since their equity is | | | equity of $140,000) | | |
| $100,000, ⅓ must be $50,000) | | | | | |

It is clear that C gets a larger capital credit if the goodwill method is used, but when the firm is finally dissolved, goodwill will be written off as a loss. If C gets 40 per cent of the profits and shares 40 per cent of the losses, his share of the $10,000 loss will be $4,000 which would reduce his equity (assuming no other changes) to $46,000. Conclusion: He should prefer the bonus method.

### Dissolution and Liquidation Problems

When a partnership is dissolved, its assets sold (realized), the creditors paid, and the investment of the owners returned to them, the firm is said to be liquidated. The law provides that in case of liquidation, a firm must first pay its creditors, must then repay any loans made by partners, and may then return to the partners their invested and earned equity. However, if any partner's share of the losses on the realization of the assets is greater than the total of his earned and invested equities, the resulting debit balance in his capital account may be offset against his loan balance, if any, and he will be paid only the balance then remaining.

If no distribution is made to the partners until all noncash assets are sold, no problem is encountered in recording the liquidation. But, if the partners wish to withdraw excess cash before the realization is completed and the final total loss known, there is a problem as to the amount each should receive. For example, assume that X, Y, and Z are partners sharing profits and losses in the ratio of 5, 3, and 2, respectively. They have been unsuccessful and have decided to quit business. Their books show the following balances on January 1.

| | | |
|---|---:|---:|
| Cash...................... | $10,000 | |
| Land...................... | 8,000 | |
| Buildings (net)............. | 34,000 | |
| Equipment (net)............ | 8,000 | |
| Accounts payable........... | | $16,000 |
| X, loan................... | | 4,000 |
| X, capital................. | | 12,000 |
| Y, capital................. | | 15,000 |
| Z, capital................. | | 13,000 |
| | $60,000 | $60,000 |

On January 13 the Equipment is sold for $10,000.

On March 1 the Land and Buildings are sold for $30,000.

If no payments are made to partners until all assets are sold, the liquidation may be recorded by these simple entries:

| | | | |
|---|---|---|---|
| Jan. 13 | Cash | 10,000 | |
| | Equipment | | 8,000 |
| | X, Capital | | 1,000 |
| | Y, Capital | | 600 |
| | Z, Capital | | 400 |
| | (To record sale of equipment and to distribute the gain to the partners in their P & L ratio) | | |
| Jan. 13 | Accounts Payable | 16,000 | |
| | Cash | | 16,000 |
| | (To pay outside creditors) | | |
| Mar. 1 | Cash | 30,000 | |
| | X, Capital | 6,000 | |
| | Y, Capital | 3,600 | |
| | Z, Capital | 2,400 | |
| | Land | | 8,000 |
| | Buildings | | 34,000 |
| | (To record sale of land and buildings and to distribute the loss to the partners in their P & L ratio) | | |

The balances in the accounts now show Cash of $34,000 and loan and capital balances as follows:

| | |
|---|---|
| X, loan................ | $ 4,000 |
| X, capital............. | 7,000 |
| Y, capital............. | 12,000 |
| Z, capital............. | 11,000 |
| | $34,000 |

The final liquidation is recorded by:

| | | | |
|---|---|---|---|
| Mar. 1 | X, Loan | 4,000 | |
| | Cash | | 4,000 |
| | X, Capital | 7,000 | |
| | Y, Capital | 12,000 | |
| | Z, Capital | 11,000 | |
| | Cash | | 30,000 |
| | (To record payment of loan of X and distribution of cash as per capital balances) | | |

But, if the partners are not sure when the assets will all be realized, they may decide to withdraw cash before the land and buildings are sold. Since the total loss is still unknown, a problem arises as to the amount which each partner should receive. As before, the first payment must be made to outside creditors. After they have been paid, the remaining $4,000 cash may be distributed to the partners in settlement of their loan and capital balances. However, no loan balance should be repaid until the accountant determines whether each partner can be charged with his share of *all possible future losses* without resulting in a debit balance in his capital account. If a partner's loan should be repaid and his share of

Exhibit 8-2
Work Sheet for Cash Distribution

| | Transaction | Cash | Noncash assets | Liabil- ities | (5) X equity | (3) Y equity | (2) Z equity |
|---|---|---|---|---|---|---|---|
| | Balances | 10,000 | 50,000 | 16,000 | 16,000 | 15,000 | 13,000 |
| Jan. 13.. | Sale of equip. | 10,000 | −8,000 | | 1,000 | 600 | 400 |
| | Balances | 20,000 | 42,000 | 16,000 | 17,000 | 15,600 | 13,400 |
| Jan. 14.. | To pay creditors | −16,000 | | −16,000 | | | |
| | Balances | 4,000 | 42,000 | | 17,000 | 15,600 | 13,400 |
| | Possible loss | | 42,000 | | −21,000 | −12,600 | −8,400 |
| | Balances | 4,000 | | | −4,000 | 3,000 | 5,000 |
| | Loss if X cannot pay (to Y and Z- ratio of 3 and 2) | | | | +4,000 | −2,400 | −1,600 |
| | Balances | 4,000 | | | | 600 | 3,400 |
| Jan. 14.. | Actual cash paid | −4,000 | | | | −600 | −3,400 |
| | Balances | | 42,000 | | 17,000 | 15,000 | 10,000 |
| Mar. 1.. | Sales of land and building | 30,000 | −42,000 | | −6,000 | −3,600 | −2,400 |
| | Balances | 30,000 | | | 11,000 | 11,400 | 7,600 |
| Mar. 2.. | Cash paid | −30,000 | | | −11,000 | −11,400 | −7,600 |

the loss on the realization of the remaining noncash assets exceeded the balance in his capital account, he would have received cash to which he was not entitled. The only way to avoid the possibility of overpaying any partner is to assume that all remaining noncash assets are worthless, distribute the resulting losses (not in the ledger accounts but on a work sheet), and pay the partners the balance which would remain in their capital and loan accounts after they had been charged their share of these possible losses.

The first step in the solution of this "liquidation in installments" is to prepare a work sheet (Exhibit 8-2) to compute the cash to be distributed to the partners. All noncash assets may be shown in a single total, and because of the right of offset, all loan and capital balances for a partner may be shown in a single total. However, when an actual payment is made to a partner with a loan balance, the charge will be made to his loan account until it is fully paid.

The journal entries to record the realization and liquidation are taken from the dated lines of the work sheet. All other lines represent balances or *possible* losses. A summary of journal entries taken from this work sheet would show cash paid to creditors, $16,000; to X, $11,000; to Y, $12,000; and to Z, $11,000. These should be and are the same as the total payments received by each under the first assumption. It should also be noted that, despite his loan balance, X received none of the first distribution of cash.

## *Financial Reports of Partnerships*

**The Income Statement.** The income statement (or profit and loss statement) of a partnership is prepared in the same form as are the statements of sole proprietorships or corporations in the same line of business. Only two minor differences exist and these are at the end of

EXHIBIT 8-3
BAKER, CRANE, AND DALE CO.
Income Statement for the Year Ending December 31, 1957

| | | | | |
|---|---|---|---|---|
| Net income from sales........................................... | | | | $186,000 |
| Less cost of goods sold.......................................... | | | | 122,000 |
| Gross profit on sales............................................ | | | | $ 64,000 |
| Less operating expenses: | | | | |
| Selling expenses......................................... | | | $18,000 | |
| General and administrative expense......................... | | | 14,000 | 32,000 |
| Net operating income........................................... | | | | $ 32,000 |
| Nonoperating expenses and income (net expense).................. | | | | 2,000 |
| Net income.................................................... | | | | $ 30,000 |

Distribution of net income:

| | A | B | C | Totals |
|---|---|---|---|---|
| Salaries as agreed.................. | $4,000 | $4,000 | $ 6,000 | $ 14,000 |
| 6 % interest on investment........... | 1,200 | 700 | 1,800 | 3,700 |
| Balance divided equally.............. | 4,100 | 4,100 | 4,100 | 12,300 |
| Totals............................ | $9,300 | $8,800 | $11,900 | $ 30,000 |

the report after the determination of the net income. Since the sole proprietorship is not subject to Federal or state income taxes and there is no distribution of the profits to be shown, the income statement is completed when the final net income is shown. The corporation is subject to

Federal income taxes, and, as a general rule, its income statement will show the computations required to find the net income, will then show the amount of income tax to be paid on the current year's business, and will end with the final "Net income after taxes" figure.

On the income statement of the partnership there will be no income tax provisions shown since the individual partners, like the sole proprietor, pay all income taxes personally. There should, however, be a section following the net income determination which shows the distribution of the net income to the several partners. For example, see Exhibit 8-3.

**The Balance Sheet.** The only difference in the form of a balance sheet for a partnership and that of a sole proprietor or a corporation appears in the presentation of the owners' equities. The statement presented on page 109 shows the basic pattern followed by a corporation. The balance sheet of a partnership presents similar details about assets and liabilities, but the net worth section describes the equity of each partner, as:

Proprietorship:
```
    John Doe, capital........................................  $30,000
    Earned equity:
        John Doe, surplus, Jan. 1, 1957...................  $12,000
        Increase in equity from 1957 operations............   8,000   20,000
    Total ownership interest, Dec. 31, 1957..............................   $50,000
    James Ford, capital.......................................  $25,000
    Earned equity:
        James Ford, surplus, Jan. 1, 1957.................  $ 6,000
        Increase in equity from 1957 operations............   3,000    9,000
    Total ownership interest, Dec. 31, 1957..............................    34,000
        Total proprietorship...............................................   $84,000
```

If a statement of changes in partners' capital is prepared to accompany the balance sheet, the details in regard to the changes may be omitted from the balance sheet and only the total equity of each partner shown, as:

```
            Proprietorship:
                John Doe, total equity.............  $50,000
                James Ford, total equity..........   34,000
                    Total equity of owners..................  $84,000
```

**Statement of Partners' Capital.** The statement of changes in partners' capital referred to above is similar to the statement of capital described on page 144 of this chapter. A statement prepared for the partnership of Doe and Ford at the end of the fiscal year, December 31, 1957, is shown in Exhibit 8-4. If no separate surplus accounts are maintained, the earned equity would be included in Capital and the statement would be simpler but less informative.

EXHIBIT 8-4
JOHN DOE AND JAMES FORD
Statement of Changes in Partners' Capital for the Year Ended December 31, 1957

|  | John Doe | | James Ford | |
| --- | --- | --- | --- | --- |
| Capital, invested equity, Jan. 1, 1957...... | $25,000 | | $25,000 | |
| Add capital invested during year......... | 5,000 | | | |
| Total invested equity................ | | $30,000 | | $25,000 |
| Surplus, earned equity, Jan. 1, 1957........ | $12,000 | | $ 6,000 | |
| Add net income for 1957............... | 10,000 | | 5,000 | |
| Total............................. | $22,000 | | $11,000 | |
| Less drawings during 1957.............. | 2,000 | | 2,000 | |
| Net earned equity.................... | | $20,000 | | $ 9,000 |
| Total equity of owners, Dec. 31, 1957....... | | $50,000 | | $34,000 |

*Joint Ventures*

When two or more persons or firms join in a temporary business under-taking, such as the development and sale of real estate or the purchase and sale of a single shipment of goods, a temporary partnership is formed. This partnership is called a joint venture but it is governed by the same laws as is the ordinary partnership previously described. Since it exists only until the particular project for which it was formed is completed, which is often a matter of only a few days or weeks, problems involved in the admission of new partners, dissolutions, installment liquidation, etc., are seldom encountered. As a result, if the venture sets up its own accounting records, no new problems are encountered. The venture books are kept in exactly the same way as are the records of any other partner-ship. The individual partners, however, may want to keep a record of their own investment in the venture. These records may be described as follows: Each member may invest cash or other assets in the venture. When he does so, he debits an account called "Investment in Joint Venture" and credits the account with the asset contributed. When the venture profits are determined, he debits his investment account and credits an account showing his income from the venture. When cash is received from the venture, he debits cash and credits his investment account. The balance in his investment account at any time should be equal to the credit in his capital account on the books of the venture and anything which increases or decreases his equity accounts on the venture books must be reflected in the investment account in his own records.

If separate venture books are not set up, each partner may record venture transactions on his own books. The entries required under these conditions are more complex and save little time. As a result, they are seldom used.

## SUMMARY

The invested and earned equities of sole proprietors or partners can be segregated as Capital and Surplus or combined into one classification and called Capital, usually the latter. A statement of capital for a sole proprietorship or partnership normally includes additional investments, major withdrawals of invested capital, drawings against earnings, and net profit for the period. Net profit for partnerships must be allocated among the partners, customarily on some basis which provides allowances for services rendered and interest on investments.

When capital balances are to be adjusted at the time a new partner is admitted, either the "goodwill" or "bonus" method can be employed. If the equity of a new partner is to be recorded in excess of the amount of his investment, *goodwill* can be recorded to balance the excess credit or a portion of the original partners' capital balances can be transferred to the new partner's capital as a *bonus*. Under other circumstances, additional equity credits, based on goodwill or bonuses, may be allowed the original partners. Various asset and equity adjustments are also necessary at the time a partnership is dissolved, since assets are seldom liquidated at book value.

## QUESTIONS

**1.** What accounts should be used to show the invested equity, the earned equity, and the amount of drawings of a sole proprietor?

**2.** What accounts are used to show the equity of a sole proprietor if the retained earnings are not separated from the invested equity?

**3.** What disposition is ordinarily made of the balance in the owner's drawings account?

**4.** Proprietorships and partnerships often eliminate the owners' surplus accounts but corporations always try to keep retained earnings separate from the invested equity accounts. Why do you think this is true?

**5.** Would you agree that the valuation of assets contributed by each partner is of relatively minor importance?

**6.** A and B are buying and selling lumber as a partnership. B claims that he is not responsible for debts incurred by A because there is no written partnership agreement. Is B responsible for A's personal debts? Is B responsible for debts incurred by A in purchasing lumber? Is B responsible for debts incurred by A in purchasing lumber if he and A have a definite understanding that A is to confine his activities strictly to sales?

**7.** What are the essential characteristics of a partnership?

**8.** Is there any difference between a partnership dissolution and a partnership liquidation? Discuss.

**9.** Which of the following statements regarding the distribution of partnership profits are acceptable?

*a.* Partnership profits are always divided equally.

*b.* Partnership profits may be divided in any agreed manner.

*c.* Partnership profits should be divided in proportion to the capital balances of the partners.

*d.* If partners make no agreement as to the division of profits, it may be assumed that profits will be divided equally.

*e.* If profits are divided in a ratio of 3 to 2 and no mention is made of losses, losses will be divided equally.

*f.* Differences in the contribution made by each partner may be recognized by allowing interest on the investment or by paying partners salaries, or both.

*g.* If the partners agree to divide profits by paying 6 per cent interest on the beginning capital balances and dividing the balance equally, interest is allowed even though the firm operates at a loss.

*h.* A partner who has a one-third interest in the firm does not necessarily receive one-third of the profits.

*i.* When a partnership is liquidated, the final distribution of cash is made in accordance with their capital balances rather than in their profit-sharing ratio.

**10.** What are the advantages and disadvantages of the partnership as a form of business organization?

**11.** Why would a firm sometimes be willing to lend money to a partnership when it would refuse the loan to a corporation in a similar financial condition?

**12.** When may a partner withdraw from a partnership and when is he liable for damages if he withdraws?

**13.** What approval is necessary before C can sell D his equity in the partnership of A, B, and C?

**14.** What entry does the partnership bookkeeper make if C sells his equity in the firm to D? Why is there no record of the amount of cash involved?

**15.** If you were in a partnership with A and B and you wished to withdraw, would you be willing to take the balance shown in your capital account in final settlement? Discuss.

**16.** Why is a revaluation of partnership assets often desirable when a partner withdraws? How would you place a value on inventories, land, buildings, patents, and franchises, and how are these assets normally shown on the books?

**17.** A, B, and C are partners sharing profits and losses in the ratio of 5, 3, and 2. A balance sheet prepared just before final liquidation showed the following liability and capital balances:

| | |
|---|---:|
| Accounts payable | $10,000 |
| A, loan | 5,000 |
| A, capital | 9,000 |
| B, capital | 16,000 |
| C, capital | 20,000 |
| | 60,000 |

*a.* If the assets are all in cash, in what order should the cash be distributed?

*b.* If there is only $15,000 in cash, how would you distribute it? Should A's loan be repaid before the other partners are paid anything?
If the noncash assets of $45,000 are sold for $25,000, how should the loss be distributed? How should the final $25,000 be distributed?

*c.* If there was $15,000 in cash and the other assets were sold for $25,000 and no distribution was made until they were all sold, how would the $40,000 be distributed?

**18.** Assume that A and B are partners and B dies. B's son wants to take his father's place in the firm. Does he have a right to do so? Can A refuse to take B's son as a partner? Can A force B's heirs to settle for the amount shown in B's capital account? Can B's heirs cause a liquidation of the firm if A refuses to accept the son and they cannot agree on a settlement? Do you think it desirable to agree on the procedure in case of the death of a partner when the partnership is formed or would it be better to wait until a partner actually dies? How can A and B protect themselves against the possibility of having to use all the firm's working capital to pay heirs of a deceased partner?

**19.** How does a joint venture differ from an ordinary partnership?

**20.** How does the corporate form of organization avoid the principal disadvantages of a partnership?

**21.** The book value of Mr. Todd's equity is as follows: capital, $16,000 and surplus, $24,000. Todd sells his interest in the partnership to Mr. Layton for $50,000 cash. What entries should be made on the partnership books?

**22.** If a new partner is to be allowed a capital credit in excess of the amount of his investment, either the "bonus method" or the "goodwill method" can be employed in the preparation of the journal entry required to record admission of the new partner. Under which method will the total equity (as shown in all the capital accounts) be equal to the total amount invested? Under which method will the total equity exceed the amount actually invested?

**23.** X, Y, and Z share profits and losses equally. The assets of their partnership are valued at $100,000; liabilities, at $40,000. What is the total owner's equity? The assets are sold for $70,000, debts are paid, and the balance of the cash distributed to the partners. What is the total loss on realization? What is the total amount received by the partners as a result of the liquidation of the business? Can you determine, from the information given, the amount each partner should receive? Why?

**24.** A's capital is $20,000; B's capital is $30,000. The partnership records show that there is a $10,000 note payable to A. After all assets are sold and all debts—except the partner's note—are paid, there is $25,000 of cash remaining. In final liquidation, how much should A and B receive?

## CHAPTER 9

# STOCKHOLDERS' EQUITY—CORPORATIONS

A corporation, in the eyes of the law, is a separate legal entity. A business organized as a corporation holds title to property and contracts debt in the business name; a corporation initiates lawsuits in the name of the company; a corporation is sued in its own name; and a corporation must pay Federal income taxes on profits earned. Proprietorships and partnerships hold property in the name or names of the owners; legal proceedings are in the names of the owners; and income taxes on business profits are a liability of the individual owners, not a liability of the business units.

## Organization of a Corporation

Proprietorships and partnerships can usually be organized without permission from the state or other governmental agencies. The owners, if they wish, may file their business name with local officials in order to make protection of that name easier; and they may be required to pay an annual license fee. A business unit that is to operate as a corporation is obliged to take more formal steps in its organization: a charter of incorporation has to be obtained from the secretary of state, bylaws must be drawn, and a board of directors has to be elected by the stockholders. The charter gives the firm its legal being, describes the extent of its activities, and itemizes the types of stock and number of shares that can be issued. The directors establish general policies, select officers who are responsible for the day-by-day management of the business, and approve budgets, financing plans, major contracts, etc. Ordinary stockholders *cannot* transact business for the corporation.

The legal form of organization affects only the accounting entries for the owner's equity, and these differences are primarily changes in terminology. The basic differences in accounting systems are caused by the nature of the operating transactions. A retail department store, for example, might operate as a sole proprietorship one year, a partnership the next year, and a corporation the third year, but during this time there would be few basic changes in the accounting entries and statements other than those changes required in the classification of owner's equity. On the other hand, a hotel and a retail department store that are both corporations have accounting entries and statements that are as different as their operating transactions and the properties owned.

### Comparative Advantages and Disadvantages

The corporate form of enterprise organization has been one of the major factors in the economic development of the United States. Similar forms of legal entities have been common in many other countries for years (for example, the British "limited" companies), but American businessmen have made much greater use of the advantages afforded by this form of organization. Recent statistics show that approximately 50 per cent of our manufacturing and wholesaling concerns are incorporated and that this 50 per cent has 75 to 90 per cent of the sales and employees. Corporations account for only 5 to 15 per cent of the total number of service and retail establishments but have 35 to 50 per cent of the total income and 40 to 50 per cent of the employees. Some of the principal advantages and disadvantages of the corporate business form are listed below.

Advantages:

1. Ownership represented by transferable shares
2. Existence of organized markets for purchase and sale of the ownership shares of larger corporations
3. Limited liability of owners
4. Unlimited life

Disadvantages:

1. Frequent separation of ownership and management in larger companies
2. Double taxation of earnings

**Ownership Represented by Transferable Shares.** A person who desires to become a member of a partnership must negotiate terms and be accepted by all of the partners. Partners are limited in their financing to the extent of their personal fortunes, what they can borrow, and what can be obtained by the admission of a new partner; and frequently it is difficult to acquire a new partner with "sufficient" funds.

Ownership shares in a private business corporation are represented by stock certificates that, under most circumstances, are freely transferable. Sale and purchase of the certificates complete the transfer of ownership. There is no need for consultation with the other shareholders; neither their approval nor that of the corporation's officers is necessary for the transfer of the certificates.

Use of certificates to represent ownership has another distinct advantage: various classes of ownership can easily be distinguished by different certificates. Owners who receive no preferences over others hold what is termed "common" stock. Shareholders with preferences are the owners of "preferred" stock. This ability to issue ownership shares of different types makes it possible for the corporation to appeal to investors with different objectives.

Representation of ownership by shares also makes it possible to divide proprietorship into low-cost units. Consequently, even a man of modest means may become interested in the purchase of a few shares at $30 or $40 each, or less.

**Existence of Organized Markets.** Once stock has been issued by a corporation, it may be freely traded between parties. Capital stock of the larger corporations is traded on the New York Stock Exchange and other organized exchanges. Shares in the smaller companies may be traded on the local stock exchanges or perhaps only "over-the-counter" by dealers, brokers, investment bankers, and others. The existence of these markets has made it possible for shareholders who so desire to sell their certificates with comparative ease; and, at the same time, provides an easily available "supply" for those who desire to purchase.

The fact that markets exist for the exchange of most stock shares provides an interest in corporate ownership that cannot attach to ownership interest in a partnership or proprietorship. The purchase and sale of a partnership interest, for example, may be an extremely slow, clumsy process as compared with the purchase and sale of corporate shares.

**Limited Liability of Owners.** Only in extremely rare cases can the owners of corporate shares be held personally liable for debts of the corporation. Generally, and almost without exception, the liabilities are those of the corporate entity alone. If the assets of the company are not sufficient for satisfaction of creditor claims, the creditors do *not* have recourse against the personal assets of the owners. This is one of the major reasons that American companies have been able to gain huge sums in the form of ownership capital, even though a majority of the investors realize they must rely almost entirely upon the honesty and integrity of the corporate management. Many of these same investors would hesitate to purchase an interest in a partnership because their personal assets could be taken if the assets of the business were insufficient to satisfy company debts.

**Unlimited Life.** Corporations can be organized for a stated period of time; most corporations, however, have perpetual existence. They continue until such time as the owners decide to liquidate or they are forced to liquidate. Death or insanity of owners or purchase and sale of issued shares on the open market have no effect on the existence of the corporation. The shares represent the ownership, and whoever has legal title to the shares thereby becomes legal owner. The acts of one owner cannot cause the dissolution of the corporation.

**Separation of Ownership and Management.** All of the stock of a corporation may be owned by one individual (a corporation sole), by members of one family (a family corporation), or by a comparatively few persons (a closely held corporation). In such instances the owners are frequently the managers or directors of the corporate business. Stock of our larger corporations, however, is widely held, sometimes by thousands or hundreds of thousands of stockholders. Complete control, in such cases, is often wielded by the corporate officers and directors, who may or may not be principal shareholders. The directors and officers are normally able to maintain control as long as stockholders with a sufficient number of shares provide them with proxies to vote as they, the managers, see fit. An organized and comparatively small minority of shareholders is sometimes able to control a corporation with ease, as long as there is no concerted effort made to recruit the other stockholders into an opposition camp.

Many shareholders never vote their stock. Many who do are well aware of the fact that they must rely on the judgment of others as to how they should vote. In many cases, the "average" stockholder has neither the time nor ability to analyze corporate conditions and arrive at his own independent judgment based on facts.

**Double Taxation.** Profits from a sole proprietorship or partnership are included on the personal tax returns of the individual owners as a part of their total taxable income; no income tax is levied against the business unit as such. This is not true in the case of a business unit organized as a corporation, for the corporation itself must pay income taxes on its profits. In addition, the owners must include most of the dividends as a part of their personal income subject to taxation. As a result, the distributed profits of a corporation are taxed twice, once to the corporation, once to the owners.

*Equity Terminology*

The invested equity of a sole proprietorship or partnership is often called "capital"; the earned equity, "surplus." The term capital may embrace both invested and earned equity. In a corporation the invested equity is known as "capital stock" and the earned equity, as "earned surplus." The two divisions of corporate equity *cannot* be combined, for the law requires that the invested portion be classified separately to indicate the amount of permanent capital that must be retained for the protection of creditors. The earned portion also must be kept separate to indicate the maximum amount that can be withdrawn as dividends. Creditors are thereby provided assurance that assets cannot be distributed to owners if invested equity would, as a result, be reduced below the amount of permanent capital.

The reduction of owner's equity by the withdrawal of cash or other property in a noncorporate enterprise is usually identified as "drawings" or "withdrawals." In a corporation, the distribution of cash or other property to the owners is known as "dividends."

### Stockholders' Equity on the Balance Sheet

The owner's equity section on the balance sheet for a corporation might appear, in summary form, as illustrated below:

```
Stockholders' equity:
  Capital stock:
    Preferred stock..............  $ 40,000
    Common stock...............    100,000  $140,000
  Surplus:
    Capital surplus..............  $ 10,000
    Earned surplus..............    60,000    70,000
    Total stockholders' equity......................  $210,000
```

These classifications of financial data will be explained in detail in the discussions that follow. Stockholders' equity, as employed above, is synonymous with owner's equity or net worth. Net worth is the most frequently used title.

### CAPITAL STOCK

The invested equity of a corporation is represented by units of ownership called "shares". Individual capital stock certificates may be for one share or any given number of shares. The total of the shares that can be marketed is referred to as the amount "authorized." Those shares that have been sold are called "issued" shares; those reacquired by the company are "treasury" shares; and those held by parties other than the corporation are "outstanding" shares, i.e., shares issued less treasury shares, if any.

### Common Stock

The holders of common stock normally have no preference as to dividends or as to assets in liquidation. They represent the true, residual ownership that must bear all the risks. If a corporation has only one class of stock, it must be common stock, since owners can have no preference over creditors.

Most common stock is "voting" common. Occasionally, however, a corporation may issue two classes of common stock: one class is voting common, the other is nonvoting common. In such cases, the so-called nonvoting common often has some preference with respect to dividends and/or the proceeds of liquidation and is essentially a type of preferred stock.

If additional shares of common stock are to be issued, common-law doctrine requires that each common shareholder be given the opportunity to preserve his proportionate interests in the voting control and in the earned equity. This legal "pre-emptive" right gives each common holder the privilege of purchasing a share of the additional issue which is proportionate to his current holdings.

### Preferred Stock

Preferred capital stock gives the holders thereof certain rights and preferences, usually as to dividends or as to assets in liquidation.

*Noncumulative preferred stock* has priority as regards dividend distributions in any one year. If a total of $100,000 of 6 per cent noncumulative preferred stock is held by owners, at least $6,000 must be distributed to the preferred shareholders, in any one year, before any amount can be paid to the common stockholders. There is *no* guarantee, however, that such dividends will be paid—even though current profits or accumulated earned surplus exceed dividend requirements. The directors are entirely within their legal rights if they decide that all funds should be retained for use in the business. They may even continue to reinvest earnings until such time as the company is able to pay both common and preferred dividends. Under such conditions, noncumulative preferred actually has priority only as to assets in liquidation, and this preference alone has little appeal to potential stockholders. As a result, issues of noncumulative preferred are infrequent at present.

*Cumulative preferred stock*, currently the most popular type of preferred, provides preference over common stock not only as to current dividends but also as to any dividend amounts unpaid in prior years. If, at the end of the year 1957, dividends had not been paid on $100,000 of 6 per cent cumulative preferred stock for three years, then the following would have to be paid to the holders of cumulative preferred before anything could be paid to the common shareholders:

| | |
|---|---:|
| Dividends in arrears, 1955 | $ 6,000 |
| Dividends in arrears, 1956 | 6,000 |
| Current dividends, 1957 | 6,000 |
| Total | $18,000 |

If the $18,000 were distributed to the cumulative preferred shareholders in 1957, the directors could then declare dividends on the common stock (assuming sufficient funds were available).

*Preferred stock may be "convertible"* into common shares on the basis of so many common shares for each share of preferred. Preferred shareholders will normally convert at any time during the conversion period that a gain can be realized. They may also convert if the conversion privilege is about to change or expire and they believe that the common will be more valuable than the preferred after the change in conversion privileges has become effective. They may also convert if the preferred is to be redeemed soon and the market value of the common into which it could be converted is greater than the redemption price.

*Preferred stock may be "callable"* as of certain dates and at stated "redemption" prices. Those who hold the stock on the call date have no choice; they must redeem their stock with the company at the established call price (redemption value). The facts pertaining to redemption, usually included on the face of the stock certificate, constitute a contract between the corporation and the shareholders. Both redemption and conversion features provide convenient means of retiring preference stock which might otherwise be unavailable for retirement except through purchase on the open market.

*Preferred stock usually has contingent voting rights;* e.g., preferred stock often carries the right to vote if dividends remain unpaid for a stated period. In such circumstances preferred may gain voting control of the corporation. Preferred holders also frequently have the right to vote on any proposal that would affect their "prior" position.

*Preference as to assets in liquidation* is frequently a right enjoyed by holders of preferred shares. In the distribution of proceeds from liquidation, the preferred shareholders will usually have a prior claim at least to the extent of their par value, before proceeds can be distributed to common holders. They may also have prior claim to an additional amount equal to dividends in arrears.

## Par Value Stock

Par value stock has a par value per share that is printed on the face of the certificate. One certificate for five $10 par shares would, for example, have a total par value of $50. If the corporation issued 10,000 such shares, the total capital value shown on the balance sheet would be $100,000. When a corporation is authorized by the secretary of state to issue a certain class of par value stock, the accounting reports must always value those shares which have been sold at total par. If sold for more than par, the premium must be stated separately.

Stock is sold at a premium when issued at a price in excess of the par value. If a share of common with a par of $50 is sold for $56, the corporation must record the extra $6 as Premium on Common Stock. If a preferred share with a par of $100 is sold for $110, the preferred must be shown on the records at par of $100 and the premium of $10 recorded in the Premium on Preferred Stock account.

The sale of stock at less than par (at a discount) makes the holders thereof personally liable to creditors to the extent of the discount. Such issues are now extremely rare and generally not permitted by state law.

## No-par Stock

The "par value" of stock must always be credited to the capital stock account at time of issue. The total par value represents a measure of corporate assets which cannot be distributed to shareholders unless all liabilities of the corporation have first been paid. This provides a margin of safety for the protection of the creditors, who cannot hold the stockholders personally liable for debts of the corporation.

Stock can be issued without a par value. In such cases, the directors must declare what portion of the sales price of the individual shares is to be credited to the capital stock account (so-called "stated" value) and what amount is to be credited to paid-in surplus. Use of no-par value stock provides the directors with a means of issuing the same stock at different prices without running afoul of state laws that do not permit the issuance of stock at less than par. Assume, for example, that the first block of a $100 *par* stock was sold for $102. Several years later the directors decide to sell more shares of the same stock, but the market for the stock is now so low that the shares could be sold for no more than $90 each. The directors would then be forced to ask the state for authorization to issue a completely new series of stock. If, however, the stock mentioned above had been no-par value stock with a stated value of $60 per share, the original block could have been sold at $102 and the additional shares at $90. The excess over the stated value, $42 and $30 per share, would be credited to Paid-in Surplus. (The additional shares could not generally be sold at less than $60, however, unless the purchaser could legally assume a personal liability to the creditors for the amount of the discount, i.e., the difference between the purchase price and the stated value.)

Another advantage of no-par stock is that the certificates do not carry a price tag. A par value on the certificate may lead some persons to believe that par represents actual worth or market value. A slight disadvantage is that in some states the paid-in surplus amount can be included with earned surplus in establishing the maximum for the dollar valuation of assets that can be distributed in the form of dividends. Even if legal, notice should be given stockholders of any dividend distributions that decrease paid-in surplus, for such a dividend actually represents a return of invested capital, not earnings.

To illustrate the point, suppose that a corporation is organized on January 1, 1958. At that time 1,000 shares of no-par common are issued at $68 per share. By resolution of the directors $40 per share is the stated value that is to be classified as capital stock and $28 per share as paid-in surplus. The entry, if all of the 1,000 shares were sold at the same time, would be:

| | | |
|---|---|---|
| Cash | 68,000 | |
| Common Stock, no-par | | 40,000 |
| Paid-in Surplus | | 28,000 |

Assume that income and expenses of this corporation were exactly equal in 1958; i.e., there was neither profit nor loss and therefore no earned surplus. At the end of 1958 the directors legally declare a dividend of $20,000. The dividend account is then closed:

| | | |
|---|---|---|
| Paid-in Surplus | 20,000 | |
| Dividends | | 20,000 |

The owners should be notified that these dividends actually are the equivalent of a return of their investment and *not* the distribution of assets earned through operations.

### Nominal Par

Nominal- or low-par stock has the usual advantages claimed for no-par stock and is frequently more economical to issue because the stock transfer tax and certain other taxes may be considerably less. The nominal par is often $1 and sometimes less—even though the stock will be sold for, say, $20 or $30 per share. Total par, as usual, would be credited to the respective capital stock account and the amount in excess of par to a premium or paid-in surplus account. (In some states the no-par stated value or the nominal par cannot be less than a certain minimum amount established by law.)

### Treasury Stock

Stock issued but reacquired and not canceled is known as treasury stock. It is a reduction in the valuation of ownership equity and *not* an asset. The treasury stock is usually carried on the books at cost, not at par or stated value. If ten shares of its own $100 par common were purchased by a corporation on the open market at $86 per share, then $860 should be debited to the Treasury Stock account. If later sold at $90, the $4 gain per share should be recorded as a credit to Paid-in Surplus. If sold at $80, the $6 loss per share would be charged to Paid-in Surplus, or to Earned Surplus if there were no Paid-in Surplus.

The cost valuation of treasury stock is sometimes deducted directly from the total par or stated value of the stock of the same issue but is usually deducted from total net worth, as shown in outline form at top of page 174.

```
Common stock, $100 par;
    100 shares authorized and issued;
        10 shares in the treasury....................  $10,000
Earned surplus.............................    8,000
                                             $18,000
        Less treasury stock.........................      860
        Total net worth...........................  $17,140
```

The treasury stock is deducted from the valuation of owner's equity to show the amount that has actually been invested and left with the company, plus any surplus. Treasury stock should not be classed as an asset, for a corporation cannot logically own a portion of itself.

### Net Worth on the Balance Sheet

Each class of stock and surplus should be shown separately in the net worth (stockholders' equity) section of the balance sheet. In addition to a descriptive title for each class of stock there should be the following information: par or stated value, number of shares authorized, number of shares issued, and number of shares, if any, that are held as treasury stock. Any surplus other than that earned must be shown separately.

The net worth section below serves to illustrate one form of presentation. Note that preference stock is listed first, earned surplus, last.

```
Net worth:
  Capital stock:
    Preferred, 5% cumulative;
      par value $60;
      1,000 shares authorized and issued;
      100 shares in the treasury....................  $ 60,000
    Common, stated value $30 per share;
      40,000 shares authorized;
      15,000 shares issued........................   450,000  $   510,000
  Surplus:
    Paid-in surplus from sale of no-par common......  $150,000
    Earned surplus................................    400,000       550,000
        Total...........................................  $1,060,000
    Less preferred treasury stock...........................       6,400
        Total net worth....................................  $1,053,600
```

### Accounting Entries for Stock Issues

The par value capital stock of a corporation may be sold at par or at a premium, and no-par stock will be assigned a stated value which does not exceed the price at which it can be sold. Assets other than cash may be received for stock, and stock may be sold on account (or subscribed). In every case the entry for the sale of stock finally results in a debit for the value of the asset received, a credit to a capital stock account for the par value (or stated value) of the stock issued, and an additional credit to a paid-in surplus account (called a "premium" in the case of par value stocks) for the excess of the selling price over its par or stated value.

Typical accounting entries for capital stock transactions are illustrated below:

1. No entry is necessary when authorization for a stock issue is received from the secretary of state (but a notation of the number of shares authorized and the par, if any, should be made in the capital stock account).

2. If 1,000 shares of $40 par common stock are issued at par for cash, the entry, in general journal form, would be:

| | | |
|---|---|---|
| Cash | 40,000 | |
|     Common Stock | | 40,000 |

3. If 2,000 shares of the same $40 par stock were later issued at $58 per share, the entry should be:

| | | |
|---|---|---|
| Cash | 116,000 | |
|     Premium on Common Stock | | 36,000 |
|     Common Stock | | 80,000 |

4. If 4,000 shares of no-par value common were issued at $64 and the board of directors had approved a resolution to place a stated value of $40 on each share, the entry would be as follows:

| | | |
|---|---|---|
| Cash | 256,000 | |
|     Common Stock, no-par | | 160,000 |
|     Paid-in Surplus | | 96,000 |

5. If 3,000 shares of $100 par, 6 per cent cumulative preferred stock are issued in exchange for a new building, the following entry would be made (assuming the current value of the building is actually $300,000):

| | | |
|---|---|---|
| Building | 300,000 | |
|     Preferred Stock, 6% cumulative | | 300,000 |

6. If 1,000 shares of $50 par, 4 per cent convertible preferred were sold for $52 per share, the required entry should be:

| | | |
|---|---|---|
| Cash | 52,000 | |
|     Preferred Stock, 4% convertible | | 50,000 |
|     Premium on 4% Convertible Preferred | | 2,000 |

7. If 5,000 shares of $20 par value stock were sold on credit (subscribed) and the shares *issued* at the time of subscription, the journal entry would be as follows:

| | | |
|---|---|---|
| Subscriptions Receivable—Common | 100,000 | |
|     Common Stock | | 100,000 |

If payments of $12,000 were received in the month following subscription, a summary general journal entry to record payment would be as shown below:

| | | |
|---|---|---|
| Cash | 12,000 | |
|      Subscriptions Receivable—Common | | 12,000 |

8. Frequently, stock sold on credit is not issued until fully paid. A net worth account entitled Capital Stock Subscribed is credited at the time of subscription; any balance in this account at statement date should be included in the stockholders' equity section immediately following the related capital stock account. As the stock is paid in full by the subscribers, this account is debited and the appropriate capital account credited. If 2,000 shares of $40 par preferred stock were subscribed at par under the conditions just described, the entry would be:

| | | |
|---|---|---|
| Subscriptions Receivable—Preferred | 80,000 | |
|      Preferred Stock Subscribed | | 80,000 |

Assume that partial payments are received in the amount of $14,000:

| | | |
|---|---|---|
| Cash | 14,000 | |
|      Subscriptions Receivable—Preferred | | 14,000 |

Still later, payments of $10,000 are received. Included in these payments is $2,000 from subscriber John Doe; this represents the balance due in full on his subscription of $4,000. In other words, his subscription is fully paid and his shares are therefore issued.

| | | |
|---|---|---|
| Cash | 10,000 | |
|      Subscriptions Receivable—Preferred | | 10,000 |
| Preferred Stock Subscribed | 4,000 | |
|      Preferred Stock | | 4,000 |

9. If 4,000 shares of $10 par common, subscribed for at $12 per share, are to be issued only when fully paid, then the initial entry would be as shown below:

| | | |
|---|---|---|
| Subscriptions Receivable—Common | 48,000 | |
|      Common Stock Subscribed | | 40,000 |
|      Premium on Common Stock | | 8,000 |

When John Doe makes a final payment of $600 on his $2,400 subscription, the entries would appear as shown:

| | | |
|---|---|---|
| Cash | 600 | |
|      Subscriptions Receivable—Common | | 600 |
| Common Stock Subscribed | 2,000 | |
|      Common Stock | | 2,000 |
|      (200 $10 par value shares fully paid) | | |

As illustrated above, the amount *over par* must always be credited to the appropriate *premium* account at the time of subscription. The amount *over stated value* would be credited to Paid-in Surplus. Subsequently, only the par value is transferred from the subscribed account to the capital stock account at the time an account becomes fully paid.

10. If 1,000 shares of no-par common are subscribed for at $34 and, by resolution of the board of directors, the stated value is to be $20:

| | | |
|---|---|---|
| Subscriptions Receivable, | | |
| No-par Common | 34,000 | |
| No-par Common Subscribed | | 20,000 |
| Paid-in Surplus | | 14,000 |

Assume that a subscription receivable of $3,400 for 100 shares has been fully paid. The following entry is then necessary to transfer the stated value to the appropriate capital stock account:

| | | |
|---|---|---|
| No-par Common Subscribed | 2,000 | |
| Common Stock, no-par | | 2,000 |

### Subscribers' Ledger

Detailed records must be maintained to show the amounts subscribed by each subscriber, the payments received, and the balance receivable, if any. If stock is issued only when fully paid, the subscribers' ledger is necessary to show when a subscription receivable has been paid in full and stock is to be issued.

This subsidiary ledger, like all others, is summarized in the general ledger by a control account. The *totals* of subscriptions and payments received would be posted to the general ledger control account periodically, while the corresponding detail would be posted to the subscribers' individual ledger accounts. The balance of the control should, of course, be equal to the sum of the subsidiary balances.

### Purchase and Sale of Issued Stock

The preceding discussions have been concerned with the original issuance of stock by corporations. Once the stock has been sold by the issuing company it may be traded on the exchanges or sold directly by one party to another. The price at which issued stock is sold or traded is the "market" price and this price may be quite different from the original issue price or the current book value. Sales of shares from one stockholder to another are not entered in the general ledger accounts of the corporation, and the price at which the stock sells is not important to the accountant. However, a stockholders' ledger is usually maintained to show the *number* of shares held by each stockholder.

## CORPORATE SURPLUS

*Earned Surplus*

Earned surplus of a corporation represents the stockholders' equity in net asset increases derived from operations and retained for use in the business. If earned surplus appears on the balance sheet, it indicates that the dollar valuation of the inward flow of assets from operations (income) has exceeded the dollar valuation of costs expired for operating purposes (expense), and that a portion of this net increase in asset valuations has been retained for use in the business, rather than distributed to the owners.

Assume the following facts for a corporation that has been in existence for 40 years:

| | |
|---|---|
| Total income for 40 years............... | $30,000,000 |
| (dollar valuation of inward flow of assets from operations) | |
| Total expenses for 40 years.............. | 27,000,000 |
| (dollar valuation of assets relinquished for operating purposes) | |
| Total of profits for 40 years............. | $ 3,000,000 |
| Less dividends........................ | 1,000,000 |
| (dollar valuation of assets distributed to owners) | |
| Earned surplus, end of 40 years........... | $ 2,000,000 |
| (dollar valuation of owner's equity in undistributed asset increase arising from operations) | |

Assets of a dollar amount equal to the dollar valuation of earned surplus can, theoretically, be distributed to the owners, for earned surplus represents the legal limit on dividends. A more practical and real limit, however, is the amount of assets not needed for the operation of the business and, for that reason, available for distribution. Earned surplus may be valued at $600,000 and, at the same time, there may be only $100,000 in cash, $70,000 of which is needed for operations. The directors may then declare cash dividends of $30,000, but certainly not dividends of $600,000.

Since earned surplus (frequently called "retained earnings") is to be an accumulation of profits less dividends, it is evident that both the P & L Summary account and the Dividends account should be closed to Earned Surplus. For example, assuming profits of $50,000 and dividends of $8,000, the entries would appear as below:

| | | |
|---|---|---|
| P & L Summary | 50,000 | |
| Earned Surplus | | 50,000 |
| Earned Surplus | 8,000 | |
| Dividends | | 8,000 |

Dividends cannot be declared if such a declaration would leave earned surplus with a negative (debit) balance. If a firm had only earned surplus of $4,000, dividends of $6,000 could not be declared or paid. If the firm had enough excess cash, dividends of $4,000 could be paid, leaving earned surplus of zero. But owner's equity cannot be reduced below the dollar valuation of the total stated capital (sum of par and no-par stated values) by the distribution of assets to the owners. Losses from operations are, however, sometimes unavoidable and the result is a reduction of owner's equity below the total stated capital. Assume, for example, a corporation organized on January 1, 1956, that issued 10,000 shares of $60 par common for $600,000 cash on that date. In 1956 the firm had a net loss of $16,000; in 1957, a net profit of $4,000. As of December 31, 1957, the net worth section would appear as illustrated:

```
Stockholders' equity:
   Common stock, $60 par value;
      10,000 shares authorized and issued..... $600,000
   Deficit earned surplus...................  (12,000)
      Net worth Dec. 31, 1957.............  $588,000
```

The stated capital of $600,000 has been reduced by operating loss—but not by dividends. Dividends could not legally be declared until the records disclosed earned surplus rather than a *deficit* earned surplus.

## Appropriated Earned Surplus

The dollar amount of earned surplus serves, in most states, as a theoretical—and legal—maximum on the dollar valuation of assets that can be distributed to shareholders. Assume the following balance sheet amounts for a corporation as of the end of its fiscal year:

| | | | | |
|---|---|---|---|---|
| Cash...................... | $    10,000 | Liabilities................. | $  200,000 |
| Other assets.............. | 990,000 | Common stock............ | 500,000 |
| | | Earned surplus........... | 300,000 |
| Total assets............. | $1,000,000 | Total equities.......... | $1,000,000 |

It is obvious that creditors have claims of $200,000 against the total dollar valuation for assets of $1,000,000. The claims or equities of the owners in the assets are valued at $800,000, the sum of the capital stock and earned surplus. The Earned Surplus account reveals that there has been an increase in net assets (assets minus liabilities) of $300,000, all of which arose *from operations;* and, consequently, there is $300,000 of asset valuation available for distribution to the owners—if *not* needed in the business, and *if* there are assets in a form that can be distributed. In the example above, the directors might very well decide not to distribute any dividends because cash is the only asset in a distributable form and the business may need all of the $10,000 for operating purposes.

The corporate directors may also decide that there is really not $300,000 of asset valuation available for distribution now or later, since they are definitely planning a $100,000 plant expansion during the next several years. This does not reduce the equity of the owners but it will result in the transformation of asset valuation to a form that will not be distributable, even at a later date. Consequently, the directors or auditors may decide this information should be revealed on the balance sheet by showing that $100,000 of the $300,000 in valuation supposedly available for dividends is definitely *not* available now nor in the foreseeable future. A journal entry to reflect this decision would be as follows:

| | | |
|---|---|---|
| Earned Surplus | 100,000 | |
|     Appropriated for Plant Expansion | | 100,000 |

If there is a slight possibility—but not yet a liability—that the corporation may have to pay out approximately $40,000 as a result of a pending lawsuit, a further appropriation of earned surplus should be made:

| | | |
|---|---|---|
| Earned Surplus | 40,000 | |
|     Appropriated for Contingencies | | 40,000 |

After these appropriations, the earned surplus portion of the net worth section would be shown as follows:

| | | |
|---|---|---|
| Net worth: | | |
|   Common stock............................................ | | $500,000 |
|   Earned surplus: | | |
|     Appropriated for plant expansion........... | $100,000 | |
|     Appropriated for contingencies.............. | 40,000 | |
|     Unappropriated balance.................... | 160,000 | 300,000 |
|      Total net worth................................ | | $800,000 |

The unappropriated balance of $160,000 would then serve to express a maximum dollar valuation of assets that the directors believe *may* be available for distribution to the owners. The amount of dividends to be paid, however, will ordinarily be determined by the amount of cash on hand—not by the surplus balance alone.

### Statement of Earned Surplus

Most corporations do not have appropriations of earned surplus. In this case a statement of earned surplus consists of simply the opening surplus balance, plus profits for the period, less all dividends declared. If appropriations of earned surplus were made in prior years, the report becomes a "statement of earned surplus—unappropriated balance" and the same procedure as outlined above is followed, except that the opening and closing balances must be identified as "unappropriated" balances. Any appropriation made during the current period would appear as a deduction on the statement and the ending balance subsequently shown as "earned surplus—unappropriated balance."

## Paid-in Surplus

Another classification of surplus frequently found in the net worth section of a corporate balance sheet is termed "capital surplus" or, preferably, "paid-in surplus." Included under the one heading of capital or paid-in surplus may be a variety of credits arising from different sources. This may be adequate if the amounts are insignificant when compared with the total net worth. If, on the other hand, the amounts are significant, they should be classified separately under descriptive titles such as those discussed below.

**Premium on Capital Stock.** When par value stock is issued at a price in excess of par, the excess over par should be credited to an appropriate premium account. If common stock with a total par value of $100,000 is issued at $106,000, the $6,000 should be classified as Premium on Common Stock. If 6 per cent cumulative preferred is issued at a premium of $10,000, this amount should be credited to Premium on 6 per cent Cumulative Preferred Stock.

**Paid-in Surplus.** This account title is usually recognized as the correct classification for that portion of the issue price of no-par stock that has not been established as stated value. For example, a corporation issues 1,000 shares of no-par value common stock at $54 per share. By resolution of the directors $40 per share is to be stated value. The journal entry to record the issue would be as follows:

| | | |
|---|---|---|
| Cash | 54,000 | |
| Common Stock, no-par | | 40,000 |
| Paid-in Surplus | | 14,000 |
| (Issue of Common Stock, no-par) | | |

## Donated and Appraisal Surplus

Occasionally, stockholders in small corporations will donate assets in order to improve the financial condition of their company. The resulting increase in the owner's equity may be recorded as a part of Paid-in or Capital Surplus. This procedure, however, is generally not acceptable, particularly if the amount is fairly significant. It is better to show such an increase under the specific heading of Donated Surplus. Assume, for instance, that a shareholder in a "family" corporation donates land valued at $16,000; the entry should then be:

| | | |
|---|---|---|
| Land | 16,000 | |
| Donated Surplus | | 16,000 |

In preparation for the sale of the business, or for some other reason, the directors of a corporation may decide to have the assets of a corporation appraised at current market value. Assume, say, that the results of an appraisal reveal that the depreciated book value of the firm's building is $40,000 less than its current market value. The following entry could then be made:

| | | |
|---|---|---|
| Building—Appraisal Increase | 40,000 | |
| Appraisal Surplus | | 40,000 |

Notice that the debit increase is *not* made in the Building account, since the original cost of fixed assets should always be maintained separately in the accounts. This type of entry is seldom made; when management desires to have such information on the balance sheet, most accountants would prefer including it simply as a footnote rather than as an increase in the fixed assets and net worth.

The appraisal increase is not, of course, depreciable for tax purposes, since the concern has incurred no additional cost. It should be written off over the remaining life of the asset, however. If we assumed that the building mentioned above had an estimated remaining life of 40 years, then the following entry would have to be made at the end of each year:

| | | |
|---|---|---|
| Appraisal Surplus | 1,000 | |
| Building—Appraisal Increase | | 1,000 |

## DIVIDENDS

When owners invest in a corporation, cash or some other asset account is debited and an appropriate equity account credited. When the reverse occurs and assets are distributed to the owners, a credit must be made to the proper asset account and a decrease recorded in the stockholders' equity. This equity decrease could be charged directly to the Earned Surplus account, since the usual assumption is that earned surplus represents equity valuation in assets that are available for distribution. For information purposes, however, the equity decreases arising from asset distributions to owners are usually maintained in a separate account, and the balance of this account is then deducted from available earned surplus on the face of the financial statement. The person reading the statement is thereby informed that owner's equity has been reduced by a specific amount as a result of dividend distributions to stockholders. For example:

XYZ CORPORATION

Statement of Earned Surplus for the Year Ended December 31, 1957

| | |
|---|---|
| Earned surplus, Jan. 1, 1957............ | $210,000 |
| Net profit for 1957.................... | 30,000 |
| Total............................ | $240,000 |
| Less dividends....................... | 10,000 |
| Earned surplus, Dec. 31, 1957......... | $230,000 |

Dividends payable become a legal liability of the corporation only when they have been declared by the directors and notice of the declaration has been made public. Even dividends in arrears on cumulative preferred stock do not represent liabilities until such time as they arc declared payable. Dividends are declared payable, on a certain date, to all parties who own stock as of a specified date. As an illustration: The directors of XYZ Corporation declared on December 10, 1957, that dividends of $10,000 would be paid January 20, 1958, to all parties on record as owners of the stock on January 12, 1958.

December 10, 1957, would be recognized as the "date of declaration" and the following would have to be entered in the general journal on that date:

| | | |
|---|---|---|
| Dividends | 10,000 | |
| Dividends Payable | | 10,000 |

January 12, 1958, would be known as the "date of record" and all owners on this date would receive dividends. A person who purchased the stock on January 13, 1958, or later would not receive a dividend. January 20, 1958, would be the "date of payment" and the following entry would be necessary to reflect payment of the liability:

| | | |
|---|---|---|
| Dividends Payable | 10,000 | |
| Cash | | 10,000 |

Dividends are normally due and payable within a relatively short time after declaration. Any amounts unpaid as of the balance sheet date must therefore be included among the *current liabilities* on the balance sheet. (A separate dividends payable account should be maintained for each class of dividends due.) When dividends are payable, the stockholders are in the unique position of being both owners and creditors of the company at the same time.

### Form of Dividends

The great majority of distributions to owners are in the form of *cash dividends* and the amount of cash on hand is, for that reason, the greatest factor in the directors' decision as to whether or not dividends should be declared.

*Property dividends* represent the distribution of assets other than cash. In the case of "closely held" corporations that are owned by a comparatively few persons, assets such as inventory items, or investments in stocks and bonds, may sometimes be distributed to the owners. In one case on record, a distillery distributed its inventory of whisky to the stockholders. Property dividends are charged to the Dividends account, with an offsetting credit to the appropriate asset account.

*Stock dividends* serve as a means of reclassifying earned surplus as stated capital. As a result, the "permanent" capital of the corporation is enlarged and, at the same time, the legal maximum available for dividend distribution is lowered. The stockholders receive additional shares, but the total equity valuation of the owners is *not* changed.

Example: The Eastern Corporation has net worth as shown below:

Common stock, $100 par;
    3,000 shares authorized; 1,000 shares issued..... $100,000
Earned surplus .............................. 260,000
    Total net worth........................... $360,000

The directors decide that there is very little chance that the present earned surplus can be decreased to any significant extent by dividend distributions, that net worth will present a somewhat stronger picture to the creditors if the permanent stated capital is enlarged, and that a market price lower than the present $400 per share would make the shares more attractive to a greater number of investors. For these reasons, two additional shares of common stock are issued for each share currently outstanding; i.e., the 2,000 shares authorized but unissued are distributed to the owners. The full par value of all stock issued must be credited to the capital stock accounts, so 2,000 times $100, or $200,000, of equity valuation must be classified as Common Stock. This necessitates a corresponding decrease in Earned Surplus and the complete entry would be as shown here:

Earned Surplus          200,000
    Common Stock          200,000

After this reclassification of ownership equity, the net worth section would appear as:

Common stock, $100 par;
    3,000 shares authorized and issued........... $300,000
Earned surplus............................... 60,000
    Total net worth........................... $360,000

Before the stock dividend there were 1,000 shares issued and outstanding, with a current market value of $400 per share. Afterwards there were 3,000 shares outstanding—or three shares for each one that was outstanding before the dividend. If the market value for one share was $400, it would be expected that after the stock dividend each share would have a market value of approximately $133 ($400 divided by three). There might be a greater demand for the lower-priced shares, however, and in such cases the market would probably be more than $133 per share.

A *stock split* also serves to increase the number of shares outstanding and thereby decreases the market value per share. It differs from a stock dividend in that it does *not* serve as a means of reclassifying surplus and, consequently, does not require an accounting entry. Assume that in the example above the board of directors and the stockholders have approved a stock split rather than a stock dividend and the corporate charter is amended to authorize a new issue of $50 par stock. The 1,000 shares of $100 par stock are retired and each stockholder is issued two shares of the new $50 stock in exchange for each share of the old $100 stock. This 2-for-1 split-up would result in a decrease of approximately 50 per cent in the market price per share but would have no effect on the total book values for capital stock or earned surplus.

### Dividends on Preferred Stock

When a corporation has only common stock and noncumulative preferred stock outstanding, the computation of dividends creates few problems. If a certain amount is available for dividends, payments to preferred holders have priority. When there is more available than needed to take care of the current annual requirements for preferred, the balance can be paid to the common stockholders.

Dividends in arrears on cumulative preferred make the computation a little more involved. Suppose that 6,000 shares of 5 per cent cumulative preferred with a $20 par are outstanding, and that dividends have not been paid since 1953. At the end of 1957 the directors declare that there is sufficient cash to pay out dividends of $32,000. How much should be distributed to preferred? How much to common?

| | |
|---|---:|
| Total available...................... | $32,000 |
| To preferred........................ | 24,000 |
| ($120,000 × 5% × 4 years) | |
| Balance to common................. | $ 8,000 |

### BOOK VALUE PER SHARE

The value of ownership interest as recorded on the ledger and statements is usually known as "book value." The computation of book value *per share*, when only common stock has been issued, is as follows: total net worth divided by number of shares issued and outstanding. Book value per share for preferred that has claims only to the extent of its stated capital is simply the preferred stated capital divided by the number of preferred shares outstanding, *which is the same amount as par*. If cumulative shares have claims for the amount of dividends in arrears, the computation becomes a little more complex. An example follows:

Net worth:
Common stock, $40 par;
    10,000 shares authorized and issued......... $400,000
Preferred stock, $20 par;
    5% cumulative;
    6,000 shares authorized and issued.......... 120,000
Earned surplus........................ .... 224,000
      Total net worth........................... $744,000

1. Assume there are no dividends in arrears: Book value per share for preferred would be the same as par, $20 ($120,000 divided by 6,000 shares). Book value per share for common would be:

Total net worth................. $744,000
Less preferred claims............ 120,000
Common equity................. $624,000 divided by 10,000
                             or $62.40 per share

2. Assume there are dividends in arrears: A footnote to the balance sheet states that dividends on the cumulative preferred stock have not been paid for 1954, 1955, 1956, and 1957, which represents a total of $24,000 in arrears. Computations of book values under these circumstances are as follows:

*a.* Preferred:

Stated value................. ....... $120,000
Claims for dividends........... 24,000
    Total claims................. $144,000
    $144,000 divided by 6,000 shares equals a
    book value of $24 per share for preferred.

*b.* Common:

Total net worth................. $744,000
Preferred claims................ ...... 144,000
    Common equity................. $600,000
    $600,000 divided by 10,000 shares gives a
    book value of $60 per share for common.

Book value per share is of interest as a means of illustrating growth in stock valuation over a period of years, and also as a comparison with market value. Since assets, and consequently net worth, are valued on the basis of cost, it is not unusual for market value to be considerably more than book value during a period of prosperity.

## LONG-TERM DEBT FINANCING

Corporate management frequently finds that funds should be obtained by borrowing rather than by issuing additional stock. If funds are needed for a long period, loans may be obtained from one or several sources by the issuance of long-term notes. Suppose that an insurance company agrees to lend the corporation $60,000 on the basis of an unsecured note. The entry for this transaction would be:

| Cash | 60,000 | |
| Notes Payable | | 60,000 |

If the insurance company demands security, a mortgage may be placed on a building and the entry would then be:

| Cash | 60,000 | |
| Mortgage Payable | | 60,000 |

When it is impossible to obtain large sums from one source, management may decide to "float" (sell) an issue of bonds. The bond certificates in one issue are identical and normally carry the following information: date of issue, interest rate, interest payment dates, principal amounts due, date due, and the seal of the issuing company. Assume, for example, that the corporate directors approve the issuing of 5,000 bonds with a face value or principal amount of $1,000 each. If all the bonds were sold at the same time, a journal entry to record the transaction would be:

| Cash | 5,000,000 | |
| Bonds Payable | | 5,000,000 |

Suppose that the bonds carry an interest rate of 4 per cent, payable semiannually. The following entry would then be made at the end of each six months:

| Bond Interest Expense | 100,000 | |
| Cash | | 100,000 |

All amounts of long-term debt that are payable after one year from the balance sheet date should be shown on the balance sheet under the heading of long-term debt. Any amounts due *within* one year after the balance sheet date must be classified as current liabilities. If the bonds are serial or installment bonds, that portion of the total liability which is due within the coming year must be classified as current and the balance as long-term.

*Classification of Bonds*

The most common types of bonds can be classified on the basis of collateral (security): (1) Debenture bonds are unsecured—except as they have priority to payment of interest and principal when compared with payments to owners and certain other classes of creditors. (2) Real estate mortgage bonds are secured by buildings and/or land which can be attached and sold if interest or principal payments are not met. Interest and principal on bonds represent fixed obligations that must be satisfied if a business is to continue, and for this reason bonds should be used as a means of acquiring funds only if the business income is fairly stable, e.g., a public utility. Otherwise, the bondholders may force the stockholders "out of business" during periods of recession or depression—or at any other time that interest or principal is not paid when due.

## SUMMARY

Most of the variations in accounting for business units are caused by differences in operations, not by the form of ownership. Accounting for a sole proprietorship, a partnership, and a corporation, all of the same size and in the same line of business, would be very similar, except for those transactions that affect invested and earned equities. The records for a sole proprietorship or a partnership can be maintained with only one "capital" account for each owner. Both business and personal assets of proprietors and partners are generally available to creditors to satisfy debts. Only business assets are normally available to corporate creditors and, for that reason, the "permanent" invested capital must be kept separate from that portion of the stockholders' equity which is the result of "retained earnings." Creditors are protected in that dividends are *not* normally allowed if the permanent stated capital of the corporation would be reduced by a distribution of assets to the owners.

The permanent capital of a corporation is usually subdivided into two major groups, common stock and preferred stock. Either common or preferred can be par, no-par, or nominal par-stock; either can be issued in exchange for cash or property or on credit. Preferred may have preference only as to assets in liquidation and current dividends, but more often than not will also have preference to all cumulative dividends in arrears. Preferred stock may also be convertible and/or callable. All equity valuation exhibited by surplus is a part of the common book value, unless preferred has claims for unpaid dividends.[1] The corporate surplus is usually classified as retained earnings (earned surplus) and capital surplus (paid-in surplus) and the latter may be subdivided into a number of more specific classifications if amounts are significant. The earned surplus is theoretically a measure of the asset amount that could legally be distributed in the form of dividends, but the amount of excess cash is actually the determining factor in most cases.

## QUESTIONS

**1.** What is the meaning of "entity"? Of "net worth"?

**2.** Why are the representation of ownership by shares and the existence of markets for trading shares listed as advantages of the corporate form of business organization?

[1] Issues of participating preferred stock are now so rare that a discussion of such stock has been omitted.

**3.** A partnership is dissolved by what events? How may a corporation be liquidated?

**4.** Creditors of proprietors and partners can look to what assets for the satisfaction of their debts? The liabilities of a corporation normally have to be satisfied from what assets?

**5.** An income tax return is not filed for a sole proprietorship; an information return is filed for a partnership. On what income tax return is the income from a proprietorship or partnership included as a part of the taxable income? Is an income tax return filed for a corporation? Corporate profits are said to be subject to "double taxation." Why?

**6.** Describe common stock and preferred stock. Explain, briefly, the characteristics of each different type of preferred stock.

**7.** If par stock is sold at a premium, what accounts are credited? If the sales price of no-par value stock is greater than the stated value, what accounts are to be credited?

**8.** List the advantages of no-par value stock as compared with par value stock; of nominal par stock as compared with par value stock.

**9.** A corporation issues common stock and later reacquires a small amount of this same stock on the open market. The cost of this stock should be charged to what account? How is it shown on the balance sheet?

**10.** What information regarding a stock issue should be presented on the statement of financial condition?

**11.** A, B, and C each subscribe to $1,000 of preferred stock; the stock is to be issued when fully paid. A month later A pays $500 on his subscription, C pays $1,000. What are the three entries required to record the above transactions?

**12.** The East Corp. has 2,000 subscribers to an issue of stock. How can they determine when Mr. Jones, one of the 2,000 subscribers, has completed payment on his subscription?

**13.** The West Corp. has not issued any stock for the past 60 years, but stock of the corporation is sold and purchased every day of the year. How? By whom? What effect do these purchases and sales have on the financial records of the company?

**14.** Many persons say that "dividends are paid out of earned surplus." Dividends must actually be paid "out of" what? What is the most common form of dividend distribution?

**15.** What is earned surplus? What sort of limit on dividends does earned surplus represent? What is usually a more realistic and meaningful limit on dividends?

**16.** Why may the directors resolve to reclassify a portion of earned surplus as appropriated earned surplus? If a corporation has both appropriated and unappropriated earned surplus, what serves to indicate the limit on dividends?

**17.** What is the difference between earned surplus and paid-in surplus?

**18.** When do dividends become a legal liability of the company? Where should the liability be classified on the balance sheet? What three dates are important in connection with dividends?

**19.** Are stock dividends really a dividend in the sense that something is distributed? What can be achieved by the issuance of a stock dividend?

**20.** What are dividends in arrears? Can there be dividends in arrears on common stock?

**21.** Define the following:

*a.* Par value per share
*b.* Book value per share
*c.* Market value per share

**22.** If stock is not to be sold in order to obtain needed long-term financing, how may the corporation obtain the desired funds?

## CHAPTER 10

# ACCOUNTING FOR SALES

In the two chapters on partnerships and corporations, the terms and problems connected with the ownership and financing of business organizations were discussed. This chapter provides a summary of terms, problems, and procedures involved in accounting for sales. It should help the student to understand the meaning and nature of the accounts which arise as a result of the various selling arrangements. Among the problems discussed are: sales for cash, c.o.d. sales, sales on open account, sales on notes or trade acceptances, installment sales, consignment sales, departmental sales and cost records, and sales through agencies and branches.

Because of the number of problems to be discussed, no attempt will be made to describe all the alternative procedures which may be used nor to discuss fully all the technical problems which may arise. Rather, an attempt will be made to describe the basic problem, the accounts involved, and *one* typical procedure for handling the problem.

## *Sales other than Merchandise*

The Sales account and the term "Sales" are used in accounting only in connection with sales of merchandise. Sales of land, buildings, equipment or other fixed assets or the sale of patents, copyrights, or any other asset should be recorded by debits to the asset received and credits to the account with the asset which is sold rather than to the sales account. Any difference between the book value and the selling price should be recorded in an account called Gain (or Loss) on Sale of Assets (usually specifically named). If the asset sold was subject to depreciation or depletion, the depreciation expense must be recorded to the date of sale, the reserve for depreciation must be closed, and the difference between the book value and the selling price must be recorded as a gain (or loss) on sale.

## THE PROBLEMS IN SALES ACCOUNTING

As a first step in studying the procedures involved in accounting for sales of merchandise, let us first consider what information is necessary and thus customarily provided by the accounting department, and what is sometimes desirable and can be provided at little additional cost.

We must know, and accounts always show:

1. The total sales and the cost of the goods sold so that statements of earnings may be prepared
2. The amount of cash received, so that we may know the amount which should be on hand
3. The amounts owed us by each of our customers, so that we may make collections properly
4. The amount of discounts allowed, so that we may properly report earnings
5. The amount of returned sales and sales allowances so that we may determine net sales and watch the cost of sales adjustments

It would be desirable to know, and accounts often show:

6. The sales and costs by departments so that the profitability of each department can be found
7. The sales and costs in various agencies and branches
8. The profitability of merchandise handled on or through consignments
9. The profitability of installment sales

The customary accounting reports do not provide the following types of data:

1. Sales by salesmen
2. Sales by sales districts or geographical areas
3. Sales by product lines
4. A breakdown of sales by exact time of sale, as day of week, or time of day
5. Size of orders of salesmen
6. Sales of particular items or lines by salesmen
7. Reasons of customers for buying a particular item or brand—what advertising caused sale
8. Comparison of actual sales with sales potential of the area
9. Per cent of business obtained in area

Information of the type indicated above is often of vital importance to management in evaluating salesmen and establishing sales quotas, in determining product lines to be carried and quantities required, in suggesting ways to increase sales by increasing number or size of orders, in calling attention to items or lines not being pushed by some salesmen, in evaluating the effectiveness of various advertising programs or merchandising practices, in judging the effectiveness of the entire selling program, and in improving merchandising and management policies and procedures. Since the provision of data of this type is not an essential part of the basic accounting process, the need for this type of information is often neglected in accounting texts. However, most of the basic information is available in the accounting department and can often be summarized and tabulated at little additional cost. This is especially true where a "punched-card" accounting system is used.

### When Does a Sale Occur?

Firms which are on a "cash basis" do not record income until the cash is actually collected. For example, when a doctor performs a service for a client, the client's account is charged for the service but no other entry is required. When the account is collected, the customer's ledger account is credited. An entry is then made debiting cash and crediting an appropriately named income account in the general ledger. But, merchandising and manufacturing concerns do not use a *cash basis* of accounting, and they record sales income when the income is earned rather than when it is collected. This raises the question, "When is the income earned and when is the entry made?"

No problem arises in the case of cash sales, for the income is earned when the cash is received and the goods delivered or set aside. If merchandise is sold on account, the income is considered earned when the asset "accounts receivable" is exchanged for the asset "merchandise inventory." In the case of installment sales, where expenses of collecting and recording are to be borne by future periods and where losses from failure to collect and losses on repossessions are quite likely to be substantial in amount, the installment sale is recorded at the time the installment contract is signed, but the income is not considered totally earned until the account is fully collected. Thus if an item which cost $200 is sold for $300 and $150 of the $300 is collected before the end of the fiscal year, only one-half of the profit of $100 is considered earned during the period in which the sale was made. The remainder of the profit will be shown in a deferred gross profit account and will be taken up as future collections are made. This problem will be illustrated and more fully explained under the section on "Installment Sales."

It is sometimes desirable to take up a portion of the income on a sale or service contract before the sale is actually made. In contracts where there is an agreement to pay costs plus fixed fees or costs plus a per cent of cost, as cost plus 10 per cent, the income which should be taken up is easily estimated. Where the sales contract calls for a fixed price, as where a building construction bid is awarded to the lowest bidder, there is no assurance that the completion of the contract will result in a profit. For this reason, it is doubtful if profits may be properly recorded until the contract is completed.

## Cash Sales of Merchandise

The simplest transaction involving the sale of merchandise is the sale of merchandise for cash. The typical merchandising business (such as the grocery, clothing, or hardware store) makes no attempt to record the cost of the merchandise at the time of the sale since to do so would slow down the selling operation and increase selling costs. Cash sales are recorded at the end of the day from cash register totals, cash register reports, or other summaries by a debit to Cash and a credit to Sales.

**Cash Short or Over.** If the amount of cash in the cash drawer at the end of the day (after removing the change fund) is not equal to the cash register (or sales ticket) total of cash receipts, the accountant will assume that the register total is correct and that the discrepancy is due to errors in making change. Since the cash on hand may be more or less than the amount shown by the register, there may be either a gain or loss resulting from the error. For example, assume that after the $50 change fund has been set aside, the cash in the register is counted and found to be $420.50. The register shows total sales of $421.50. The entry is:

| | | |
|---|---|---|
| Cash | $420.50 | (Actual count) |
| Cash Short or Over | 1.00 | (Difference) |
| Sales | $421.50 | (Register total) |
| (To record cash sales for day) | | |

On days when the cash on hand exceeds the total shown by the register, the Cash Short or Over account is *credited* with the difference. At the end of the fiscal period the balance in the account indicates whether the account is to be considered an expense or miscellaneous income for the period.

## Sales on Account

When merchandise is sold on open account, which means that the buyer gives only an oral or implied promise to pay, the transaction is recorded by a debit (or charge) to the customer's account and a credit to Sales. If there are only a few customers who buy on open account, the accounts with the individual customers may be kept in the general ledger. If there are many such customers, their accounts are kept in a separate subsidiary ledger (accounts receivable ledger) and only the total is shown in the Accounts Receivable account in the general ledger.

When hand-kept records are used, the sales invoices are typically recorded in order in a sales journal such as the one shown below:

Sales Journal

| Date | Customer's Name | Address | Terms | Inv. No. | Amount |
|------|-----------------|---------|-------|----------|--------|
| Jan.  1 | James Ford | Albany, Ore. | 2/10, n/30 | 126 | 156 |
| 6 | John Doe | Canby, Ore. | n/30 | 127 | 25 |
| 15 | Richard Green | Dale, Ore. | 1/10, n/30 | 128 | 150 |
| | | | | | 331 |

The address column is often unnecessary and a column for "terms" is unnecessary if all terms are the same. As explained earlier, the individual items must be posted to the individual accounts of the customers and the column total must be debited to the Accounts Receivable account and credited to the Sales account.

If perpetual inventories are kept, a second amount column is used to record the cost of the articles sold. The items in this column are posted to the individual inventory ledger sheets and the column total is posted as a debit to the Cost of Sales account and a credit to the inventory control account (Merchandise Inventory or Finished Goods).

Many problems arise in connection with the handling of sales on account. Some of these are:

What is the procedure if there is a sales tax?

What procedure is followed if freight is sometimes paid for the purchaser and added to his bill?

What amounts are used if the customer is allowed trade or cash discounts?

What is done if the sale is a c.o.d. sale?

What is done if the customer agrees to accept a trade acceptance or gives a note in settlement?

What entries are required when unsatisfactory merchandise is returned?

How can the cost of recording sales and preparing statements be reduced?

What information is available as a result of normal accounting procedures and what additional sales data can be obtained at reasonable cost?

**Sales Taxes.** When sales taxes are to be collected from the customer, a sales journal similar to the one illustrated above but having three amount columns may be used. The first column shows the amount of the sale, the second shows the amount of sales tax, and the third shows the total due from the customer. Details of the third column are posted to the individual customer accounts and the total is posted to the debit of the Accounts Receivable control account. The total of the first column is posted to the credit of the Sales account to show the total sales income and the total of the second column is posted to the credit of a Sales Taxes Payable account to show the liability for taxes on sales made.

**Freight Paid by Seller and Charged to Customer.** If freight or postage charges are sometimes *paid for the customer and added to his bill*, the problem may be easily handled by setting up additional columns. For example:

Sales Journal

| Date | Customer | Invoice | Accts. Rec. Dr. | Postage Cr. | Freight Out—Cr. | Sales Cr. |
|------|----------|---------|-----------------|-------------|-----------------|-----------|
| Jan. 1 | John Doe | 126 | 125.50 | .50 | | 125.00 |
| 6 | Joe Green | 127 | 156.00 | | 6.00 | 150.00 |
| | | | 281.50 | .50 | 6.00 | 275.00 |

The details of the accounts receivable column are posted to the individual customer accounts as usual and the column total is posted to the control account. If all postage paid is charged to the Postage Expense account, the total of the postage column may be credited to this expense account, thus reducing the account balance to the actual expense to the firm. In a similar manner, if all freight on sales is charged to Freight Out (an expense account), crediting this account for amounts for which the firm is to be reimbursed will correctly state the expense. Sales is, of course, credited for the total of the sales column.

**Discounts on Sales.** Two types of discounts are commonly granted customers: "trade discounts," which are always considered price adjustments; and "cash discounts," which are allowances granted for prompt payment.

Assume that a customer is quoted a price of $600 for an item, less 10 and 5 per cent trade discounts. The terms of sale are 2/10, n/30 (read two ten, net thirty) which means that he will be allowed a 2 per cent discount if the invoice is paid within ten days (after date of invoice, usually) and that the full amount is due in 30 days.

The sale should be entered at $600 less the 10 and 5 per cent discounts, or

$$\$600 - 10\% \text{ of } \$600 = \$540$$
$$\$540 - 5\% \text{ of } \$540 = \$513$$

If 10 and 5 per cent trade discounts are commonly granted, the net decimal equivalent may be found and used to figure the net amount in a single step. This is done by multiplying the complement of the first discount by the complement of the second discount, in this case $0.90 \times 0.95$ or 0.855. The figure 0.855 or 85.5 per cent is called the "*net* decimal equivalent" of a chain discount of 10 and 5 per cent.

If the $600 sale in the first example is entered by a debit to Accounts

Receivable and a credit to Sales for $513, the seller may expect to be paid $513 less 2 per cent of $513, or $502.74, if the bill is paid within ten days and the full amount of $513 if the customer takes more than ten days to pay. The receipt of the cash within the discount period will be recorded by a debit to Cash for the amount actually received ($502.74), a debit to Discount on Sales for the discount allowed ($10.26), and a credit to the customer's account for the full amount originally charged to him ($513).

When a part of merchandise sold is returned or when freight charges are paid by the wrong party, there may be some confusion as to the amount on which the discount is to be figured. Always see that the discount is figured on the *merchandise* bought and kept. Two examples will illustrate the problems involved:

1. Assume a sale to John Ford of $2,000; terms, 2/10, n/30. We allowed Ford credit for merchandise returned, $400. He pays his account within the discount period. On what amount is he allowed a discount? The amount of merchandise bought and kept: $2,000 − $400 = $1,600.

The entry for the receipt of the cash:

| | | |
|---|---:|---:|
| Cash | 1,568 | |
| Discount on Sales | 32 | |
|     Acct. Rec.—John Ford | | 1,600 |

Since Ford's account was debited for $2,000 at the time of the sale, and credited for $400 at the time of the return (the offsetting credit was Returned Sales and Allowances), the credit of $1,600 when the payment is received will bring his account to a zero balance.

2. Assume a sale to Joe Green of $3,000; terms 2/10, n/30; freight terms f.o.b. shipping point. As a courtesy to Green we prepaid the freight, $60, and charged the amount to his account. He returned $300 worth of merchandise and was given credit for this amount. He now pays his bill. On what amount should the discount be figured? The amount of *merchandise* bought and kept: $3,000 − $300 = $2,700. Green's account shows:

Joe Green

| Sales | $3,000 | Return | $300 |
|---|---:|---|---:|
| Freight | 60 | | |

The entry for the receipt of cash will be:

| | | |
|---|---:|---:|
| Cash | 2,706 | |
| Discount on Sales | 54 | |
|     Acct. Rec.—J. Green | | 2,760 |
|    Computation: | | |
|      Balance in acc. | $2,760 | |
|      Discount (2% of 2,700) | 54 | |
|      Cash due from Green | $2,706 | |

Note that Green is not allowed a discount on the $60 although it is to be repaid. It is obvious that we cannot profitably pay $60 for freight and allow a customer to repay only $58.80 of the amount.

A good businessman should know the difference between a cash discount and ordinary interest and should never fail to take advantage of discounts offered. For example: Assume that you have purchased an item costing $3,000; terms 2/10, n/30; and you find that you do not have the cash on hand to take advantage of the discount but will be able to pay the invoice when due. Assume, also, that you can borrrow the money at your bank at 6 per cent. Should you borrow money at 6 per cent to take advantage of a 2 per cent discount? The answer is definitely "yes." This is the reason:

$3,000 $\times$ 2% = $60 discount
$3,000 $-$ $60 = $2,940 amount needed for 20 days
6% interest on $2,940 for 20 days = $9.80
Amount saved by taking discount..........  $60.00
Cost of borrowing money.................    9.80
Net saving.............................  $50.20

In this connection it is important to note that credit rating reports show whether a firm takes discounts to which it is not entitled or fails to take discounts to which it is entitled. Firms which attempt to take discounts after the discount period has expired damage their credit ratings. Firms which fail to take discounts to which they are entitled fall into three categories:

1. Carelessly or poorly managed firms which lose discounts inadvertently

2. Firms whose managers are ignorant of the savings to be obtained

3. Firms which have no bank credit and are unable to pay in time to take the discount

When a firm's statements show a satisfactory current financial position and credit reports show that discounts are not being taken, you should seriously question the accuracy or honesty of the financial reports. Remember that no business which appears to be in good condition should fail to take advantage of cash discounts.

**C.o.d. Sales.** When merchandise is sold c.o.d. and is delivered by the company's own delivery men, the simplest procedure is to make a note of the merchandise as it is given to the delivery man and to record the transaction as a cash sale when he turns in his receipts at the end of each day.

If c.o.d. sales are made to out-of-town customers, a C.o.d. Accounts Receivable account may be charged for all sales and credited for all collections. It is not necessary to set up individual accounts with each customer since we never need to find the amount owed us by an individual customer.

C.o.d. sales which are shipped by freight may be made by sending a sight draft with an order bill of lading to the customer's bank. The customer must present the bill of lading before the merchandise can be obtained, and he must go to the bank and pay the sight draft to obtain the bill of lading.

**Trade Acceptances.** In many cases the customer agrees to give a written promise to pay for the merchandise delivered to him. These written promises to pay are called notes or trade acceptances. There is no difference in the accounting procedure involved for notes or trade acceptances and both are shown in the accounts and statements as notes receivable. There are some differences in the parties involved and in the physical appearance of the forms, however.

A trade acceptance is a note which arises out of a sale of merchandise at the time of the sale. It is drawn up by the seller of the merchandise (the drawer) and must be accepted by the buyer (the drawee). It is payable to the seller who is thus both the drawer and the payee. The buyer indicates his acceptance by writing across the face of the paper:

> "Accepted (date)
> Payable at (place)
> Signed by (signature)"

A trade note receivable may be received at the time of a sale but is often received at the time the account is due where the buyer wants additional time for payment of a bill. It is drawn up by the buyer (the maker) and is made payable to the seller or to his order (the payee).

Both notes and acceptances may be discounted at the holder's bank if the holder needs cash before the maturity date of the notes. The bank will charge a fee based on the maturity value of the note and the number of days to maturity. The holder who thus discounts his notes at the bank will debit Cash for the amount received, debit Interest Expense if he receives less than the face of the note or credit Interest Income if he receives more than the face of the note, and credit Notes Receivable for the face of the note. He will be contingently liable with the maker of the note and will be expected to pay the bank the maturity value of the note plus any charges involved if the party who is primarily liable refuses to pay.

**Returned Sales and Allowances.** When merchandise is sold, the usual entry is a debit to Cash (or Accounts Receivable) and a credit to Sales. If a customer returns merchandise and his money is returned to him (or he is given credit on his account) the original entry for the sale could be reversed. This would mean that the sales account would be credited when a sale is made and debited if the merchandise is returned. However, if this were done, the balance in the Sales account would show the *net* sales, and both total sales and the amount of merchandise returned would be obscured. Since sales returns and allowances are important as a check on the quality of merchandise being sold, the effect of adjustment policies, and as an indication of customer dissatisfaction, it is important that the amount returned be known. For this reason, a separate account is usually maintained so that both gross sales and sales returns and allowances figures may be readily available.

Sometimes a customer is granted an "allowance" due to damaged or defective merchandise without there being an actual return of the goods. The entries made if a cash allowance is made (or if the customer's account is credited) are the same as if the merchandise were actually returned. An account called Returned Sales and Allowances is often used to make it clear that both types of transactions are included. However, if an error is made in a sales invoice amount, the correction is made directly to the Sales account since this involves neither a return nor an allowance and is not an indication of damaged or defective goods nor of customer dissatisfaction.

If there are a large number of sales returns and allowances, a special column may be desirable in the cash payments journal and a separate journal, similar to the sales journal, may be needed for returns and allowances of charge customers. If such a journal is used, the individual items are posted to the customers' accounts in the accounts receivable ledger. At the end of the month, the total is posted as a debit to Returned Sales and Allowances and a credit to the Accounts Receivable control account in the general ledger.

For management purposes, the usual accounting entries need to be supplemented by analyses showing what items are being returned, why they are being returned, and what customers are returning them. These data may suggest changes in the product, changes in suppliers, changes in merchandising practices (advertising or guarantees), or perhaps dropping certain customers.

**Accounts Receivable Records.** Most retail and wholesale businesses selling on account find the problem of recording sales and the receipt of payments on account their largest single record-keeping problem. For this reason, many firms begin the mechanization of their record keeping with machines for handling accounts receivable records. Since all the major office machines companies manufacture machines to handle the problem and dozens of variations in procedures are possible, it is impossible to describe more than a typical plan for recording account sales.

The sales tickets or sales invoices flow to the accounting department where an adding machine tape is run on them. The accounts receivable bookkeeper then selects the ledger card for the first customer, picks up the old balance from the ledger card, writes the amount of the charge from the invoice, depresses the proper keys and the machine moves to the proper column, prints, and takes a new balance. He then picks up the old balance again, subtracts it from the new balance (which is still in the machine), and takes a final total, which is the amount of the invoice. This amount adds in another adding register and the total of the register is checked against the adding machine prelist. This procedure provides a check on the pickup of both the old balance and the new invoice amount. Under this system the sales journal is made as a carbon or ribbon copy of the entry in the subsidiary ledger. Statements, which usually occupy a minor place in accounting texts but are a major record-keeping problem, are made from the same printing as the ledger record. This may be done by the use of carbon paper, repeat-printing devices, or a new chemically treated paper which makes "carbon" copies without the use of carbon paper. General ledger entries are, as usual, made from the totals of the invoices recorded.

A popular variation of the procedures described for handling account sales provides a "line balance" check and a distribution record in addition to the records described. Under this method, the prelist, old balance, charge, and new balance are prepared as before. After picking up the old balance for the second time, the invoice amount is entered in a distribution column (as, for example, a departmental sales analysis) and a new total is taken. If the old balance and the charge as entered in the distribution columns are equal to the new balance, the machine prints an asterisk or a zero balance and the carriage positions itself for the next entry. If they are not equal, the error must be corrected before posting can be continued.

Any business which has a substantial number of active accounts should consider the use of accounting machines for this phase of record keeping. Most of the machines are quite flexible and, through the use of tabulator stops and control bars, can be made to handle accounts receivable, accounts payable, and general ledger records. Many machines have typewriter keyboards and can be used to handle almost any accounting problem.

In addition to machines of the type indicated above, some firms are now punching the accounting data into cards which can be sorted and tabulated in any desired way. This type of machine is especially suited to the problem of providing statistical data for sales management. For example, it is a simple problem to analyze sales by products, by salesmen, by sales districts, by distribution channels, by time of sale, by geographical area, or in any way which will help the sales department know exactly what, when, where, or how its sales are made. This type of information is especially valuable in planning programs of advertising, planning routes and establishing sales quotas, determining product requirements, evaluating promotional methods, aging receivables, etc.

## DEPARTMENTAL SALES

Many firms have found it desirable to set up their operations by departments so that the operating efficiency of each department (and department manager) can be evaluated and the contribution of each department to the total earnings can be estimated. This has been found to be very effective in encouraging sound and efficient operating procedures and provides management with much more valuable data than are available where all operations are lumped together.

Although the typical text for accounting majors devotes a chapter to this subject, the basic ideas can be described in a few paragraphs. From a record-keeping standpoint, it simply means that there must be Sales, Purchases, Returned Sales, Returned Purchases, Freight In, and Inventory accounts for each department, and all journals must contain additional columns to make this departmentalization possible. If this is done, departmental gross profits are readily obtainable. The profit and loss statement will show a column or set of columns for each department and a set of columns for the totals of all departments.

It may also be desirable to show a departmental breakdown of selling and administrative expenses so that departmental net profits may be found. Some of these expenses, such as sales salaries, are easily departmentalized and may be set up in separate accounts when paid. Other expenses, such as advertising, office salaries, officers' salaries, rent, taxes, or insurance expense are much more difficult to prorate and many bases may be used. For example, rent and other occupancy costs may be allocated to the departments on the basis of square feet of floor space used, advertising may be allocated on a basis of column inches (or time) used, etc.

The above discussion should serve to show that many of the expense allocations are arbitrary and are questionable. Still if they are consistently followed, the progress of a department can be roughly measured and its contribution approximated. It will be quickly seen, however, that some of the costs cannot be controlled by the department manager and it is doubtful whether any real value comes from the allocation of these costs to the departments.

One of the most common errors made by the beginner in departmental accounting is the assumption that a department which is operating at a loss should be discontinued. This conclusion could lead to some serious errors in management. Let us briefly consider why this is so:

1. The basis of allocation of many costs is arbitrary and sometimes incorrect. The use of different bases would give different net profit amounts. Are the bases used valid?

2. There is no relationship between the expenses allocated to a department and the expenses which would be avoided if the department were closed. For example, if 20 per cent of the administrative expense is allocated to department B, how much would the president's salary (an administrative expense) be cut if the department is closed?

3. All departments help to carry the overhead. If one department is discontinued, the other departments must carry a larger share of the burden.

4. Although some expenses may not be decreased by discontinuing a department, the income certainly would be. Even sales of other departments might be affected. For example, if the meat department is discontinued in a grocery store, customers who do not like to make two stops may buy all their groceries where they can get meat.

5. The department may be using up fixed assets which could not be readily sold. If the losses do not exceed the depreciation, the department is not causing a depletion of the working capital. If the department is breaking even, the fixed assets are being "sold" at book value. This may be much better than trying to sell them outright.

6. It may not be possible to discontinue a department and sell its fixed assets because they form an integral part of the factory.

7. Some departments are operated at cost or even at a loss as a management policy or merchandising strategy because they serve to bring customers into the store, e.g., the cafeteria of a department store.

For these reasons it must be clear that any decision to discontinue an unprofitable department must be carefully considered on other bases than the reported net profit of the particular department. We must analyze the costs which would be avoided and weigh them against the income which would be lost before any intelligent decision may be reached.

## ACCOUNTING FOR THE COST OF GOODS SOLD

There are two principal methods used for determining the cost of goods sold. The most obvious solution is to record the cost of the item sold at the time the sale is made. This is done by a debit to Cost of Goods Sold and a credit to Inventory for the cost price of the item sold at the same time that Cash (or Accounts Receivable) is debited and Sales credited for the selling price. This procedure is called the "perpetual inventory" method of accounting since the accountant knows at all times the value of the inventory on hand. Because of the time required to record the cost of each item sold, this system is clearly unsatisfactory in businesses, such as drug or grocery stores, which sell a very large number of small items. These stores estimate their cost of goods sold by taking a physical inventory of the goods on hand at the beginning of a period, adding to this the cost of goods purchased to obtain the total available for sale, and subtracting the amount unsold at the end of the period to find the cost of goods sold during the period.

The use of a physical count of goods on hand to determine goods sold means that items which are stolen or lost appear as a part of the cost of goods sold. If the final inventory is valued at "cost or market, whichever is lower," a drop in market (replacement costs) will result in decreasing the value of goods on hand and in increasing the figure shown as the cost of goods sold.

**Estimating the Inventory.** Because the "physical inventory" procedure requires that an inventory be taken before a profit and loss statement can be prepared and because taking an inventory is an expensive and time-consuming procedure, many firms not using perpetual inventories prepare only one profit and loss statement per year. While this is sufficient for tax purposes, it does not provide management with data quickly enough for the figures to be of most value in management decisions. To overcome this problem and to make possible monthly or quarterly financial reports, a method of estimating retail store inventories has been devised. This requires that a record be kept of the cost and selling price of goods purchased, any additional markups, and all markdowns. This information is summarized as follows to determine the inventory at any time:

|  | Cost | Retail |
|---|---|---|
| Beginning inventory | $12,000 | $16,000 |
| Purchases | 30,000 | 40,000 |
| Freight in | 1,000 | |
| Markups (net) | | 2,000 |
| Total | $43,000 | $58,000 |
| Less: Sales (from sales record) | | −40,000 |
| Markdowns | | −1,000 |
| Final inventory | X | $17,000 |

To find X, the final inventory at cost, we need only solve the ratio:

$$\frac{43,000}{58,000} = \frac{X}{17,000}$$
$$X = \$12,600$$

Stated in another way, we may say that the *total cost* is 43/58ths or 74.1 per cent of the total *retail price*. The *cost* of the final inventory is 74.1 per cent of the remaining *retail* value. And, 74.1 per cent of $17,000 is $12,600.

## INSTALLMENT SALES

Firms which sell goods with a large unit cost, such as refrigerators, ranges, heating or air-conditioning equipment, furniture, automobiles, etc., often find that their sales can be tremendously increased by allowing their customers to buy with only a small down payment with the balance due in weekly or monthly installments. In the case of installment sales (as contrasted with "lay-away" sales) the merchandise is immediately placed at the disposal of the customer. To protect his equity, the merchant often delivers title to the property and takes a chattel mortgage from the buyer. More often, the merchandise is sold under a contract whereby the merchant retains title to the goods until they are fully paid for. In either case, the sale is recorded at the time the goods are turned over to the buyer, and, in either case, the merchant has a right to reclaim or repossess the goods if the buyer fails to pay for them as agreed.

While it is permissible for income tax purposes to consider the gross profit on installment sales as income of the period in which the sale is made, the fact that the cost of servicing the accounts is quite large and the losses on repossessions may completely wipe out any profits on the sale has led many firms to adopt procedures which take up the gross profit as collections are made.

If only an occasional sale is made on the installment basis, it hardly seems practical to set up the special accounts and record-keeping procedures required to record installments, and sales entries may be made in the regular accounts receivable and sales accounts. Where installment sales make up an important part of total sales, the proper matching of costs against the income produced is seriously distorted and the comparability of the accountant's statement of income and costs is lost unless profits are taken up as the accounts are collected. For this reason, basic procedures for a theoretically sound system of installment accounting are briefly described here.

Since the items which are sold on an installment basis are ordinarily things which have a large unit value (as refrigerators, television sets, etc.), it is feasible to record both the cost and the selling price as the article is sold. The following illustration assumes that perpetual inventories are thus kept, that the installment sales are kept separate from regular sales on account, and that installment accounts receivable are kept separate from regular accounts receivable.

**Purchases.** When the goods are bought by the merchant, the purchase is recorded by a debit to the Inventory account for the total cost (including freight) and a credit to Cash or to Accounts Payable.

**Sales.** Installment sales may be recorded in an installment sales journal similar to the following:

Installment Sales Journal

| Date | Customer | Acct. No. | Sales | Cost |
|------|----------|-----------|-------|------|
| Jan. 6 | John Ford | 5501 | 300 | 240 |
| 8 | Joseph Green | 5502 | 400 | 320 |
| 12 | Jason Hason | 5503 | 360 | 288 |
| | | | 1,060 | 848 |

Each sale is entered at the total agreed selling price. Carrying charges, if any, are included in the total. Interest charges based on the unpaid balance should not be included.

For example, on January 6 a refrigerator which cost $230 plus freight of $10 was sold to John Ford. He made a down payment of $30 and agreed to pay $27 a month for 10 months. Notice that the total sales price is entered in the installment sales journal. The cash received is entered as a receipt on account in the cash receipts record. The items in the installment sales journal are posted daily to the inventory records (at cost) and the customers' accounts (at the sales price) in the installment accounts receivable subsidiary ledgers. The totals of the columns are posted as follows:

| | | |
|---|---|---|
| Installment Accounts Receivable | 1,060 | |
| Installment Sales | | 1,060 |
| Cost of Installment Sales | 848 | |
| Inventory | | 848 |

**Collections on Account.** When the down payment is received, Cash is debited and Installment Accounts Receivable is credited for the amounts received. The weekly or monthly installments are entered in the same manner. Since the gross profits are to be taken up as collections are made, and since the gross profit rate may vary from one fiscal period to the next, it is necessary that we be able to determine the amount collected on the sales of each year. This may be done by having one Installment Accounts Receivable controlling account and separate subsidiary ledgers for the accounts of each year. The amount of gross profit considered earned is determined by reducing the deferred gross profit balance to the amount appropriate for the end-of-year receivables balances. This will be more fully explained later.

**Trade-ins and Repossessions.** If trade-ins are accepted as a part of the down payment, the inventory account is debited for their fair market value, the customer's account is credited for the agreed amount, and the excessive allowance, if any, is debited to the deferred gross profit account for that year.

To record repossessions, the most logical procedure requires that the merchandise be brought back on the books at its fair value, the accounts receivable balance be closed by a credit equal to the amount still owed, the remaining deferred gross profit on the item be canceled, and any difference be charged (or credited) to Loss (or Gains) on Repossessions. The computations involved are shown in the illustrative problem.

**End-of-year Entries.** At the close of the fiscal period when all journals have been posted, the Cost of Installment Sales account will show the total cost of goods sold on installments and the Installment Sales account will show the total sales on installments. Assume that these accounts for 1956 appear as:

| Cost of Installment Sales | Installment Sales |
|---|---|
| $96,000 (From cost column of Inst. Sales Journal) | $120,000 (From sales column of Inst. Sales Journal) |

An entry is now made closing both accounts and setting up the difference between them in an account called Deferred Gross Profit—1956. In this example the deferred gross profit for 1956 is $24,000 and the entry described is:

| | | |
|---|---|---|
| Installment Sales | 120,000 | |
| Cost of Installment Sales | | 96,000 |
| Deferred Gross Profit—1956 | | 24,000 |

**Realized Gross Profit.** As soon as the entries described above have been made, the deferred gross profit rate for 1956 is determined—$24,000 on sales of $120,000 equals 20 per cent.

When the credit of $120,000 was made to Installment Sales (above), the offsetting debit was made to Installment Accounts Receivable. If this entire amount had been collected, the entire amount of deferred gross profit ($24,000) would have been realized. But, assume that only $108,000 has been collected. The realized gross profit, which is 20 cents on each dollar collected, is 20 per cent of $108,000, or $21,600. The amount of deferred gross profit which has been realized is now entered as:

| | | |
|---|---|---|
| Deferred Gross Profit—1956 | 21,600 | |
| Realized Gross Profit—1956 | | 21,600 |

This leaves a balance in the Deferred Gross Profit account of $2,400 ($24,000 − $21,600).

In practice, the easiest way to compute the realized gross profit is to find the total remaining in Installment Accounts Receivable for each year by checking the balances in the subsidiary ledger accounts. For 1956 this total should be $12,000. (Sales of $120,000 minus collections of $108,000). If $12,000 remains to be collected and the deferred gross profit rate is 20 per cent, then $2,400 (20 per cent of $12,000) is still unrealized. Since the deferred gross profit for 1956 is $24,000 and only $2,400 is still unrealized, the realized portion is $21,600 ($24,000 — $2,400) and this amount is taken up as illustrated before.

## ILLUSTRATIVE PROBLEM—INSTALLMENT ACCOUNTING

1. Beginning-of-year balances:

```
Inventory.......................................  15,000
Installment accounts receivable—1955............   3,000
Installment accounts receivable—1956............  12,000
Deferred gross profit—1955 (25%)......................    750
Deferred gross profit—1956 (20%).....................  2,400
```

Check the balances marked (1) in the ledger accounts and follow through the debits and credits for each of the following transactions for 1957:

2. Purchases of merchandise, $68,000

```
Inventory                                        68,000
     Accounts Payable                                      68,000
(From Purchases Journal—recording total cost of goods purchased)
```

3. Total installment sales, $80,000; cost, $60,000

```
Installment Accounts Receivable—1957             80,000
     Installment Sales                                     80,000
Cost of Installment Sales                        60,000
     Inventory                                             60,000
(From the Installment Sales Journal—total selling price and total cost
of sales)
```

4. Total collections on account, $73,000

```
Cash                                             73,000
     Installment Accounts Receivable                       73,000
(From Cash Receipts Journal—to record total collections)
```

5. Repossessions on 1956 sales: $600 in accounts receivable; fair value of merchandise, $380

```
     Inventory                                      380
     Loss on Repossessions                          100
     Deferred Gross Profit—1956                     120
          Installment Accounts Receivable                    600

     (From General Journal—Computation:
       Balance owed on account.......................$600
       Deferred gross profit rate, 20%
          20% of $600..............................   120
       Unrecovered cost.............................  $480
       Fair market value............................   380
       Loss on repossession.........................  $100
```

6. To close Installment Sales and Cost of Installment Sales and set up Deferred Gross Profit—1957

| | | |
|---|---|---|
| Installment Sales | 80,000 | |
| Cost of Installment Sales | | 60,000 |
| Deferred Gross Profit—1957 | | 20,000 |

(End-of-year entry determined by balances in accounts to be closed)
Deferred Gross Profit rate = 20,000 on 80,000 = 25 %

7. To take up realized gross profit. End-of-year receivables balances from schedule of ledger accounts (Installment Accounts Receivable) for each year:

| | | |
|---|---|---|
| Deferred Gross Profit—1955 | 750 | |
| Deferred Gross Profit—1956 | 1,800 | |
| Deferred Gross Profit—1957 | 15,250 | |
| Realized Gross Profit | | 17,800 |

Computation:

| | *1955(25 %)* | *1956(20 %)* | *1957(25 %)* |
|---|---|---|---|
| Accts. Rec. Balances—End of 1957............ | $  0 | $2,400 | $19,000 |
| Present balance in Deferred Gross Profit........ | 750 | 2,280 | 20,000 |
| Actual present Deferred Gross Profit | | | |
| 1955, 25 % of Acct. Rec. balance of zero....... | 0 | | |
| 1956, 20 % of Acct. Rec. balance of $2,400..... | | 480 | |
| 1957, 25 % of Acct. Rec. balance of $19,000.... | | | 4,750 |
| Gross Profit realized through 1957 collections..... | $750 | $1,800 | $15,250 |

## GENERAL LEDGER FOR INSTALLMENT SALES

### Accounts

**Inventory**

| | |
|---|---|
| (1) $15,000 | (3) $60,000 |
| (2)  68,000 | |
| (5)    380 | |

**Installment Accounts Receivable**

| | |
|---|---|
| (1) 1955 $ 3,000 | (4) $73,000 |
| (1) 1956  12,000 | (5)    600 |
| (3) 1957  80,000 | |

**Deferred Gross Profit—1955 (25 %)**

| | |
|---|---|
| (7) $   750 | (1) $   750 |

**Deferred Gross Profit—1956 (20 %)**

| | |
|---|---|
| (5) $   120 | (1) $ 2,400 |
| (7)   1,800 | |

**Deferred Gross Profit—1957 (25 %)**

| | |
|---|---|
| (7) $15,250 | (6) $20,000 |

**Cash**

| | |
|---|---|
| (4) $73,000 | |

**Accounts Payable**

| | |
|---|---|
| | (2) $68,000 |

**Installment Sales**

| | |
|---|---|
| (6) $80,000 | (3) $80,000 |

**Cost of Installment Sales**

| | |
|---|---|
| (3) $60,000 | (6) $60,000 |

**Loss on Repossessions**

| | |
|---|---|
| (5) $   100 | |

**Realized Gross Profit**

| | |
|---|---|
| | (7) 1953—$   750 |
| | (7) 1954—  1,800 |
| | (7) 1955— 15,250 |

After all the entries outlined above have been made, the Loss on Repossessions balance of $100 and the Realized Gross Profit (on installments) balance of $17,800 are transferred to the Profit and Loss Summary along with other cost and income accounts, and the net profit is determined in the usual way.

*Installment Sales Accounts on the Statements*

1. Installment Accounts Receivable. Amounts due within one year are current assets. Amounts due after the close of the next fiscal year are sometimes shown as "other assets." Since the amount may be small and difficult to determine, the entire amount is usually shown as current.

2. Realized Gross Profit. The realized gross profit amounts, by years, are added to the gross profits on regular operations on the profit and loss statement.

3. Installment Sales and Cost of Installment Sales. Appear on a schedule supporting the realized gross profit figures (see 2).

4. Loss on Repossessions. Appears on profit and loss statement as a deduction from total gross profit amounts (before deducting selling and general expenses).

5. Deferred Gross Profit. Appears on the balance sheet as a deferred credit. Will be credited to realized gross profit as collections are made or canceled as repossessions are made.

6. If perpetual inventories are not used, the cost of installment sales will be computed from Merchandise (beginning) Inventory + Net Purchases + Freight in + Repossessed Merchandise—Merchandise (ending) Inventory. These accounts will provide the cost figure to be subtracted from installment sales to find the Deferred Gross Profit.

### ACCOUNTING FOR AGENCIES AND BRANCHES

One very common procedure for increasing sales is to establish agencies or branches in the territory to be served.

**Agencies.** The distinction between an agency and a branch office is not clear cut because there is no set procedural pattern and no generally followed administrative pattern. We may say, however, that a true agency is much like establishing a permanent office for a traveling salesman. The agency has no permanent stock of goods but only samples and catalogs. Sales are approved and accounts carried on the home office books and deliveries are made from home office stocks. The agency manager, who is essentially a sales representative, keeps a record of cash disbursements and has his checking account reimbursed periodically in the same manner as a petty cash fund is kept. No other accounting records are kept by the agency. The home office may follow either of two common procedures:

1. It may record all sales and expenses in its regular expense and

income accounts and make no record of agency operations. If this is done, total expenses, total income, and total profits will be correctly reported but no data will be available regarding the profitability of the individual agencies.

2. Income and expense accounts may be established for each agency so that the profitability of each agency can be determined and the work of each agency manager evaluated.

In either case the procedures followed are quite simple and can be readily understood by anyone who is familiar with basic record-keeping methods.

**Branches.** The true branch is operated in the same way as an independently owned business. The branch manager buys and sells, and carries his bank account, his accounts receivable, and his accounts payable, etc., in the usual manner. Since the branch is owned and established by the home office, it is quite logical that the Home Office account should replace the usual net worth accounts. This new account is credited for everything received from the home office and debited for payments made to the home office. When the books are closed, the profits are credited to Home Office just as they would ordinarily be credited to Surplus, and losses are debited to Home Office just as they would be debited to the owner's equity accounts in any type of business.

*Illustrative Problem*

The following simple set of transactions illustrates the basic entries for a branch. Entries for the home office will be discussed later.

1. The branch is established, cash of $2,000 is provided, the building and equipment are rented for $300, and merchandise worth $8,000 is received from the home office.

| | | |
|---|---|---|
| Cash | 2,000 | |
|     Home Office | | 2,000 |
| Rent Expense | 300 | |
|     Cash | | 300 |
| Shipments from Home Office | 8,000 | |
|     Home Office | | 8,000 |

2. Merchandise costing $6,000 is puchased on account from outside sources. (Note: Many branches carry merchandise other than that provided by the home office).

| | | |
|---|---|---|
| Purchases | 6,000 | |
|     Accounts Payable | | 6,000 |

3. Sales of $15,000 are made: $6,000 for cash and $9,000 on account.

| | | |
|---|---|---|
| Cash | 6,000 | |
| Accounts Receivable | 9,000 | |
| Sales | | 15,000 |

4. Expenses of $600 are paid.

| | | |
|---|---|---|
| Miscellaneous Expense | 600 | |
| Cash | | 600 |

5. Accounts receivable are collected, $8,000; and accounts payable paid, $5,000.

| | | |
|---|---|---|
| Cash | 8,000 | |
| Accounts Receivable | | 8,000 |
| Accounts Payable | 5,000 | |
| Cash | | 5,000 |

6. An inventory is taken and the books are closed. The inventory is $3,000.

| | | |
|---|---|---|
| Profit and Loss | 14,900 | |
| Shipments from Home Office | | 8,000 |
| Purchases | | 6,000 |
| Rent Expense | | 300 |
| Miscellaneous Expense | | 600 |
| (To close the cost and expense accounts) | | |

| | | |
|---|---|---|
| Merchandise Inventory | 3,000 | |
| Sales | 15,000 | |
| Profit and Loss | | 18,000 |
| (To set up inventory and close income accounts) | | |

| | | |
|---|---|---|
| Profit and Loss | 3,100 | |
| Home Office | | 3,100 |
| (To transfer net income to the home office account) | | |

The home office is faced with the problem of determining the profitability of each branch and keeping a record of the assets owned and at the various branches. Assuming the branch is billed for the goods at cost, its entries for the transactions given above are:

| | | |
|---|---|---|
| 1. Branch A | 2,000 | |
| Cash | | 2,000 |
| Branch A | 8,000 | |
| Inventory | | 8,000 |
| (If perpetual inventories are not kept, the credit could be made to Shipments to Branches) | | |

2, 3, 4, and 5, no entries

| | | |
|---|---|---|
| 6. Branch A | 3,100 | |
| Profit on branches | | 3,100 |
| (To take up profit earned by branch A) | | |

Additional problems arise if the branch is billed for the goods at other than cost, if shipments are made from one branch to another at the request of the home office, and if fixed assets used by the branch are carried on the books of the home office. These problems are fully treated in advanced accounting texts.

*Statements Prepared by Home Office.* On combined profit and loss statements, prepared by the home office, columns are shown for each branch and for the home office and a total is shown for the entire organization. In the "total" columns, the accounts Shipments from Home Office, a cost account for the branches, and Shipments to Branches, a minus cost account for the home office, are eliminated.

On the combined balance sheet, the Home Office accounts of the various branches are offset against the Branch Office accounts on the home office books. In this way, all reciprocal amounts are eliminated in the final statements for the company.

## SALES ON CONSIGNMENT

A method of selling which is of increasing importance to the manufacturer or farmer is the use of consignments. Under a consignment contract, the merchandise is transferred from the owner (the consignor) to a merchant or broker (the consignee) who acts as the agent of the owner in selling the goods. For example, a farmer who raises onions may deliver his produce to a commission merchant who sells the product for the farmer and charges a commission based on the selling price (or an agreed amount) for his work; or, a seed company leaves seeds and a display rack at the grocer's with the understanding that the grocer will sell the seeds and pay only for those sold, and the company will pick up the rack and surplus seeds at the end of the planting season; or, a manufacturer of hats will send a merchant a complete line of hats which the merchant will attempt to sell and on which he will be paid a sales commission.

In every case the unsold merchandise belongs to the *consignor* and is included in his inventory at the end of the fiscal period. Merchandise sent out on consignment should not be entered as a sale by the consignor and should not be considered a purchase by the consignee. Persons studying the statements of firms handling consignments should be certain that the consignor does not include merchandise out on consignment as sales and that the consignee does not include consigned goods in his merchandise inventory.

### Reasons for Consignments

From the point of view of the farmer or the manufacturer, consignments have the following advantages:

1. When a new product or one which may not find consumer acceptance is developed, the merchant may be unwilling to buy a stock of the items but would be willing to accept and try to sell them if the producer retains title and will pick up all the unsold items. This means that new products may be more easily introduced because they do not have to be *sold* to the merchant.

2. The producer retains title and is therefore able to control the selling price, thus assuring no price cutting on his product.

3. The producer may control the operating policies of the merchant if the consigned goods are the major item sold, as when shoe or hat stores get their merchandise on consignment.

4. The producer does not run a great risk of credit losses since he does not relinquish title to the goods and may reclaim his goods if the merchant becomes bankrupt.

5. A chain operation may be built up at much less total cost and in a manner which encourages the initiative of the various managers, since each manager may be the owner of his store.

From the point of view of the merchant or commission agent, the procedure is also quite attractive:

1. New products may be tried without the risk of loss on unsalable items.

2. Goods subject to wide price fluctuations, as fruit or farm produce, may be handled without risk of loss to the agent.

3. A large inventory may be carried without a large investment, thus enabling many persons to enter businesses from which they would otherwise be barred. For example, a service station may carry a complete line of tires on consignment even when the operator has very limited financial resources and would not be able to handle tires if he had to purchase a stock outright.

4. Merchants may be able to carry complete lines for the entire season when they would otherwise let their stocks be depleted toward the end of the season. For example, a grocer can carry a complete line of garden and flower seeds if he knows that seeds left at the end of the season will not be his loss. This increases sales of both consignor and consignee.

## Record Keeping for Consignments

The most obvious procedure for handling small consignments can be illustrated by the procedure commonly used for the sale of garden and flower seeds as mentioned above. With the approval of the grocer, the salesman for the seed company sets up his display rack in the grocery store, fills the rack and makes a notation in his route book. The grocer checks to see that the rack is full but makes no entry in his records. The grocer sells the seeds along with other grocery items and runs them through as regular sales. The salesman calls on the grocer each week, refills the rack and charges the grocer for the seeds sold, determined by the quantities required to fill the rack. The grocer records this as a purchase and the salesman records the sale. At the end of the fiscal period, the grocer ignores the seed rack in taking inventory but counts the packages missing and makes an entry debiting Purchases and crediting Accounts Payable to record the liability for the merchandise sold.

The farmer or manufacturer who has only an occasional shipment on consignment may follow a similar simple plan.

When the merchandise is shipped to the consignee, a memorandum is kept showing the quantity and cost of goods and the freight paid. When freight is paid on the shipment, it is charged to Freight Out and Cash is credited. When the goods are sold, the consignor will receive an "account sales" from the consignee showing the amount received, amount sold, and expenses incurred. He will also receive a remittance for the amount due him (sales less expenses and commission). He will then debit Cash and the various expenses and credit Sales. If the merchandise is not all sold at the end of his fiscal period, all freight and other expenses *on the unsold portion* will be removed from the expense accounts and included in the value of the inventory on consignment.

The entries for the consignee are even more simply made. He sets up an account with the consignor which he charges for any expenses (freight, drayage, etc.) on the consignment. No other entry is made until the goods are sold. When a sale is made, Cash is debited, the Commission Earned account is credited for the agreed commission, and the account with the consignor is credited for the balance. When the weekly or monthly *account sales* is prepared, the consignor's account is debited and cash is credited for the remittance. The amount in the consignor's account before the remittance will be the credit made at the time of the sale less the debits made when expenses were paid for the consignor.

Where consignments are of considerable importance in the total sales of a manufacturer, more elaborate record-keeping procedures are justified. These procedures are fully treated in most advanced accounting texts.

### QUESTIONS

**1.** Why is the sale of a delivery truck by the Houston Furniture Company recorded as a credit to Delivery Equipment while the sale of a delivery truck by the Houston Motor Company is recorded as a credit to Sales?

**2.** What debits and credits are required when a depreciable fixed asset is sold?

**3.** The usual income statement shows only the total sales for the fiscal period. How could analyses showing *where* sold, *when* sold, *who* sold, *why* sold, and size of order be of value in business management?

**4.** Is a sale of merchandise on account considered income of the period in which the merchandise is delivered or of the period in which the account is collected?

**5.** Explain the purpose of a Cash Short and Over account and the entries required to record cash sales when cash is short and when cash is over (or long).

**6.** If a simple sales journal having only one amount column is being used to record sales on account, would it ever contain sales of assets other than merchandise? Would it contain cash sales? When and how would postings be made to the subsidiary accounts receivable ledger? When would the total be posted? And to what general ledger accounts would the total be posted? Would the postings you have described leave the balance in the control account in agreement with the total of the individual accounts in the subsidiary ledger?

**7.** Explain how the prepayment of freight or postage for a customer can be easily handled through the use of appropriate columns in the sales journal. What entry do you think would be made when stamps are actually purchased or the freight bill actually paid? Can you figure out an alternative procedure for handling prepaid freight problems?

**8.** What is the difference between a "cash discount" and a trade discount? How are terms "2/10, n/30" read and what does this mean?

**9.** What is the decimal equivalent of a chain discount of 20 and 10 per cent? What is the *net* decimal equivalent; i.e., what single per cent when multiplied by the amount of an invoice will give the same result as would be obtained by taking off 20 and 10 per cent?

**10.** If merchandise with a list price of $2,000 less trade discounts of 20 per cent and 10 per cent is purchased on terms of 2/10, n/30, what entry (with amounts) is made to record the purchase? What entry would be made when the account is paid, assuming it is paid within the discount period? What entry is made if the account is not paid until the thirtieth day after the date of the invoice?

**11.** Why is it not necessary to set up a subsidiary ledger account for each c.o.d. customer? What procedure can be used to handle local c.o.d. sales?

**12.** Explain the difference between ordinary notes and trade acceptances. What entries are made when merchandise is sold and a trade acceptance received in settlement of the account?

**13.** What are the advantages of departmental accounting records? What accounts are necessary to provide gross profit figures by departments?

**14.** Why should a businessman question departmental net operating income amounts?

**15.** How would you decide whether departments which are operating at a loss should be discontinued?

**16.** How is the cost of goods sold determined by firms not using the "perpetual inventory" system? If some goods are stolen by shoplifters, how does this loss appear in the income statement?

**17.** Explain how retail stores use the "retail method" of estimating inventories.

**18.** A firm using perpetual inventories and selling largerly on installments has the following transactions. What debits and credits are required?

*a.* Installment sales $80,000; cost of sales $60,000.

*b.* Cash received as down payments $10,000.

*c.* Collections on installment accounts receivable, all for the current year, $50,000.

*d.* At year end, to close Installment Sales and Cost of Installment Sales and set up Deferred Gross Profit on Installment Sales.

*e.* To transfer realized gross profit to the Realized Gross Profit account.

**19.** Explain the meaning and nature of each of the following accounts:

*a.* Installment Sales
*b.* Cost of Installment Sales
*c.* Installment Accounts Receivable
*d.* Repossessed Merchandise
*e.* Deferred Gross Profit on Installment Sales
*f.* Realized Gross Profit

**20.** Explain the use of the following accounts found on the books of a branch office:

*a.* Shipments from Home Office
*b.* Home Office

**21.** How does a branch close the profit and loss summary account if a profit has been earned? If there has been a loss?

**22.** What are the advantages of consignments as a method of selling (*a*) to the consignor? (*b*) to the consignee?

**23.** Who owns consigned merchandise and how is it shown in the inventory?

**24.** What is the purpose of an "account sales"?

**25.** Explain what records the consignor makes when he ships merchandise on consignment. When he pays freight? When he receives an account sales showing goods sold, commissions, and cash remitted?

CHAPTER 11

# PRODUCT COST ACCOUNTING

Product cost accounting includes the records and procedures by which the costs of materials, labor, and manufacturing expenses are charged to inventories (in process and finished goods) and subsequently to cost of goods sold. It provides a means for management to trace the costs of manufacturing in order to determine how the profit or loss arose. In its more advanced forms cost accounting becomes a part of scientific management, for one of the aims of scientific management is to gather information that will make it possible to realize the most efficient use of the productive facilities.

The reasons for the adoption of cost accounting and the extent to which it is used are determined to a degree by the nature of the business operations. A custom manufacturer that produces to customer orders on a "cost plus" basis must develop product costs in order to arrive at sales prices. Those manufacturing concerns that produce to customer orders on a "fixed price" basis need cost data to determine if the units were sold at a profit or loss and to provide a basis for establishing future sales prices. Firms that continually manufacture the same variety of products in volume lots use cost data as an aid in the control of operations, as well as for pricing and determining profits. Repetition in production makes it possible to estimate in advance what costs should be and to compare the actual results with these estimates.

Product cost accounting supplements the financial accounting system for a manufacturing concern by breaking down many costs normally carried only as period totals in the general records and charging these costs to the units of product manufactured. A general accounting system can provide management with the total cost of the manufactured products, but only a general accounting system supplemented by a cost accounting system can provide unit production costs; for product cost accounting serves to allocate material, labor, and other manufacturing costs to the products in such a fashion that various unit and operational costs can be developed to aid management.

A trading enterprise has only one inventory, merchandise held for

217

resale, but a manufacturing concern normally has *three* inventory classifications:

1. Raw materials and purchased parts in the stock rooms, usually called the "materials" inventory

2. Partially completed units on the production floor, known as the "in process" inventory

3. Completed units in the warehouse ready for sale, called the "finished goods" inventory

### FINANCIAL STATEMENTS AND GENERAL ACCOUNTING FOR A MANUFACTURING CONCERN

If a manufacturing concern has only financial accounting records, its statements must be prepared on the basis of information obtained from the general accounts and periodic inventory counts. The physical inventory of materials can be valued on the basis of purchase invoice prices, but the valuations established for the in process and finished goods inventories must include the costs of direct labor and manufacturing expenses, as well as material costs. When adequate cost records are not available, the amounts included in the valuation of the in process and finished goods inventories must be estimated.

For purposes of illustration, assume that the selected general ledger accounts presented below are for the Todd Company, a manufacturing concern that maintains a general accounting system with a subsidiary ledger for manufacturing expenses and prepares statements on a calendar year basis.

| Materials Inventory | In Process Inventory | Finished Goods Inventory |
|---|---|---|
| 1-1-57   $60,000 | 1-1-57   $52,000 | 1-1-57   $85,000 |

| Material Purchases | Direct Labor | Manufacturing Expenses |
|---|---|---|
| Total for 1957   $80,000 | Total for 1957   $158,000 | Total for 1957   $124,000 |

Physical inventory counts were made as of the last day of the year and the following valuations established:

Materials inventory
    (per invoice prices)                 $67,000
In process inventory (estimated)      65,000
Finished goods inventory
    (estimated)                    95,000
("Materials" is customarily intended to include both raw materials and purchased parts)

The first of three schedules which support the income statement can be prepared entirely from the inventory and account data provided above. This schedule (Exhibit 11-1) illustrates the computation of the cost of materials used during a period. It is essentially the same as determining the cost of goods sold for a trading firm; i.e., the amount purchased is added to the amount on hand at the beginning, and the ending inventory is deducted from the total available to find the amount sold or used.

EXHIBIT 11-1

TODD COMPANY

Schedule of Materials Used for the Year 1957

| | |
|---|---:|
| Materials inventory, Jan. 1, 1957. . . . . . . . . . | $ 60,000 |
| Material purchases. . . . . . . . . . . . . . . . . . . . . . | 180,000 |
| Available for use. . . . . . . . . . . . . . . . . . . . . . . . | $240,000 |
| Materials inventory, Dec. 31, 1957. . . . . . . . . | 67,000 |
| Cost of materials used. . . . . . . . . . . . . . . . . | $173,000 |

The Manufacturing Expenses account shown in the preceding example is a general ledger control account. The detail in Exhibit 11-2 was taken from the individual accounts in the subsidiary ledger for manufacturing expenses.

EXHIBIT 11-2

TODD COMPANY

Schedule of Manufacturing Expenses for the Year 1957

| | |
|---|---:|
| Indirect labor. . . . . . . . . . . . . . . . . . . . . . . . . . . . . . . . . . . . . . . . . . . . . . . . . . . . | $ 39,000 |
| Factory supplies. . . . . . . . . . . . . . . . . . . . . . . . . . . . . . . . . . . . . . . . . . . . . . . . . | 18,600 |
| Factory utilities. . . . . . . . . . . . . . . . . . . . . . . . . . . . . . . . . . . . . . . . . . . . . . . . . | 22,000 |
| Maintenance and repairs on machinery and equipment. . . . . . . . . . | 12,400 |
| Depreciation—factory building. . . . . . . . . . . . . . . . . . . . . . . . . . . . . . . . . . | 9,800 |
| Depreciation—machinery and equipment. . . . . . . . . . . . . . . . . . . . . . | 14,000 |
| Taxes and insurance on manufacturing facilities. . . . . . . . . . . . . . . . | 8,200 |
| Total manufacturing expenses. . . . . . . . . . . . . . . . . . . . . . . . . . . . . . | $124,000 |

The two schedules (Exhibits 11-1 and 11-2) provide information on the costs added to production during 1957 in the form of materials and manufacturing expenses. Direct labor cost added can be obtained from the general ledger accounts, as can the amount of the opening in process inventory. After the ending in process inventory valuation has been established, all the necessary data are available for computation of the cost of units that were completed; i.e., the cost of unfinished units on hand at the beginning, plus the costs added to production during the period, less the cost of unfinished units on hand at the end, equals the cost of goods manufactured ("goods" are not considered manufactured until they are finished and ready for sale).

After the cost of goods manufactured has been computed (Exhibit 11-3), it is possible to develop the cost of goods sold, as shown on the income statement presented in Exhibit 11-4. The other data on the income statement are similar to those for a trading enterprise. (Returns, allow-

Exhibit 11-3

Todd Company

Schedule of Cost of Goods Manufactured for the Year 1957

| | | | |
|---|---|---:|---:|
| In process inventory, Jan. 1, 1957 | | | $ 52,000 |
| Costs added to production: | | | |
| Materials used* | | $173,000 | |
| Direct labor | | 158,000 | |
| Manufacturing expenses* | | 124,000 | 455,000 |
| Total costs in process | | | $507,000 |
| In process inventory, Dec. 31, 1957 | | | 65,000 |
| Cost of goods manufactured | | | $442,000 |

\* See supporting schedules for details.

Exhibit 11-4

Todd Company

Income Statement for the Year 1957

| | | | |
|---|---:|---:|---:|
| Sales, net | | | $540,000 |
| Cost of goods sold: | | | |
| Finished goods inventory Jan. 1, 1957 | | $ 85,000 | |
| Cost of goods manufactured* | | 442,000 | |
| Available for sale | | $527,000 | |
| Finished goods inventory Dec. 31, 1957 | | 95,000 | 432,000 |
| Gross profit | | | $108,000 |
| Selling expenses: | | | |
| Sales salaries | $17,000 | | |
| Advertising | 10,400 | | |
| Other | 4,600 | $ 32,000 | |
| Administrative expenses: | | | |
| Office salaries | $19,300 | | |
| Depreciation—office facilities | 2,000 | | |
| Taxes and insurance—office facilities | 2,200 | | |
| Other | 2,500 | 26,000 | 58,000 |
| Net profit | | | $ 50,000 |

\* See the supporting schedule for details.

ances, discounts, and numerous other typical accounts have been omitted in order to simplify the example.)

General accounting records alone will *not* reveal if various products are being manufactured profitably. The income statement of the Todd Company, for example, shows a net profit of $50,000; but if the company manufactures ten different products, six of them may have been produced and sold at a profit of $80,000 while the other four were produced and sold at a loss of $30,000. Only additional records provide product costs that can be compared with related sales prices. These same records can also be employed as a means of analyzing changes in efficiency and as a means of indicating needed improvements, such as alterations in product design, changes in plant layout, etc.

The balance sheet for the Todd Company would be similar to those prepared for most trading concerns, except that the current asset section would include three inventories, materials inventory, in process inventory, and finished goods inventory, rather than only one merchandise inventory.

## DETAILED COST RECORDS

Product cost accounting consists of the records and procedures necessary to develop various unit costs and other manufacturing control data. These records and procedures are in addition to the general accounting system, for cost accounting does not replace financial accounting. A manufacturing concern may have only a financial accounting system or both financial and cost accounting systems. If a manufacturing firm has both systems, all cost data that appear in the detailed cost records must also appear in the general records in summary form (unless the firm has a "statistical" cost system which is not integrated with the general ledger). In other words, the cost accounting records contain a detailed "breakdown" of certain costs that appear in the general ledger in summary form.

### Material Costs

Raw materials are usually considered as materials that are to be shaped, formed, or altered in the production processes. Sheet steel in metal fabrication and crude oil in refining are examples of raw materials. Purchased parts normally are assembled or shaped components that can be used in the form in which they are acquired, e.g., motors and bodies purchased by an automobile assembly plant. Major components, such as car motors, are sometimes referred to as purchased subassemblies. All of these, however, fall under the broad classification of "materials," as the word is employed in accounting.

In a complete cost accounting system, a stock ledger card is maintained for each significant item of material that is acquired. These cards show both quantities and dollar amounts for the materials acquired, issued, and on hand. The dollar costs applied to the items issued from stock may be charged on the basis of the FIFO (first-in first-out), LIFO (last-in first-out), or average cost methods. When the FIFO method of costing is employed, materials issued are charged out on the basis of the first or earliest prices that have not yet been used to cost materials issued. Under the LIFO method, the last or latest cost prices not yet applied are charged to current issues of materials. In a period of rising prices the FIFO method will normally result in a relatively lower cost of materials used and the LIFO method in a relatively higher cost. When prices are falling, the cost of materials used will be lower if the LIFO method is utilized rather than the FIFO method.

If the average method of costing materials is adopted, a new average is computed each time there is a purchase, and the current average is used to cost materials issued. The average cost method is frequently employed because the application of costs from the detailed stock ledger cards is somewhat simpler than if FIFO or LIFO is employed, and also because this method provides unit costs that are influenced by both "first" and "last" prices. The average cost method will, during a period of changing prices, customarily produce a cost of materials used that is between the costs computed under FIFO and LIFO. A perpetual inventory stock ledger card with average costs is illustrated in Exhibit 11-5.

EXHIBIT 11-5

| Stock Ledger Card | | | | | | | | | |
|---|---|---|---|---|---|---|---|---|---|
| Description: Item X | | | | | | | Stock Number A-600 | | |
| 1958 date | Received | | | Issued | | | On hand | | |
| | Quantity | Unit cost | Amount | Quantity | Unit cost | Amount | Quantity | Unit cost | Amount |
| 1-1 | | | | | | | 60 | $1.10 | $ 66.00 |
| 1-10 | 100 | $1.06 | $106.00 | | | | 160 | 1.075 | 172.00 |
| 1-18 | | | | 120 | $1.075 | $129.00 | 40 | 1.075 | 43.00 |
| 1-20 | 100 | 1.09 | 109.00 | | | | 140 | 1.086 | 152.00 |
| 1-27 | | | | 90 | 1.086 | 97.74 | 50 | 1.086 | 54.26 |

Unit costs on materials received would be taken from the purchase invoices, e.g., $1.06 and $1.09 as shown above. The quantity purchased is added to the quantity on hand (60 plus 100 equals 160); the total cost of the materials purchased is added to the cost of what is on hand ($106 plus $66 equals $172); and the dollar amount on hand is divided by the quantity on hand to compute the *average unit cost* ($172 divided by 160 equals $1.075 each). Materials issued are costed on the basis of the last unit cost shown under the "on hand" or "balance" column. This cost is entered on a material requisition, which serves as an original record of the materials withdrawn from stock. An example is presented in Exhibit 11-6.

When materials are first received, the purchase invoices provide data for both the journal entries and the amounts to be entered on the stock ledger cards. The entry in general journal form would be as shown below:

Materials Inventory x
    Accounts Payable—A. B. Co. x
(Credit purchase of materials)

EXHIBIT 11-6

| Material Requisition | | | |
|---|---|---|---|
| Requisition No. 86 | | Job Order No. 61 | |
| Description | Quantity | Unit cost | Total |
| Item X | 120 | 1.075 | 129.00 |
| Signed    A. Foreman | | Date    1-4-58 | |

At the end of each month, a summary of the material requisitions would show the dollar amounts charged to the various job lots (or processes) and the total dollar amount of all materials issued. This total serves as the basis for a general journal entry such as the following:

Goods in Process                           x
    Materials Inventory                        x
  (Cost of materials used this month)

These entries indicate that all materials received are charged, and all materials issued are credited, to the Materials Inventory control account. At the same time the perpetual inventory stock ledger cards show the corresponding detail as being "received" and "issued." The sum of all the dollar balances on the stock ledger cards should, consequently, be equal to the balance of the inventory control account in the general ledger.

Materials issued may be classed as either "direct" or "indirect." Most materials that become a part of the finished product are called "direct materials," e.g., lumber used in manufacturing furniture. Those incidental materials that are necessary to production, but generally do not become a part of the product are known as "indirect materials," e.g., sandpaper used in manufacturing furniture.

*Direct Labor Costs*

The payroll entry for a manufacturing company might appear as entered below in general journal form:

Direct Labor                               8,000
Indirect Labor                             1,500
Sales Salaries                             2,800
Office Salaries                            2,700
    Wages Payable (or Cash)                        13,100
    Income Taxes Withheld                           1,525
    FOASI Withheld                                    375
(Payroll for period)

In a product cost accounting system the labor costs must be accumulated by individual job lots or processes, as well as in summary form in the general ledger. To accomplish this, each employee who works directly on the product must keep "job time tickets" which indicate the amount of time he has worked on each job lot, or the payroll department must maintain records of the labor hours and cost for each processing department. If job time tickets are used, the indicated hours are multiplied by the appropriate wage rates and the labor costs are then summarized by jobs or processes—just as material requisitions are summarized. The total of all direct labor costs per the time tickets should equal the amount charged to the Direct Labor account on the basis of data from the daily timecards. Direct labor hours and costs per the timecards should be reconciled each day with the hours and costs entered on the labor time tickets. This procedure will localize errors and permit early completion of the summary at the end of the month.

Indirect labor costs customarily consist of the salaries and wages of the factory superintendent, foremen, inspectors, and others who do not work directly on the products but whose services are nevertheless necessary for production purposes.

## Manufacturing Expenses

The total of all manufacturing expenses (sometimes called "indirect" costs) could be allocated to the various units produced with some degree of accuracy at the end of each year, assuming that all such expenses for a twelve-month period were to be spread equitably over all items manufactured during that period. But since the quantity and value of production varies from month to month, it is impractical to charge all of the expenses for one month to the production for that month. Charges for building depreciation, taxes, and insurance, for instance, may be the same each month, but output in July may be twice that in January. Under such circumstances it is generally considered inequitable to charge twice as much of these manufacturing expenses to each unit produced in January as compared with each unit produced in July. If January were a slow month, there also might be a comparatively large amount of maintenance and repair work done in preparation for the busy season. This work would benefit production for many months and should not be charged only to items manufactured in January.

It would, in addition, be extremely difficult to attempt to allocate the actual costs of manufacturing expenses to each group of products *as it is finished*. Unit costs, however, are needed by management as soon as possible after production is finished. To meet this need, the indirect costs are charged to production on the basis of a predetermined rate. Those manufacturing expenses to be charged on the basis of such a rate are usually estimated in advance for the coming year, assuming a certain level of activity. The estimated total is then divided by the total labor hours or labor cost expected at that level of activity. This provides an amount per hour or a percentage of labor cost that can be used to apply the manufacturing expenses to jobs as they are completed. Computations of two *predetermined rates* are illustrated below (the estimated amounts are assumed to be for the coming year):

$$(1) \quad \frac{\text{Estimated manufacturing expenses}}{\text{Estimated direct labor hours}} = \frac{\$54,000}{45,000} = \$1.20/\text{hour}$$

or

$$(2) \quad \frac{\text{Estimated manufacturing expenses}}{\text{Estimated direct labor cost}} = \frac{\$54,000}{\$90,000} = 60\% \text{ of D.L. cost}$$

If a job completed during the next year required 200 direct labor hours at a labor cost of $406, the amount of expense or "burden" to be charged against that particular job would be computed as:

(1)          200 hours × $1.20 per hour = $240

or

(2)          $406 D.L. cost × a 60% burden rate = $243.60

The latter method is the more commonly used since direct labor cost figures are readily available. The labor hours basis is generally more accurate because numerous manufacturing expenses are charged on a time basis, yet many firms do not feel that the additional work involved in summarizing the direct labor hours is worth while. There are several other methods for the computation of predetermined expense rates, but none of them is widely used.

Before estimates can be made of manufacturing expenses and direct labor, it is necessary to estimate the volume of production that will be utilized as the basis for the estimates. The so-called "normal capacity" basis, one of the more commonly employed bases, requires an estimate of the average annual sales for the next several years. Once the sales estimates have been completed, it is then possible to estimate the amount of production that would be required to meet the expected sales demand. Estimated normal (or "average") annual production in units can, subsequently, be converted to direct labor hours and costs necessary for that volume of production. The example below illustrates a simple computation for a factory that manufactures only three products. All figures represent *estimated* data based on an appraisal of what is expected during the next year (or some other future period). It has been assumed that none of the manufacturing expenses are to be charged as "direct" costs; i.e., all of them are to be charged to product lots by use of a predetermined rate.

| Product | Annual production | Hours per unit | Total hours | Average wage | Labor cost |
|---------|-------------------|----------------|-------------|--------------|------------|
| A | 5,000 units | 3 | 15,000 | $2/hr. | $30,000 |
| B | 1,000 units | 10 | 10,000 | 2/hr. | 20,000 |
| C | 4,000 units | 5 | 20,000 | 2/hr. | 40,000 |
| | | | 45,000 | | $90,000 |

Next to be estimated is the amount of indirect costs that will be incurred at a normal capacity of 45,000 direct labor hours per year. If "fixed" expenses such as straight-line depreciation, insurance, and taxes on manufacturing facilities are estimated at $31,500 per year, and "variable" expenses such as power, supplies and indirect labor are estimated at $22,500 per year, the predetermined rate would be computed as follows (assuming that direct labor hours are to be the basis for application of the manufacturing expenses):

$$\text{Fixed expenses:} \quad \frac{\$31,500}{45,000} = 70 \text{ cents per hour}$$

$$\text{Variable expenses:} \frac{\$22,500}{45,000} = 50 \text{ cents per hour}$$

$$\text{Predetermined rate} \qquad \$1.20 \text{ per hour}$$

## Overapplied and Underapplied Expense

The amount of manufacturing expense applied on the basis of a predetermined rate will always be different from the amount of expense actually incurred, because (1) actual production volume will not be the same as the estimated normal capacity, (2) the prices paid will seldom be exactly the same as estimated, and (3) the degree of efficiency will vary from that expected. Assume, for example, with the estimates discussed in the previous section, that the actual manufacturing expenses amount to $58,000 in a year when there were 40,000 direct labor hours worked, and, consequently, $48,000 charged to the In Process account (40,000 × $1.20). The Manufacturing Expenses control account would appear, in summary, as follows:

Manufacturing Expenses

| Actual: | | Applied to cost of product: | |
|---------|---|-----------------------------|---|
| Fixed expenses | $31,500 | 40,000 × $0.70 = | $28,000 |
| Variable expenses | 26,500 | 40,000 × 0.50 = | 20,000 |
| Total cost | $58,000 | 40,000 × $1.20 = | $48,000 |

Manufacturing expenses have been underapplied by $10,000 ($58,000 expense actually incurred less $48,000 applied on the basis of the predetermined rate of $1.20 per hour). The amount underapplied can be analyzed as follows:

Idle capacity loss:
Fixed costs incurred.......................................... $31,500
Less fixed costs applied (40,000 × $0.70)..................... $28,000  $ 3,500
Budget variation loss:
Variable costs incurred...................................... $26,500
Variable costs applied (40,000 × $0.50)..................... 20,000   6,500
Amount underapplied.......................................... $10,000

The idle capacity loss of $3,500 indicates that the plant operated at 5,000 hours less than normal capacity and that this amount should be charged on the income statement as a "loss" rather than as a product cost. Should the plant operate at more than the normal capacity of 45,000 direct labor hours, there would be an "overcapacity gain," and the fixed costs would then be considered overapplied.

The variable expenses in this illustration were also underapplied. It had been determined that variable expenses should be 50 cents per direct labor hour worked, regardless of the volume of production, for the total of variable expenses supposedly varies in proportion to the volume of production and should, therefore, remain constant on a per unit basis. But the $26,500 of costs actually incurred exceeded the amount of variable expense applied by $6,500. If the difference of $6,500 was due to inefficiencies and waste, the amount should appear on the income statement as a loss. If some of the original estimates were incorrect, the resulting differences should be included as a part of the cost of goods manufactured. Prices paid cannot ordinarily be controlled and price increases should be charged as manufacturing cost and not as a part of the budget variation loss. Only a great deal of analysis can determine the various causes underlying a "budget variation" and, consequently, such additional work is usually performed only if the variation is significant. When relatively insignificant, the entire amount is often included in the cost of goods manufactured without analyzing the causes of the variation

### JOB ORDER COST ACCOUNTING

In some businesses, such as machine shops or furniture factories, numerous "jobs" or "job lots" may pass through the various departments or work centers during a relatively short time. Employees in a lathe department, for instance, might be working on several different products simultaneously. Under such circumstances the different products are processed in job lots. Each job lot is a certain number of like units in process, and each lot is represented by a numbered job order cost sheet.

*Summary Cost Records and Accounting Entries*

A job order cost sheet is used to accumulate costs for each job lot that is manufactured. In its simplest form it is a "recap" of the material and labor costs that have been accumulated on separate summaries, such as those following, plus the amount of manufacturing expense applied on the basis of a predetermined rate.

EXHIBIT 11-7

| Summary of Material Requisitions | | | | | | January 1958 |
|---|---|---|---|---|---|---|
| Date 1958 | Req. No. | Job Order Numbers | | | | |
| | | 59 | 60 | 61 | 62 | 63 | Total |

| Date 1958 | Req. No. | 59 | 60 | 61 | 62 | 63 | Total |
|---|---|---|---|---|---|---|---|
| 1-2 | 84 | $ 64.00 | | | | | $ 64.00 |
| 1-3 | 85 | | $ 57.00 | | | | 57.00 |
| 1-4 | 86 | | | $129.00 | | | 129.00 |
| { (and so on) | | | | | | | { |
| Totals: | | $214.70 | $629.50 | $410.00 | $541.80 | $1,100.00 | $2,896.00 |

The summary of material requisitions (Exhibit 11-7) serves not only to accumulate material costs by job lots but also to provide the total for all materials used during the period. The following journal entry would be based on this total:

| | | |
|---|---|---|
| Goods in Process | 2,896 | |
| Materials Inventory | | 2,896 |
| (Materials put into process during January) | | |

EXHIBIT 11-8

| Summary of Job Time Tickets | | | | | | | | January 1958 |
|---|---|---|---|---|---|---|---|---|
| Date 1958 | Job Order Numbers | | | | | | | |
| | 57 | 58 | 59 | 60 | 61 | 62 | 63 | Total |

| Date 1958 | 57 | 58 | 59 | 60 | 61 | 62 | 63 | Total |
|---|---|---|---|---|---|---|---|---|
| 1-2 | $21.70 | $54.60 | $ 11.80 | | | | | $ 88.10 |
| 1-3 | | 9.10 | 49.00 | $ 33.20 | | | | 91.30 |
| 1-4 | | | 19.65 | 24.60 | $ 42.30 | | | 86.55 |
| { (and so on) | | | | | | | | { |
| Totals: | $21.70 | $63.70 | $306.10 | $511.04 | $600.00 | $486.30 | $741.16 | $2,730.00 |

The summary of job time tickets (Exhibit 11-8) can also serve as the basis for a general journal entry, as well as the source of direct labor costs applied to each job lot during the period. The entry for the total direct labor cost would be:

| | | |
|---|---|---|
| Goods in Process | 2,730 | |
| Direct Labor | | 2,730 |
| (Direct labor put into process during January) | | |

The amount of direct labor cost per the summary should, of course, agree with the amount charged to the Direct Labor account during the period. Sixty per cent of the direct labor cost would be the basis for the application of manufacturing expense:

| | | |
|---|---|---|
| Goods in Process | 1,638 | |
| Manufacturing Expense | | 1,638 |
| (60% of $2,730, the direct labor cost for January) | | |

Assume that job lot number 61 has been completed and a job order sheet prepared. After the pertinent data *from the preceding summaries* and the applied manufacturing expense have been entered, the job order cost sheet would appear as illustrated in Exhibit 11-9:

EXHIBIT 11-9

| The MFG Company—Job Cost Sheet | | | Job Order No. 61 | |
|---|---|---|---|---|
| Product: B | | | Date started: 12-21-57 | |
| Quantity: 100 | | | Date completed: 1-19-58 | |

| Costs added: | Dec. 1957 | Jan. 1958 | | Total |
|---|---|---|---|---|
| Material costs | $206.00 | $ 410.00 | | $ 616.00 |
| Direct labor costs | 250.00 | 600.00 | | 850.00 |
| Mfg. expense applied (60% of D.L. cost) | 150.00 | 360.00 | | 510.00 |
| Total cost | $606.00 | $1,370.00 | | $1,976.00 |

Unit cost: $1,976.00 ÷ 100 = $19.76

The job cost sheet (Exhibit 11-9) shows that job lot number 61 was in process as of December 31, 1957, and was valued at $606 as of that date, and that $1,370 of additional cost was added in January before the job was completed. After completion in January this cost sheet and others representing finished jobs would have been pulled from the in process files and summarized as follows:

Summary of Job Lots Completed during January, 1958

| Job | Cost |
|---|---|
| 57 | $ 249.60 |
| 58 | 174.00 |
| 59 | 842.70 |
| 60 | 1,597.20 |
| 61 | 1,976.00 |
| (and so on) | |
| Total cost | $8,200.00 |

A similar summary could be made of the "in process" job order cost sheets in order to reconcile these with the balance of the Goods in Process account.

The total cost of jobs completed throughout the month would be transferred to the Finished Goods Inventory account by a general journal entry:

```
Finished Goods                          8,200
     Goods in Process                          8,200
(Cost of jobs completed in January)
```

In the case of job order number 61, the following information would be transcribed from the job order cost sheet to the "received" column on the appropriate stock ledger card for finished goods: quantity of 100, unit cost of $19.76, and total cost of $1,976. The unit costs used to charge out the cost of finished goods issued would depend upon the method of costing employed, probably FIFO, LIFO, or average costs. If a summary of the cost of goods sold showed a total of $8,600 for the month of January, a general journal entry would reflect the change as follows:

```
Cost of Goods Sold                      8,600
     Finished Goods                            8,600
(Cost of finished units sold during January)
```

Any significant variation in manufacturing expense caused by a difference between actual and normal capacity would be charged or credited to an account such as Capacity Loss or Gain and shown on the income statement as a separate item. Any significant variation caused by waste and inefficiency would also be recorded and presented as a separate item, but any difference resulting from inaccuracies in the original estimates, of course, should be included directly in the cost of goods manufactured.

## The Flow of Products and Costs

Materials are received and stored in the stock rooms and issued to the production floor on the basis of requisitions. While in process, direct labor and manufacturing facilities are used to convert the materials to finished goods. When completed, the items are transferred to the finished goods warehouse to await sale. This flow can be diagramed as follows, assuming a very simple plant layout:

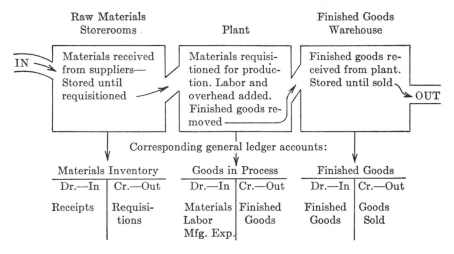

The illustration shows how the flow of materials and products within the factory is reflected by a corresponding flow of costs within the general ledger accounts. (These costs must usually be obtained from summaries of requisitions, time tickets, completed job orders, and cost of goods sold.) Balances of the three general ledger control accounts shown above should always be in agreement with the related subsidiary detail; i.e., Materials Inventory and the perpetual inventory of materials should always be in agreement, Goods in Process and a schedule of costs from the "in process" job order cost sheets should agree, and Finished Goods should reconcile with the perpetual inventory of finished goods. The flow chart shown in Exhibit 11-10 illustrates these points; this exhibit should be examined before the discussion of process costs.

## PROCESS COST ACCOUNTING

Job order cost accounting must be employed in plants or departments where a variety of products may pass through the same work centers simultaneously. In departments where *only one* product passes through for an extended period of time, it is normally more practicable and convenient to adopt process cost accounting. Where all departments within one plant have this characteristic, the costs for the entire manufacturing operation can be recorded on the basis of process cost accounting; e.g., sawmills, refineries, and cigarette, paint, and chemical manufacturers usually need only process costing. Many plants, however, must use both job order and process costing, since some departments will process only one product and other departments will regularly process a variety of work.

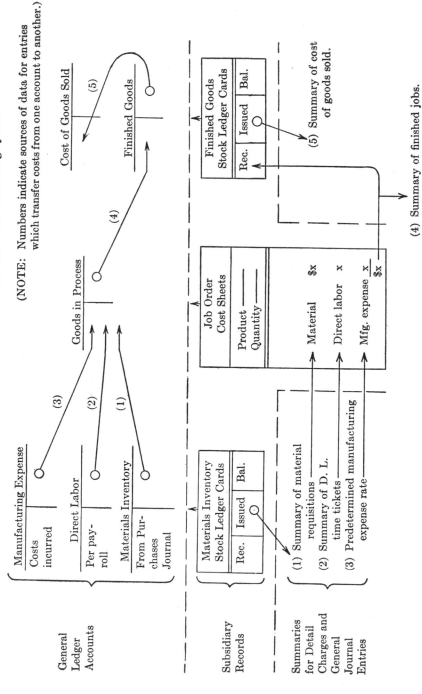

Exhibit 11-10. Diagram of the Flow of Costs in a Job Order Cost Accounting System

(NOTE: Numbers indicate sources of data for entries which transfer costs from one account to another.)

General Ledger Accounts

Manufacturing Expense
Costs incurred

Direct Labor
Per pay-roll

Materials Inventory
From Pur-chases Journal

Goods in Process

Cost of Goods Sold

Finished Goods

Subsidiary Records

Materials Inventory Stock Ledger Cards
| Rec. | Issued | Bal. |
| --- | --- | --- |

Job Order Cost Sheets

Product
Quantity

| Material | $x |
| --- | --- |
| Direct labor | x |
| Mfg. expense | x |
| | $x |

Finished Goods Stock Ledger Cards
| Rec. | Issued | Bal. |
| --- | --- | --- |

Summaries for Detail Charges and General Journal Entries

(1) Summary of material requisitions
(2) Summary of D. L. time tickets
(3) Predetermined manufacturing expense rate

(4) Summary of finished jobs.

(5) Summary of cost of goods sold.

*Accumulation by Processes of Costs for a Period*

Costs under a job order system are accumulated by individual job lots on the basis of job order cost sheets. In a processing plant where one product continually passes through the same process or processes, there is usually no practical means or need to separate the continuous flow into job lots. Instead of collecting costs by job lots, they are accumulated by processes (or departments) for a period of time. When total costs for one process for a given period have been accumulated, it is then possible to divide the total costs by the number of units produced in order to compute the unit cost for a period. Process costs are, therefore, *average unit costs* for a given period of time. If one product is processed continuously through one department during a period of one month, there can be only one average unit cost. Under job order production there would be ten different unit costs if a product were manufactured in ten different job lots during one month.

There is customarily less detailed paper work necessary when process costing can be employed, since costs can be charged to a relatively few processes rather than to numerous job lots. Consequently, the process, rather than the job lot, becomes the key to the system. All materials, direct and indirect, can be requisitioned by process or department. There is no need to separate direct and indirect materials, for under job order systems material is distinguished as indirect only because it cannot be associated with specific job lots. For the same reason, direct and indirect work are often combined and charged to the processes simply as "labor." If all materials and labor, direct and indirect, are charged directly to the processes, other manufacturing costs can be charged to the product on the basis of a predetermined rate. This assumption has been followed in the illustration which follows.

*Accounting Entries for Application of Costs*

The form for the accumulation of costs by processes (or departments) can be identified as a "production report." An illustrative problem will serve to explain how costs are collected for this report. Assume, first, the following general journal entries for the XYZ Chemical Company at the end of April, 1958: In the cost accounting for this company all labor costs are accumulated originally in departmental labor accounts and then transferred to the "process" accounts. Actual manufacturing expenses, other than indirect materials and labor, are also charged to departmental accounts. The amounts applied to production are then credited to the departmental expense accounts and debited to the process accounts. In this way it is possible to develop the amount of manufacturing expense which is under- or overapplied for *each* department or process.

| | | |
|---|---|---|
| Process 1 | 36,000 | |
| Process 2 | 8,500 | |
|     Materials Inventory | | 44,500 |

(Direct and indirect materials
withdrawn from stock
for use in production
per the monthly summary
of material requisitions)

| | | |
|---|---|---|
| Process 1 | 27,750 | |
| Process 2 | 23,000 | |
|     Labor—Process 1 | | 27,750 |
|     Labor—Process 2 | | 23,000 |

(Direct and indirect labor costs
within the two process departments
per charges made
by the payroll department)

| | | |
|---|---|---|
| Process 1 | 16,650 | |
| Process 2 | 17,250 | |
|     Manufacturing Exp.—Process 1 | | 16,650 |
|     Manufacturing Exp.—Process 2 | | 17,250 |

(Process 1: predetermined rate
of 60% times labor cost of $27,750
equals $16,650.
Process 2: predetermined rate
of 75% times labor cost of $23,000
equals $17,250)

During the month a certain number of units were completed in Process 1 and a certain number were transferred to Process 2. In the same period a number of units were completed in Process 2 and a certain number transferred to finished goods. It is therefore necessary that the accounting records reflect a corresponding transfer of costs from process to process and from process to finished goods. Before journal entries can be made to reflect these changes, it is necessary to compute unit production costs to be used in the evaluation of the amounts transferred and also of the amounts still in process. The flow chart shown in Exhibit 11-11 illustrates both the sources for the cost data and the subsequent transfers of these costs.

*Computation of Equivalent Units*

The number of "units to be accounted for" depends upon the amount of basic material that was on hand at the beginning plus the amount that has been added to operations during the period. In this example it has been assumed that all material is introduced at the very beginning of the operation, that there was enough material in process when the month began to manufacture 2,000 finished units, and that enough was added for 18,000 more. In other words all material costs are introduced as soon

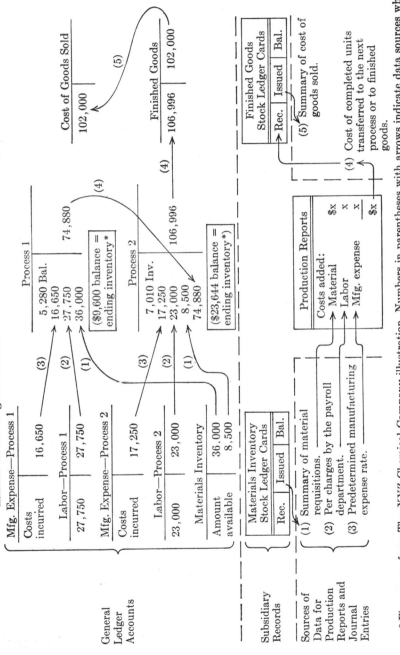

Eхнiвiт 11-11. Diagram of the Flow of Costs in a Process Accounting System*

**General Ledger Accounts**

Mfg. Expense—Process 1

| Costs incurred | 16,650 |
|---|---|

Labor—Process 1

| 27,750 | 27,750 |
|---|---|

Mfg. Expense—Process 2

| Costs incurred | 17,250 |
|---|---|

Labor—Process 2

| 23,000 | 23,000 |
|---|---|

Materials Inventory

| Amount available | 36,000 | 8,500 |
|---|---|---|

Process 1

| | 5,280 Bal. | |
|---|---|---|
| (3) | 16,650 | |
| (2) | 27,750 | |
| (1) | 36,000 | 74,880 |

($9,600 balance = ending inventory*)

Process 2

| | 7,010 Inv. | |
|---|---|---|
| (3) | 17,250 | |
| (2) | 23,000 | |
| (1) | 8,500 | |
| | 74,880 | 106,996 |

($23,644 balance = ending inventory*)

Cost of Goods Sold

| 102,000 | |
|---|---|

(5)

Finished Goods

| (4) | 106,996 | 102,000 |
|---|---|---|

**Subsidiary Records**

Materials Inventory Stock Ledger Cards

| Rec. | Issued | Bal. |
|---|---|---|

Production Reports

| Costs added: | |
|---|---|
| Material | $x |
| Labor | x |
| Mfg. expense | x |
| | $x |

Finished Goods Stock Ledger Cards

| Rec. | Issued | Bal. |
|---|---|---|

**Sources of Data for Production Reports and Journal Entries**

(1) Summary of material requisitions.
(2) Per charges by the payroll department.
(3) Predetermined manufacturing expense rate.
(4) Cost of completed units transferred to the next process or to finished goods.
(5) Summary of cost of goods sold.

* Figures are from The XYZ Chemical Company illustration. Numbers in parentheses with arrows indicate data sources which are described in bottom portion of diagram.

235

as the materials go into process, but the materials must be converted to finished goods by the application of labor and other costs.

Units in process obviously do not yet have all costs applied; and, to develop a unit production cost, it is necessary to estimate the stage of completion of all unfinished units. The production report for Process 1 (Exhibit 11-12) indicates that the 2,000 units on hand at the beginning of the period included only one-fourth of the labor and expense required for completion in Process 1. These units are assumed to be among the 17,000 completed and transferred during the period, which means that 15,000 units (17,000 less 2,000) were put into process and completed during the period and that the 2,000 units already in process were completed by application of three-fourths the usual labor and overhead (since one-fourth had already been applied during the previous period). The 3,000 "material" units still in process at the end of the month are estimated to include only two-thirds the labor and expense necessary for completion in Process 1—the amount of labor and expense equivalent to that necessary for the production of 2,000 units 100 per cent complete. This gives a total of $(2,000 \times 3/4) + 15,000 + (3,000 \times 2/3)$ or 18,500 equivalent units processed in department 1.

In Process 2 (see Exhibit 11-13) enough material was in process at the beginning of the month to manufacture 1,000 complete units, but only one-half of the labor and expense needed to complete the conversion had been applied. During the month the remaining one-half of the required labor and overhead was added to the opening inventory of 1,000 units— the equivalent of that needed to finish completely 500 units, 13,000 were started and finished, and 4,000 units were estimated to be three-eighths finished at the end of April. This gives a total of $(1,000 \times 1/2) + 13,000 + (4,000 \times 3/8)$ or 15,000 equivalent units processed in April.

## Production Reports and Transfer Entries

After the data have been summarized and computations completed, the production reports serve as the basis for the following general journal entries:

| | | |
|---|---|---|
| Process 2 | 74,880 | |
| Process 1 | | 74,880 |
| (Per the production reports for Process 1— leaving $10,800 in Process 1) | | |
| Finished Goods | 106,996 | |
| Process 2 | | 106,996 |
| (Per the production report for Process 2— leaving $23,644 in Process 2) | | |

The quantity, unit cost, and total cost of completed units, per the

EXHIBIT 11-12
XYZ CHEMICAL COMPANY
Production Report—Process 1
April, 1958

### Units

| Units to be accounted for: | | Units accounted for: | |
|---|---|---|---|
| In process, April 1 (¼ processed) | 2,000 | Completed and transferred to Process 2 | 17,000 |
| Placed in process in April | 18,000 | Still in process, April 30 (⅔ processed) | 3,000 |
| Total to be accounted for | 20,000 | Total units accounted for | 20,000 |

### Costs

| Costs to be accounted for: | | | Costs accounted for: | |
|---|---|---|---|---|
| Materials in process, April 1 | | $ 4,000 | 2,000 units in process, April 1: | |
| Processing costs on 2,000 units (¼ finished) | | 1,280 | Materials, 2,000 × $2.00 | $ 4,000 |
| Inventory, April 1 | | $ 5,280 | Processing costs to April 1 | 1,280 |
| Materials placed in process in April | | 36,000 | Processing costs in April (¾ of 2,000) × $2.40* | 3,600 |
| Processing costs for April | | | Total cost of first 2,000 units | $ 8,880 |
| Labor | $27,750 | | 15,000 units started and completed: | |
| Manufacturing Expense | 16,650 | 44,400 | Materials, 15,000 × $2.00 | $30,000 |
| | | | Processing costs 15,000 × $2.40 | 36,000 |
| | | | Total cost of 15,000 | $66,000 |
| | | | Total cost of 17,000 units to Process 2 | $74,880 |
| | | | 3,000 units still in process: | |
| | | | Materials, 3,000 × $2.00 | $ 6,000 |
| | | | Processing costs (⅔ × 3,000) × 2.40* | 4,800 |
| | | | Total in process inventory | $10,800 |
| Total costs to be accounted for | | $85,680 | Total costs accounted for | $85,680 |

* Computation of processing costs per unit for April, 1958.

Process 1:

| Equivalent units | | Processing costs | |
|---|---|---|---|
| 2,000 × ¾ = | 1,500 equiv. units | Labor | $27,750 |
| 15,000 × 1 = | 15,000 | Mfg. expense | 16,650 |
| 3,000 × ⅔ = | 2,000 equiv. units | Total proc. cost | $44,400 |
| Total | 18,500 | 44,400/18,500 = $2.40 per unit | |

EXHIBIT 11-13
XYZ CHEMICAL COMPANY
Production Report—Process 2
April, 1958

## Units

| Units to be accounted for: | | Units accounted for: | |
|---|---|---|---|
| In process, April 1 (½ processed)................... | 1,000 | Completed and sent to finished goods.................... | 14,000 |
| Received from Process 1...... | 17,000 | Still in process, April 30 (⅜ completed)................ | 4,000 |
| Total to be accounted for..... | 18,000 | Total accounted for.......... | 18,000 |

## Costs

| Costs to be accounted for: | | | Costs accounted for: | | |
|---|---|---|---|---|---|
| Materials in process, April 1: | | | 1,000 units in process, April 1: | | |
| From Process 1............$ | 4,760 | | Materials in process........ | $ | 5,260 |
| Added in Process 2........ | 500 | | Processing costs to April 1.. | | 1,750 |
| Processing costs on 1,000 (½ completed)............ | 1,750 | | Processing costs for April: (½ of 1,000) × 2.68⅓*)... | | 1,342 |
| Inventory in process, April 1................ $ | | 7,010 | Total cost of first 1,000 units................. | $ | 8,352 |
| Materials placed in process in April | | | 13,000 units started and completed: | | |
| From Process 1............ | 74,880 | | Materials, 13,000 × $4.9047† | $ | 63,761 |
| Added in Process 2........ | 8,500 | | Processing costs, 13,000 × 2.68⅓............... | | 34,883 |
| Processing costs for April: | | | Total cost of 13,000 units. | $ | 78,644 |
| Labor........... $23,000 | | | Total cost of 14,000 units to | | |
| Mfg. Expense..... 17,250 | 40,250 | | finished goods............. | | $106,996 |
| | | | 4,000 units still in process 2: | | |
| | | | Materials, 4,000 × $4.9047. | $ | 19,619 |
| | | | Processing costs (⅜ of 4,000) × 2.68⅓............. | | 4,025 |
| | | | Total cost still in process.. | $ | 23,644 |
| Total costs to be accounted for. | $130,640 | | Total costs accounted for..... | | $130,640 |

* Computation of processing costs per unit for April, 1958.

Process 2:

| Equivalent units | | Processing costs | |
|---|---|---|---|
| 1,000 × ½ = | 500 equiv. units | Labor | $23,000 |
| 13,000 × 1 = 13,000 | | Mfg. expenses | 17,250 |
| 4,000 × ⅜ = | 1,500 equiv. units | Total proc. cost | $40,250 |
| Total | 15,000 | 40,250/15,000 = $2.68⅓ per unit | |

† Materials costs on 17,000 units started in April:

| | | |
|---|---|---|
| Costs from Process 1 | $74,880 | Cost per unit: |
| Added at beginning of 2 | 8,500 | $83,380/17,000 = $4.9047 |
| Total for 17,000 units | $83,380 | |

production report for the last process, are entered on the finished goods stock ledger cards. Unit costs so recorded could then be charged out of finished goods on the basis of the FIFO, LIFO, or average cost method for the cost of goods sold. If the XYZ Chemical Company sold finished units with a total cost of $102,000, as shown by a summary for the period, the following journal entry would be made:

        Cost of Goods Sold          102,000
                Finished Goods                  102,000
            (Per the summary for April)

Differences between the actual costs incurred for manufacturing expenses and the amounts applied on the basis of the predetermined "burden" rates would be shown as a separate loss item or included as a part of the cost of goods manufactured, depending upon the circumstances and the extent of the differences. If the differences were so small as to be insignificant, they would probably be charged as part of the cost of goods manufactured for the period.

## STANDARD COSTS

The unit costs developed under job order and process cost systems, such as those illustrated in the preceding sections, can be used for comparison with prior unit costs for the same product and with predetermined estimates of what the costs should be. In this way management can determine if costs are increasing or decreasing and if they appear to be more or less than they should be. When the actual costs incurred are charged to the In Process and Finished Goods Inventories, the cost accounting system is applying "historical" costs, i.e., those costs actually incurred.

Another form of costs—"standard" costs—can also be applied under a job order or process cost accounting system. Estimates are made in advance of what the unit costs *should be* if there is *efficient use* of materials, labor, and other facilities. These standard costs are then used for charges in both the general ledger accounts and in the subsidiary detail—not just for comparison with historical unit costs. Charges to the In Process and Finished Goods accounts are at standard, and any differences between the standard and actual costs are entered in separate variance accounts which identify the cause of the variance. Suppose, for example, that material with a predetermined standard cost of $1,000 is purchased for $1,020. The entry in general journal form to record this would appear as follows:

        Materials Inventory                  1,000
        Materials Price Variance              20
                Vouchers Payable                  **1,020**
            (Actual cost $1,020; standard cost $1,000)

If the standard material cost on a job lot had been set at $800, but the material requisitions showed that $850 had been charged against the job, the following entry would be made (assuming no other material was issued during the period):

| | | |
|---|---|---|
| Goods in Process | 800 | |
| Materials Use Variance | 50 | |
| Materials Inventory | | 850 |
| (Material used $50 in excess of standard) | | |

Labor standards are established on the basis of the time that should be required to do a job and on the hourly wages paid the classification of workers who normally perform the work. Suppose that a job with a standard labor cost of $1,600 has a total actual labor cost of $1,750 charged against it. Analysis reveals that $110 of the variance is the result of over standard hours and that $40 results from the inclusion on the job of several men who are paid more than the standard rate. The journal entry to record the necessary data would be:

| | | |
|---|---|---|
| Goods in Process | 1,600 | |
| Labor Efficiency Variance | 110 | |
| Labor Rate Variance | 40 | |
| Direct Labor | | 1,750 |
| (To record standard labor cost and variances) | | |

Earlier in the chapter a method for analyzing an overapplied or underapplied manufacturing expense balance was discussed. When standard costs are employed the analysis becomes slightly more complicated, since a portion of the under- or overapplied balance results from the difference between the actual and standard hours. For purposes of illustration assume the following for a manufacturing firm that employs standard costs:

Normal activity for a period is estimated as 10,000 direct labor hours. At this level of activity it is expected that variable manufacturing expenses will total $6,000. Fixed manufacturing expenses are estimated at $4,000 for each period, regardless of volume. At the end of the current period there have been 9,400 hours actually worked and manufacturing expense of $11,000 actually incurred. Standard hours for the amount produced is 9,000 hours. Under these conditions:

1. Overhead rates are determined as follows:

$$\text{Variable expense rate} = \frac{\$6,000}{10,000} = \$0.60/\text{D.L. hour}$$

$$\text{Fixed expense rate} = \frac{\$4,000}{10,000} = \$0.40/\text{D.L. hour}$$

$$\text{Predetermined rate} \qquad \overline{\$1.00/\text{D.L. hour}}$$

2. The general ledger account is as shown below:

Manufacturing Expenses

| Actually | Applied: |
|---|---|
| incurred: $11,000 | 9,000 × $1 = $9,000 |

(underapplied by $2,000)

3. Analysis of the underapplied balance is as follows:

(a) Budget variation loss:

Expenses actually incurred.............................. $11,000
Assumed to be fixed expense........................... 4,000

Variable expense—actual................................ $ 7,000
Budget allowance at actual:
$0.60 (variable rate) × 9,400 hours =.................. 5,640

Excess of actual variable expenses over budger allowance............ $1,360

(b) Capacity variation loss:

Normal capacity hours................................. 10,000
Hours actually worked................................. 9,400

Idle capacity hours................................. 600
Idle capacity loss:
$0.40 (fixed rate) × 600 hours =.............................. 240

(c) Efficiency variation loss:

Hours actually worked................................ 9,400
Standard hours....................................... 9,000

Over standard hours................................. 400
Efficiency loss:
$1 (predetermined rate) × 400 hours =....................... 400

Underapplied balance....................................... $2,000

4. Journal entries to record the above information would be as follows:

Goods in Process                9,000
    Manufacturing Expenses          9,000
    (To record overhead charged to production
    on an estimated basis)

Budget Variation                1,360
Capacity Variation              240
Efficiency Variation            400
    Manufacturing Expenses          2,000
    (To record variance losses; actual hours were
    less than the normal activity basis but more
    than standard)

Systems with standard costs may be more expensive to install than systems with historical costs, but the additional cost is often more than offset by the greater amount of useful data obtained. In the first place, a detailed, scientific study of costs is required in order to use standards. This in itself may by very beneficial by bringing to light inefficiency and opportunities for improvement. Variances from standard cannot be ignored, because all costs must be accounted for, and when variances are recorded in separate accounts, they serve as "red flags" to warn management that something is amiss.

## SUMMARY

A manufacturing concern with only general financial accounting records can compute the total cost of materials used, the total cost of goods manufactured, and the total cost of goods sold. But, only with a product cost accounting system can such a firm develop unit product costs, including unit costs for material, labor, and manufacturing expense. In departments where various lines of product are processed more or less simultaneously, costs must be charged to job lots and summarized on job order cost sheets. In departments where one product is processed for an extended period of time, costs are usually charged to the process and summarized on production reports. Process costs are, therefore, average costs for the period of time covered by the production reports.

Unit product costs make it possible for management to determine whether some given item is being manufactured at a gain or a loss and whether the costs of production on it are increasing or decreasing. A complete cost system will make it possible to locate changes in efficiency. Standard costs are particularly useful in this respect since any variances from the predetermined estimates of what costs should be are recorded as separate account information. When actual costs are more than standard, the excess may be considered an inefficiency or waste loss which is distinguished as a "variance" on the statements rather than being included as a part of the cost of goods manufactured.

Cost accounting is an extremely complex field and many important phases of the subject have been ignored entirely in this brief discussion. Those elements and principles of costing that are included have been treated in a very rudimentary fashion in order to place emphasis on the relationships between the flow of products within a plant and the flow of costs within the cost accounting records.

The following are typical of many cost subjects that have not been discussed: development of unit costs by departments under a job order system, treatment of by-product costs and income, treatment of cost of units lost in production, estimated cost systems, flexible budgets for use in developing predetermined burden rates, distribution cost accounting systems, break-even analysis, differential cost analysis, allocation of controllable expenses to departments or work centers (so-called "responsibility" accounting), statistical costing, use of consumption reports and formula costing in a process cost system, allocation of service department costs, treatment of semivariable expenses in the computation of predetermined burden rates, etc., and last, but far from least important, the many and varied aspects and problems found in the field of standard costs.

## QUESTIONS

**1.** What information regarding production costs can be supplied by a financial accounting system? What additional information can be derived from a product cost accounting system?

**2.** Can there be a financial accounting system without a cost accounting system? A cost accounting system without a financial accounting system?

**3.** Most manufacturing concerns will usually have three inventories. Why?

**4.** Manufactured items include two major classifications of cost which are not included in the valuation of a merchandise inventory for a retail concern. What are they? What title takes the place of "cost of purchases" on an income statement for a manufacturing firm?

**5.** A business manufactures 100 different products. How can it be determined if each one of these products is being manufactured profitably?

**6.** What internal form is used to record withdrawals from stock and charges to job lots or processes? What is another name for a perpetual inventory card?

**7.** What form is used as the basis for charging direct labor hours to specific job lots?

**8.** Why is it usually considered impractical to charge the cost of manufacturing expenses actually incurred to the specific job lots? How are manufacturing expenses usually charged to job lots?

**9.** Why is it necessary to estimate the volume of production *before* estimates of manufacturing expenses and direct labor are prepared? What is "normal capacity"?

**10.** Manufacturing expenses may be overapplied or underapplied. Explain.

**11.** A predetermined expense rate is often subdivided into what two components? Which costs continue even when a plant is not operating?

**12.** What is the meaning of each of the following terms: Idle capacity loss? Overcapacity gain? Budget variation loss? Budget variation gain?

**13.** Under what conditions is a job order cost accounting system employed? When is a process system used? Can both systems be used in the same plant?

**14.** What information is obtained from summaries of material requisitions and job time tickets? From job cost sheets?

**15.** What form serves as the means of accumulating costs charged to a specific job lot? The unit costs shown on these forms are entered in what perpetual inventory records?

**16.** A manufacturing concern with a complete cost accounting system sells 260 units of a certain product. What form is the source of the cost that is charged to Cost of Goods Sold?

**17.** "Direct" and "indirect" labor and materials are distinguished one from the other in a job order system, but no such distinctions are usually made in a process accounting system. Why?

**18.** What is the meaning of equivalent units? Why are they necessary to the computation of average unit costs in a process system?

**19.** Why is it usually necessary to compute average unit costs for material, labor, and expenses under a process cost accounting system?

**20.** Can standard costs be applied under either a job order or process cost system?

**21.** Do standard costs usually represent what costs are expected to be or what costs should be?

**22.** What is the purpose of the variance accounts described in the discussion of standard costs?

**23.** How do standard costs serve as a basis for "management by exception"?

**24.** Why are variances caused by errors in the original rates or standards usually included as a part of the cost of goods manufactured, rather than as separate items on the statements?

## CHAPTER 12

# ACCOUNTING FOR TAXES

Taxes represent expenditures for services rendered or to be rendered, directly or indirectly, by various governmental agencies. These agencies maintain roads, provide fire and police protection, operate public schools, conserve our natural resources, maintain judicial systems, prepare and preserve public records, and maintain national defense—to name only a few. The "rates" charged for these services are generally not subject to control by business, since managers are seldom in a position to "shop around" for lower tax rates, as they do for lower prices on merchandise and other items. Alert managers may, however, be able to control the *total* amount of taxes, at least within certain restricted limits.

The discussions that follow are not necessarily complete explanations of the various phases of the relatively few tax topics introduced. These discussions are intended only as brief descriptions of some of the provisions of the laws and regulations which are frequently encountered by many taxpayers; they are *not* intended for use as source material in the solution of tax problems.

## Property Taxes

Business units and individuals are normally required to pay property taxes on real and personal property owned by them. Real property usually consists of land and buildings. Personal property is generally considered as movable property, such as inventories, machinery, equipment, and furnishings. The amount of taxes assessed against real and personal property by local authorities is customarily determined by: (1) a mill levy and (2) the property values established for taxing purposes. The amount of tax can be increased or decreased by a change in the mill rate or by a change in the taxable value of the properties—or by changes in both.

In cash basis accounting the property taxes are charged as expense in the year of payment. Under accrual accounting the amount is often prorated (1) to the accounting periods that are within the period between assessment dates or (2) to the accounting periods that are within the period which represents the fiscal year of the taxing body, for example, July 1 to June 30.

*Payroll Taxes*

Before the 1930s an employee who had gross pay of $100 usually received $100 in payment. His employer was not required to withhold taxes, was not required to pay various payroll taxes, and was not required to file numerous payroll tax returns. Today most employers must:

1. Withhold income and social security taxes from gross pay.

2. Provide, with each payroll check, a stub or slip that itemizes the gross amount earned, the amounts withheld, and the net paid.

3. Record this same information on the individual payroll ledger cards which are maintained for each employee.

4. Place in a depository bank, each month or each quarter, the amount withheld during the period for social security and income taxes.

5. File a quarterly return for income and social security taxes withheld. This return includes the name, social security number, and amount of taxable wages for each employee.

6. File a quarterly return for state unemployment insurance. This return must also include names, social security numbers, and taxable wages.

7. File monthly or quarterly returns for workmen's compensation (sometimes called state industrial accident insurance).

8. File an annual return for Federal unemployment insurance.

9. Prepare for each person employed during the calendar year a summary statement (W-2) of gross pay, income tax withheld, and deductions for Federal Old-Age and Survivors Insurance, and forward copies of these completed W-2 forms to the employees and to the Internal · Revenue Service. The latter copies must be accompanied by reconciliation reports.

10. Withhold required amounts for union dues, purchase of bonds, pension plans, etc.

The cost of maintaining adequate payroll records, filing the numerous reports, and paying the various taxes is now an accepted part of business operation and record-keeping procedure.

**Federal Old-Age and Survivors Insurance Tax.** Federal Old-Age and Survivors Insurance taxes are also known as FICA (Federal Insurance and Contributions Act) taxes, as FOAB (Federal old-age benefits) taxes, and as social security taxes (although state unemployment insurance taxes are also, in a sense, "social security" taxes). In 1957 most employers of one or more persons must pay an FOASI tax equal to $2\frac{1}{4}$ per cent of the first $4,200 paid each employee and must withhold a like amount from each employee's pay.

When an employee who has been covered by FOASI retires, he is entitled to monthly old-age benefits; or if a husband dies before retirement age, his wife is entitled to benefits for dependent children under 18 years of age. Wives, husbands, and parents who are sixty-five or over may be entitled to survivors' benefit payments which are based on the earnings of a deceased spouse or child who had worked in covered employment. Women, in cases where the benefits are payable at age sixty-five, e.g., a retired working woman, widow, or retired worker's wife, may elect to start receiving social security payments at age sixty-two. If this election is made, the payments are permanently reduced, except that a wife's reduced benefit is changed to a widow's unreduced benefit if her husband predeceases her.

Maximum benefits payable during recent years were as follows: A retired worker, age sixty-five or over, whose "average monthly wages" were $350 per month or more, would be entitled to $108.50 per month in retirement benefits. If the worker's wife is also sixty-five or over, the couple would receive $162.80 per month. A widow over sixty-five could draw $81.40 per month if her deceased husband had "average monthly wages" of $350 or more. A widow of any age with two or more dependent children under 18 could receive the maximum benefit of $200 per month.

Agricultural workers are covered by old-age and survivors' insurance regulations if they are paid $150 or more in a calendar year by one employer. Nonfarm domestic workers must be covered only if they receive more than $50 in a calendar quarter. Student workers in college living groups are exempt.

Most self-employed persons who have net earnings of $400 or more in a calendar year are required to pay a $3\frac{3}{8}$ per cent FOASI self-employment tax on such earnings, up to a maximum of $4,200; the maximum is decreased by the amount of any wages which were subject to FOASI withholdings. Self-employed individuals who are subject to the tax are eligible for the same benefits as wage earners who work in covered employment.

**Unemployment Insurance Taxes.** The employers' maximum unemployment insurance tax expense is equal to 3 per cent of the first $3,000 of gross wages earned by each employee during a calendar year. Only 0.3 per cent of the gross taxable wages is paid to the Federal government, while 2.7 per cent or less is paid quarterly to the state governments, which actually administer the plans in accordance with Federal law and regulations. A company that has relatively few employees who draw benefits against its reserve may receive a "merit rating" of considerably less than 2.7 per cent. Only those who employ four or more persons are required to pay the annual Federal unemployment tax, but state unemployment taxes must frequently be paid by those who employ only two or three. (Only five states withhold amounts *from employees* for unemployment insurance.)

The weekly benefits drawn by unemployed persons who have been in covered employment will vary according to the wages they have earned. Full-time agricultural labor and certain other specified types of work are not covered by unemployment insurance.

**Workmen's Compensation Insurance.** State governments usually require that specified employers insure their employees for on-the-job accidents and occupational diseases. This insurance, sometimes called state industrial accident insurance, may be carried with the state or, when permitted, with private insurance companies. Premiums are paid in accordance with a schedule which reflects the accident potentials of different classifications of work. An employer, for instance, might pay 7 cents on each $100 of clerical wages and $6 on each $100 of wages paid to men felling trees in the woods. Benefits paid employees will, of course, vary according to the severity and duration of on-the-job injuries or occupational illnesses.

Premium cost is sometimes charged to an insurance expense account. It is, however, considered as part of the total payroll tax expense by many employers, since it is imposed by law and insures the employees, not the employer.

**Accounting Entries for Payroll and Payroll Taxes.** Assume that during 1957 Mr. X employs ten men in work that is subject to both social security taxes and workmen's compensation. The FOASI rate is $2\frac{1}{4}$ per cent, the SUI rate is the 2.7 per cent maximum, the FUI rate is 0.3 per cent, and the workmen's compensation rate for the type of work performed is $2\frac{3}{4}$ per cent. If the withholding tables indicated that a total of $120.50 is to be withheld for Federal income taxes, the payroll entry for $1,000 of gross pay would be as follows:

| | | |
|---|---:|---:|
| Wages | 1,000.00 | |
|     Income Tax Withheld | | 120.50 |
|     FOASI Withheld | | 22.50 |
|     Cash (or Wages Payable) | | 857.00 |

The accrual for the employer's payroll taxes would be as shown below:

| | | |
|---|---:|---:|
| Payroll Taxes Expense | 80.00 | |
|     FOASI Payable | | 22.50 |
|     SUI Payable | | 27.00 |
|     FUI Payable | | 3.00 |
|     Workmen's Compensation Payable | | 27.50 |

## ACCOUNTING FOR FEDERAL INCOME TAXES ON BUSINESS PROFITS

The computation of payroll taxes and the preparation of payroll tax returns require much bookkeeping that would otherwise be unnecessary.

Little additional accounting is usually required, however, for the preparation of Federal income tax returns—*if* a firm maintains a complete set of general financial accounting records. Tax regulations do not describe the methods of bookkeeping that should be maintained, but they do require that each taxpayer keep such records as are necessary for the accurate preparation of returns. Any method of accounting can be used as long as it clearly reflects taxable income and is used consistently.

Each taxpayer, individual or business, should, *at the very minimum,* do the following: (1) use a bank checking account for disbursements and receipts; (2) make a complete record of all assets acquired—description, date acquired, and cost; and (3) retain all canceled checks, receipts, bills, invoices, statements, contracts, notes, deeds, mortgages, and other items that serve as evidence to support transactions.

The discussions that follow deal only with Federal income taxes.

## Methods of Accounting

The cash basis of accounting is generally employed by individuals and many service-type businesses—and it must be used by such taxpayers if no books or records of accounts are maintained. Under this method all expenses, other than expired costs for insurance and fixed assets, are usually reported as of the time payment is made, and all income is reported as of the time cash or its equivalent is received. Some items are, however, considered as income even though cash has not actually been received. Interest on a savings account, for example, is taxable income to the depositor as of the time his account is credited.

When inventories are an income-producing factor, businesses cannot report on the *cash basis* for income tax purposes. In such instances, most firms report on the *accrual basis* by recording all income as of the time it is earned, all significant expenses as of the time incurred, and by taking inventories into account for the computation of cost of goods sold. Business units that sell tangible items on a time-payment plan can, if they so desire, report on the *installment basis* and include gross profit on sales in taxable income as receivables are collected, as explained in Chapter 10.

## Procedures for Reporting Taxable Business Income

All business income is subject to Federal income taxes, but the methods for filing the required information and for payment of taxes vary according to the form of legal organization. This factor has little influence, however, on the computation of net taxable income.

In the case of corporate entities, returns are filed and taxes paid in the name of the business. The annual return filed with the Federal government includes comparative balance sheets, a statement of income and expense, numerous detailed schedules which support summary totals in the statements, and various other data. Corporate income taxes are currently imposed by the Federal government at the rate of 30 per cent on the first $25,000 of net taxable income and at 52 per cent on all amounts over $25,000.

Partners must file an information return (a U.S. Partnership Return of Income), but income taxes on each partner's proportionate share of the profits are paid by him as an individual. The information return for a partnership contains balance sheets, an income statement, and various supporting schedules and sundry data, including a schedule of the partners' shares of the taxable income. Payments to partners in the form of salaries and interest allowances can be deducted as an expense item on the income statement but must then be included on the schedule of partners' shares in taxable income.

A sole proprietorship neither files a return nor pays Federal income tax. Instead, the annual statement of income and expense is included as "schedule C" of the owner's individual return. Balance sheets are not required.

## Accounting Profit and Net Taxable Income

Business profit computed in accordance with generally accepted accounting principles and net taxable income (gross income less allowable deductions) are often the same. Business units must normally include all income received or earned in gross income for tax purposes; and the Federal tax law, as compiled in the Internal Revenue Code, states that "all the ordinary and necessary expenses paid or incurred during the taxable year in carrying on any trade or business" are deductible in the computation of taxable income. Specific provisions of the Code, however, allow certain income to be excluded from gross income and also place limitations on expense items that are customarily considered as "ordinary and necessary." Consequently, accounting profit and net taxable income are sometimes quite different. A few of the factors in the tax law and regulations which cause these differences are briefly described in the paragraphs that follow.

## Capital Gains and Losses on Sales of Capital Assets

"Capital assets" are defined, for income tax purposes, as all assets *other than* (1) inventory items held for resale to customers, (2) real and depreciable property used in a trade or business, (3) accounts and notes receivable acquired in exchange for the sale of stock in trade or for services rendered, and (4) several other items which are rather uncommon. But sales of land and depreciable property used in a trade or business and held more than six months can be treated as sales of capital assets and included in the computation of capital gains and losses, if the gains exceed the losses on the sale of such items. Sales of livestock, unharvested crops, and timber may also be treated as sales of capital assets under certain specified conditions. Gains on the sale of personal property such as jewelry, furniture, and automobiles would be included as capital gains; but losses on the sale of such property would not be included, since such losses are personal and therefore not deductible.

Gains and losses on capital assets held six months or less are *short-term* capital gains and losses; gains and losses on capital assets held more than six months are *long-term* capital gains and losses. If short-term losses exceed short-term gains, there is a *net* short-term capital loss; if long-term gains exceed long-term losses, there is a *net* long-term capital gain. If the reverse were true in each instance, there would be a *net* short-term capital gain and a *net* long-term capital loss. Both net gains and net losses are included in gross income at 100 per cent. But, when net long-term capital gain exceeds net short-term capital loss, 50 per cent of the excess may be deducted by individuals; i.e., only 50 per cent of the excess of net long-term capital gain over net short-term capital loss must be included in taxable income. Several examples follow.

Assume that a taxpayer pays $400 cash for two shares of stock on Jan. 10, 1957. One share is sold for $300 on July 10, 1957 and the other share is sold a day later for the same amount. The $100 gain on the sale of the first share is a short-term gain and must be included in full. The second share was held more than six months, however, and the taxpayer is entitled to a deduction for $50, or one-half the excess of the net long-term capital gain over the net short-term capital loss (in this case zero, since there is a net short-term capital gain rather than a loss). In total, $150 of capital gain is included in the taxable income of the individual.

A taxpayer sells for $3,000 personal jewelry which had been purchased at a cost of $1,000 many years before. In the same tax year he receives $5,400 as payment in full for land that he had acquired as an investment five months earlier at a cost of $6,000. The net long-term capital gain of $2,000 exceeds the net short-term loss of $600 by $1,400 and the taxpayer is entitled to a deduction equal to one-half this excess. Therefore, only $700 must be included in taxable income.

The computation of the amount of long-term capital gain which is included in the taxable income of an individual who is a sole proprietor or partner is illustrated in the schedule at the top of page 251.

The sales of land and depreciable property used in a business are, as mentioned, included in the computation of net capital gain or loss *only* when all such assets which have been held *more* than six months have been sold at a *net gain*. If such assets, considered as a group, have been sold at a loss, the loss is considered an "ordinary" loss (as contrasted with a "capital" loss) and the transactions are excluded from the schedule of

Schedule of Capital Gains and Losses

Sale of assets held more than six months:
Land and depreciable property used in taxpayer's business:

| | | |
|---|---:|---:|
| Gain on sale of land........................................... | | $60,000 |
| Loss on sale of machinery...................................... | | 40,000 |
| Long-term gain............................................ | | $20,000 |

Other business assets:

| | | |
|---|---:|---:|
| Loss on sale of XYZ stock................................. | $8,000 | |
| Gain on sale of ABC bonds............................... | 2,000 | |
| Long-term loss............................................. | | 6,000 |
| Net long-term capital gain...................................... | | $14,000 |

Sale of assets held six months or less:
Personal assets:

| | | |
|---|---:|---:|
| Loss on sale of Todd Company stock........................ | $7,000 | |
| Gain on sale of Machinery Sales Company stock............. | 3,000 | |
| Net short-term capital loss...................................... | | 4,000 |
| Excess of net long-term capital gain over net short-term capital loss........ | | $10,000 |
| Less 50% deduction allowed....................................... | | 5,000 |
| Amount included in taxable income................................. | | $ 5,000 |

capital gains and losses. Also excluded are the ordinary gains and losses on the sales of such assets which have been held for six months or less. Ordinary gains and losses are fully included in the computation of taxable income.

*Alternative Capital Gains Tax of 25 Per Cent*

The effective tax rate *on the excess* of net long-term capital gain over net short-term capital loss is *limited to 25 per cent*. An individual whose upper brackets of income are taxed at more than 50 per cent should compute the so-called "alternative tax" when long-term capital gain is included in taxable income, for 50 per cent of one-half the net long-term capital gain included in income is equal to a 25 per cent effective rate. The computation of the alternative tax is based on a 25 per cent rate for the excess of net long-term capital gains over short-term losses and regular rates for other income.

Assume, for example, that a single taxpayer has net taxable income of $32,000 (including one-half of the $2,000 excess of net long-term capital gain over net short-term capital loss) and that the tax rate on the last $6,000 is currently 62 per cent. One-half of the $2,000 excess (or $1,000) is therefore assumed to be taxed at 62 per cent or $620. When the alternative tax is computed, the taxpayer is required, however, to pay only $500 on the gain; i.e., the tax can be limited to 25 per cent of the $2,000 excess.

The alternative computation should be always made for corporations that are reporting long-term gain, since the minimum corporate income tax rate of 30 per cent exceeds the "alternative" rate of 25 per cent on long-term capital gains, which in the case of a corporation, must be *fully* included in income.

## Capital Loss "Carry-over"

"Capital loss" arises (1) if net long-term capital loss exceeds net short-term gain, (2) if net short-term loss exceeds net long-term gain, or (3) if there is both a net short-term loss and a net long-term loss. The amount of capital loss deductible against ordinary income in any one year is limited to $1,000 for a taxpayer other than a corporation, but any unused deduction can be carried forward for five years and, in each year, can be used as a deduction equal to the amount of capital gains plus $1,000. Assume that in 1957 a taxpayer has an excess of capital losses over capital gains of $4,000. He can deduct $1,000 from ordinary income in 1957 and carry $3,000 forward to 1958, a year in which he has $800 of net long-term capital gain. The capital loss "carry-over" is first applied to offset the $800 capital gain and an additional $1,000 can be deducted from ordinary income. This leaves a loss of $1,200 ($3,000 less $800 and $1,000) to carry forward to 1959.

A corporation may also carry a capital loss forward for five years, but none of it can be used as a deduction from ordinary income. On a corporate return, capital loss can be offset only against capital gain. Suppose, for example, that a corporation had a capital loss of $4,000 in 1957. None of it could be applied against ordinary income, so $4,000 would be carried forward to 1958. If there were $800 of capital gain in 1958, $800 of the amount carried forward could be offset against this gain and $3,200 carried forward to 1959.

Capital gains and losses of a corporation can be included only in the computation of the corporate income tax. Capital gains and losses incurred by a sole proprietorship or partnership are *not* included in the computation of business profit for tax purposes (usually called ordinary income) but are, instead, included in the computation of net taxable income for the owners as individuals.

One of the intended purposes of the long-term gain provisions is to encourage the sale of capital assets, for many taxpayers would be reluctant to sell certain assets if all of the gain were to be taxed at regular rates. These provisions are also a recognition that gain on capital assets usually accrues gradually and that it is, therefore, unfair to tax all the gain from such sales as though it accrued within one year.

## Income from Dividends and Interest

Dividend income received from most domestic corporations should be excluded from the computation of taxable income for a proprietorship or partnership. The amount excluded must then be included on the individual returns, along with other dividend income received directly by the owners. This procedure permits the exclusion of certain amounts from the total of *all* dividend income received by an individual who is a proprietor or partner.

Corporations are allowed to deduct 85 per cent of the amount of dividends received from most domestic corporations which are subject to the income tax. They must, however, include all interest received in taxable income, except that received from obligations of a state or a political subdivision of a state, such as a city. This latter exclusion applies to all taxpayers.

## *Methods of Costing Inventory Items*

Year-end inventories are usually valued on the basis of cost or the lower of cost or market. The "cost" of inventory items, on hand and charged to cost of goods sold, is normally determined on the basis of the first-in first-out method, the last-in first-out method, or the average cost method. All three methods are generally acceptable for both regular accounting purposes and for income tax reporting. High income tax rates during recent years have caused many firms to adopt LIFO costs in order to increase their cost of goods sold and thereby lower taxable profits. (See pages 131 to 134 for more detailed discussion of inventory valuation.)

## *Depreciation Methods*

Depreciation methods acceptable for accounting purposes are generally recognized for income tax purposes, for example, the straight-line method, the machine-hour method, and the unit-of-production method. The straight-line method, the most common of the three, is illustrated by the following example.

A company purchased a new machine for $12,000 on January 1, 1957. The machine has an estimated physical life of five years, but due to expected obsolescence, an estimated useful life of four years, or an annual depreciation rate of 25 per cent. Salvage value at the end of four years is estimated as $2,000. The annual allowable depreciation charge would be computed as follows: $12,000 less $2,000 divided by four years equals $2,500 per year (or $10,000 times 25 per cent equals $2,500).

Tax regulations now allow "accelerated" depreciation methods for *new* assets having a useful life of three years or more. These methods cannot be employed if the assets are acquired secondhand. Under the "declining-balance" method a uniform rate is applied to book value as of the beginning of each period. This rate cannot exceed twice the amount of the straight-line rate and it must be applied to the declining balance over the expected useful life. Declining-balance depreciation charges on a $12,000 machine with a four-year useful life would be as shown below:

| Year | Book value at beginning of year | Rate, per cent | Annual depreciation |
|------|------|------|------|
| 1957 | $12,000 | 50 | $6,000 |
| 1958 | 6,000 | 50 | 3,000 |
| 1959 | 3,000 | 50 | 1,500 |
| 1960 | 1,500 | 50 | 750 |

The above rate of 50 per cent is twice the straight-line rate of 25 per cent (100% ÷ 4 years) and represents the maximum rate allowable. The book value of $750 at the end of 1960 ($1,500 less $750) is the assumed salvage value and no additional depreciation charges would be allowed after 1960.

Another method of obtaining accelerated depreciation charges during the early years is known as the "sum-of-the-years digits" method, which requires that salvage value be deducted from original cost and that the balance be spread over the expected useful life. Assume, for example, that a company buys a new truck for $3,400, that salvage value is estimated as $400, and that the useful life is expected to be five years. Depreciation under this method would then be computed as follows:

| Years | Fraction of depreciable cost | Depreciation |
|------|------|------|
| 1st | $5/15$ of $3,000 | $1,000 |
| 2d | $4/15$ of 3,000 | 800 |
| 3d | $3/15$ of 3,000 | 600 |
| 4th | $2/15$ of 3,000 | 400 |
| 5th | $1/15$ of 3,000 | 200 |
| 15 | $15/15$ | $3,000 |

The two accelerated methods of depreciation described above are often accepted for regular accounting purposes, although there is considerable contention among professional accountants that the use of these methods frequently violates the principle that costs should be expired in accordance with services rendered. However, many businessmen, particularly in new concerns, prefer using the accelerated methods in order to lower taxes during the relatively short periods in which installment payments must be made on new assets.

*Net Operating Loss "Carry-backs" and "Carry-overs"*

A net loss in the operation of a business for one year can be used to offset the income of other years. This so-called "net operating loss" can be carried back two years and carried forward five years. Assume, for example, that a taxpayer who operates a sole proprietorship had a net operating loss of $6,000 in 1957 and that in the years 1955 through 1958 he had no income or deductions other than those from the business. His 1955 net profit of $2,000 from operations could then be offset by the net operating loss "carry-back," leaving $4,000 of carry-back to apply against his net taxable income of $3,000 reported for 1956. The $3,000 consisted of net operating profit from the business of $2,500 and taxable long-term capital gains of $500 (one-half of $1,000). Before the carry-back is applied against income for 1956 the amount of capital gain excluded must be added back; i.e., $500 plus $3,000 equals $3,500, the adjusted income for 1956. After the $4,000 is applied there is a balance of $500 that can be used as a deduction against earned income in 1958. To summarize:

| | | |
|---|---:|---:|
| Net operating loss, 1957 | | $6,000 |
| Net operating loss carry-back to 1955 | | $6,000 |
| Less net operating profit for 1955 | | 2,000 |
| Unused carry-back | | $4,000 |
| Net operating loss carry-back to 1956 | | $4,000 |
| Less: Taxable income | $3,000 | |
| Add back excluded capital gain | 500 | 3,500 |
| Unused carry-back | | $ 500 |
| Net operating loss carry-over to 1958 | | $ 500 |

The taxpayer would receive refunds of income taxes paid for 1955 and 1956 after submitting claims supported by a schedule such as the one outlined above.

There are numerous other adjustments and refinements that frequently complicate the computation of net operating loss carry-backs and carry-overs—particularly for an individual who is a proprietor or partner. Such computations are ordinarily less complicated for a corporation, since adjustments are not usually necessary. The most common adjustment on the return of an individual, that for long-term gains, does not appear on a corporate return, since the 50 per cent reduction in long-term capital gains is not available to corporations. (*But* the 25 per cent maximum for the alternative capital gains tax applies to corporations as well as other taxpayers.)

### Charitable and Political Contributions

Political contributions are not an allowable deduction for a business or an individual. Charitable contributions are not allowed as a deduction in the computation of net income for a proprietorship or a partnership, but such contributions may be included among the itemized personal deductions of the owners on their individual returns. Corporations are allowed a deduction for charitable contributions in an amount equal to 5 per cent of net taxable income computed without benefit of the deduction for charitable contributions. Any excess over 5 per cent can be carried forward and deducted in the two succeeding years, as long as the total deduction in any one year does not exceed the 5 per cent maximum.

### Typical Adjustments in Reporting Business Income

John Jones operates a wholesale concern as a sole proprietor. His business income statement, based on accrual principles of accounting, appears below. Jones recorded the political contributions as a business expense because he felt they were made in behalf of a candidate who favors legislation that would benefit his business. The charitable contributions, made in the name of the business, were considered by Jones as a form of advertising. The dividend income was received on stocks which were purchased with business funds and are held as business assets. "Gain on the sale of securities and fixed assets" represents the excess of sales prices over book values on the sale of common stock and a truck, both of which had been owned for more than six months.

EXHIBIT 12-1

JONES WHOLESALE CO.

Income Statement for the Year 1957

| | | |
|---|---:|---:|
| Sales income | | $124,600 |
| Cost of goods sold | | 68,200 |
| Gross profit | | $ 56,400 |
| Expenses: | | |
| Salaries and wages | $27,100 | |
| Bad debts (estimated) | 890 | |
| Taxes and interest | 1,410 | |
| Depreciation | 9,600 | |
| Political contributions | 300 | |
| Charitable contributions | 760 | |
| Other expense | 340 | 40,400 |
| Net operating profit | | $ 16,000 |
| Other income: | | |
| Dividend income | $ 1,600 | |
| Gain on the sale of securities and fixed assets | 4,400 | 6,000 |
| Net profit | | $ 22,000 |

When the "ordinary income" for tax purposes is reported, the contributions, dividend income, and long-term capital gain would be excluded, as shown in Exhibit 12-2.

Exhibit 12-2

John Jones, d.b.a. Jones Wholesale Co.

Schedule of Income and Deductions for the Year 1958

| | | |
|---|---:|---:|
| Sales income | | $124,600 |
| Cost of goods sold | | 68,200 |
| Gross profit | | $ 56,400 |
| Deductions: | | |
| Salaries and wages | $27,100 | |
| Bad debts | 890 | |
| Taxes and interest | 1,410 | |
| Depreciation | 9,600 | |
| Other expense | 340 | 39,340 |
| Ordinary income | | $ 17,060 |

The ordinary income would be included on the owner's personal income tax return along with any other taxable income he had earned or received. Dividend income and capital gains would also be included, along with any like items arising from other sources. The charitable contributions would be included if the taxpayer itemized his personal deductions.

If this firm were a partnership, the information return filed for the business would show the dollar amount of each of the following that was to be included by the partners on their individual returns: ordinary income, dividend income, capital gains, and charitable contributions.

## REPORTING INCOME AND DEDUCTIONS FOR AN INDIVIDUAL

Generally speaking, every resident of the United States who has $600 or more of gross income during a taxable year must file a U.S. Individual Income Tax Return. The computation of taxable income for an individual can be outlined as follows:

*Gross income less deductions from gross income = adjusted gross income*

*Adjusted gross income less personal deductions and exemptions*

*= taxable income*

Some of the items commonly included under each of these headings are described below.

### Gross Income

All income which is not specifically exempt must be included in the gross income of an individual, e.g., wages, salaries, commissions, rents, tips, prizes, interest, dividends, profits from business or profession, capital gains, etc. Some of this income may, however, be excluded under certain conditions.

**Sick Pay.** Wages received while absent from work because of illness or accident may be excluded from gross income *if* the payments are made under an employer-financed accident and health plan. The exclusion is limited to a maximum of $100 per week and does not apply to the first seven days if the absence is caused by sickness which does not require hospitalization during this time.

**Interest.** Interest received or credited to a taxpayer's account must, with few exceptions, be included in gross income. The gradual increase in United States savings or war bonds may be reported as interest income each year or the entire increase may be reported for the year in which the bonds are cashed. Interest from obligations issued by states and their political subdivisions is fully exempt.

**Dividends.** Fifty dollars of dividend income from domestic corporations can be excluded from gross income if the corporations "qualify" according to tax regulations. Four per cent of the amount of such dividends included in gross income can ordinarily be deducted as a credit against the tax due.

**Profits from Business or Profession.** For income tax purposes, the profit of a proprietorship or partnership is computed without contributions, certain dividend income, and capital gains and losses. These items are, however, included in the computation of taxable income on the individual returns of the owners or partners.

**Capital Gains and Losses.** Gain on the sale of a *personal asset*, such as a family car or painting, should be included as capital gain, but loss on the sale of such an asset is *not* deductible. However, both gain and loss on the sale of *investments* are included—gain and loss on the sale of securities or real estate, for example. The capital gains and losses realized as an individual are grouped with any capital gains and losses from proprietorships or partnerships. If the net long-term capital gain then exceeds the net short-term loss, only 50 per cent of the excess has to be included in taxable income. If losses exceed gains, only $1,000 of the loss can be deducted from the ordinary income of the current year, but the balance can be carried forward for five years to offset future capital gains and income. If the "carry-over" to any one year exceeds the capital gains, then $1,000 of the carry-over can be deducted from ordinary income.

**Exempt Income.** The following are examples of exempt income which is *not* reported for Federal income tax purposes: Federal Old-Age and Survivors Insurance benefits, state unemployment benefits, workmen's compensation and other insurance benefits for injury or sickness, insurance dividends, the amount received as beneficiary of a life insurance policy (usually), interest on obligations issued by states or their political subdivisions, gifts, inheritances, etc.

## Deductions from Gross Income

A taxpayer engaged in a business should have all allowable expenses incurred in the operation of the business included as deductions in the computation of the profit which becomes a part of gross income on his individual return. A taxpayer who works as an employee is entitled to deduct the following from his gross income:

**Reimbursed Expenses.** An employee is usually reimbursed for expenses he incurs on behalf of his employer. When such reimbursed funds are included in gross income they can be deducted in arriving at adjusted gross income. (They are often omitted entirely, despite the fact that such omissions are not permitted by the tax regulations.) When an employee is not reimbursed for all "nontravel" expenses incurred on behalf of his employer, the excess can be deducted only as a personal deduction.

**Local Transportation Expenses.** Local transportation costs, incurred in the performance of services for an employer, are deductions from gross income, even though such costs are not reimbursed.

**Out-of-town Travel Expenses.** When an employee travels away from the city where he normally works and remains away at least overnight, he is entitled to a deduction from gross income for any out-of-town travel expenses incurred on behalf of his employer. "Out-of-town travel expenses" means the cost of fares, lodging, meals, tips, and any other expenses necessary to travel; it does not include entertainment expense or personal expenses such as laundry. These can be deducted from gross income only if they have been included in gross income as reimbursed expenses.

## Personal Deductions

Gross income less deductions from gross income equals adjusted gross income. For the majority of taxpayers gross income and adjusted gross income are the same, since most taxpayers work as employees and have no deductions from gross income. All taxpayers, however, are entitled to "personal" deductions from adjusted gross income, for the law allows each taxpayer a *standard deduction* even though personal deductions of an allowable nature have not been incurred. The standard deduction is equal to 10 per cent of adjusted gross income (or a maximum of $1,000 in most cases) and should, of course, always be used by a taxpayer whose actual deductions are less than this amount. *If more*, the personal deductions should be "itemized" and the total deducted. The more common personal deductions (often called nonbusiness deductions) are discussed below:

**Charitable Contributions.** The total deduction for "charitable" contributions to nonprofit organizations is generally limited to 20 per cent of adjusted gross income. An extra 10 per cent is allowed for contributions made to churches and tax-exempt schools and hospitals. This, in effect, raises the limit to 30 per cent of adjusted gross income.

**Interest.** Interest on personal debt is generally deductible, e.g., interest on bank loans, on home mortgages, on contracts and notes for the purchase of automobiles and furniture, etc.

**Taxes.** Most non-Federal taxes can usually be deducted, e.g., property taxes, sales taxes, state income taxes, state gasoline taxes, etc. Federal excise taxes and social security taxes cannot be deducted.

**Medical and Dental Expenses.** Only that portion of the cost of medical and dental care which *exceeds* three per cent of adjusted gross income is deductible; and only that portion of the cost of drugs and medicines which exceeds one per cent of adjusted gross income can be included as a part of the cost of medical and dental care. The type and amount of expense that can be deducted is limited by law. Special rules apply to taxpayers sixty-five years of age or over.

**Other Deductions.** Expenses for the care of children and certain other dependents can be deducted under certain conditions. Uninsured theft and casualty losses (by fire, flood, wind, etc.) of personal property, such as cars, clothing, and cash, are generally deductible. Those "ordinary and necessary" expenses incurred for an employer's benefit which are not deductible from gross income can usually be taken as personal deductions. Typical of these expenses are the following: cost of small tools and safety equipment required for use on the job, unreimbursed cost of entertaining customers, and the cost of dues paid to unions or professional societies. Also deductible are those nonbusiness expenses which are considered as *ordinary and necessary* to the production of income or to the management of property held for the production of income.

### Exemptions for Taxpayers and Dependents

A taxpayer is allowed a deduction of $600 for each "exemption." A single taxpayer with no dependents is entitled to one exemption. A husband and wife who file a joint return are entitled to two exemptions. They would also be entitled to an exemption for each child who received more than one-half of his or her support from them and who is (1) under nineteen or (2) over nineteen but qualifies as a student or (3) over nineteen but with gross income of less than $600. A child who qualifies as an exemption for his parents but who has taxable income would also be able to take an exemption for himself on his own return. The same individual is thus claimed as a $600 exemption on two returns.

Exemptions are also allowed for certain relatives or for one who is a member of the taxpayer's household, if the relative or member of the household received more than one-half of his or her support from the taxpayer and had less than $600 of gross income. An additional exemption is allowed a taxpayer who is sixty-five or over or a taxpayer who is blind.

## Taxable Income and Joint Returns

Adjusted gross income less personal (nonbusiness) deductions and exemptions is equal to taxable income. Taxable income multiplied by the applicable tax rate (or rates) yields the amount of tax due. (The applicable rates—graduated from 20 to 91 per cent—are included in schedules and tables furnished by the government.) No computation is necessary for the many taxpayers whose adjusted gross income is less than $5,000 and who do not itemize deductions. These taxpayers use a table which includes allowances for both the standard deduction and the number of exemptions claimed.

A man and wife should normally file a joint return in order to lower their tax liability. On a joint return their taxable income is divided, each half is multiplied by the graduated rates which are applicable to that amount, and the result is multiplied by two. This means that the maximum tax rate on joint income will be comparatively lower. Suppose, for example, that a married man who has taxable income of $8,000 files a joint return with his wife, who has no income. Their income would be subject to a maximum tax rate of 22 per cent, whereas a single man who had the same amount of taxable income would be subject to a maximum rate of 30 per cent.

## COMPUTATION OF TAXABLE INCOME FOR AN INDIVIDUAL

John L. Jones, age fifty, is vice-president of a Middle Western manufacturing firm. His spouse, Joyce C. Jones, age forty-six, is a housewife and the mother of their two children: Todd Evan Jones, age twenty, a college student, who earned $730 during 1957; and Leslie Kay Jones, age sixteen, a high school student, who earned $610 during 1957. John's mother-in-law, Mary Morton, lives with the Jones family. She is sixty-eight years of age, unemployed, and her only income during 1957 consisted of $200 from dividends and interest.

A W-2 form received from the Thomas Manufacturing Corp. shows that John was paid a salary of $20,000 during 1957 (his salary had been continued under an employer-financed health plan while he was ill and absent from work for approximately one month), plus $840 in the form of reimbursements for out-of-town travel. Certain other expenses incurred for the benefit of his employer were not reimbursed.

John is the sole owner of the Jones Wholesale Co. (see the income statements on pages 256 and 257) and is also a partner in the Smith and

Jones Supply Co. He had additional income from the following sources in 1957: dividends from common stock, interest from a savings account and city bonds, and income from rental property.

Detailed information about the preceding income and deductions, and allowable personal deductions, will be found in the computation of taxable income for John Jones and his wife in Exhibit 12-3. (This computation is based on tax regulations in effect as of the end of 1956.) The form of presentation shown is intended only as a means of illustrating the points involved and does not necessarily represent the form of presentation that would be required in the actual preparation of an income tax return. ("Gross income" does not appear in the computation as a separate total, since the "deductions from gross income" are subtracted from the specific items of income to which they relate.)

EXHIBIT 12-3

Gross Income Less Deductions from Gross Income

1. Salary from the Thomas Manufacturing Corp.:

| | | |
|---|---:|---:|
| Gross (including reimbursed expenses)..................... $20,840 | | |
| Less: Reimbursed expense for out-of-town travel...... | $840 | |
| Unreimbursed expense for local transportation... | 160 | |
| Excludable sick pay; maximum of $100 per week for three weeks........................... | 300 | 1,300 |
| Balance................................................. | | $19,540 |

2. Profit from businesses:

| | | |
|---|---:|---:|
| Ordinary income from Jones Wholesale Co., a sole proprietorship........................................ | $17,060 | |
| Taxpayer's share of ordinary loss from the Smith and Jones Supply Co., a partnership........................ | (6,140) | |
| Total.................................................... | | 10,920 |

3. Dividends from "qualifying" corporations:

| | | |
|---|---:|---:|
| Received by Jones Wholesale Co. on securities held as company investments: | | |
| American Telephone & Telegraph................. $1,000 | | |
| North American Aviation........................ | 600 $ 1,600 | |
| Received directly by John Jones on stock held as an individual: | | |
| General Motors Corp................................. | 450 | |
| Total of dividends received.......................... | $ 2,050 | |
| Less exclusion permitted by law....................... | 50 | |
| Balance included in taxable income.................... | | 2,000 |

4. Income from interest on:

| | | |
|---|---:|---:|
| Savings account...................................... | $    140 | |
| Corvallis City bonds (excluded)...................... | | |
| Total.................................................... | | 140 |

5. Capital gains and losses:

| | |
|---|---:|
| Gain on sale of equipment by the Jones Wholesale Co. (equipment had been held more than six months)........ | $ 2,400 |

EXHIBIT 12-3 (*Continued*)

| | | |
|---|---:|---:|
| Taxpayer's share of loss on sale of truck by the Smith and Jones Supply Co. (truck had been held more than six months)...................................... | (700) | |
| Long-term capital gain on the above sales of depreciable property (if the gain on the sale of such assets held six months or more exceeds the loss, the excess is treated as long-term capital gain).................... | $ 1,700 | |
| Gain on the sale of American Telephone & Telegraph stock which had been held several years by the Jones Wholesale Co........................................ | 2,000 | |
| Net long-term capital gain from business endeavors......... | $ 3,700 | |
| Short-term loss on the sale of preferred stocks owned by Jones for less than six months....................... | (500) | |
| Net long-term capital gain before carry-over............... | $ 3,200 | |
| Less capital loss carry-over from 1956 (balance of loss on 1956 sale of stocks that could not be offset against ordinary income for 1956 because of $1,000 limitation)........................................... | 400 | |
| Net long-term capital gain*............................. | $ 2,800 | |
| 50% of above is included in taxable income...................... | | 1,400 |

6. Income from rental units:

| | | | |
|---|---:|---:|---:|
| Gross rental income..................................... | | $ 3,120 | |
| Less: Depreciation................................ | $ 600 | | |
| Repairs.................................... | 200 | | |
| Taxes and insurance....................... | 320 | 1,120 | |
| Net rental income......................................... | | | 2,000 |
| Adjusted gross income........................................... | | | $36,000 |

\* In 1957 the taxpayers sold their residence for $25,000 and purchased a new one for $34,000. The residence sold had a cost basis of $15,000 but under a special provision of the law, the $10,000 gain does not have to be included in current taxable income. The gain is deducted from the cost of the new house, leaving $24,000 as the basis for the computation of gain or loss on the sale of the new residence, if and when it is sold.

## Personal (*Nonbusiness*) Deductions

The personal deductions of the taxpayers are itemized as shown in Exhibit 12-4, since the total of these deductions exceeds $1,000, which is the maximum amount that can be taken as a "standard deduction." If the taxpayers' adjusted gross income had been less than $10,000, the personal deductions would be itemized as long as they exceeded 10 per cent of the adjusted gross income.

The computation of the tax on $14,000 has been shown in detail to illustrate how the graduated rates are applied. In actual practice the computation would be simplified by the use of a tax rate schedule prepared by the government.

EXHIBIT 12-4

1. Charitable contributions to:
   Red Cross (by Jones Wholesale Co.)...................... $   760
   Boy Scouts............................................        208
   Church................................................        642
       Total...........................................            $ 1,610
2. Interest paid on:
   Home mortgage......................................... $   900
   Car contract..........................................        140
   Furniture contract....................................         80
       Total...........................................              1,120
3. Taxes:
   Property taxes on home................................ $   310
   State income taxes....................................        860
   State sales taxes.....................................        274
   State gasoline taxes..................................         66
       Total...........................................              1,510
4. Medical and dental expenses:
   Cost of medicines and drugs........................... $   240
   Less 1 % of adjusted gross income.....................        360
       Net allowable...................................           none
   Other medical and dental expenses..................... $1,710
   Less amounts paid or reimbursed by insurance company......        500
       Net expense.....................................         $1,210
   Less 3 % of adjusted gross income.....................      1,080
       Allowable deduction.............................                130
5. Other deductions:
   Casualty loss—family car damaged in collision.............. $   607
   Less amount paid by insurance company.................        507
       Net cost .......................................  $   100
   Casualty loss—plants killed by frost..................        183
   Cost of entertaining customers not reimbursed by the employer        297
   Dues paid by Jones as a member of a professional society....         50
       Total...........................................                630
       Total personal deductions.......................            $ 5,000

*Exemptions*

John L. Jones, husband........................................ $   600
Joyce C. Jones, wife..........................................        600
Todd Evan Jones, son..........................................        600
Leslie Kay Jones, daughter....................................        600
Mary Morton, mother-in-law....................................        600
    Total exemptions.........................................            $ 3,000

*Computation of net taxable income*

Adjusted gross income......................................... $36,000
Less: Itemized personal deductions............................ $5,000
    Exemptions............................................    3,000    8,000
Net taxable income............................................ $28,000

Exhibit 12-4 (*Continued*)

*Computation of tax liability on a joint return*

One-half of taxable income ........................................... $14,000

|  | | Rates | | Tax | |
|---|---|---|---|---|---|
| First | $ 2,000 | × 20% | = $ | 400 | |
| Second | 2,000 | × 22 | = | 440 | |
| Third | 2,000 | × 26 | = | 520 | |
| Fourth | 2,000 | × 30 | = | 600 | |
| Fifth | 2,000 | × 34 | = | 680 | |
| Sixth | 2,000 | × 38 | = | 760 | |
| Seventh | 2,000 | × 43 | = | 860 | |
|  | $14,000 | | | $4,260 | |

Tax liability: $4,260 multiplied by two............................... $ 8,520

Amount due with return:

   Tax liability............................................................ $ 8,520

   Less: Dividends received credit—4% of $2,000 dividend income......... 80

                                                      $ 8,440

   Less: Tax withheld by employer............................. $3,000

       Amount paid on declaration of estimated tax............. 5,000   8,000

   Balance to be paid................................................... $ 440

Taxpayers with a certain amount of income not subject to withholding are required to file a Declaration of Estimated Tax and to make quarterly prepayments on the estimated amount of tax which will not be withheld.

Income for the Jones children would be reported on their individual returns. Each would be entitled to a standard deduction (neither had personal deductions to itemize) and a personal exemption of $600. The individual returns serve as claims for refunds when the amounts withheld exceed the total tax liabilities. If any additional amounts are due they should be paid at the time the returns are filed.

## TAXES ON RIGHT TO TRANSFER PROPERTY

The Federal *estate tax* (often called an inheritance tax) is a tax on the right to transfer property at death. It is measured by the amount of property included in the "taxable estate" of a deceased resident, but there is no tax liability unless the gross estate exceeds $60,000 or the total of exemptions and deductions which are allowable. A gross estate generally consists of all property, tangible or intangible, owned by a decedent at time of death. (Life insurance benefits, payable to beneficiaries other than the estate, are normally not a part of the estate.) The property included in the gross estate is appraised at its fair market value as of the date of death or at an alternative valuation date established within one year after the decedent's death. Deductions from the gross estate include funeral and administrative expenses, debts of the decedent, transfers to charitable, religious, and educational institutions, and the value of property transferred to a surviving spouse; the latter cannot exceed 50 per cent of the so-called "adjusted gross estate."

Gross estate less exemptions and deductions equals the amount of the taxable estate, which is taxed on the basis of graduated rates that range from a low of 3 per cent to a high of 77 per cent. The credits against the tax include those for state inheritance taxes and Federal gift taxes paid on property included in the estate.

The Federal *gift tax* is also a tax on the right to transfer property. It is a tax which is imposed upon the donor and is usually measured by the fair market value of the gifts. The donor, however, is allowed to deduct the following from the gross value of his gifts: an annual exclusion of $3,000, a specific exemption of $30,000 (which may be deducted in whole or in part in any one year), the amount of gifts to charitable and similar nonprofit organizations, and generally, in the case of a married person, an amount equal to one-half the value of gifts to a spouse. The amount of taxable gifts is taxed on the basis of graduated rates which vary from a low of $2\frac{1}{4}$ per cent to a high of $57\frac{3}{4}$ per cent. These rates are applied in any one year to the cumulative gifts to date, and a credit is then taken for gift taxes paid in prior years. This eliminates the possibility of avoiding the higher tax rates by spreading gifts over a period of years.

## SUMMARY

All businesses must generally pay property taxes and payroll taxes, regardless of their form of organization. A business organized as a corporation must also pay income taxes on profits, while a business organized as a sole proprietorship or partnership does not. Profits from a proprietorship or partnership do not escape taxation, however, for such profits must be included in the taxable income of the owners on their individual income tax returns. Certain items cannot be entered in the computation of such profits (usually called ordinary income), but most of these items must, nevertheless, be included on the individual income tax returns of the owners.

Taxable income of an individual is equal to gross income less (1) deductions from gross income, (2) personal nonbusiness deductions, and (3) allowable exemptions. A businessman who is a proprietor or partner normally has many deductions from gross income (his business expenses), but an employee usually has none or only a few, such as reimbursed expenses or out-of-town travel costs. All individuals, however, are entitled to an allowance for personal deductions, either in the form of a "standard" deduction or in the form of "itemized" deductions. All individual taxpayers are also entitled to one or more exemptions of $600 each. After the allowable deductions and exemptions are taken, the net taxable income is taxed on the basis of graduated rates.

The Federal government taxes not only income but also the right to transfer property, either before or after death. A living donor is taxed on gifts in excess of a certain amount. The estate of a decedent is taxed on certain property transferred at death, if the fair market value of the property exceeds a stated minimum.

## QUESTIONS

**1.** What is usually the basis for the computation of property tax assessments?

**2.** Who can receive benefits from Federal Old-Age and Survivors Insurance?

**3.** What is the maximum rate paid on state unemployment insurance? How can this rate be lowered?

**4.** What is the purpose of workmen's compensation insurance? How are the rates determined?

**5.** A certain company is required to pay FOASI taxes, SUI taxes (at the maximum rate), FUI taxes, and workmen's compensation (at 4 per cent). What is the company's *total* payroll cost if the gross payroll for the period is $10,000? Assume that none of the employees have earned more than $3,000.

**6.** Which method of accounting will most clearly reflect income earned? Under which method is gross profit deferred?

**7.** Which legal forms of business organizations are responsible for filing income tax returns? Which form of organization is required to pay income taxes?

**8.** Explain the meaning of "net long-term capital gain" and of "net short-term capital loss." If the former exceeds the latter, what percentage of the excess is included in the taxable income of an individual?

**9.** An individual has net long-term loss of $8,400 and net short-term gain of $5,200. How is the excess reported for tax purposes?

**10.** A taxpayer has net long-term capital gain of $6,000 and net short-term capital loss of $4,000. What should be the maximum effective tax on the excess, $250 or $500?

**11.** What are typical items that should be excluded from the computation of profit reported by a sole proprietorship or a partnership?

**12.** Which method of costing inventory items will generally result in lower income taxes for a year in which prices are continually rising?

**13.** Under which of the two accelerated depreciation methods is it unnecessary to estimate salvage or trade-in value?

**14.** For what reason or reasons would a firm use accelerated depreciation?

**15.** What is the purpose of net operating loss carry-backs and carry-overs?

**16.** What deductions from gross income are allowed a taxpayer who is a proprietor or partner? A taxpayer who is an employee?

**17.** Are taxpayers required to report gain on the sale of a family car? Loss?

**18.** Why do many persons contend that at least a portion of dividend income should be excluded from the taxable income of an individual?

**19.** Under what conditions can the sales of land and depreciable property be included in the computation of capital gains and losses?

**20.** When should a taxpayer itemize personal deductions?

**21.** What are the limits on charitable contributions and on medical and dental expenses?

**22.** A man and wife furnish over one-half the support for their two children who are both under 19 years of age. How many exemptions could be claimed on a joint return?

**23.** Why does a joint return usually result in a lower tax liability for a man and wife?

**24.** Should gifts and inheritances be included in the computation of Federal income tax?

**25.** There will be no estate tax unless the current value of the decedent's gross estate exceeds what amount?

**26.** A father, during a period of 30 years, presented gifts to his children with a total value of $120,000, but was not required to pay any Federal gift tax. How is this possible? (Assume that the law remains the same during the 30-year period.)

# PART 3

# THE ANALYSIS OF FINANCIAL DATA

## CHAPTER 13

# ANALYSIS OF FINANCIAL STATEMENTS

Business decisions may be based upon "intuition" or upon an intelligent analysis of factual data. Where intuition is used successfully, it is based upon a subconscious weighing of a great number of factors which the businessman believes significant. These factors may include such things as the fact that stock prices are rising, the impression that business is declining because there has been an increase in the number of clearance sales or number of firms going out of business, or an impression of public reaction to news events and an interpretation through personal experience or observation of the probable effect on market conditions. Although the businessman may not realize it, his decision is not based on pure intuition but rather upon the total effect and evaluation of multitudinous impressions. Intuition is not used successfully if this subconscious evaluation is not present.

## The Need for Financial Data

The person who attempts to use an intelligent analysis and interpretation of factual data as a basis for his decisions simply recognizes that impressions may be misleading and personal observations may be too limited to serve his thinking. He recognizes the limitations of his own experiences and the tendency for an individual to see cause and effect relationships where occurrences closely follow one another and where wider experience or observation would reveal no causal relationship. He attempts to verify or to correct his impressions by using all factual data which are available but he does not limit his thinking to an elaborate treatment of a mass of quantitative (numerical) data, or he will find his decisions are no better than, if as good as, those based on *intuition*, for the person using *intuition* never limits his thinking to the use of any particular set of facts.

Where the necessary figure-facts involve the finances of a business, the accounting department may be expected to furnish the necessary data, usually in the form of special reports or standard financial statements. In matters which do not involve financial transactions, such as statistical quality control, acceptance sampling, analysis of time series, estimating sales potentials, etc., the help of a statistician or a person with some understanding of statistical techniques will be required.

**Management Needs.** In almost every case the service rendered by the accounting department is in the form of a financial report or statement which is to be analyzed by the person receiving it and, in the light of existing economic conditions, market trends, imminent legislation, competition, ability and efficiency of management, etc., used as a basis for making a business decision. While there is no question that the accountant's thorough knowledge of accounting principles, conventions, and procedures places him in the best position for understanding, analyzing, and interpreting financial data, in questions involving management decisions the accountant is no more responsible for interpreting the statements than are the other executives of the business. The accounting department collects and records the data, prepares the financial statements, and often computes a number of useful rates and ratios, but neither the head accountant nor the controller (nor the chief accounting officer, whatever his title may be) is solely responsible for interpreting the financial data in terms of policies to be laid down or action to be taken. Since the accountant usually does not make the final decision on the action to be taken, it is obvious that other executives of the firm must also be in a position to analyze and make their own interpretations of financial data. We may safely say that every business executive who expects to take a part in policy-making decisions must have an understanding of the figure-facts upon which most intelligent decisions finally rest.

As an example of what has just been said, assume that the president of a manufacturing concern, who has come up through the sales department, finds that his business is faced with an acute shortage of working capital. He knows that working capital may be obtained from retained earnings and he decides that increased sales will increase earnings and pull the business out of its temporary financial straits. To increase sales, he instructs his credit manager to be more lenient in granting credit. In order to avoid losing sales he decides to increase his inventories. As a result of his actions, he has a larger balance in accounts receivable and a much larger investment in inventories, and his working capital position is now much worse than it was before he set out to "improve" it.

**The Need of the Stockholders.** The statements appearing in the annual reports of a corporation are read and interpreted by the stockholders, often without benefit of the accountant's explanations and interpretations. On the basis of the data shown and their own understanding of economic conditions existing during the period covered, the stockholders must judge the efficiency of the managers of their business. If they feel that the business has been poorly managed, they may attempt to bring about changes through the election of new men to the board of directors; or if this is not possible, they may decide to sell their stockholdings. In some cases they may feel that the business is facing a relatively unprofitable period and because of its financial position may be unable to survive. This may cause them to sell their stock. In the same way, the belief that a business is in a strong position or will soon become profitable may cause the prospective stockholder to buy stocks or the present stockholder to buy more shares. These people are not accountants but they need an understanding of accounting terminology, accounting statements and their meanings, and some knowledge of analysis.

**Lending Agencies.** Where financial statements are used as a basis for credit, the lending agency or the mercantile creditor must have an understanding of statements analysis. He must know the meanings of the accounts and whether they are properly classified on the statements given to him; he must understand the weaknesses and limitations of financial statements in general; and must have some idea of what ratios, rates, or amounts he should expect in the business which he is considering. He must also be able to weigh the financial data presented and, in the light of economic conditions and his appraisal of the character and ability of the men responsible for the business (owners or managers), must decide whether to make the loan or grant the credit line requested. The men making these decisions are bank loan officers or credit managers. They are not accountants. Yet, the analysis of financial statements and their interpretation in terms of the appropriate action to be taken are at the very heart of their jobs.

In the same way it may be shown that government officials, labor leaders, legislators, lawyers, bondholders and prospective bondholders, and even the general public need to have some understanding of financial statements. The purpose of these chapters on the analysis and interpretation of financial statements is to give the nonaccounting major who may become a business excutive an understanding of the techniques most likely to enable him to see the essential facts in the financial data available as a basis for his decisions in order that his decisions may more often be the correct ones.

*Historical Background of Statement Analysis*

From the time of the first written description of accounting up through colonial days, businesses were relatively small and were owned by a single proprietor or small group of partners. As a result, financial records and reports were of minor importance as a management tool. There was no need for reports to stockholders; and financial reports were of almost no importance as a basis of credit since there were no commercial banks, no mercantile credit agencies, and the owners were personally liable for the debts of their business enterprises. For these reasons, the analysis of financial statements is a relatively new area of study. The techniques being used are still being developed and improved and they are far from being fully perfected. New reports and statements are being developed as the value of figure-facts as a basis for decision making becomes more and more evident.

The importance of financial statement analysis in making business decisions depends upon the existence of each of the following conditions:

1. There must be a system of record keeping which will provide the financial data necessary for us to know:

   *a.* The properties which the business owns
   *b.* The debts which the business owes
   *c.* The equity which the owners have in the properties which they nominally own
   *d.* The sources of income and the amount of income from each source
   *e.* The reasons for the expenses and the amount paid (or the cost) of each

2. There must be persons trained to accumulate these data and to present them in an understandable form.

3. There must be businesses of sufficient size to make it necessary for the owners to have more financial data than they can retain in their heads.

4. There must be absentee ownership if statements are to be important for owners in judging the efficiency of their managers.

5. There must be businesses willing to sell on credit if statements are to be of importance to credit men and there must be agencies which can be depended upon to furnish reliable information about the prospective customer.

6. There must be banks willing to lend money if analysis is to be of importance in obtaining loans.

7. There must be some form of pressure put upon businessmen to cause them to keep accurate records.

8. There must be some degree of uniformity in the way records are kept if the reports are to be really meaningful.

9. There must be businesses of sufficient size to make necessary widespread ownership and to make the borrowing of large amounts an ordinary occurrence.

10. There must be legal action possible against those who knowingly use false financial data to obtain funds or merchandise from others.

11. There must be a recognized need on the part of businessmen, stockholders, investors and others for figure-facts as a basis of business decisions.

12. There must be a realization of the limitations of the data available and the inadequacy of *historical* data as a sole basis for business decisions.

Most of these conditions have already been substantially achieved. Reliable data are available or can be collected. Credit agencies, banks, and large-scale operations have created the need. The legal machinery has been set up, and businessmen are rapidly learning how to make full use of their financial records. The development of the accounting system has already been briefly described. The following paragraphs will explain how the other conditions have been achieved and how they are making the ability to interpret financial data more and more important.

**The Beginning of Commercial Banks.** When the first commercial bank was established in Philadelphia in 1781, the corporation, with its provision for limited liability, was still of almost no importance as a form of business organization. Loans were made on the basis of the total estimated wealth of the owner or the owners since suit could be brought against the individual if the loan was not repaid. The prospective borrower who appeared at the bank with a request for a loan knew that his request would be granted or refused on the basis of his reputation for character, business ability, and wealth, and upon his ability to get a satisfactory endorser on his note; or upon his ability to furnish the bank with sufficient collateral to guarantee the repayment of the debt. He did not expect to furnish the bank with any detailed statements of properties owned, debts, sources of income, or net worth. If he had provided such information, the banker would have had no procedures for studying these data and no standards by which to judge the business's financial condition. It is quite likely that the prospective borrower did not have this information and that he, himself, had only a hazy notion of his financial standing.

It was not until after the Civil War that bankers began to see the desirability of granting loans on the basis of the financial condition of the individual businesses. This was brought about by a number of factors:

1. The old procedure of requiring endorsers was time-consuming and unsatisfactory because it required bringing in outsiders on private deals, it eliminated many potential customers, and it provided no protection for the bank when A signed for B and B signed for A, etc.

2. The increasing importance of the corporation and the limited liability of the individual stockholder made more important the problem of determining whether the assets of the corporation would alone be sufficient to guarantee the loan.

3. Businessmen were seeing the need for keeping better records and were slowly becoming accustomed to having financial data about their

businesses placed in the hands of persons who had a legitimate need for knowledge as a basis for bank or mercantile credit.

By 1900 it had become a general practice for bank loans to be made on the basis of financial statements, and by 1915 the Federal Reserve System had given this practice its backing and a significant boost in importance when it advised member banks that only notes based on financial reports would be eligible for rediscount with the Federal Reserve Branch. Thus banks which needed to sell the notes taken from their customers were almost forced to make loans on the basis of financial statements. This naturally led to some standardization of form for reporting which in turn led to more uniform accounting procedures.

**Mercantile Credit Agencies.** In colonial days mercantile credit, like bank credit, was based on the general wealth of the customer. This was due to exactly the same reasons: (1) the unlimited liability of the proprietor or partners made total wealth of most significance; (2) the typical customer, not required to make annual income tax returns and having a relatively small business unit, was often ignorant of exact financial data about his business; and (3) there were no credit agencies, such as Dun and Bradstreet, which could furnish reliable information at a reasonable price.

When the prospective customer lived at some distance from the creditor, it was obviously impossible for the creditor to obtain the personal evaluation which was, and still is, a significant factor in granting all credit. The creditor (manufacturer or wholesaler) attempted to overcome this handicap by securing opinions from local men (bankers, lawyers, ministers and merchants) in regard to the character and ability of the prospective customer. In addition to the load imposed on friends of the customer, this method had obvious disadvantages to the creditor. The information obtained was often limited and almost never gave any factual data, there was no uniformity in reporting the information given, and such facts and opinions as were given were often biased or only partially true.

To meet this need for reliable information from an unbiased observer, the mercantile credit agencies were developed. The first one, The Mercantile Agency, was established in New York City in 1841. Others soon followed. At the present time, Dun and Bradstreet, the successor to The Mercantile Agency and The Bradstreet Company (1849), and Standard and Poor are among the principal agencies for providing this type of credit information.

**The Increasing Importance of the Corporation.** Perhaps no factor has been more responsible for the development of financial statement analysis than has the constantly increasing importance of the corporation as a form of business organization.

During our colonial period and for many years thereafter the typical business was a small trading or shipping enterprise requiring a relatively small capital investment and capable of being operated by a single individual or family. The sole proprietorship and the partnership were almost the only types of business organization used. There were some joint stock companies (a form of partnership with transferable shares) and corporations, while not unknown, were limited almost exclusively to charitable, educational, or other nonprofit organizations.

As soon as American business reached the point where an individual or a small group of individuals was no longer able to supply the capital needed to build the railroad lines or to build and equip the mills and factories, businessmen began to see the need for a better form of organization. There is no point at which the corporate form of organization may be said to have been "born" but the famous Dartmouth College case which was decided by the Supreme Court in 1819 is generally considered the most significant date in its rapid development. In this case it was held that the corporation is "an artificial being, invisible, intangible, and existing only in contemplation of law" and capable of suing and being sued and of owning property in its own name. Since that date the corporation has grown from a position of no practical importance to a point where it is now estimated that 65 per cent of the total volume of business in the United States is accounted for by business units organized as corporations.

It is quite evident that the corporation, while still far from the most common type of business form, is the most important form in businesses requiring large investments and, consequently, is the form used by practically all major industrial concerns, railroads and other carriers, and all types of public utilities. Perhaps the reason for the importance of this development to financial statement analysis is, however, not so evident.

The effects of the corporation may be organized and summarized by considering the business condition created or made possible by the widespread use of this form of organization:

1. The corporation allows widespread ownership of shares in business since its life is not limited to the lives of its owners. This allows absentee ownership and the absentee owners need financial data to judge the efficiency of their managers.

2. The relatively unlimited funds available to the corporation made possible the development of business enterprises of a size never before dreamed possible. Familiarity with details of assets owned, costs, and hundreds of facts which formerly could be well known by a single proprietor became an impossibility. Only through written reports and financial statements could the managers hope to keep informed of the finances of the business which they were to control.

3. The limited liability offered the stockholder made it important for the prospective mercantile or bank creditor to consider the assets, the liabilities, the earnings record, and the economic future of the business, since the personal wealth of individual owners was no longer a safeguard. Each business had to pass or be rejected on the basis of its own financial standing, and that standing was revealed to a large extent, but certainly never completely, in its financial reports.

4. The limited liability offered the owners also created a need for legislation to protect the creditor and the public interest from the unscrupulous or ill-advised corporation. These laws caused the corporation to come under the close scrutiny of Federal and state regulatory agencies, and these agencies require reports and statements. And, since these agencies had the authority to specify how the reports were to be prepared, a much greater uniformity in accounting procedure and terminology resulted. This has spread to businesses other than corporations, and though far short of its possible final outcome, has resulted in more nearly comparable statements for particular businesses or industrial groups.

5. As a legal entity able to hold property in its own name and act as an individual in all business matters, the corporation became subject to Federal income taxes when the Sixteenth Amendment was passed in 1913. The requirement that the corporation pay an annual tax on the profits which it had earned made necessary the use of an accounting system capable of providing the required information, and, while no particular type of record is required, the income tax has led to a much more widespread use of the double-entry system of record keeping. It has also done a great deal, through specifying how profits are to be determined, to standardize accounting procedures. This, also, has resulted in more comparable statements and reports.

**The Federal Reserve Act of 1913.** The Federal Reserve Act of 1913 resulted in the establishment of twelve regional reserve banks in which each national bank of the district is required to own a stock interest equal to 6 per cent of its own paid-in capital and surplus. Each member bank is required to maintain a reserve deposited in cash in its Federal Reserve branch which is equal to 25 per cent of its total deposits, subject to some variation. These deposits provide the principal source of funds for the Federal Reserve branch bank. In return for their use, the member banks have the privilege of borrowing from their branch reserve bank by rediscounting certain notes received from the member bank's own customers. To rediscount these notes the member bank must file an application for rediscount which states that the note is, in its opinion, eligible for rediscount. A number of requirements must be met to make the note eligible, the ones of principal interest here being:

1. Every application must contain a statement by the member bank as to whether it has on file a statement showing the financial worth of the person or firm primarily liable on the note.

2. A Federal Reserve bank may require statements showing a reasonable excess of quick assets over current liabilities.

3. The proceeds of the note must not have been used to provide permanent or fixed assets of a business nor be used for any purely speculative purpose.

4. "Eligible paper" not rediscounted may be used by the member bank as collateral for its own notes to the reserve branch.

The statement that the financial reports of the borrower were on file and had been used as a basis for the original loan was at one time considered essential for the paper to be eligible for rediscount, and proof of liquidity is still the principal factor in determining the eligibility of paper for rediscount. Because of the emphasis on the ratio of current assets to current liabilities, this ratio has often been called the "banker's ratio." There is some question as to whether the ratio shows what it was originally believed to show and we may be certain that it has been overemphasized. It is now clear that the current ratio does not necessarily reflect the ability of a business to pay its current obligations since the liquidity of a business depends upon the liquidity of the particular assets and not solely upon the current ratio. Thus, the liquidity of inventories, for example, must be judged by the inventory turnover, economic conditions, and the types of inventories held (raw materials may be more or less liquid than finished products) rather than by the current ratio alone. Nevertheless, the effect which this attempt at judging liquidity has had on financial statement analysis has been tremendous.

The practice of granting cash discounts has led to a substantial increase in the use of bank credit. In most cases the buyer finds that it is profitable for him to borrow from the bank to take advantage of the discount offered. If he does not pay within the discount period, the seller may finance the sale through a bank loan. In either case, the bank is likely to be called upon for temporary funds. As a result of this borrowing, commercial banks began in about 1890 to establish credit departments to evaluate the financial position of prospective customers, especially those desiring unsecured loans. By 1900 it had become customary for a borrower to furnish the bank with financial data. As previously noted, the requirement of the Federal Reserve Act that financial data about the borrower be on file helped to promote a trend already well begun.

**Legislation Promoting Statement Analysis.** The analysis of financial data has received three important boosts from the Congress of the United States. The first boost was the establishment of the Federal Reserve System. The importance of this Act has already been noted.

The second boost, which came at almost the same time, was provided by the Sixteenth Amendment and the subsequent income tax legislation which made it necessary for each business to report its profits each year. No other factor has ever had such a tremendous effect on the importance of record keeping. Firms which had formerly made no real attempt to keep records of financial transactions were faced with the problem of reporting their profits and keeping records which would substantiate their reported income and expense. While the law has never specified the form to be used or the type of accounting system required, it does specify the procedures which are satisfactory in computing bad debt losses, depreciation costs, and reporting income and expense. This has done a great deal to standardize accounting procedures and methods of computing costs and income to be reported in a given fiscal period.

It is unfortunately true that many small businesses make little use of the accountant's services other than to use his data in making out the income tax returns and the other reports required by the government. Many firms which first began to take their record keeping seriously when they were forced into it by the government have now learned the value of financial data in solving business problems and are making their records a starting point for policy decisions.

A third important boost was given financial analysis by the Securities Act of 1933 and the Securities Exchange Act of 1934. As a result of these Acts a business with new issues of securities to be sold on a public exchange is required to file a registration statement and a prospectus. Also, businesses whose securities are listed for sale must file annual reports prepared in accordance with the regulations prescribed by the Securities and Exchange Commission. The immediate result of this legislation was to standardize reports issued to the Commission and to make available the financial statements of our major corporations. Although the Commission has no authority over the reports issued to stockholders, there can be no great variation between the reports filed for the SEC and those presented to stockholders without arousing the stockholders to the possibility of deception. The practical effect of the legislation has been, therefore, to bring about a much greater uniformity in all the reports issued by these corporations, and many firms not registered with the Commission have brought their own record keeping and reporting procedures in line with the procedures required of the larger corporations.

**The Development of Accountancy.** Although the double-entry system of accounting has been known for five hundred years or more, the profession of accountancy has developed within the past seventy years. The first accountants kept the records of the single firm by whom they were employed. The honesty and accuracy of the accountant's work were judged by his employer and were matters of no interest to outsiders for they were not stockholders, and if they were creditors, they did not depend upon the business assets alone for a return of their money. With the growth of the corporate form of organization and the development of larger and larger commercial and industrial units, it became more and more important to have an unbiased outsider examine the records of these businesses to see that the records were accurately and honestly kept and that the reports prepared from them fairly presented the financial position of the business concerned. The need for this assurance of accuracy by stockholders, bondholders, investment bankers, and large commercial creditors, together with the need for expert help in planning accounting systems and control procedures, finally led to the development of accountancy as a profession.

The first public accountants in the United States began practicing in the twenty years following the Civil War. By 1895 the number had increased to a point where the need for public control and licensing of those qualified to practice was recognized. As a result of this need for protection against the unqualified, and in recognition of those whose work could be depended upon, the State of New York passed the first state law for the licensing of Certified Public Accountants. Since that date, all states have passed laws that require the examination and licensing of Certified Public Accountants. Though persons less well qualified are permitted to practice public accounting in most states, they are in no case called "Certified Public Accountants."

Accountants engaged in private practice are, of course, not required to pass an examination since their work is done for a single firm and is not necessarily relied upon by stockholders and creditors. This does not mean that unaudited reports are not used in granting credit, however, for the reports furnished credit managers are generally prepared by the private accountant and most of them are not checked by an outside accounting expert.

**Cost Plus Contracts.** In recent years, the widespread use of "cost plus" contracts, particularly on government orders for war material, has given a significant boost to cost accounting. Since the amount to be paid is usually cost plus a stated per cent of cost or plus a fixed fee, the manufacturer must have adequate cost records to determine the amount which he is to receive. These records must also be kept in such a way as to enable the government to check their accuracy and adequacy. War contracts were also subject to renegotiation and adequate cost records were necessary as a basis for adjustment. The result of these two problems has been that many firms which were forced to keep better cost records to satisfy the government are now finding that the figures which they are able to obtain are of equal importance in evaluating their operational policies and in improving the efficiency of their plants.

## The Limitations of Financial Statements

There is no question but that the person who uses facts, including financial figure-facts, as a basis for his thinking will have a sounder basis than the person who uses only impressions gained through personal observation. There is, however, a tendency to attempt to form conclusions on the basis of an analysis of financial reports alone. This cannot be done successfully—and students who attempt it or teachers who imply that it can be done make a serious error and contribute to a misunderstanding of the real purpose of financial statement analysis.

**The Need for Additional Information.** The financial statements of a firm present important information regarding its operations and financial condition but they never reveal the entire picture. For this reason, it is impossible for a person to make really intelligent decisions about a firm if his information is limited entirely to the data presented on its financial statements. The importance of this fact to the outside analyst cannot be overemphasized. Among the factors which must be considered are:

1. The effects of recent or impending legislative action
2. The effects of wars, cancellations of war contracts, and reconversion problems
3. The possible lack of raw materials for processing
4. The market value of pledged assets
5. The present value of fixed properties in estimating the real value of the owner's equity
6. The present value of inventories in evaluating ownership
7. The effect and likelihood of new products or competition
8. The adequacy of insurance coverage
9. The record for honesty and integrity of the managers, as partially revealed by fires, bankruptcies, etc.
10. The apparent discrepancies between reported financial condition and the financial condition indicated by actual business practices
11. The depth and quality of management ability and the likelihood of changes in the administrative setup
12. The relative standing or progress of a firm in comparison with its competitors

Each of the following cases illustrates a typical condition where additional data are needed and where the failure to go beyond the statements could lead to costly errors or erroneous conclusions:

1. The Hayden Farm has reported excellent earnings for the past fourteen years—but the statements do not reveal that its principal crop has just been (or will soon be) removed from the price support program.

2. The Ace Manufacturing Company made an excellent showing from 1941 to 1956 —but the statements do not reveal that it has completed all contracts for war materials and is now faced with finding new products and establishing a sales organization.

3. The Pokee Lumber Co., a small sawmill operation, seems to be in excellent shape—but the statements do not show that it has completed cutting all of its own timber and must now buy its logs at much higher costs or perhaps close down if no logs can be obtained.

4. A mortgage holder has a $50,000 mortgage on land with a book value of only $20,000—but the records do not show that the land has a current market value of over $100,000 and his investment is quite safe.

5. The stockholders of the Sleepy Lumber Co. have been asked to trade their stock for shares of equal book value of a larger firm and are about to make the trade—but their statements do not reflect the present market value of their timber holdings purchased during the depression and which, through undercutting (cutting less than growth) and price changes, are now worth over 100 times their original cost.

6. Mr. Lawton, a partner in Johnson & Lawton Co. is considering selling his equity in the firm for the balance shown in his capital account— but the accounts do not reflect the present value of any of the fixed properties or the current replacement value of the inventories and his net worth is significantly understated.

7. The Flamingo Motor Court has been earning a nice profit and the fixed debt, though large, is being retired as planned—but the statements do not show that a newer, larger, and better located court is just about to open in the same small town.

8. The Johnson Co. has a first mortgage on the building of Ace Company. The mortgage is for $20,000 and the buildings have a market value of $40,000. The investment seems safe enough—but the statements do not show that there is only $15,000 of fire insurance on the building.

9. The statements of Hokum and Company look very good—but they do not show that the manager of Hokum has taken out bankruptcy three times in other cities and has had at least two successful fires. He could be dishonest.

10. The Hokum Company appears to be in good current position and should have no trouble meeting its current debts—but the statements do not show the fact that it has failed to take advantage of purchase discounts, which generally means a lack of cash or a lack of business ability but could also mean that the records are false.

11. The Ace Company, under the management of Mr. Howard D. Ace,

has been very successful and you are planning to invest in the firm. The records do not show that Mr. Ace is seventy-two years old and is planning to retire. There is no one in the firm of comparable ability and Howard, Jr., who is almost completely incompetent, is the principal stockholder and is likely to be the next chief executive officer.

12. The Motor Mfg. Co. is in good condition as indicated by all its statements and the company has earned a reasonable rate of profit in each of the past ten years—but the statements do not show that compared to other firms in the industry it has the poorest record of all and is gradually losing its share of the total business. It is simply riding a wave of prosperity due to economic factors and is profitable in spite of extremely poor management.

A classic example of the need for additional data is provided by the X Manufacturing Company. In January, 1946, the president of the company stated that his firm was "as sound as a dollar" but was suffering from a temporary shortage of working capital. Upon investigation it was found that the company had been organized shortly before World War II to manufacture a patented machine. The machine was not salable, but before the company was in serious difficulty it received a flood of contracts to manufacture parts for airplanes, torpedo parts, and various types of metal products needed by our military forces. The president of the company was an optimistic, enthusiastic, and talented engineer, and the plant was well equipped and well run. Profits were good and dividends were paid regularly from 1939 to 1945. From its financial reports the business appeared to have been quite successful. There was a shortage of working capital due to a liberal dividend policy and a lack of foresight in regard to reconversion costs, but the company president believed this condition to be temporary.

Though no serious condition was revealed by the statements, it was felt that a reappraisal of management planning was needed. It was found that no plans had been made for a new product until the war contracts were completely finished. A new product had then been quickly selected and reconversion had been started. The following questions had not been answered:

1. Will the products planned for postwar production make the most effective use of the plant facilities?

2. Will the manufacture of the products planned require the skills possessed by the present labor force?

3. Will the working capital be adequate to pay reconversion costs and to carry the larger finished goods and receivables balances likely in the postwar period?

4. Are there sources of capital available to meet reconversion and other costs?

5. Will the marketing or distribution setup (which is practically non-existent because production is all sold to the government) be adequate when the product must be sold to many customers?

6. Do the products planned cover a number of areas so that cyclical fluctuations may be minimized? Do they require so many different channels of distribution that they cannot be profitably marketed?

7. Does the firm have available, or can it get, the materials needed for the postwar production?

In the case of the X Manufacturing Company it was found that the products planned did not use the plant or labor force efficiently. They could not be marketed by the company's present sales organization and no plans had been made to enlarge the sales force. They consisted of products to be sold by door-to-door salesmen to housewives, products to be sold to large manufacturers, and products to be sold to retailers. In addition, the current financial position, though adequate for operating conditions in 1945, was not good enough to provide for the costs of reconversion and for the larger inventories and receivable balances which were sure to come with selling nonmilitary goods. There had been no arrangements made or even contemplated for financing the sales organization which would be required for marketing the new product. No arrangements had been made for capital to purchase government-owned equipment in the plant and no sources of materials had been arranged for in spite of the fact that the materials needed were likely to be difficult to obtain.

Although the final appraisal of any company will depend to a large extent upon whether we are being asked to sell the company raw materials on open account, are planning an unsecured bank loan, are planning an investment in the company's stock, or are planning a long-term secured loan, we must conclude that despite its good earnings record and fair present position, this company's financial management is weak and its long-range outlook is poor.

**The Inadequacy of Historical Records.** Another limitation of accounting which we must recognize is the inadequacy of historical data as a guide to future policy. No amount of processing can make records of past sales reveal future demand or price trends, and accounting is largely concerned with recording and summarizing past events. However, the preparation of budgets and forecasts is becoming increasingly common and accounting data make a significant contribution to their preparation.

**Changing Price Levels.** The fact that the dollar is constantly changing in value presents a serious problem in analyzing accounting data. Transactions are recorded in dollars of varying value but they are shown on the balance sheet and added as if they were of equal value. Even the income statement is affected by these changing values for how can we say we have matched costs against the income produced if the sales are in 1957 dollars while the depreciation charged on the building and machinery is in 1935 depression dollars. Accountants have suggested adjusting all values for price-level changes but many problems are involved and little progress has been made. The failure to devise a satisfactory method of adjusting for price-level changes leaves problems in presentation and analysis of data for which we have no good solution. For example:

1. There is no satisfactory way of showing the values of the properties owned in terms of the present value of money. A building lot bought in 1932 for $10,000, now worth $30,000 (due to the increase in the value of the particular location and/or the decreasing value of the dollar) will ordinarily be shown at its original cost.

2. Depreciation may be charged to recover the original cost of a fixed asset (such as a machine or factory building) whose replacement will cost perhaps twice as much as the original equipment.

3. Sales amounts may show increases while sales volume is actually decreasing.

4. Statements of firms which bought their fixed assets at different times are not really comparable.

5. Profits reported may be due to price-level changes and small depreciation charges resulting from favorable purchases of fixed assets rather than good merchandising practices.

6. Established firms which bought their fixed properties when prices were low provide formidable competition for newcomers who must pay current high prices for their fixed assets. But they also pay more income taxes!

This should indicate that financial data provide a starting point for our thinking, but the mathematical manipulation of figures and all the tables, graphs, and ratios ever devised *do not provide a substitute for thinking*. Let us recognize the limitations of our tools, but let us not throw them away because they cannot accomplish the job by themselves. Decisions based on facts are better, in the long run, than any other type.

### *Viewpoints and Procedures*

The principal users of financial data may be classified into four major groups based on the type of problem for which the user is attempting to find an answer. These groups are (1) managers, (2) owners or prospective owners (stockholders), (3) short-term creditors, and (4) long-term creditors or bondholders. Each person's analysis is determined by his viewpoint and limited by the data available to him.

**The Viewpoint of Management.** The managers of a firm are primarily interested in improving the operating efficiency, controlling the assets owned, keeping the properties owned and the equities in them in proper relationship, and planning the future operating and financial policies. They have access to all records and make use of detailed studies of all expenses, income, cash requirements, inventories, etc., in addition to the procedures described in the following chapters.

**The Viewpoint of the Stockholders.** The owners of a proprietorship or partnership are also usually the managers, but most stockholders of a large corporation view the operation of their business as owners rather than as managers. They are interested in evaluating the efficiency of their managers to determine the possible need for change. They are also interested in the profitability of their investment and the long-term outlook of the firm. Their decision to buy or sell their stock will be determined by these findings.

**The Viewpoint of the Short-term Creditor.** Commercial banks and trade creditors furnish a large part of a firm's working capital. Since they expect to be paid within a very short time, they are primarily interested in the current position of the firm and have a relatively minor interest in its long-term outlook. For this reason, they concentrate on the procedures which will reveal the ability of the firm to meet its current obligations.

**The Viewpoint of Long-term Creditors.** Long-term creditors are interested in both the current earnings and the prospective earnings of a firm. It is obvious that interest payments depend upon the firm's earnings. It is not so obvious that the final repayment of the principal is dependent upon future earnings to a greater extent than it is upon the *present value* of the firm's fixed assets. Because of the size of their investments and the relatively small number of investments made, they have sufficient time for a much more thorough analysis than the typical short-term credit investigation. And because of the long period of time before they will get a return of their principal, they are much more interested in long-range plans and economic outlook.

Although each analyst's procedures depend upon his viewpoint and the data which are available to him, most analyses begin with a balance sheet or an income statement. The first step in the analysis is to make certain that all accounts are properly classified. Chapters 14, 15, and 16 review the meaning and classification of common account titles and describe the procedures most often used in the analysis of balance sheet and income statement data.

## SUMMARY

The importance of financial statements as a source of factual data has increased tremendously in recent years. The increasing importance of the corporation as a form of business organization has been a major factor in this development. Other factors are the development of accountancy, the development of commercial banks and credit agencies, Federal legislation requiring annual reports on earnings and SEC regulations promoting uniformity of accounting statements, and the requirement of the Federal Reserve banks that borrowers submit financial reports.

The accounting department gathers the financial facts and summarizes them for the use of management, but they are not solely responsible for business decisions based on these data. All businessmen must understand business reports and must be able to make their own interpretations. One of the greatest needs is the recognition of the limitations of statement data and a clear understanding of the effect of accepted principles and conventions on the values shown. Without this understanding, one may mistake book values for actual market values, may think that the "net worth" section of the balance sheet shows the present value of the owner's equity, may be easily misled by the "reported" net income during periods of rapid price-level changes, or may make innumerable mistakes in interpreting the meaning of reserves, surplus, and other accounts.

## QUESTIONS

**1.** Would you agree that a good analysis of a firm's financial condition must be based solely upon the factual data found on the company's financial reports?

**2.** Explain how each of the following items has a bearing on the interpretation of financial reports:

  *a.* Economic conditions
  *b.* Competition and new products
  *c.* Character of managers or owners
  *d.* Experience or background of managers
  *e.* Fire record
  *f.* Insurance carried
  *g.* Depth of management
  *h.* Raw material supply—availability of materials
  *i.* War, end of war, or legislation

**3.** Would you agree that a businessman who has a competent accounting department has no need for a knowledge of accounting since he never helps record the data or prepare financial statements?

**4.** Explain how each of the following developments has contributed to the increasing importance of financial analysis:

  *a.* Double-entry accounting
  *b.* Commercial banks

c. Mercantile credit agencies
d. The development of accountancy as a profession
e. The Federal Reserve banks
f. Income tax legislation
g. The increasing importance of the corporate form of organization—absentee owners, size, limited liability, regulation
h. Cash discounts
i. Securities Exchange Act

**5.** John Fulton is retiring as a partner in the firm of Fulton, Cohen, and Kelly. He has agreed to sell his interest to the remaining partners. Explain why each of the following facts should be considered in determining the real value of his equity:

a. The land and buildings were purchased in 1934
b. Inventories are valued at cost (LIFO) or market, whichever is lower
c. All "investments" are shown at cost
d. A direct write-off method has always been used for bad debts
e. The firm has earned net profits of above 25 per cent on the owner's equity for the past 8 years

**6.** How do changing price levels add to the difficulty of interpreting balance sheet and income statement data?

**7.** The analyses made by the various users of financial statements depend upon the purpose or viewpoint of the analyst. What factors are of primary importance to each of the following groups:

a. Short-term creditors
b. Long-term creditors
c. Stockholders
d. Managers
e. Government

## CHAPTER 14

# ANALYSIS OF THE INCOME STATEMENT

The content and arrangement of the operating statements of merchandising and manufacturing firms were described and illustrated in Chapter 6. Procedures used in analyzing and interpreting these reports are now presented.

## Comparative Income Statements

**Increase-Decrease Statements.** The significance of an amount shown on a financial statement comes largely as a result of a comparison of this amount with some base or standard rather than from the amount alone; e.g., what decision could you make about a firm if you knew that their net sales for 1957 amounted to $367,200? Is this good or bad, high or low? Has management done a good job? Have good merchandising practices been followed? Has our new advertising program been effective? Are we doing better or worse? It is obvious that we cannot begin to answer any of these questions because we have no basis for comparison of what we did in 1957 with what we have done before, with what we had planned to do, or with what our competitors are doing. Unless we can establish some basis for comparison, the figures on our income and expense statement are of little value for management purposes.

Several types of reports are available for providing management with satisfactory bases for evaluating operating statements. One of the most commonly used devices is the comparative income and expense statement with columns showing operating results for the current and preceding period, a column showing the amount of increase or decrease in each item, and a fourth column showing the per cent of increase or decrease (see Exhibit 14-1).

In the preparation of this report, the earlier year is always considered the base. The amount of increase or decrease is figured by subtracting the 1956 figure from the 1957 amount, and the per cent of increase is figured by dividing the amount of change by the value for the base year, 1956. The selling and administrative expenses would frequently be itemized or would be supported by itemized schedules.

From a report of this type it is easy to see that the net sales have increased $60,200 or 20.7 per cent for 1957. The total cost of goods sold has increased only 11.3 per cent so the margin on sales has increased. This increase in gross profit has been accompanied by a 10.0 per cent increase in selling expenses and a 13.3 per cent increase in administrative expenses and has resulted in net operating profits of more than twice the amount

EXHIBIT 14-1

ACE COMPANY

Comparative Income and Expense Statement for the Years 1956 and 1957

|  | 1956 | 1957 | Increase or decrease | Per cent change |
|---|---|---|---|---|
| Gross sales........................ | $306,000 | $367,200 | $61,200 | 20.0 |
| Less returned sales & allow....... | 6,000 | 7,000 | 1,000 | 16.7 |
| Net sales...................... | $300,000 | $360,200 | $60,200 | 20.7 |
| Cost of goods sold: | | | | |
| Inventory at beginning........... | $ 40,000 | $ 42,000 | $ 2,000 | 5.0 |
| Purchases (net)................ | 180,000 | 196,000 | 16,000 | 8.9 |
| Transportation in.............. | 4,000 | 5,000 | 1,000 | 25.0 |
| Total...................... | $224,000 | $243,000 | $19,000 | 8.5 |
| Less inventory at end of year..... | 42,000 | 40,500 | −1,500 | −3.6 |
| Cost of goods sold.............. | $182,000 | $202,500 | $20,500 | 11.3 |
| Gross profit on sales.............. | $118,000 | $157,700 | $39,700 | 33.6 |
| Operating expenses: | | | | |
| Selling expenses................ | $ 60,000 | $ 66,000 | $ 6,000 | 10.0 |
| Administrative expenses.......... | 30,000 | 34,000 | 4,000 | 13.3 |
| Total expenses................ | $ 90,000 | $100,000 | $10,000 | 11.1 |
| Net profit on operations........... | $ 28,000 | $ 57,700 | $29,700 | 106.1 |
| Other income.................... | 3,000 | 4,000 | 1,000 | 33.3 |
|  | $ 31,000 | $ 61,700 | $30,700 | 99.0 |
| Other expenses.................. | 4,000 | 6,000 | 2,000 | 50.0 |
| Net income for year.............. | $ 27,000 | $ 55,700 | $28,700 | 106.3 |

for the preceding year. With this type of information we are in a position to begin to answer some of our original questions about the effectiveness of management and the value of our operating policies, and our accounting reports begin to reveal their true value.

However, it should be remembered that the accounting department does not provide us with all the information which we may wish; e.g., we know that there has been a 20.7 per cent increase in net sales but our records do not show whether this change has been due to an increase in prices or to an increase in the physical quantities of goods sold. It is quite likely to have been due in part to increases in both prices and quantities sold, but it is possible that the quantity of goods sold has actually decreased. It may be desirable to adjust the sales figures for price changes so that a truer picture of changes in volume may be seen. This price "deflation," as it is called, may be accomplished by dividing the net sales figures for each year by an appropriate price index for the year. The price indices to be used may be those found in published sources or if no suitable index is available, may be especially constructed for the firm by the firm's own statistical research department.

**Trend Percentages.** Where it is desirable to watch the movement of statement items over a period of years, it is sometimes convenient to express each year's value as a per cent of the value for some base year as illustrated in the simplified statement shown in Exhibit 14-2.

EXHIBIT 14-2

ACME COMPANY

Statement of Income and Expense with Trend Percentages for 1953 through 1957

| Item | Dollar amount | | | | | Trend percentage | | | | |
|------|------|------|------|------|------|------|------|------|------|------|
|  | 1953 | 1954 | 1955 | 1956 | 1957 | 1953 | 1954 | 1955 | 1956 | 1957 |
| Net sales............ | 2,000 | 2,400 | 2,500 | 2,800 | 3,600 | 100 | 120 | 125 | 140 | 180 |
| Cost of sales......... | 1,200 | 1,400 | 1,500 | 1,600 | 2,000 | 100 | 117 | 125 | 133 | 167 |
| Gross profit.......... | 800 | 1,000 | 1,000 | 1,200 | 1,600 | 100 | 125 | 125 | 150 | 200 |
| Selling expenses...... | 300 | 350 | 360 | 390 | 420 | 100 | 117 | 120 | 130 | 140 |
| Admin. expenses..... | 200 | 220 | 240 | 280 | 300 | 100 | 110 | 120 | 140 | 150 |
| Total expenses..... | 500 | 570 | 600 | 670 | 720 | 100 | 114 | 120 | 134 | 144 |
| Net oper. income..... | 300 | 430 | 400 | 530 | 880 | 100 | 143 | 133 | 177 | 293 |

This type of statement may be quickly and easily prepared. The first step is to select some year or period as the base period. Any year may be used but the earliest year is generally considered best unless the amounts for this year are clearly not typical amounts and thus not suitable as a base. When the base period has been selected, the trend percentages are computed by expressing each figure as a per cent of the base year amount. For example, the trend percentages for net sales were found by dividing each "dollar amount" by $2,000, the base year value, and expressing the quotient in "per cent"; or, for 1954, 2,400/2,000 = 1.20 or 120 per cent.

The value of this type of statement for studying *relative* changes is readily apparent and would be even more apparent if larger and more difficult amounts to compare had been used in the Dollar Amount columns.

It would be possible to express each figure as a per cent of the preceding year rather than as a per cent of some constant base year, and this is sometimes done. However, the procedure illustrated is believed to be more effective.

It has also been found quite helpful to present significant items from such a statement in a graphic form so that the movement may be even more clearly seen. A line diagram showing sales, cost of goods sold, and selling expenses for a ten-year period would make the increases and decreases in amount much more quickly and clearly seen.

## Common-size Statements

The cost and expense amounts on any operating statement must be considered in relation to the total income which has been produced through incurring these costs. For example, if you were asked to decide whether sales salaries for your firm were too high or too low, you could not reach your decision from the single fact that the sales salaries for the year amounted to $200,000, for this amount is neither large nor small until it can be compared with the amount of income which the salesmen produced. In a similar manner it can be shown that each item on the profit and loss statement must be compared to the total income before its full meaning is apparent. For this reason, profit and loss statements which are to be used by management are often prepared with an additional column in which each amount is expressed as a per cent of net sales for the period. This type of statement, called a "common-size" profit and loss statement or a "100 per cent" statement, is illustrated in Exhibit 14-3.

The advantages of this type of statement are apparent. Some of the points which are now more readily seen are:

1. The returned sales and allowances, though slightly greater than for the preceding year, are actually slightly smaller in proportion to the goods sold.

2. The inventory at the end of 1957 is only 11.2 per cent of sales as compared with 14.0 per cent for the preceding year, thus indicating that there is no tendency to build up stocks which are not salable.

3. The total cost of goods sold is 56.2 per cent of sales as compared with 60.7 per cent for 1956. This means that sales have not been increased by price slashing and that we are getting a greater margin on goods sold than in the preceding period.

4. The margin on sales is up from 39.3 to 43.8 per cent, thus giving us a much better chance to increase net profits.

5. Both selling and administrative expenses have increased in amount but have decreased in proportion to sales produced.

6. As a result of a higher margin and relatively lower operating expenses, the net operating income is now 16.0 per cent or 16 cents per dollar of sales as compared with 9.3 cents per dollar of sales for 1956.

In addition to the figures shown, it would be desirable to prepare itemized lists of selling expenses and general or administrative expenses showing not only the amounts but also the relative importance of each item. For example, a schedule of selling expenses for the Ace Company might show a detailed breakdown of selling expenses (see Exhibit 14-4).

From an analysis such as this, it is easy to see that the most significant change has been a doubling of the advertising budget. Salaries have remained constant but have decreased relatively, travel expenses have

EXHIBIT 14-3

ACE COMPANY

Common-size Income and Expense Statement for the Years 1956 and 1957

|  | 1956 | | 1957 | |
|---|---|---|---|---|
|  | Amount | Per cent | Amount | Per cent |
| Gross sales.......................... | $306,000 | 102.0 | $367,200 | 101.9 |
| Less returned sales & allowances.... | 6,000 | 2.0 | 7,000 | 1.9 |
| Net sales ......................... | $300,000 | 100.0 | $360,200 | 100.0 |
| Cost of goods sold: | | | | |
| Inventory, Jan. 1................... | $ 40,000 | 13.3 | $ 42,000 | 11.7 |
| Purchases (net)................... | 180,000 | 60.0 | 196,000 | 54.4 |
| Transportation in................. | 4,000 | 1.3 | 5,000 | 1.4 |
| Total........................ | $224,000 | 74.7 | $243,000 | 67.4 |
| Less inventory, Dec. 31........... | 42,000 | 14.0 | 40,500 | 11.2 |
| Cost of goods sold................ | $182,000 | 60.7 | $202,500 | 56.2 |
| Gross profit on sales................ | $118,000 | 39.3 | $157,700 | 43.8 |
| Operating expenses: | | | | |
| Selling expenses................... | $ 60,000 | 20.0 | $ 66,000 | 18.3 |
| Administrative expenses........... | 30,000 | 10.0 | 34,000 | 9.4 |
| Total expenses.................. | $ 90,000 | 30.0 | $100,000 | 27.8 |
| Net profit on operations............. | $ 28,000 | 9.3 | $ 57,700 | 16.0 |
| Other income...................... | 3,000 | 1.0 | 4,000 | 1.1 |
| Total........................ | $ 31,000 | 10.3 | $ 61.700 | 17.1 |
| Other expenses..................... | 4,000 | 1.3 | 6,000 | 1.7 |
| Net income for year................ | $ 27,000 | 9.0 | $ 55,700 | 15.4 |

been decreased both absolutely and relatively, delivery expenses have increased slightly as the volume of sales increased, and miscellaneous selling expenses are down slightly. The increase in advertising has brought it up to 18.2 per cent of the total selling expense and to 3.3 per cent of sales. The new sales program has increased the total income so that, though there has been a $6,000 increase in total selling expenses, the total selling costs now amount to only 18.3 cents per dollar of sales as compared with 20 cents for 1956. This is the type of information which, together with information about market conditions, economic outlook, price trends, etc., must form the basis for business decisions.

**The Use of Standards.** Another value of the common-size income and expense statement is that these statements may be more easily compared with statements of a competitor or statements of the industry. One way of estimating whether a firm is trying to operate on too small a margin, whether it is paying too much for salaries, or what would be a reasonable rental (or occupancy cost) for the store is to compare the

EXHIBIT 14-4
ACE COMPANY
Schedule of Selling Expenses for 1956 and 1957

| Item | Amount | | Increase or decrease | | Per cent of total | | Per cent of net sales | |
|---|---|---|---|---|---|---|---|---|
| | 1956 | 1957 | Amount | Per cent | 1956 | 1957 | 1956 | 1957 |
| Sales salaries....... | $40,000 | $40,000 | | | 66.7 | 60.6 | 13.3 | 11.1 |
| Travel ........... | 4,000 | 3,000 | $−1,000 | −25.0 | 6.7 | 4.5 | 1.3 | 0.8 |
| Advertising........ | 6,000 | 12,000 | 6,000 | 100.0 | 10.0 | 18.2 | 2.0 | 3.3 |
| Delivery expense... | 6,000 | 7,200 | 1,200 | 20.0 | 10.0 | 10.9 | 2.0 | 2.0 |
| Misc. selling exp ... | 4,000 | 3,800 | −200 | −5.0 | 6.7 | 5.8 | 1.3 | 1.1 |
| Total.......... | $60,000 | $66,000 | $  6,000 | 10.0 | 100.0 | 100.0 | 20.0 | 18.3 |

firm's "per cent of net sales" figures with figures for the industry as a whole or for firms which are of similar size and which operate under similar conditions.

To help in this type of problem, many trade associations publish common-size statements which may be used for comparison. Dun and Bradstreet also publish trade studies with typical operating statements for various lines of business. Among the firms surveyed by Dun and Bradstreet and reported in their "Cost of Doing Business" series are: sporting goods stores, jewelry stores, bars and taverns, grocery stores, men's furnishings, farm supply stores, gasoline service stations, lumber and building material dealers, grocery and meat stores, retail shoe stores, and children's and infants' wear stores.

The Dun and Bradstreet report for lumber and building material dealers,[1] as a typical example, shows seven tables of operating data with dealers grouped according to rate of profit earned, by class of customer, by sales volume, by form of organization, by population of city, by credit policy, and by geographical region. The purpose of the series is "to make available to small businessmen yardsticks which they can use to measure the success with which they are operating their businesses" and to make

[1] Cost of Doing Business, Survey Number 9, Dun and Bradstreet, Inc.

it possible for the small retailer "to spot unfavorable tendencies in time to take corrective action."

*Eliminating the Effect of Price Changes*

In many cases a study of the trend of sales, cost of sales, merchandise inventory, and many operating expenses over a period of years can be made much more meaningful if the effect of price changes can be eliminated. For example, variations in sales or in inventories are due both to variations in the physical quantities of goods and to variations in prices. A grocery store which is selling twice as much in 1956 as it did in 1940 should have a dollar volume of approximately four times the 1940 figure, since prices have also doubled. If the dollar volume of sales is only twice the 1940 figure, there has been no increase in the actual quantities sold.

To study changes in physical quantities, variations due to price changes must be eliminated. This may be accomplished through the use of index numbers. In many cases suitable price indices may be obtained through published sources, such as the Wholesale Price Index or the Consumer Price Index of the Bureau of Labor Statistics. Each of these indices is made up of a number of components which may be weighted and combined in a variety of ways. Where no suitable index can be found, the firm may construct an index of its own prices.

One method of constructing a suitable index of prices is to select a representative list of items sold, find the typical quantity of each sold in a year, and the selling price in each year covered by the study. The typical quantity is multiplied by the price for each item for each year and total typical values (price times quantity) are obtained. The total for one of the years is given a value of 100 and the other totals are expressed as a per cent of the base year total. Exhibit 14-5 is an example.

EXHIBIT 14-5
Computation of a Price Index

| Commodity | Typical quantity sold | Price charged | | | Typical value (price × quantity) | | |
|---|---|---|---|---|---|---|---|
| | | 1954 | 1955 | 1956 | 1954 | 1955 | 1956 |
| A | 20 | $ 6 | $ 7 | $ 5 | $   120 | $   140 | $   100 |
| B | 40 | 10 | 11 | 12 | 400 | 440 | 480 |
| C | 10 | 15 | 18 | 20 | 150 | 180 | 200 |
| D | 30 | 20 | 21 | 24 | 600 | 630 | 720 |
| Totals...... | ... | ... | ... | ... | $1,270 | $1,390 | $1,500 |
| Price index... | ... | ... | ... | ... | 100.0 | 109.4 | 118.1 |

From this index it may be seen that 1955 prices were about 9 per cent higher than prices in 1954, and 1956 prices are 18 per cent higher than 1954 prices. Sales for 1955 should show a 9 per cent gain over 1954 even if there has been no increase in the actual quantity of goods sold, and 1956 sales should show an 18 per cent increase over 1954. If the actual sales for the three years were $420,000, $446,000, and $462,000, respectively, let us eliminate the effect of price changes and see what changes in volume have actually occurred.

Elimination of the Effect of Price Changes

| | 1954 | 1955 | 1956 |
|---|---|---|---|
| Sales (in thousands)............ | $420 | $446 | $462 |
| Price index................... | 100 | 109 | 118 |
| Deflated sales................ | $420 | $409 | $391 |
| Sales volume index............ | 100 | 97 | 93 |

The "deflated" sales figure is found by dividing the actual sales by the price index and multiplying by 100. The index of sales volume is found by expressing the deflated sales figure for each year as a per cent of deflated sales in the base year.

In spite of an apparent increase in sales over the three-year period, there has been a constant decrease in the volume of goods handled. Sales for 1955 were actually only 97 per cent as great as 1954 sales, and 1956 sales were only 93 per cent as great as 1954. These facts could not be seen from a study of the trend of the dollar volume of goods sold.

As a second example, assume that the inventory of raw materials (in thousands of dollars) of a manufacturer over a seven-year period from 1950 to 1956 and an index of cost prices (1952 = 100.0) for the same years were as follows:

Actual Inventories and Price Index

| | 1950 | 1951 | 1952 | 1953 | 1954 | 1955 | 1956 |
|---|---|---|---|---|---|---|---|
| Inventory............... | $399 | $420 | $488 | $755 | $653 | $519 | $540 |
| Index of cost prices..... | 94.4 | 99.0 | 100.0 | 103.8 | 103.8 | 106.2 | 108.5 |

Has there been an increase in the quantity of goods on hand? Is the inventory larger in 1956 than it was in 1950? What per cent increase has there been in actual quantities of goods on hand? What has been the per cent of increase in prices?

Inventories Adjusted for Price Changes

| | 1950 | 1951 | 1952 | 1953 | 1954 | 1955 | 1956 |
|---|---|---|---|---|---|---|---|
| Adjusted inventory............. | $423 | $424 | $488 | $727 | $629 | $489 | $498 |
| Inventory volume index........ | 100 | 100 | 115 | 172 | 149 | 116 | 118 |

From the index numbers it may be seen that prices are up from 94.4 in 1950 to 108.5 in 1956. This is an increase of 14.1 points or 16 per cent. The adjusted inventories show that the quantity of goods on hand remained fairly constant through 1951, rose slightly in 1952, reached a peak in 1953 and by 1956 had dropped back to about 18 per cent above the 1950 level. Using the original base year, 1952, as a guide, 1956 inventory volume is up only slightly more than 2 per cent ($488 to $498).

*Analysis of Variation in Gross Profit*

Another technique which may be of some value in studying the effect of price and volume changes is the analysis of variation in gross profits. These techniques may be illustrated by the following simple problem:

In 1956 the Dover Company sold 600 articles which cost $1.20 for $1.50 each. Assume also that in 1957 the quantity sold increased 8 per cent, the cost of each item sold increased 10 per cent, and the selling price was increased by 16 per cent.

|  | 1956 | Change | 1957 |
|---|---|---|---|
| Sold...................... | 600 | + 8% | 648 |
| Unit cost................. | $1.20 | +10% | $1.32 |
| Unit sales price........... | $1.50 | +16% | $1.74 |

A comparative income statement for the Dover Company for the two years shows:

|  | 1956 | 1957 | Change |
|---|---|---|---|
| Sales................. | $900.00 | $1,127.52 | $227.52 |
| Cost of sales.......... | 720.00 | 855.36 | 135.36 |
| Gross profit........... | $180.00 | $ 272.16 | $ 92.16 |

It is evident that the increase in sales ($227.52) is due to both a price increase and a volume increase and that the changes in cost of sales and gross profit are also due to these same factors. In this problem, we were given the per cent of increase in volume, in cost prices, and in selling prices. In actual practice we may know only one of these factors. But it is possible to determine the approximate increase or decrease in volume, in cost prices, or in selling prices if only one of the changes is known. The following pattern is used in any case:

Analysis of Variation in Gross Profit

|          | 1956    | 1957      | Change    |
|----------|---------|-----------|-----------|
| Sales............... | $900.00 | $1,127.52 | $227.52 |
| Cost of sales........ | 720.00  | 855.36    | 135.36   |
| Gross profit........ | $180.00 | $ 272.16  | $ 92.16  |

$$\begin{array}{l} \$1,127.52 \\ \underline{*\quad 972.00\ (a)} \end{array} \Big\} \$155.52$$

$$\begin{array}{l} \$\quad 900.00 \\ \underline{*\quad 972.00\ (b)} \end{array} \Big\} \$ 72.00$$

$$\begin{array}{l} \$\quad 855.36 \\ \underline{*\quad 777.60\ (c)} \end{array} \Big\} \$ 77.76$$

$$\begin{array}{l} \$\quad 720.00 \\ \underline{*\quad 777.60\ (d)} \end{array} \Big\} \$ 57.60$$

P = Price
V = Volume

\* This year's figure at last year's prices.

The first step is to write the actual sales and cost of sales figures for the two years on the top line of each bracket. The second step is to compute the figures marked (a) and (b), and (c) and (d). If the per cent increase in selling prices is known, (a) is found first. If the per cent increase in costs is known, (c) is found first. If the volume change is known, (b) and (d) may both be found. Assume that we know selling prices are up 16 per cent.

Since we are assuming that 1957 sales prices are 116 per cent of 1956 prices, we may find what 1957 sales would have been at 1956 prices by dividing the 1957 sales amount by 116 and multiplying by 100. This gives the figure 972. This figure is copied in the blanks marked (a) and (b). Now since 1956 sales were $900 and 1957 sales at 1956 prices (no price change) were $972, we know that the $72 increase was due to volume and $72/900 = 0.08$. Thus the volume increase was 8 per cent. We now increase the 1956 cost of sales figure ($720) by 8 per cent to get the 1957 costs if volume alone had changed. This answer is written in spaces (c) and (d). By comparing 1957 costs ($855.36) with what the costs would have been without price changes ($777.60), we find that costs are up $77.76 ($855.36 − $777.60) or 10 per cent over the costs without price changes. These are the same figures we used in setting up the problems so we know they are all correct.

By subtracting the computed amounts from the actual sales and cost figures, we find that sales increased $155.52 due to price increases and $72.00 due to increased volume, thus explaining the $227.52 increase in sales. Cost of sales increased $77.76 due to a 10 per cent increase in cost prices and was up $57.60 due to increased volume. This fact explains the $135.36 increase in costs. The $92.16 increase in gross profits resulted from a 16 per cent increase in selling prices, a 10 per cent increase in costs, and an 8 per cent increase in volume.

If we had known only that there had been a 10 per cent increase in cost prices, we would have computed the figure marked (c) by dividing $855.36 by 110 and multiplying by 100. This answer would have been copied in spaces (c) and (d). We would have then found that $777.60 is 108 per cent of $720.00, or the volume increase was 8 per cent. Figure (b) could then have been computed by increasing $900 by 8 per cent. This amount would then be copied in (a) to complete the analysis.

If we had known that the volume had increased 8 per cent, we could have computed (b) and (d) by increasing the $900 and $720 by 8 per cent. These answers could then be copied in (a) and (c) to complete the table.

## The Break-even Point

From a management point of view, one of the most important applications of statement analysis is the determination of the volume of sales at which the firm's total income will exactly equal its total operating costs. This is the volume of business necessary for the firm to avoid operating at a loss and is the point above which the firm will begin to show a profit. This is called the "break-even point" analysis. It can be used to compute the approximate profit which will be earned or the approximate loss which will be suffered at various levels of production. If the amount of sales can be forecast, the profit or loss can be estimated and the wisdom of proposed plant expansions and proposed financial plans, such as bond issues, sales of capital stock, or dividend policies, can be evaluated.

The analysis requires more information than is presented on the income statement and involves considerable use of judgment. The first step is to classify each expense item as fixed or variable with production. Fixed expenses are those which would remain constant at any reasonable level of production. Variable expenses are those which increase as production increases and decrease as production is decreased; e.g., the following classifications might be found in a particular firm:

| *Fixed Expenses* | *Variable Expenses* |
|---|---|
| Rent, taxes, and insurance | Materials used |
| Indirect labor | Supplies used |
| Heat and lights | Direct labor |
| Depreciation (if based on life in years) | Depreciation (if based on production) |
| Superintendence | Power |
| Administrative expenses | Payroll taxes (labor) |
| Certain selling expenses | Freight in |
| Etc. | Freight on sales |

**Computation of Break-even Point.** When the total fixed expense has been determined, the total variable expense at various levels of production should be estimated and the amount of variable expense per dollar of sales found; e.g., assume that the fixed expenses of the Roper Company are $162,000 and variable expenses are 40 cents per dollar of sales. If the plant, operating at practical capacity, can produce 12,000 units per year

EXHIBIT 14-6
Break-even Point Analysis

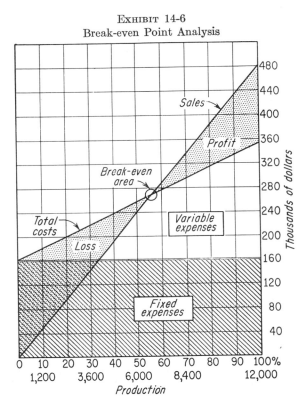

and these units sell for $40 each, the variable costs at 100 per cent of capacity will be 40 per cent of $480,000 or $192,000. These data may be presented in a diagram as shown in Exhibit 14-6.

Note that the fixed expenses are constant at all levels of production. Variable expenses are equal to 40 per cent of the sales dollar (if selling price is $40 each) or $16.00 per unit produced. The total operating expense at capacity is thus $354,000 ($162,000 + 40% of $480,000, or $162,000 + $16.00 times 12,000). The sales line runs from zero to $480,000 when 12,000 units are sold at $40 each. The point at which the total income is just equal to the total operating cost can be estimated at *6,750* units or *56 per cent* of capacity.

The point can be computed without the use of a chart using the following reasoning:

At the break-even point the total operating costs are exactly equal to the total sales. Variable expenses are equal to 40 per cent of sales, so fixed expenses must be equal to 60 per cent of sales at the break-even point. We know that fixed expenses are $162,000. If $162,000 is 60 per cent, then 100 per cent (or sales income required to break even) is 100 times 162,000/60 or $270,000. At $40 per unit, this would mean a production of 6,750 units. This would be 6,750/12,000 or slightly over 56 per cent of capacity.

Because of the fact that some variable expenses are not perfectly related to production and some fixed expenses are subject to increase when production reaches certain levels, the exact value of the break-even point cannot be determined. To emphasize this fact, the point at which the total income line crosses the total cost line may be enclosed in an ellipse and called the break-even area. Perhaps the exact point is not actually necessary. The important thing is that management must realize that profits are not directly variable with sales. In our example, sales of $480,000 would mean an operating profit of $126,000. This is better than a 25 per cent profit on net sales. But, if sales dropped to $300,000 could we expect a profit of 25 per cent of $300,000 or $75,000? The following table answers the question:

Costs and Incomes at Selected Levels of Activity

| Sales.................... | $200,000 | $300,000 | $400,000 | $480,000 |
|---|---|---|---|---|
| Fixed costs.............. | 162,000 | 162,000 | 162,000 | 162,000 |
| Variable costs........... | 80,000 | 120,000 | 160,000 | 192,000 |
| Net profit............... | ($ 42,000) | $ 18,000 | $ 78,000 | $126,000 |

Net profit on sales of $300,000 is seen to be only about $18,000 instead of $75,000 and a loss of $42,000 could be expected if sales drop to $200,000. This emphasizes the important effect of sales volume on net profits in firms which have high fixed charges.

**Practical Value of Break-even Point Analysis.** If the company described above is operating at 50 per cent of capacity and is selling 6,000 units per year, it has total sales of $240,000 and total operating costs of $162,000 + $16 times 6,000 or $258,000, and is operating at a loss of $18,000 per year. The cost per unit sold is $258,000/6,000 or $43 and the selling price per unit is $40. Assume that they have an opportunity to sell an additional 3,000 units per year in South America if they will reduce the price on these units to $35 each, which is $8 below present total unit cost. Could they profitably take this contract, assuming that the sale to the South American dealer would have no effect on their domestic sales?

```
Total sales.........  $40 × 6,000  $240,000
                       35 × 3,000   105,000
                                   $345,000
Total costs:
   Fixed...............  $162,000
   Variable............   144,000   306,000
Net profit....................   $ 39,000
```

Accepting the order for 3,000 additional units at $35 would result in a profit of $39,000 as compared to expected losses of $18,000, in spite of the fact that the selling price is $8 less than the present unit cost.

As another example, assume that the Roper Company is operating at 80 per cent of capacity. Its sales amount to 9,600 units at $40 each or $384,000. Its total costs are $162,000 plus $16 times 9,600 or $315,600, and it is making a profit of $68,400. It is believed that if the selling price were reduced to $35 per unit, operations could be increased to practical capacity. Would this be profitable?

```
Sales............  12,000 units at $35  $420,000
Costs: Fixed.............  $162,000
       Variable...........   192,000   354,000
Net profit........................   $ 66,000
```

The profit which would be earned if prices were cut to $35 would be $66,000 as compared with present profits of $68,400. This means that profits would be decreased if prices were to be dropped to get the added quantity of sales.

As a third example, assume that the Roper Company is operating at practical capacity, has sales of $480,000, and is making a profit of $126,000. An expansion is being considered. If the proposed machinery is purchased, fixed costs will be increased to $210,000 and variable costs will be reduced to $12 per unit, or 30 cents per sales dollar if prices are kept at $40 per unit. Sales can be increased to 15,000 units. Would the proposed expansion prove profitable?

The break-even point after the proposed expansion would be computed as follows: ($X$ equals sales at the break-even point)

$$X = 210,000 + 0.30X$$
$$0.70X = 210,000$$
$$X = \$300,000$$

and $\dfrac{300,000}{40} = 7,500$ units to break even

Maximum profits under proposed expansion are:

```
Sales............  15,000 units at $40   $600,000
Costs: Fixed..............  $210,000
       Variable...........   180,000    390,000
Net profit........................    $210,000
```

This means an increase in profits of $84,000 ($210,000 − 126,000) if sales can be increased to 15,000 units. Sales of 7,500 units are necessary to break even, while at the present time sales of 7,500 units would produce dollar sales of $300,000 and a profit of $18,000. Sales of 12,000 are now producing a profit of $126,000. If the machinery were bought and sales were not increased, the profits would not be changed since

$$\$480,000 - (210,000 \text{ plus } 30\% \text{ of } \$480,000) = \$126,000$$

also. There is no danger in the proposed expansion if sales can be maintained at their present levels. Greater profits will result if sales can be increased, but the firm will have a higher break-even point and will make less profit and incur losses sooner if sales volume should decrease. On the basis of these facts and on sales forecasts, a sound decision can be made.

### Graphic Presentation of Income Data

Many graphic devices are available for the presentation of the data found on an income statement. Probably the most commonly used chart is one which shows the distribution of the income dollar to the various groups who help to produce the firm's goods or services and are thus entitled to a share of its income. This type of chart is prepared from an income statement organized as shown in Exhibit 14-7.

EXHIBIT 14-7

SLEGEL COMPANY

Income Statement—Distribution of the Income Dollar

for the Year Ended December 31, 1957

|  | Amount | Per cent |
|---|---|---|
| Total net income for 1957 |  | $200,000 | 100.0 |
| Distribution of net income: |  |  |
| To suppliers of merchandise and materials | $120,000 | 60.0 |
| To employees for wages and salaries | 46,000 | 23.0 |
| To government for taxes | 12,000 | 6.0 |
| Allowance for depreciation of plant and equipment | 8,000 | 4.0 |
| To owners as a return on their investment | 8,000 | 4.0 |
| Total | 194,000 |  |
| Net retained in business for growth and expansion | $ 6,000 | 3.0 |

The share of each participant may be presented in a number of ways: A large paper dollar may be used to represent total income and pieces may be cut from it to show the per cent going to each factor involved in producing the income. Coins may be placed in several stacks whose heights are proportional to the share of each participant, or a silver dollar or large circle may be cut into wedge-shaped pieces which are proportional to the share received by each. Two or more years may be compared by the use of additional circles, and the size of the circle may be proportional to the total income. This last refinement is of doubtful value, however, because of the difficulty of estimating the relative areas of circles of various sizes.

From a management viewpoint, a Z chart is one of the most effective methods of summarizing income data and presenting a quick picture of the trend of sales or other important income statement items. To illustrate how the Z chart is used, assume the following monthly sales figures for the Nelson Company. The data are graphically presented in Exhibit 14-8.

| Month | Sales | | Cumulative sales | | 12-month moving total |
|---|---|---|---|---|---|
| | 1956 | 1957 | 1956 | 1957 | |
| January..... | $ 7,600 | $ 9,400 | $ 7,600 | $ 9,400 | $106,200 |
| February.... | 5,800 | 7,400 | 13,400 | 16,800 | 107,800 |
| March....... | 8,200 | 10,100 | 21,600 | 26,900 | 109,700 |
| April........ | 8,800 | 7,500 | 30,400 | 34,400 | 108,400 |
| May........ | 9,900 | 9,200 | 40,300 | 43,600 | 107,700 |
| June........ | 8,400 | 9,600 | 48,700 | 53,200 | 108,900 |
| July........ | 5,200 | 7,600 | 53,900 | 60,800 | 111,300 |
| August...... | 4,800 | 7,200 | 58,700 | 68,000 | 113,700 |
| September... | 8,600 | 11,800 | 67,300 | 79,800 | 116,900 |
| October..... | 10,700 | 13,500 | 78,000 | 93,300 | 119,700 |
| November... | 11,800 | 14,600 | 89,800 | 107,900 | 122,500 |
| December... | 14,600 | 12,700 | 104,400 | 120,600 | 120,600 |
| | $104,400 | $120,600 | | | |

To emphasize the month-to-month variation, a column is set up for each month and bars are drawn for each month as that month's sales data are obtained. A colored line could be used to enter corresponding figures for the preceding year.

The cumulative sales line shows the total sales from January 1 (the first day of the fiscal year) to the end of the current month. The distance between the lines measures the amount by which 1957 sales exceed the 1956 sales.

The total sales for the year 1956 is plotted on the left-hand scale at the point marked $A$. This line is then extended across the chart to the point marked $B$. A twelve-month moving total is found for the end of each month of 1957. The January figure, for example, is obtained by subtracting the January, 1956, value ($7,600) from the 1956 total and replacing it with the January, 1957, figure ($9,400). This value ($106,200) is then plotted at the right-hand side of the January column. If January, 1957, is better than the January, 1956, figure which it replaced, the point will be above the line $AB$. When February sales figures are obtained, the total for the twelve months ending February 28, 1957, is computed in the same way ($106,200 − 5,800 + 7,400 = $107,800), and this figure is entered at the right-hand side of the February column. If this point is above line *AB*, the total sales for January and February, 1957, must exceed the total

EXHIBIT 14-8

Sales of Nelson Company, 1956 and 1957

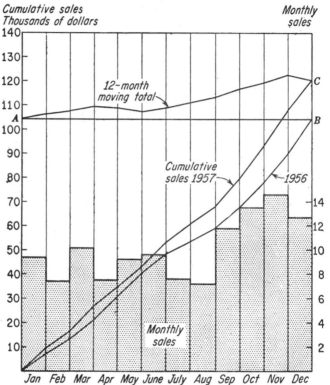

for the corresponding months of the preceding year. If the line drawn across the February column rises, the February, 1957, sales must exceed the 1956 February value, etc. Similar plottings are made for each month as the sales data come in, and all plotted points are connected by straight lines.

At any time during 1957 the chart will reveal many valuable trends and comparisons. For example, let us assume that data have been entered through June, 1957. What facts can be obtained from the chart?

1. The bars represent the monthly sales for each month of the year and emphasize the month-to-month variation. If colored lines are used to present the sales of the preceding year, the difference between the months is shown by the difference between the red and black lines.

2. The cumulative sales line shows that total sales through June, 1957, exceeded total sales for the same period in 1956. The distance between the lines measures the difference. (The lines for a particular month are parallel when the monthly sales in that month are the same for the two years. Diverging lines, as in March, indicate that the 1957 March value exceeds the 1956 value.)

3. The twelve-month moving total is above the line AB and has been above this line all through 1957. This means that even though April and May were below the preceding year, the 1957 total has, so far, always exceeded the 1956 total to that same date. When the moving total line slopes upward, as in January, February, March, and June, the 1957 values are higher than the corresponding 1956 values. The down-sloping line for April and May shows that sales in these months were not as good as in 1956; the steeper the slope, the greater is the change.

4. Total sales for the two years are shown by the points B and C. The difference between these points measures the total increase for 1957.

## SUMMARY

The significance of amounts shown on the income statement comes largely from comparisons with figures for prior years or with industry standards. Comparative statements showing increases and decreases of specific items, trend percentages, and common-size statements are among the most widely used procedures for making these comparisons possible.

Many changes in statement amounts are largely due to price-level changes. These changes may often be minimized by the use of index numbers. Variations in gross profits may be analyzed to determine the approximate effect of changes in volume, sales prices, and cost of goods sold on the amount earned.

An analysis of operating cost totals into variable and fixed expenses makes possible the computation of the volume of sales required to break even and the probable profit which can be realized at various levels of operation. Using these procedures, the effect of proposed changes in plant equipment or sales policy may be evaluated. Many graphic devices are available for depicting trends in earnings, dividends, sales, etc., or for presenting other income and expense data. The value of the income statement as a tool of management is largely determined by the analyst's ability to make the comparisons and analyses described.

## QUESTIONS

**1.** Net sales of the Ace Company increased from $200,000 in 1956 to $216,000 in 1957. Which of the following statements are true, which are false, and which are doubtful?

*a.* Net sales increased $16,000.

*b.* Net sales increased 108 per cent.

*c.* Net sales in 1957 are 108 per cent more than net sales for 1956.

*d.* Net sales increased 8 per cent.

*e.* There has been an 8 per cent increase in the quantity of goods sold.

*f.* The increase in net sales may have occurred in spite of a decrease in physical volume.

*g.* The current (or latest) year should be used as the base in figuring the per cent of change.

*h.* Changes in dollar volume may be due to price changes, to changes in physical quantities sold, or to a combination of both.

**2.** Which year should be selected as the base year in computing trend percentages?

**3.** Trend percentages for a company were computed for the years from 1953 through 1957. Figures for selling expenses for this period were 100, 106, 121, 132, and 143. Which of the following statements are true, which are false, and which are doubtful?

*a.* The trend is upward and therefore indicates an unsatisfactory condition.

*b.* Selling expenses increased 6 per cent from 1953 to 1954.

*c.* Selling expenses increased 11 per cent from 1956 to 1957.

*d.* Good management always tries to minimize expenses.

*e.* It is more important to maximize current and long-run profits than to minimize expenses.

*f.* Increases in expense amounts must always be evaluated in terms of their effect on net income.

*g.* The trend figures shown were computed by expressing selling expenses for each year as a per cent of the preceding year.

**4.** On a common-size statement, what figure is used as the base or 100 per cent? Why is this figure used rather than gross sales or some other amount?

**5.** What are the advantages of common-size statements over income statements in absolute amounts?

**6.** Explain how the effect of price changes on net sales can be eliminated through the use of index numbers of prices charged.

**7.** How are expenses classified when a break-even chart is to be prepared?

**8.** What is meant by the terms fixed expenses, variable expenses, semifixed expenses?

**9.** What is the break-even point? Why is it important that a break-even point be computed?

**10.** If a company has a profit of $40,000 on sales of $400,000, do you think it likely that profits would have been $20,000 on sales of $200,000? Why not?

**11.** If the Ajax Company has fixed operating expenses of $180,000 and the variable expenses amount to 40 per cent of sales at the break-even point, what is the break-even point for the firm? What profit should the company earn if sales are $600,000 for the year?

**12.** Does the break-even point analysis help to show how a relatively small increase in volume may result in a large percentage increase in net profits?

**13.** The Jan Company has fixed expenses of $240,000. Variable expenses are $6 per unit sold. If each unit sells for $14, how many units must be sold for the firm to break even? What profit would the firm make if it sells 30,500 units? How much would it make if it can increase sales to 31,000 units? Does it seem reasonable that this small increase in volume could double the net profit?

## CHAPTER 15

# ANALYSIS OF BALANCE SHEET DATA

The preparation of the balance sheet has been described and illustrated in Chapter 6. Although the various forms and arrangements were fully described, little time was spent in discussing the proper classification of individual items. Now that the accounts used by partnerships and corporations and accounts needed to record the more complex manufacturing and selling problems have been described, a more thorough study of account classification can be made.

## THE CLASSIFICATION OF BALANCE SHEET ACCOUNTS

The problem of the proper classification of balance sheet accounts is of great significance to the analyst because the financial statements of an individual firm cannot be compared with those of another firm using a different classification system or following different conventions in the classification of the individual accounts. For example, a balance sheet of a large West Coast lumber company shows "Provision for Federal taxes on income" as a current liability but deducts from this amount $22 million of United States government tax notes which have been purchased to be used to pay this liability. Following this procedure, current assets total $78 million and current liabilities total $21 million, which gives a current ratio of 78 to 21 or about 3.7 to 1. Some analysts believe this classification procedure a violation of the basic principle that both assets and liabilities should be shown in their full amounts and no offsets should be made. If a change is made to agree with this point of view, the treasury tax notes would be included in the current assets and not deducted from the tax liability. This would increase the current assets to $100 million and would increase the total current liabilities to $43 million. As a result, the current ratio would be 100 to 43 or about 2.3 to 1. Thus, it is obviously impossible to compare ratios or percentages of one firm with those of another firm unless the statements themselves are comparable. And it is impossible to establish standards or meaningful averages from a group of statements unless all the statements have been prepared in a uniform way.

Because of the need for uniform treatment of account balances, the first step in the analysis of a balance sheet is to reclassify the accounts in accordance with the subheadings and classification principles which the analyst has established. These principles cannot be established for all persons for all viewpoints, and no attempt will be made here to say that a particular account must be classified in a particular way for all analysts. For instance, if the business has notes receivable from officers and the managers know that these notes will be paid within the next six or eight months, there is no reason why they should not think of them as current assets and as current sources of cash. But the banker, who may doubt that the notes will be paid soon and who may be inclined to think such loans or advances poor business policy, would be quite likely to consider such notes as "Other" assets or noncurrent receivables.

Let us assume that balance sheet classifications as prescribed by the Securities and Exchange Commission are satisfactory for our purposes. These headings are:

|  |  |
|---|---|
| *Assets* | *Liabilities, capital shares, and surplus* |
| 1. Current assets | 1. Current liabilities |
| 2. Investments | 2. Deferred income |
| 3. Fixed assets | 3. Long-term debt |
| 4. Intangible assets | 4. Other liabilities |
| 5. Deferred charges | 5. Reserves not shown elsewhere |
| 6. Other assets | 6. Capital shares |
|  | 7. Surplus |
|  |    *a.* Paid-in |
|  |    *b.* Appraisal |
|  |    *c.* Other capital surplus |
|  |    *d.* Earned surplus |
|  |       (1) Appropriated |
|  |       (2) Unappropriated |

When a balance sheet is to be completely analyzed, the items presented must be fitted into the desired classifications. In examining balance sheets the analyst may find many different account titles or balance sheet descriptions which he must be able to understand and classify properly. The most commonly used balance sheet accounts are shown in the list which follows. The accompanying discussion will help to clarify the meaning of these accounts and will suggest some questions which should be raised, especially when the statements are not prepared by CPAs.

LIST OF BALANCE SHEET ACCOUNTS

1. Cash
2. Accounts Receivable
3. Notes Receivable
4. Allowance (Reserve) for Bad Debts
5. Accrued Receivables
6. Merchandise Inventory
7. Marketable Securities
8. Investments in Subsidiaries
9. Investments (other)
10. Land
11. Buildings
12. Equipment
13. Accumulated Depreciation
14. Allowance for Depletion
15. Patents and Copyrights
16. Goodwill
17. Franchises
18. Allowance for Amortization of Intangible Assets
19. Pension (and other) Funds
20. Fixed Assets Not Used in Operations
21. Prepaid Expenses
22. Organization Expense
23. Bond Discount and Expense
24. Accounts Payable
25. Notes Payable
26. Accrued Liabilities
27. Dividends Payable
28. Estimated Income Tax Payable
29. Payroll Taxes Payable
30. Bonds Payable
31. Mortgages Payable
32. Deferred Credits to Income
33. Contingency Reserves
34. Capital Stock
35. Earned Surplus (Unappropriated)
36. Appropriated Surplus
37. Capital (or Paid-in) Surplus
38. Donated Surplus
39. Appraisal Surplus
40. Dividends Paid or Drawings

*Current Assets*

*1. Cash.* The amount shown for Cash represents the amount of cash on hand and in the bank. Since the petty cash fund is normally included, the analyst should know that the fund was replenished before the statements were prepared. If this has not been done, the expenses will be understated and the cash will be overstated. The amounts, however, will not be very large. Items which may not be deposited at a bank at their face value should not be counted as cash. This means that IOUs from employees or officers, stamps, and notes for advances are not properly included in Cash. If accounts are carried in several banks, accounting convention requires that an overdraft in one bank be shown as a current liability and not offset against balances in other banks. This problem, while important to the accounting theorist, is of relatively minor importance to the analyst. More significant problems include:

Is any of the cash unavailable because it is in closed banks or in foreign countries restricting its movement?

Is any of the cash really a part of a special fund or earmarked for special purposes and thus not available for the purpose for which the analyst would have it used?

Do bank loans require minimum bank balances which reduce the amount of cash which is actually available for paying operating costs?

*2. Accounts Receivable* generally represent amounts due from the sale of merchandise. These amounts are properly shown as current assets. Other receivables, and especially those due from affiliated companies, may or may not be considered current. If the debt is owed by an officer or a director or by an affiliated company which is not in a satisfactory current position, it is quite likely that the amount will not be received within one year and thus should not be classified as a current asset.

If accounts receivable have been pledged as security on a loan or assigned to a finance company, the analyst should be certain that the liability is not deducted and only the net equity in accounts receivable shown as an asset. If accounts receivable are assigned, the balance sheet should show the unassigned receivables, the assigned receivables, and the amount owed the finance company, as:

| *Current assets* | | *Current liabilities* | |
|---|---|---|---|
| Accounts receivable*........ | $44,000 | Notes payable............... | $5,000 |

\* Includes $8,000 assigned as security for notes payable of $5,000.

or

| *Current assets* | | *Current liabilities* | |
|---|---|---|---|
| Accounts receivable.......... | $36,000 | Notes Payable to X Finance | |
| Assigned accounts receivable... | 8,000 | Company. Secured by assigned | |
| Total.................... | $44,000 | accounts receivable......... | $5,000 |

If accounts receivable are sold outright to a commercial factor, the accounts sold are no longer included among the assets and there is no obligation to pay the factor.

*3. Notes Receivable* should be classified in the same way as accounts receivable and the same problems are involved. Some analysts feel that businesses which normally sell on open account do not have notes receivable on their books except for those received in settlement of past-due accounts. For this reason, they feel that where notes are not normally received they should not be considered current assets. The most logical basis for classification seems to be whether the amount will be collected within the next fiscal year. This may mean that a banker who is inclined toward conservatism would classify all notes other than usual trade notes as "other" assets while management would classify all notes which it expects to collect within a year as current assets, regardless of how they originated.

When notes receivable are discounted at the bank in order to obtain needed cash, the firm is contingently liable for the maturity value of the note. If the note is not paid by the maker, the bank will look to the firm which discounted the note for settlement. As a general rule, the amount of notes receivable discounted is deducted from the total notes receivable in the current asset section. Some analysts prefer to show the total notes receivable as a current asset and consider the liability for notes discounted as a current liability. The latter method would, of course, result in a lower current ratio in any case except where the current liabilities equal or exceed the current assets.

In some cases the amount shown for notes receivable includes only those notes which have not been discounted. The liability for discounted notes will then be indicated in a footnote.

Installment sales often result in accounts or notes collectible over a period of 18 to 36 months. Theoretically, amounts due after more than a year should not be shown as current assets. Actually, if the terms are usual for the trade, all installment accounts will probably be included in the current assets.

*4. The Allowance for Bad Debts* is the estimated amount of uncollectible trade accounts and notes receivable. In some cases the allowance is deducted from the accounts receivable balance alone, but where the notes receivable are trade notes and do not represent loans to officers, directors, employees, etc., there is no reason why the allowance should not apply to notes as well as to open accounts. If the annual charge to bad debts is based on a percentage of sales (or account sales), the balance in the Allowance for Bad Debts may get out of proportion to expected losses. But if the expense amount is obtained by aging the receivables and bringing the allowance up to the estimated losses, the allowance may be very accurately stated but the expense charged to current operations, since it depends upon the balance already in the "reserve," may be out of proportion to the income (sales) for the period. No perfect method of estimating bad debt losses and the resulting allowance for bad debts has yet been devised. As a rule, accountants prefer to have the loss on bad debts proportional to the account sales and correct the per cent figure used whenever the balance in the allowance begins to get out of line with the balance in the receivables accounts.

*5. Accrued Receivables.* When an income has been earned but has not yet been collected, the amount receivable is called an accrued receivable and is considered a current asset. The income earned is added to the income account through an adjustment which debits the accrued receivable account and credits the proper income account. Accrued rent and accrued interest are the most common accounts of this type.

*6. Merchandise Inventory.* All inventories of goods held for resale, whether unprocessed, partially processed, or finished goods, are considered current assets. There may be some question about the propriety of this procedure in the case of slow-moving inventories which will not be processed and sold within a year or merchandise (such as antiques) which has such a slow rate of turnover that the annual sales may not equal one inventory. The question of most importance to the analyst, however, is the principle used in evaluating the inventory. Several procedures are available. When taking a physical count of the stock, the prices assigned are usually "cost or market, whichever is lower." The "cost" used may be the cost of the specific article or one of a number of different cost bases. When perpetual inventories are kept, articles removed from stock may be recorded at the price of the earliest purchase (FIFO) or at the price of the latest purchase (LIFO). If FIFO is used, the items in the inventory will be valued at the most recent cost prices, while LIFO will result in showing the inventory at the most remote purchase prices. "Or market" is variously understood to mean present selling price or present replacement price. Except in case of securities, it should be understood to mean the present selling price in the market which furnished the firm with its product. Profits on price rises are never anticipated and merchandise may be shown at cost prices which are far below the present replacement cost. In no case should the inventory value shown be taken as the "true" value.

The valuation method used has an important effect upon the value of the inventory shown on the balance sheet and the earnings reported for each fiscal period. The use of FIFO increases the amplitude of the annual earnings cycle because the costs assigned in a period of rising prices are the lowest costs and the profits reported are overstated. In a period of falling prices, the costs assigned will be the highest costs and profits will be understated. The use of LIFO will result in evening up the annual profits reported. However, the choice of the valuation procedure to be used has no effect on the earnings over the life of the firm and both methods are approved by the Federal government.

*7. Marketable Securities.* In a highly seasonal business large amounts of working capital may be needed to carry the business through its peak. These funds may be borrowed or the firm may provide enough working capital for its peak load and try to invest the surplus cash during its off season. These funds which are not needed in operating the business because of seasonal or temporary economic conditions may be invested in securities in order to make some use of the cash which would otherwise be idle. Since the money may be needed at short notice, it is essential

that these investments be readily marketable. Such temporary investments are considered current assets; they are not classified as "Investments" since this term is reserved for more or less permanent investments.

*Investments*

8. *Investments in Subsidiaries.* Investments in subsidiaries, even
though readily salable, are not included in "Marketable Securities"
for the investment cannot be sold without destroying the relationship
between the parent and the subsidiary. In consolidated statements the
investment in the subsidiary is eliminated in the consolidating working
papers and does not appear on the consolidated statements. The amount
of the investment in other corporations, or in an affiliate if not eliminated
in the consolidated statements, may be shown at cost, at the present
market value, or at an amount which recognizes the profits earned and
the dividends paid by the company whose stock is held. In many cases
the value assigned to the stocks held is the original cost of the stock and
may bear little relationship to the present market price of the stock. An
intelligent analysis of the balance sheet requires that information regarding the valuation of investments and their present market value be
known.

9. *Investments* other than investments in stock of subsidiary or affiliated
companies may include bonds issued by governmental units or by other
business organizations. When these bonds are purchased at a discount
(or a premium) they are entered at cost and the discount is amortized
over their remaining life. For example, assume that ten-year 4 per cent
bonds of X Company, par value $100,000, are purchased on January 1
for $96,000. The entry to record the purchase would be:

| | | |
|---|---|---|
| Investment in X Co. Bonds | 96,000 | |
| Cash | | 96,000 |

At the time the first annual interest payment is received the entry is:

| | | |
|---|---|---|
| Cash | 4,000 | |
| Investment in X Co. Bonds | 400 | |
| Interest earned | | 4,400 |

By the time the bonds mature their carrying value will be equal to
their par value and the additional earning will have been spread over
the period the bonds were held. Other investments may also include
stocks owned and buildings or land, etc., not used in operating the
business.

*Fixed Assets*

10. *Land.* The land owned by a business is almost always carried at cost.
Occasionally the amount shown will reflect the result of an appraisal,

however. If carried at cost, the amount will include the price of the land, legal fees and other costs of purchasing the land, the net cost of demolishing unwanted buildings or of clearing the land, special assessments for paving or sewer, etc., and taxes incurred during the period before the land is placed in use. Again, the value at which the asset is carried on the books may be unrelated to the present value of the land—and loans depend for their security on the actual value of the property rather than upon the cost. If it is necessary to know the present value of land, the analyst must have it appraised by an expert. It is futile for the analyst to object to the accounting convention which requires that the land be shown at cost.

Generally, land is not subject to depreciation; though farm lands may depreciate, building sites represent space and are not valued by the fertility of the soil. Mining lands, however, are subject to depletion.

*11. Buildings.* Buildings, like land, are included in the fixed assets. They are shown at cost adjusted for estimated depreciation to date. The cost of a building includes cost of excavation and all costs of erection of the structure, including architect fees, building permits, etc., and taxes on the building before it is ready for use. The cost of a second-hand building includes all repair costs incurred to put the building in usable condition. Where land and buildings are purchased for a lump sum, a reasonable allocation must be made to the Land and the Building accounts and the accounts must be kept separate because the cost of the buildings may be recovered through depreciation charges while the cost of land may not. Buildings located at mines or on leased properties are depreciated over the life of the depletable asset or life of the lease where this is less than the life of the building. The analyst must remember that the value shown for buildings is the historical cost, and the accumulated depreciation simply shows the total depreciation charged as an expense up to the date of the statement. The depreciated value (or book value) is sometimes far more and sometimes far less than the amount for which the building would sell.

*12. Equipment,* store fixtures, office furniture and fixtures, machinery, delivery trucks, etc., are all shown in separate accounts but they are all fixed assets. They are all carried at original cost less an allowance for estimated depreciation. The cost includes the stated price plus freight, insurance while in transit, installation costs, costs of test runs, and any other expenses incurred in getting the equipment ready for use. The cost of used equipment should also include the cost of any repairs necessary to place it in usable condition.

*13. Accumulated Depreciation.* The balance shown under the account generally called Accumulated Depreciation on Buildings (or Equipment, or Furniture and Fixtures, etc.) represents the total depreciation charged as an expense on the asset **group** indicated. Many beginning business students think that the "Reserve for Depreciation" account represents an amount, or fund, set aside for the replacement of the asset when it is worn out or becomes obsolete and must be replaced. This is not correct. In order to avoid this misunderstanding as to the meaning of the account, there is a trend toward the use of the terms "Allowance for Depreciation," "Estimated Depreciation" or "Accumulated Depreciation" instead of the words *Reserve for Depreciation*, which were formerly more widely used.

As a general rule, the amount of depreciation charged in a given period is found as follows:

$$\frac{\text{Cost of asset} - \text{scrap or trade-in value}}{\text{Life of asset}} = \text{depreciation expense}$$

This gives the amount of depreciation per unit of life. If the life is expressed in years, it will give the depreciation per year. The annual depreciation is then divided by 12 to get monthly depreciation or by 4 to get quarterly depreciation. If the life is expressed in hours that the asset will run or the number of products it will produce, the depreciation per unit is multiplied by the hours used or products manufactured to get the depreciation for the period. This charge for depreciation gets on the books through an adjusting entry debiting "Depreciation Expense on ————" and crediting the "Accumulated Depreciation on ————." At the end of the fiscal period, the temporary account "Depreciation Expense on ————" is closed to the Profit and Loss Summary. The "Reserve" remains on the books until the asset is sold, junked, or otherwise disposed of. It is always deducted from the cost of asset to get the "net," "book," or "depreciated" value.

In every case the amount recovered over the life of an asset is planned to equal the total cost of using the asset. If prices are rising, the cost of *replacing* the asset may be far greater than the original cost. For this reason many businessmen feel that depreciation charges should cover estimated replacement cost rather than actual cost. No matter how it is determined the balance in the Accumulated Depreciation shows only the total depreciation charged off. It does not represent a replacement fund.

*14. Allowance for Depletion.* Fixed properties such as mines or forests, which are actually used up or consumed to produce the firm's product, are said to be "depleted." As in the case of depreciable properties, their original cost, which is shown by the asset account, must be recovered over the useful life of the property. As the asset is consumed, a periodic charge is made to a depletion expense account and an offsetting credit is made to an "Allowance (or Reserve) for Depletion." And, as in the case of depreciation reserves, this amount is always subtracted from the cost of the asset to arrive at the book value (or unrecovered cost) of the asset. When a building or other asset used in connection with mines, etc., will have no value after the mines are fully depleted, the estimated life of the building can be no longer than the remaining life of the mine, and depreciation on the building should be prorated on the basis of the life of the mine or the life of the building depending upon which is the shorter period.

## Intangible Assets

*15. Patents and Copyrights.* Patents are originally shown at cost. If a patent is purchased, the cost is easily obtained. Where they are developed by the firm, the cost includes research costs, attorney fees, cost of blue-prints, etc., and is much more difficult to determine. Since a patent which cannot be protected has no value, the cost of lawsuits incurred in defending a patent are also considered a part of the cost of the patent. In no case does the total dollar amount shown represent the "true" value of the patent as the cost is often far less than the benefits to be obtained from the exclusive right to produce a given article. While the legal life of a patent is seventeen years, the value of a patent may disappear long before its legal life is ended. For this reason, the cost of a patent must be recovered over the period which is expected to be benefited by the patent, which, in any case, should be no more than seventeen years. Unlike depreciable assets, the cost of a patent is ordinarily written off as a charge to patent expense and a credit directly to the patent account. This process of writing off the cost of an intangible asset is called amortization.

Copyrights give the holder a right to publish or reproduce books, songs, art works, etc. for a period of 28 years and may be renewed for a like period. When copyrights are purchased, they are entered at cost. The cost of obtaining one's own copyright is so low (about $4) that it is hardly worthwhile to capitalize the expenditure. As in the case of patents, their cost is amortized over their expected useful life by a charge to an expense account and a credit directly to the asset account.

*16. Goodwill.* Goodwill is an intangible asset whose presence is made evident by the ability of the firm to earn more than the normal rate of return on its investment. It is seldom entered in the books unless it is purchased; that is, unless an old, well-known firm is purchased for more than the net value of the tangible assets obtained, or a partner is bought out for an amount greater than his tangible net worth. The amount shown for goodwill is usually ignored in any analysis of debt-paying ability since in case of liquidation it has no value. It is often written off against the earned surplus, either in one entry or over a period of years where the amount is large.

*17. Franchises.* Cities or other governmental units often grant a firm, such as an electric power company, an exclusive right to use city streets and alleys to provide electric power, telephone service, etc., within the area. Such a grant is called a franchise. The firm may be granted the right without cost or may pay the governmental unit or some other firm for the franchise. In any case, the franchise is entered at cost. If the right runs for a given period of time, the cost is amortized over this period. If it may be revoked at any time at the option of the grantor, it should be written off within a short time. If the franchise grants a perpetual right, its value does not decrease and its cost may properly remain permanently in the asset account. The value in the franchise account should always show the unrecovered cost.

*18. Allowance for Amortization of Intangible Assets.* Balance sheets occasionally contain reserves for the amortization of some intangible asset, such as an "Allowance (or Reserve) for the Amortization of Patents." These "reserves," when used, are properly shown on the balance sheet as deductions from the related asset accounts. As previously explained, however, it is perhaps less confusing to charge the annual write-off to an expense account and credit the amount directly to the asset account, as shown for Patents and Copyrights.

When bonds are sold at a discount and the amount of the discount is shown as an asset, this asset is an intangible one but is shown on the balance sheet as a "deferred charge." The balance in the bond discount account is amortized, just as is the balance of other intangibles, by an entry which transfers a proportionate share of the bond discount from the asset account to a bond interest expense account. This charges the total cost of using the money (interest plus discount) to the interest expense account. No amortization reserves are needed for the amortization of bond discounts and they are seldom used for any intangibles.

## Other Assets

*19. Pension (and Other) Funds.* When a firm sets aside funds which are to be used for a specific purpose, the amount is removed from the cash account and set up in an appropriately named fund account. The actual cash is turned over to a trustee, who may hold the amount in cash or may invest in securities which will, through their earnings, help to increase the fund balance. It should be remembered that while a Reserve for Bond Sinking Fund merely indicates that some portion of the Earned Surplus balance has been appropriated, the appearance of a "Bond Sinking Fund" means that cash has actually been set aside. Even though these funds may be in cash, they are not to be considered current assets since they cannot be used to pay the current debts of the firm. They are usually classified as "Other Assets" or as "Investments."

*20. Fixed Assets Not Used in Operations.* Occasionally a firm holds fixed properties which are not used in producing the firm's goods or services; e.g., a manufacturer may purchase a plant site which is to be used at some future date. This type of asset is not considered a "fixed" asset but is shown as an "other" asset or an investment. Costs incurred in holding the property until it is put to use are capitalized, that is, are charged to the asset account. If machinery or other equipment no longer used is still of value and still has a value (unrecovered cost) on the books, the unrecovered cost should be shown as an *other* asset and the original cost and related depreciation reserve are no longer shown with the *fixed* assets.

### Deferred Charges (and Prepaid Expenses)

*21. Prepaid Expenses.* Many of the costs incurred in a given fiscal period will benefit both that period and other subsequent periods. When such costs are incurred, the charge may be made to either an expense or an asset account. In either case, an adjustment is required at the end of the fiscal period to make the expense account show the expired cost and to show the unexpired cost in an asset account. These asset balances, which will be used and will become expenses in future periods, are called prepaid expenses. They have also been called "deferred charges" since they will be "charged" to expense accounts in a later period.

Most analysts now consider prepaid expenses to be properly included in the current assets. Some believe that they should not be considered current assets since they cannot be used to pay current debts. The analyst may include them in current assets or in a separate section for deferred charges and prepaid expenses but they should be consistently classified if the statements are to be comparable. It should also be noted that their inclusion in the current asset section will improve the appearance of the current ratio. This should cause no real problem since the analyst will evaluate the current position with this fact in mind.

Prepaid insurance, supplies, prepaid rent, and prepaid interest are among the most common of the prepaid expense items.

*22. Organization Expense.* The costs of organizing a corporation, including fees paid to lawyers and to the state, are charged to an asset account since they are incurred *before* the firm begins to earn any income and since they benefit the corporation for its entire life. They are "intangible" but are generally shown under the "Deferred Charge" heading. Although they have an unlimited life, they are usually written off against the earned surplus during the first five years of operations. If such write-offs occur, the debit should not be considered an operating expense, but should appear on the surplus statement or at the bottom of the income statement below the net income figure.

*23. Bond Discount and Expense.* When bonds are issued at less than face value, the net amount received is debited to cash, the face of the bond issue is credited to Bonds Payable, and the difference is charged to Bond

Discount and Expense. Since the bond issue benefits a number of periods, the costs of the issue should be allocated to all the periods benefited. To do this, the original discount and issuing costs are charged to an asset account which is gradually amortized over the life of the issue. Each period is then charged with its current interest cost and a proportionate part of the original discount. The balance in the Bond Discount and Expense account at any time shows the part of the original cost which has not yet been transferred to an expense account.

## Current Liabilities

*24. Accounts Payable.* No problem is incurred in the evaluation of accounts payable. The balance is generally considered to include only amounts payable for goods purchased. Amounts payable for utilities, taxes, wages, stocks purchased, etc., should be shown in separate accounts. The analyst should be aware that some firms fail to include recent purchases in their inventories and do not record the purchase until the following period. This has no effect on costs shown but decreases both the inventory and the accounts payable balances. This improves the current ratio, increases the inventory turnover rate, and makes the current position seem much more favorable than it really is.

*25. Notes Payable.* Notes are usually issued to trade creditors in payment for goods or to banks for loans. They are occasionally issued for purchases of fixed assets or to officers and directors for loans. The balance sheet should make clear, by appropriate wording of account titles, why the notes were issued since the source of funds used is of significance to the analyst. The use of notes to settle past-due accounts, the giving of notes or acceptances when others are buying on open account, and the use of funds from officers, directors, or employees instead of regular lending agencies may be considered evidence of financial weakness. Unfortunately, published reports usually do not give these details. If any notes are secured by the pledge of assets, this fact should be indicated in a footnote and the details about the assets pledged, including their present market value, should be given.

*26. Accrued Liabilities.* At the end of each fiscal period all expenses which have been incurred but which have not been paid should be entered through adjusting entries. These entries invariably result in a debit to the appropriate expense and a credit to set up the accrued liability. Accrued taxes, accrued wages, accrued interest, and accrued rents payable are perhaps the most common of the accrued liabilities. They should always be considered current liabilities just as accrued receivables are always considered current assets.

*27. Dividends Payable.* When the board of directors declares a cash dividend, the accountant records the declaration by a debit to Dividends

Paid (or directly to Earned Surplus) and a credit to Dividends Payable. The amount of the dividend becomes a current liability at the time the dividend is declared. Since the dividend is normally paid at a later date, the unpaid amount may appear in the accounts at the end of the fiscal period and, if so, will appear on the balance sheet among the current debts. If stock dividends are declared, the firm will not use current assets for their payment and they, therefore, are not current liabilities. The amount of the stock to be issued will appear in the net worth section as "Stock Dividends Payable" under the appropriate capital stock subsection.

*28. Estimated Income Tax Payable.* At the end of each fiscal period, corporations must estimate their income tax liability and transfer a portion of the net income earned to an account showing the estimated income tax liability. This account is sometimes called "Reserve for Income Taxes" but its nature is more clearly indicated by the title "Estimated Income Tax Payable." When the exact amount of the tax is determined in the following period, the tax is paid and the liability is canceled. Any difference between the estimated and actual liabilities is properly considered an "extraordinary" gain or loss but may be considered a miscellaneous current item if of an insignificant amount.

*29. Payroll Taxes Payable.* The balances in these accounts show the amounts owed the Federal and state governments for unemployment contributions and old-age and survivors insurance (Federal Insurance Contributions Act). The unemployment insurance usually amounts to about 3 per cent on the first $3,000 paid to each employee; about one-tenth going to the Federal government and the balance to the state. The Federal Insurance Contributions Act (called FICA, OAB, FOAB, FOASI, or social security) imposes a tax which amounts to $2\frac{1}{4}$ per cent (beginning January 1, 1957) on the first $4,200 to be withheld from the employee's wages. This is matched by the employer and paid by the employer to the Federal government. Firms on an accrual basis show the tax due and unpaid on all wages and salaries, including those accrued but not yet paid.

In addition to payroll taxes which may be unpaid, the employer often has a liability for Federal and state income taxes which he has withheld from the employees' pay as required by law but which he has not yet paid to the government. This liability is shown as Federal (or State) Income Tax Withheld.

*Long-term Debt*

*30. Bonds Payable.* Bonds are sold to obtain long-term creditor funds of relatively large amounts. They are most often of $1,000 units and are usually secured by a mortgage on certain fixed properties. The mortgage agreement, called the bond indenture, is held by a trustee who represents the bondholders in their dealings with the firm. Debenture bonds are unlike mortgage bonds in that they are secured only by the general credit of the company. Bonds not due within twelve months of the balance sheet date are included under long-term debt. Those coming due within a year are considered current debt if they are to be repaid from current funds. If they are to be refunded (or reissued), they are not current liabilities but should be shown under long-term debt with footnotes explaining what is to be done to retire them. Currently maturing issues of serial bonds are considered current liabilities.

*31. Mortgages Payable.* Mortgages payable are similar to bonds payable except that there is a mortgage and a note instead of a mortgage and an issue of bonds. They are normally for smaller amounts since the note is held by a single person or firm and often arises as a result of a purchase of land, buildings, or equipment. As in the case of bonds, principal payments due within a year are considered current liabilities while those due at a later time are included under long-term debt.

## Deferred Credits

*32. Deferred Credits to Income.* Income which has been collected but not earned results in a liability to the person or firm from whom the collection was made. There is some question as to whether this liability is current or whether it is more properly shown under a separate "deferred credit" heading. If the income is to be earned through allowing the customer to use a fixed asset, as when rent is collected in advance, the obligation will not require the use of current funds and should be considered a deferred credit. If earning the income will require the use of current assets, as for magazine subscriptions collected in advance, there is a logical basis for considering the amount a current liability. Since the amounts are most often quite small, the analyst may consider the question of greater theoretical than practical importance.

*33. Contingency Reserves.* A number of firms report reserves in the equity section of the balance sheet. These may include "Reserves for Contingencies," "Self-insurance Reserves," and simply "Reserves." The subject of *reserves* is one of the most difficult of all accounting problems and is the source of a great deal of confusion for the beginning student. In general, it may be said that there are three kinds of accounts which are often called reserves:

1. Valuation accounts or reserves, which include Reserves for Depreciation and Reserves for Bad Debts, are used in the valuation of asset accounts and are correctly shown as deductions from the appropriate assets. The use of the word "reserve" in connection with these accounts

is becoming less common as terms such as Allowance for Depreciation or Allowance for Bad Debts gain in acceptance.

2. Liability accounts or reserves, which include Reserve for Income Taxes (or Estimated Income Taxes Payable) and Reserves for Employee Pension Funds, which show the estimated amount of the firm's liability on the obligation indicated. Here again the use of the word *reserves* is being gradually discontinued.

3. Surplus reserves, which include such accounts as Reserve for Retirement of Bonds, Reserve for Plant Expansion, Reserve for Working Capital, and possibly General Contingency Reserves. These are appropriations of Earned Surplus.

Reserves for contingencies should be made to fit under one of these three classifications. If the contingency is a decline in inventory prices, the reserve may be subtracted from the inventory if the decline has occurred or is believed likely. It is a surplus reserve if it represents only a possibility of a decline. If the contingency is a lawsuit and the firm expects to lose, it represents an estimate of a liability. If the reserve is simply called a Reserve for Contingencies, it is an appropriation of surplus.

Many balance sheets show Reserves for Contingencies as a separate section on the liability side and let the reader make his own decision as to their meanings. The result is that most readers simply do not know what the item represents.

### Owner Equity Accounts

*34. Capital Stock.* The various kinds of Capital Stock and the meaning of the terms used in describing stock issues were explained in Chapter 9. The balance sheet should show the various types of stock with the number of shares authorized, the number issued, and the amount for each type. Footnotes or parenthetical notes should be used to describe the stock fully. Dividends in arrears on cumulative preferred stock should also be noted in footnotes, but it should be remembered that these dividends do not represent liabilities until they are actually declared by the board of directors.

Stock which has been issued, fully paid for, and later reacquired is called "treasury" stock. Treasury stock is occasionally shown as an asset since it may be resold for cash. It is more properly shown, at cost, as a deduction at the bottom of the net worth section of the balance sheet.

The capital stock section of the balance sheet should reveal the equity of the owners which arose as a result of their investment. This is not always possible since premiums on stock are often included under Paid-in Surplus in the surplus section, and because stock dividends result in a transfer of earned surplus to the stock accounts when they are declared and paid.

*35. Unappropriated Earned Surplus.* The unappropriated earned surplus balance (or Retained Earnings) represents the equity which the stockholders have in the company which arose as a result of profitable operations and which they may legally withdraw as dividends. However, it does not show the amount of cash available to pay the dividends and it is quite possible to have a surplus balance with no cash on hand, or to have a large cash balance and no surplus. If the earnings have been reinvested in fixed properties, the firm may not be able to pay a dividend even though a surplus exists. Firms which pay out all their earnings cannot grow except through the sale of additional stock.

*36. Appropriated Surplus.* Because a surplus balance does not necessarily indicate the ability to pay a dividend, the directors sometimes transfer a part of the Unappropriated Earned Surplus balance to a Reserve for Working Capital, Reserve for Plant Expansion, Reserve for Contingencies, or some other surplus reserve account. This is purely a book entry. No funds are involved—no cash is required. The result is simply that the Unappropriated Earned Surplus balance shown on statements is reduced and there is a possible decrease in the stockholders' clamor for dividends. We cannot say that the amount of dividends payable is actually reduced since the entry can be reversed at will.

Occasionally an appropriation of surplus is made in accordance with the terms of a bond indenture. This results in a debit to the Earned Surplus and a credit to the Reserve for Bond Sinking Fund for the agreed amount. This entry cannot be reversed until the bonds are retired and does result in a decrease in the amount of dividends which may be paid until that time. If the dividends are decreased, the funds which would have been used to pay them remain in the business and the firm is more likely to be able to pay the bonds when they fall due. If a special fund is to be created to pay the bonds at maturity, this fund is created by a debit to Bond Sinking Fund and a credit to Cash. When the bonds mature, the fund is converted to cash, the bonds are paid off, and the surplus reserve may be returned to Earned Surplus or permanently appropriated through a stock dividend.

No "reserve" balance is ever to be understood as an amount of money set aside for a specific purpose; such amounts are called "funds" of some sort (as Bond Sinking Fund or Employee Pension Fund) and have debit balances. *All* reserve accounts have *credit* balances.

*Capital Surplus*

*37. Paid-in Surplus.* When the stock of a corporation is sold for more than its par or stated value, the assets are increased by an amount greater than the value shown for the stock. This equity of the owners is shown on the statements as paid-in surplus or capital surplus. All "profits" or "losses" which result from transactions involving the sale or purchase of the company's own stock are shown under the Paid-in Surplus (or Capital Surplus) heading even though some of the accounts, such as Discounts on Stock, have debit balances and must be deducted from the total for the other accounts.

*38. Donated Surplus.* Donated surplus amounts usually arise out of donations of stock or of fixed properties to the firm; e.g., if a firm is in need of funds, all stockholders may decide to donate 10 per cent of their stock to the firm. The stock is then sold and cash is debited and Donated Surplus credited for the proceeds. Or, if a city wishes to attract a large manufacturing concern, it may donate a tract of land to the firm for its building site. This land is brought on the firm's books by a debit to Land and a credit to Donated Surplus for the fair market value of the property.

*39. Appraisal Surplus.* This account arises from a reappraisal of the fixed assets of the firm. For instance, if land purchased in 1932 is carried on the books at its original cost of $10,000 and it is presently valued at $100,000, it may be argued that it would be more accurate to show the land at its present market value and to record the book increase in net worth by a credit to an account which may be called Surplus from Reappraisal of Land. There is considerable question as to whether such an entry is desirable, however. And it should be remembered that a banker does not depend upon the book value of assets but rather upon an expert's appraisal of their value when he makes a decision in regard to their value as security for a loan.

*40. Dividends Paid or Drawings.* The distributions made of a firm's earnings are shown on the Surplus Statement (or Statement of Capital, if a proprietorship or partnership), as dividends (or drawings). In the case of a corporation, the account is called Dividends, Dividends Paid, Dividends Declared, or some similar title. While there is an important difference between the declaration and the payment of a dividend, the amount shown is usually the amount *declared* for the period. Obviously, if all dividends declared are immediately paid, the dividends paid are equal to dividends declared, and the term "paid" is more meaningful to the layman. While dividends paid do not appear (except as a footnote) on the balance sheet, details of changes in capital due to profits or losses and *drawings* are often shown on the balance sheet of a proprietorship or partnership.

*Total Owner Equity.* Since the assets owned are *not shown* at their *current market value*, it would be incorrect to think that the owner's equity as shown on the balance sheet is the *actual value* of the ownership interest. If the firm were to go out of business and the assets had to be sold at a forced sale, it is quite possible that the losses incurred could completely wipe out the equity of the owners. It is also possible that land, buildings, and equipment might sell for far more than their book value and possibly even far more than their original cost.

## COMPARATIVE BALANCE SHEETS

As in the case of the profit and loss statements previously described, the value of a balance sheet is tremendously increased if the analyst has some basis for comparison. For example, an inventory of $240,000 is neither large nor small by itself; the amount is much more meaningful if it can be compared with the inventory for the past year or the past four or five years and we can observe whether the dollar amount has increased or decreased during the period. We also need to determine whether any of the increase or decrease is due to price changes or to an actual change in physical quantities, and whether the inventory has increased or decreased in proportion to other assets or to the amount of goods sold during the period.

A number of types of comparative balance sheets are commonly used to help bring out the year-to-year changes in balance sheet amounts and to give the analyst a better basis for evaluating the financial position of a firm from information available to him. Among the most widely used are the statements showing amounts and per cents of increase or decrease, statements showing trend percentages, and common-size (or 100 per cent) statements to make possible comparisons with other firms or industry standards.

Simplified balance sheets for the Ace Corporation from 1953 to 1957 will be used to illustrate the procedures used in preparing each type of statement. The basic data are presented in Exhibit 15-1. From these data and from company history we learn that the company operated at a profit in 1953. At the end of 1953, they borrowed $50,000 on 6 per cent bonds; the funds were used early in 1954 to buy a long-established competitor. Land, buildings, equipment, accounts receivable, and inventories were acquired by the purchase. The goodwill arose from the payment of $20,000 in excess of the book value of the net assets required. To help finance the expansion, $40,000 of 6 per cent preferred stock was sold at a premium of $2,000. In 1957, $15,000 was borrowed on a short-term note to help meet a temporary, seasonal demand for cash.

### Increase-Decrease Statements

To call attention to changes between balances of the current and preceding year, an "increase-decrease" statement (Exhibit 15-2) is generally prepared. The statement provides columns to show the balance sheet amounts at the two dates to be compared, a column showing the

EXHIBIT 15-1
ACE CORPORATION
Comparative Balance Sheets
December 31, 1953–1957

| | 1953 | 1954 | 1955 | 1956 | 1957 |
|---|---|---|---|---|---|
| *Assets* | | | | | |
| Current assets: | | | | | |
| Cash................... | $ 73,200 | $ 26,200 | $ 38,300 | $ 34,400 | $ 37,600 |
| Accounts receivable (net) | 23,600 | 51,300 | 58,200 | 64,300 | 56,800 |
| Merchandise inventory... | 34,400 | 82,300 | 54,200 | 46,000 | 42,500 |
| Other current assets...... | 300 | 520 | 390 | 280 | 600 |
| Total current assets.... | $131,500 | $160,320 | $151,090 | $144,980 | $137,500 |
| Investments: | | | | | |
| Investment in Subsidiary | | | | | |
| Company stock........ | | | 22,500 | 23,700 | 26,800 |
| Fixed assets: | | | | | |
| Land................... | | $ 8,000 | $ 8,000 | $ 8,000 | $ 8,000 |
| Buildings (net).......... | | 26,400 | 23,000 | 22,250 | 21,500 |
| Equipment (net)......... | $ 4,600 | 10,000 | 9,100 | 8,200 | 7,300 |
| Total fixed assets...... | $ 4,600 | $ 44,400 | $ 40,100 | $ 38,450 | $ 36,800 |
| Intangible assets: | | | | | |
| Patents................. | $ 3,300 | $ 3,100 | $ 2,900 | $ 2,700 | $ 2,500 |
| Goodwill............... | | 20,000 | 20,000 | 20,000 | 20,000 |
| Total intangible assets.. | $ 3,300 | $ 23,100 | $ 22,900 | $ 22,700 | $ 22,500 |
| Deferred charges: | | | | | |
| Discount on bonds....... | 2,000 | 1,850 | 1,700 | 1,550 | 1,400 |
| Total assets.............. | $141,400 | $229,670 | $238,290 | $231,380 | $225,000 |
| | | | | | |
| *Liabilities and net worth* | | | | | |
| Current liabilities: | | | | | |
| Accounts payable........ | $ 2,900 | $ 42,600 | $ 39,100 | $ 42,300 | $ 23,600 |
| Notes payable.......... | | | | | 15,000 |
| Other current liabilities... | | 670 | 3,590 | 12,600 | 4,200 |
| Total current liabilities. | $ 2,900 | $ 43,270 | $ 42,690 | $ 54,900 | $ 42,800 |
| Long-term debt: | | | | | |
| 6% first mortgage bonds.. | 50,000 | 50,000 | 50,000 | 50,000 | 50,000 |
| Total liabilities........... | $ 52,900 | $ 93,270 | $ 92,690 | $104,900 | $ 92,800 |
| Net worth: | | | | | |
| 6% preferred stock....... | | $ 40,000 | $ 40,000 | $ 40,000 | $ 40,000 |
| Common stock.......... | $ 80,000 | 80,000 | 80,000 | 80,000 | 80,000 |
| Earned surplus.......... | 8,500 | 14,400 | 23,600 | 4,480 | 10,200 |
| Paid-in surplus.......... | | 2,000 | 2,000 | 2,000 | 2,000 |
| Total net worth........... | $ 88,500 | $136,400 | $145,600 | $126,480 | $132,200 |
| Total liabilities & net worth. | $141,400 | $229,670 | $238,290 | $231,380 | $225,000 |

Exhibit 15-2
ACE CORPORATION
Comparative Balance Sheets
December 31, 1956 and 1957

| | 1956 | 1957 | Increase or (decrease) | Per cent increase or decrease |
|---|---|---|---|---|
| *Assets* | | | | |
| Current assets: | | | | |
| Cash. | $ 34,400 | $ 37,600 | $ 3,200 | 9.3 |
| Accounts rec. (net) | 64,300 | 56,800 | (7,500) | −11.7 |
| Merchandise inventory | 46,000 | 42,500 | (3,500) | −7.0 |
| Other current assets | 280 | 600 | 320 | 114.3 |
| Total current assets | $144,980 | $137,500 | ($7,480) | −5.0 |
| Investments: | | | | |
| Investment in Subsidiary Company stock | 23,700 | 26,800 | 3,100 | 13.1 |
| Fixed assets: | | | | |
| Land | $ 8,000 | $ 8,000 | | |
| Buildings (net) | 22,250 | 21,500 | ($750) | −3.4 |
| Equipment (net) | 8,200 | 7,300 | (900) | −11.0 |
| Total fixed assets | $ 38,450 | $ 36,800 | ($1,650) | −4.3 |
| Intangible assets: | | | | |
| Patents | 2,700 | 2,500 | (200) | −7.4 |
| Goodwill | 20,000 | 20,000 | | |
| Total intangible assets | $ 22,700 | $ 22,500 | ($200) | −0.9 |
| Deferred charges: | | | | |
| Discount on bonds | 1,550 | 1,400 | (150) | −9.7 |
| Total assets | $231,380 | $225,000 | $ (6,380) | −2.8 |
| | | | | |
| *Liabilities and net worth* | | | | |
| Current liabilities: | | | | |
| Accounts payable | $ 42,300 | $ 23,600 | ($18,700) | −44.2 |
| Notes payable | | 15,000 | 15,000 | * |
| Other current liabilities | 12,600 | 4,200 | (8,400) | −66.7 |
| Total current liabilities | $ 54,900 | $ 42,800 | ($12,100) | −22.0 |
| Long-term debt: | | | | |
| 6% first mortgage bonds | 50,000 | 50,000 | | |
| Total liabilities | $104,900 | $ 92,800 | ($12,100) | −11.5 |
| Net worth: | | | | |
| 6% preferred stock | $ 40,000 | $ 40,000 | | |
| Common stock | 80,000 | 80,000 | | |
| Earned surplus | 4,480 | 10,200 | $ 5,720 | 127.7 |
| Paid-in surplus | 2,000 | 2,000 | | |
| Total net worth | $126,480 | $132,200 | $ 5,720 | 4.5 |
| Total liabilities and net worth | $231,380 | $225,000 | ($ 6,380) | −2.8 |

* It is not possible to compute a per cent increase when the base year value is zero.

amount of increase or decrease, and a fourth column showing the per cent change. The use of columns showing both absolute and relative changes helps to emphasize the fact that some changes may be of large dollar amounts but of little significance relatively, while others may be very small in actual dollars but quite large relatively; e.g., the cash account has increased $3,200, but this is only about a 9 per cent increase in cash and may be of little significance. The "other current assets" have increased only $320, but this is an increase of more than 114 per cent. This, too, is likely to be a change of no real importance. On the other hand, the accounts receivable balance is down $7,500 or 11.7 per cent. This amount is significant both in amount and percentagewise, and, if sales have not fallen off sharply, should indicate an important improvement in collections or in credit policies. The amounts and per cents of change serve only to focus the analyst's attention on each change. It is not possible to state at what point a change becomes important. But changes which are not large in either dollars or per cent can usually be ignored. In every case in which the amount or the per cent of change seems significant, the analyst should carefully consider the probable reasons for the change, and should investigate all cases which he believes of real importance.

No problems of any significance are found in the preparation of this type of statement. In every case, the earlier year is considered the base year and is divided into the amount of increase or decrease to get the per cent of change. Answers are normally carried no farther than one decimal place, as 9.3 per cent. No "per cent change" figures can be computed if the base year amount is zero or a negative value (the surplus account occasionally has a negative, or deficit, balance), and, while amounts may *increase* by almost any per cent, there can never be more than a 100 per cent *decrease*.

### Trend Percentage Statements

Trend percentages are often computed to enable the analyst to watch the movement of selected items of importance. In the example given (Exhibit 15-3), trend values for all items in the original statement are given; some are of minor importance and might well be omitted in actual practice. Because of the fact that the 1953 values were before the purchase of the competitor and thus represent a situation not comparable with that of later years, the data for 1953 were ignored and 1954 values were used as the base year. One of the difficulties of this type of analysis is that often no single year can be selected which will provide a satisfactory base or reference point for all items.

The computations are always done by dividing the base year value into each given year value and expressing the result as a per cent. Again,

EXHIBIT 15-3
ACE CORPORATION
Comparative Balance Sheets—Trend Percentages
December 31, 1954–1957

| | 1954 | 1955 | 1956 | 1957 |
|---|---|---|---|---|
| *Assets* | | | | |
| Current assets: | | | | |
| Cash.............................. | 100.0% | 146.2% | 131.3% | 143.5% |
| Accounts receivable (net)............. | 100.0 | 113.5 | 125.3 | 110.7 |
| Merchandise inventory............... | 100.0 | 65.9 | 55.9 | 51.6 |
| Other current assets................. | 100.0 | 75.0 | 53.8 | 115.3 |
| Total current assets............... | 100.0% | 94.2% | 90.4% | 85.8% |
| Investments: | | | | |
| Investment in Subsidiary Company stock | | * | * | * |
| Fixed assets: | | | | |
| Land.............................. | 100.0% | 100.0% | 100.0% | 100.0% |
| Buildings (net)...................... | 100.0 | 87.1 | 84.0 | 81.4 |
| Equipment (net)..................... | 100.0 | 91.0 | 82.0 | 73.0 |
| Total fixed assets................. | 100.0% | 90.3% | 86.6% | 82.9% |
| Intangible assets: | | | | |
| Patents............................ | 100.0% | 93.5 | 87.1 | 80.6 |
| Goodwill........................... | 100.0 | 100.0 | 100.0 | 100.0 |
| Total intangible assets.............. | 100.0% | 99.1% | 98.3% | 97.4% |
| Deferred charges: | | | | |
| Discount on bonds................... | 100.0 | 91.9 | 83.8 | 75.7 |
| Total assets.......................... | 100.0% | 103.8% | 100.7% | 98.0% |
| | | | | |
| *Liabilities and net worth* | | | | |
| Current liabilities: | | | | |
| Accounts payable.................... | 100.0% | 91.8% | 99.3% | 55.4% |
| Notes payable....................... | * | * | * | * |
| Other current liabilities............... | 100.0 | 535.8 | 1,880.6 | 626.9 |
| Total current liabilities............. | 100.0% | 98.7% | 126.9% | 98.9% |
| Long-term debt: | | | | |
| 6% first mortgage bonds............. | 100.0 | 100.0 | 100.0 | 100.0 |
| Total liabilities........................ | 100.0% | 99.4% | 112.5% | 99.5% |
| Net worth: | | | | |
| 6% preferred stock................... | 100.0% | 100.0% | 100.0% | 100.0% |
| Common stock...................... | 100.0 | 100.0 | 100.0 | 100.0 |
| Earned surplus...................... | 100.0 | 163.9 | 31.1 | 70.8 |
| Paid-in surplus...................... | 100.0 | 100.0 | 100.0 | 100.0 |
| Total net worth....................... | 100.0% | 106.7% | 92.7% | 96.9% |
| Total liabilities and net worth........... | 100.0% | 103.8% | 100.7% | 98.0% |

* No balance in base year.

no values can be obtained if base year amounts are zero or negative amounts. The trend values may be presented along with the dollar amounts to avoid the appearance of significance when large per cent changes occur in small, unimportant items. However, as pointed out before, trend values are usually computed only for the items and totals which are likely to be of importance, as: cash, receivables, inventories, total current assets, accounts payable, total current liabilities, etc.

## Common-size Statements

The two comparative statements described in the preceding paragraphs have their chief value in the fact that they focus attention on the year-to-year changes of each item or total. Common-size or 100 per cent statements (Exhibit 15-4) have their chief value in that they make possible a comparison of the firm's financial position with that of a competitor, with industry standards, or with the analyst's (perhaps a bank loan officer's) idea of what the firm should be like.

You should recall that the asset side of the balance sheet shows the use which the firm has made of the funds placed at its disposal. Every firm requires a combination of land, labor, capital, and management to produce the goods or the services which it expects to sell. There are, obviously, certain patterns which we may expect firms in a given industry to follow, e.g., a wholesale grocer may be expected to have an investment in land, buildings, equipment, and merchandise. These are combined with the labor of the employees and the management skills of the business executives to produce the firm's service. A farmer, on the other hand, may be expected to have a different combination of the same factors to produce his product. While the amounts invested in each type of asset will depend upon the size of the business, it is reasonable to think that the *per cent* invested in each type of asset will be quite similar for each line of business, if the businesses operate under similar conditions.

The fact that each type of asset owned is stated as a per cent of the total assets owned makes quite clear the disposition which the firm has made of its funds. If the firm's operations are similar to its competitors, it is possible to compare the per cent which each firm has in inventories, the per cent that is in accounts receivable, the size of its fixed asset investment, etc. These comparisons are extremely valuable in detecting points where the firm being investigated may be out of line. Where valid industry standards are available, the value is even greater. For instance, it is extremely important to know that a particular firm has 23.2 per cent of its total assets in inventory while the average (usually median) for the industry is only 16.2 per cent, and the middle 50 per cent of the firms in the industry range between 12.6 per cent (the 25th percentile or quartile 1) and 21.2 per cent (the 75th percentile or quartile 3).

EXHIBIT 15-4
ACE CORPORATION
Balance Sheet—With Common-size Per Cents
December 31, 1957

| Assets | Amount | Per cent of total |
|---|---|---|
| Current assets: | | |
| Cash.......................................... | $ 37,600 | 16.7 |
| Accounts receivable (net)........................... | 56,800 | 25.2 |
| Merchandise inventory........................... | 42,500 | 18.9 |
| Other current assets.............................. | 600 | 0.3 |
| Total current assets............................. | $137,500 | 61.1 |
| Investments: | | |
| Investment in Subsidiary Company stock.............. | $ 26,800 | 11.9 |
| Fixed assets: | | |
| Land.......................................... | $ 8,000 | 3.6 |
| Buildings (net)...................................... | 21,500 | 9.6 |
| Equipment (net)................................... | 7,300 | 3.2 |
| Total fixed assets................................ | $ 36,800 | 16.4 |
| Intangible assets: | | |
| Patents......................................... | $ 2,500 | 1.1 |
| Goodwill......................................... | 20,000 | 8.9 |
| Total intangible assets........................... | $ 22,500 | 10.0 |
| Deferred charges: | | |
| Discount on bonds................................ | 1,400 | 0.6 |
| Total assets....................................... | $225,000 | 100.0 |

*Liabilities and net worth*

| | Amount | Per cent of total |
|---|---|---|
| Current liabilities: | | |
| Accounts payable................................... | $ 23,600 | 10.5 |
| Notes payable....................................... | 15,000 | 6.7 |
| Other current liabilities............................. | 4,200 | 1.9 |
| Total current liabilities........................... | $ 42,800 | 19.0 |
| Long-term debt: | | |
| 6% first mortgage bonds............................. | 50,000 | 22.2 |
| Total liabilities...................................... | $ 92,800 | 41.2 |
| Net worth: | | |
| 6% preferred stock................................. | $ 40,000 | 17.8 |
| Common stock...................................... | 80,000 | 35.6 |
| Earned surplus..................................... | 10,200 | 4.5 |
| Paid-in surplus..................................... | 2,000 | 0.9 |
| Total net worth..................................... | $132,200 | 58.8 |
| Total liabilities and net worth........................ | $225,000 | 100.0 |

However, no real value is to be obtained from comparing firms which are not operated in a comparable manner. For example, if one firm owns its plant or store building, manufactures or mines a large part of its product, etc., while its competitor rents its plant and buys its materials from another producer, it would be foolish to compare the per cent invested in each asset and to conclude that one firm is out of line because it does not follow the pattern set by the other (or group of others).

If the asset side of the balance sheet shows the disposition of funds, the equity side shows where the funds were obtained; i.e., what amounts were provided by the various creditors, the total amount invested by the owners, and what amount came from the earnings which were retained in the business. The common-size statement shows what per cent of the funds came from each source. Patterns in financing may always be observed in given lines of business; e.g., it is well known that firms which have irregular and uncertain earnings cannot be financed to any great extent by bond issues or other fixed obligations, while firms with regular and sometimes virtually assured earnings, as public utilities, can depend upon bond issues for a major portion of their funds.

The existence of an unusual amount of creditor financing is often taken as a sign of weakness by a banker or prospective creditor. But the condition may be desirable from the stockholder's viewpoint, because it often enables him to earn a much higher *rate* of return on his investment. This is true because the amount paid for the use of long-term creditor funds is usually quite small. The process of using creditor funds to increase the rate of return of the owners is called "trading on the equity." It should be pointed out, however, that the hopes of increasing earnings more than the cost of the borrowed funds are not always realized. Where losses occur, the firm using borrowed funds may not be able to pay its interest costs and consequently may be forced out of business. This may be summarized by saying that, from the creditor's viewpoint, the use of an unusually large proportion of borrowed funds (including current pay-ables) is not desirable and indicates a lack of strength. From the owner's viewpoint, it indicates the presence of danger but may be more profitable than more conservative financing arrangements.

Regardless of the decisions reached, the fact remains that the common-size statement provides a clear and concise presentation of the relative importance of each asset or group of assets, and the relative importance of each source of funds being used (i.e., the various liabilities and owners' equities).

Some students have felt that they could form much more valid opinions about a firm's financial position if they were told what per cent each asset should be. A little reflection, however, will indicate that this is impossible. The following paragraphs will help to make this clear.

*Cash.* Cash is an unproductive asset. The firm must pay the bank, other lending agencies, and the stockholders for the use of funds furnished by them, but it earns nothing on cash in its checking account and very little on a savings account. So the balance of cash apparently should be small. But cash is needed to pay the employees, to meet current bills, and to pay the accounts payable as they come due, and if the cash balance is too small, this cannot be done. So a large cash balance appears needed. As a matter of fact, the cash balance should be kept as small as possible, yet large enough to meet all obligations as they come due. The failure to take cash discounts on purchases, the presence of notes payable for past-due accounts, or a reputation for "slow pay" are all indicative of too little cash. Factoring (or selling) of accounts receivable when not the trade practice, and other desperate financing, such as loans from officers, etc., may also indicate a shortage of cash. On the other hand, the presence of investments in readily marketable securities should indicate adequate cash since additional cash could be obtained at short notice. However, an investment in government bonds, etc., carried for several years even during the peak of the season would indicate an excessive amount of working capital and a poor or relatively unprofitable use of the owner's investment.

*Inventories.* Large inventories lead to excessive handling costs, insurance and property taxes, and losses from obsolescence and deterioration. They also tie up funds which might be much more profitably invested elsewhere. They indicate the possibility of unrecorded losses since they may contain a large amount of unsalable goods. On the other hand, inventories which are too small may mean lost sales. They may also indicate the lack of working capital and hand-to-mouth buying practices which are expensive in terms of small-quantity buying and freight advantages lost and, perhaps, in delayed production. Lost time in the factory and worker dissatisfaction are an expensive price to pay for low inventories. Should the inventories be large or small?

*Accounts Receivable.* If the balance is large, it may indicate poor credit and collection procedures, inefficient handling of the accounts receivable, or the presence of many accounts which will never be collected. If the balance is too small, it may indicate that the firm does not have sufficient working capital to carry the accounts of its potential customers and that sales are being lost because of this. In other words, management may insist on cash at time of sale and, as a result, many who would purchase on credit are not accommodated. In a similar way, it may be shown that almost every individual account should desirably be small and just about equally desirably be large. Even accounts payable, if large, show that funds are being used at no cost to the firm—which seems somewhat favorable. And the presence of a large creditor equity may mean a very high rate of return on the owner's equity. Some of these problems will be more fully discussed in the following chapter. For the present, we may simply say that there is no substitute for a clear understanding of the accounts and their meanings and for an intelligent evaluation of many factors which may have an effect on decisions. Percentages and ratios focus attention on a particular problem or relationship—they don't provide the answer.

### Comparative Common-size Statements

Common-size statements are sometimes made for a period of years to show the changing importance of the various assets and the changing pattern of financial structure. While this may be done, it should be noted that the per cent which each item is of a total is influenced not only by changes in the item itself but by changes in the total as well. This means, for example, that inventories might make up 23 per cent of the total assets in 1956 and only 20 per cent of the total assets in 1957 even though the inventories have actually increased, simply because total assets have increased even more. For this reason, the value of 100 per cent statements over a period of years is questionable.

### Composition of Current Assets

In addition to statements showing the "per cent of total assets," it is sometimes desirable to prepare statements which use section totals, such as total current assets, as the base and show each item as a per cent of the section total. This type of analysis is particularly well suited for a study of current assets.

COMPOSITION OF CURRENT ASSETS

| | Amount | Per cent of total |
|---|---|---|
| Cash | $ 37,600 | 27.3 |
| Accounts receivable | 56,800 | 41.4 |
| Merchandise inventory | 42,500 | 30.9 |
| Other current assets | 600 | 0.4 |
| Total current assets | $137,500 | 100.0 |

## STATEMENT OF SOURCES AND APPLICATIONS OF FUNDS

The statement of financial position illustrated in Chapter 6 emphasizes the close relationship of this type of balance sheet to the statement of sources and applications of funds. In a recent statement of financial condition (balance sheet) of the Briggs Manufacturing Company, the investment of the stockholders was shown first. It consisted of two parts:

No-par value common stock outstanding........... $12,507,149
Income invested in the business.................    41,917,983
                                                  $54,425,132

The next section was headed "This Investment Was Used as Follows" and was made up of three parts:

1. Working capital............................. $20,446,701
   (Current assets minus current liabilities)
2. Land, building, and equipment.................  32,317,531
3. Other assets..................................   1,660,900
                                                  $54,425,132

Stated in another way, the statement says that *during the life of the business*, funds have been used (applied) to provide working capital; land, buildings, and equipment; and other assets. These funds were provided by the sale of stock and by earnings which had been retained in the business. However, it is often desirable to study the sources and applications of funds for a shorter period of time, such as one year, five years, or for the period the present managers have been in control, and to analyze more carefully and more fully the sources of funds and how they were used. This type of analysis considers total earnings as a source and dividends paid as an application, instead of showing the net funds provided through earnings. Other than this, and the fact that it covers a definite period of time while the balance sheet covers the entire life of the business, the two statements are quite similar in content.

The statement is prepared by analyzing the changes in amounts between balance sheets prepared at the beginning and end of the period of time covered by the report. For example, let us take a simple problem such as the following to get the basic idea of the statement.

COMPARATIVE BALANCE SHEETS

|  | Dec. 31, 1955 | Dec. 31, 1956 | Change |
|---|---|---|---|
| *Assets* | | | |
| Current assets.......... | $260,000 | $292,000 | $  32,000 |
| Land................. | 40,000 | 52,000 | 12,000 |
| Building (net).......... | 160,000 | 268,000 | 108,000 |
| Equipment (net)........ | 300,000 | 264,000 | −36,000 |
|  | $760,000 | $876,000 | |
| *Equities* | | | |
| Current liabilities....... | $120,000 | $106,000 | $−14,000 |
| Capital stock........... | 500,000 | 600,000 | 100,000 |
| Surplus............... | 140,000 | 170,000 | 30,000 |
|  | $760,000 | $876,000 | |

From these data it may be seen that the current assets have increased $32,000 while current liabilities have decreased $14,000. This means that there has been an increase of $46,000 in the working capital. An investigation of the changes in all noncurrent account balances reveals the facts which follow. The land account has increased $12,000 due to the purchase of additional land. The building account has increased $108,000 due to the purchase of buildings of $120,000 and depreciation charged off of $12,000, making a net increase of $108,000. The equipment account has decreased $36,000 due to the sale of equipment having a book value of $20,000, and additional depreciation of $16,000; the equipment was sold for $18,000. The capital stock account increased $100,000 due to the sale of 1,000 shares of $100 par value stock. The surplus account increased $30,000. This was the result of a profit of $60,000 and dividends paid of $30,000. These changes may be summarized as follows:

Changes requiring use of funds:

| | |
|---|---:|
| To increase the working capital................. | $ 46,000 |
| To purchase land............................. | 12,000 |
| To pay dividends............................. | 30,000 |
| To purchase building......................... | 120,000 |
| | $208,000 |

These funds were provided by:

| | | |
|---|---:|---:|
| Sale of equipment............................. | | $ 18,000 |
| Sale of stock (1,000 shares at $100).............. | | 100,000 |
| From operations: | | |
| Profits to surplus.................... | $60,000 | |
| Plus depreciation..................... | 28,000 | |
| Plus loss on sale of equipment......... | 2,000 | 90,000 |
| | | $208,000 |

The only part of this analysis which is at all difficult to understand is the addition of the depreciation and the loss on sale of equipment to the profits carried to surplus. This correction is due to the fact that both these amounts were deducted in determining the final profit but neither of them required the use of funds during the current period. The income less the expenses actually paid or owed amounted to $90,000.

The Statement of Sources and Applications of Funds of the Woodbury Company (Exhibit 15-5) illustrates the most common arrangement of the report.

The depreciation charged to expense and the loss on the sales of fixed assets were added back to the "funds provided by operations" because they had previously been deducted in computing the profits carried to Surplus, and they, unlike other expenses, did not require the use of current funds. If the loss on the sale of the fixed assets had been shown on the surplus statement rather than the income statement, it would not have been necessary to add this loss back to the "profits provided by operations." But depreciation is always shown on the income statement and must always be added back.

The increase in working capital was shown as an *application* of funds since it means that larger amounts are tied up in inventories, receivables, etc., or have been used to reduce current debt. A decrease in working capital would have been considered a source of funds since a business which is able to decrease its accounts receivable or its inventories or to go further in debt to current creditors has a greater buying power than it would have if it could not do these things.

EXHIBIT 15-5

WOODBURY MANUFACTURING COMPANY

Statement of Sources and Applications of Funds

for the Year Ended December 31, 1956

Funds were provided by:

| | | |
|---|---:|---:|
| Operations (as per P & L statement) | $130,000 | |
| Add: Depreciation charged | 62,000 | |
| Loss on sale of equipment | 12,000 | $204,000 |
| Sale of 1,000 shares of common stock at $26 | | 26,000 |
| Issue of bonds | $100,000 | |
| Less bond discount & expense | 6,000 | 94,000 |
| Sale of equipment (book value $42,000) | | 30,000 |
| Total funds provided | | $354,000 |

Funds were applied to:

| | |
|---|---:|
| Payment of dividends | $ 80,000 |
| Purchase of land | 12,000 |
| Erection of building | 120,000 |
| Purchase of equipment | 56,000 |
| Increase in working capital | 86,000 |
| Total funds applied | $354,000 |

The statement illustrated is often supported by a schedule of the individual current asset and current liability accounts showing the beginning and ending balances in each account, the amount of change in each, and the total increase or decrease in the net working capital.

*Preparation of Statements of Sources and Applications of Funds*

Normally the statement of sources and applications of funds covers one fiscal year but changes over any period of time may be analyzed. Most accountants prepare rather complicated working papers showing the balance sheet accounts at the beginning and end of the period, a pair of columns showing increases or decreases in each account, another pair of columns in which all changes not affecting funds are eliminated, two more columns showing working capital increases and decreases, and a final pair of columns showing applications and sources (provisions) of funds. This type of solution is unnecessary in any except the most difficult of problems and will not be illustrated here. The statement may be prepared directly from the two balance sheets. As an example, let us use the balance sheets of Ace Corporation for December 31, 1956 and 1957, as shown in Exhibit 15-1. In addition to the balance sheet, the following data from the income statement and the surplus account or surplus statement are needed regardless of the procedure used to prepare the report:

Depreciation:

| | | |
|---|---|---:|
| Buildings | $ | 750 |
| Equipment | | 900 |
| Patent amortization | | 200 |
| Profits carried to Surplus | | 14,520 |
| Dividends paid: | | |
| Common stock | | 6,400 |
| Preferred stock | | 2,400 |

In 1956 the corporation had a net working capital of $90,080 ($144,980 minus $54,900). In 1957 the net working capital was $94,700 ($137,500 minus $42,800). There has been an increase in the net working capital of $4,620 ($94,700 minus $90,080). The statement may be set up in outline form and the increase in working capital shown as an application:

Funds were provided by:

_____

_____

Funds were applied to:
Increase in net working capital $4,620

We may now ignore all the current items and determine whether the changes in the other items involved the use of funds.

If the investment in Subsidiary Company is carried at cost, funds have been used to increase this investment—$3,100.

There has been no change in Land.

The changes in Buildings and Equipment were due to depreciation. There have been no sales or purchases of either. Total depreciation was $1,650.

Patents have been written down $200 and, although this was deducted from the profits, no funds were required.

Goodwill has not changed.

The Discount on Bonds has been written off to the interest expense account but no current funds were required.

Skip the current liabilities.

There has been no change in bonds outstanding.

No new stock has been issued.

The change in Surplus can be explained by a profit of $14,520 less total dividends paid of $8,800.

No change in Paid-in Surplus.

We are now ready to put this information in statement form, using the form illustrated for the Woodbury Manufacturing Company (see Exhibit 15-6).

EXHIBIT 15-6
ACE CORPORATION
Statement of Sources and Applications of Funds
for the Year Ended December 31, 1957

Funds were provided by:

| | | |
|---|---:|---:|
| Operations (as per income statement).............. | $14,520 | |
| Add: Depreciation............................... | 1,650 | |
| Patent amortization....................... | 200 | |
| Bond discount amortized................... | 150 | |
| Total provided by operations.......................... | | $16,520 |

Funds were applied to:

| | | |
|---|---:|---:|
| Payment of dividends........................... | $ 8,800 | |
| Increase net working capital..................... | 4,620 | |
| Investment in Subsidiary Company stock.......... | 3,100 | |
| Total funds applied................................. | | $16,520 |

This is a simple example involving very few sources and applications of funds. A more complicated problem and a slightly different form will be illustrated in the second example.

## Second Illustration—Changes in Net Working Capital

Because of the difficulty encountered in attempting to define the term "funds," many "funds" statements are now called "statements of changes in net working capital." When this title is used, the things which have increased working capital (sources) are listed first. The things which have decreased working capital (applications) are listed next and the difference between the two totals is obtained. This is simply called the net increase (or decrease) in working capital. To illustrate this procedure, a second example, based on the following balance sheets and additional data, is given.

EXHIBIT 15-7
BALLARD COMPANY
Comparative Balance Sheets
December 31, 1956 and 1957

| | 1956 | 1957 |
|---|---:|---:|
| *Assets* | | |
| Current assets: | | |
| Cash.................................... | $ 24,600 | $ 26,000 |
| Accounts receivable (net)................. | 16,200 | 18,400 |
| Merchandise inventory.................... | 31,300 | 33,400 |
| Other current assets..................... | 1,200 | 900 |
| Total current assets.................... | $ 73,300 | $ 78,700 |

Exhibit 15-7 (*Continued*)

Fixed assets:

| | | |
|---|---:|---:|
| Equipment (net) | $ 42,000 | $ 46,000 |
| Buildings (net) | 116,000 | 142,000 |
| Land | 12,000 | 12,000 |
|     Total fixed assets | $170,000 | $200,000 |
| Investments (long-term) (at cost) | $ 16,000 | $ 12,000 |

Intangible assets:

| | | |
|---|---:|---:|
| Patents | $ 6,000 | $ 5,400 |
| Goodwill | 5,000 | 4,000 |
|     Total intangible assets | $ 11,000 | $ 9,400 |
| Total assets | $270,300 | $300,100 |

*Liabilities and net worth*

Current liabilities:

| | | |
|---|---:|---:|
| Accounts payable | $ 20,400 | $ 21,000 |
| Notes payable | 8,000 | 12,000 |
| Accrued payables | 3,200 | 2,800 |
|     Total current liabilities | $ 31,600 | $ 35,800 |

Long-term debt:

| | | |
|---|---:|---:|
| First mortgage note payable | 40,000 | 36,000 |

Net worth:

| | | |
|---|---:|---:|
| Preferred stock (6%, $100 par) | 60,000 | 60,000 |
| Common stock ($100 par) | 80,000 | 100,000 |
| Earned surplus | 46,700 | 52,300 |
| Paid-in surplus | 12,000 | 16,000 |
| Total liabilities and net worth | $270,300 | $300,100 |

## Additional data from the income statement and surplus account:

| | |
|---|---:|
| Net profit as per income statement | $18,200 |
| Depreciation: | |
|     Equipment | 4,300 |
|     Buildings | 22,000 |
| Patent amortization | 600 |
| Goodwill written off to Surplus | 1,000 |

Gain on sale of long-term investment, included in net profit figure, $800. No fixed assets were sold

200 shares of common stock were sold at $120 per share

| | |
|---|---:|
| Dividends paid: | |
|     Preferred | 3,600 |
|     Common | 8,000 |

## The form to be used for the report will show:

| | |
|---|---:|
| Net working capital was increased by | xx |
| Net working capital was decreased by | xx |
| Net increase (or decrease) in net working capital | xx |

We may begin by finding what our final answer will be. In 1956 the net working capital was $41,700 ($73,300 minus $31,600). In 1957 the net working capital was $42,900 ($78,700 minus $35,800). There has been an increase in the net working capital of $1,200 and our statement must check to this answer. We may now analyze the changes in the non-current items.

Equipment (net) increased $4,000 despite depreciation of $4,300. No fixed assets were sold. Equipment purchased must have been $8,300.

Buildings (net) increased $26,000. Depreciation alone would have caused a decrease of $22,000. Buildings purchased or capitalized building costs must have been $48,000.

Investments costing $4,000 were sold. The profit was $800. The selling price must have been $4,800.

Patent amortization charged as an expense but using no funds was $600.

The Goodwill was written off against Surplus and the change may be ignored.

A payment of $4,000 was made on the first mortgage note payable.

No preferred stock was issued.

Common stock with a par value of $20,000 was sold for $24,000, explaining the change in the Common Stock and Paid-in Surplus balances.

The change in Earned Surplus was due to profits earned of $18,200 less the write-off of Goodwill and the dividends paid.

We may now put this information in the form of a statement (see Exhibit 15-8).

Exhibit 15-8

BALLARD COMPANY

Statement of Changes in Net Working Capital

for the Year Ended December 31, 1957

Net working capital was increased by:

| | | |
|---|---:|---:|
| Operations (as per income statement)............ | $18,200 | |
| Add: Depreciation......................... | 26,300 | |
| Patent amortization.................... | 600 | |
| | $45,100 | |
| Less: Gain on sale of investment.............. | 800 | $44,300 |
| Sale of long-term investment (cost $4,000)............... | | 4,800 |
| Sale of 200 shares of common stock at $120.............. | | 24,000 |
| Total......................................... | | $73,100 |

Net working capital was decreased by:

| | |
|---|---:|
| Payment of dividends................................ | $11,600 |
| Purchase of equipment................................ | 8,300 |
| Purchase of buildings................................ | 48,000 |
| Payment on mortgage................................ | 4,000 |
| Total......................................... | $71,900 |
| Net increase in net working capital........................ | $ 1,200 |

In many cases the data are presented in graphic form to illustrate how funds were provided by stockholders, bond issues, earnings, or sale of fixed properties no longer needed; how these funds were used to pay dividends, to retire bonded debt, to purchase land, or to purchase buildings and equipment; and the final effect of these transactions on the net working capital of the firm.

## THE STATEMENT OF AFFAIRS

When an analyst examines the balance sheet of a business, he must remember that the assets are not shown at their "true" value—in fact, there is no such thing as *true* value. The cash is an actual count of cash on hand and in the bank; the accounts receivable are shown at the sale price less a reasonable allowance for bad debts; the merchandise inventory is shown according to some conventional procedure but the value may vary widely under different methods of valuation; the land is shown at original cost; depreciable assets are shown at original cost less the total cost thus far charged to depreciation; and investments may be shown at cost, at present market value, or by the "equity" method. Very few assets are shown at amounts which even approximate what the business could actually get for them if it were to be forced to sell them.

But many decisions need to be based on the security which the business can actually give. This is especially true in cases where the firm is in extreme financial difficulty. It is also true when a large loan is contemplated and it is realized that book values of fixed assets do not give an accurate picture of the security. As an example, a firm which owns land and buildings purchased many years ago in the depths of the depression may have clear title to property worth ten or even 100 times as much as the book value of the assets. On the other hand, assets purchased during periods of inflation or unwisely purchased during a real estate boom may be shown on the books at far more than they would actually be worth. Large loans, and especially loans to firms in precarious condition, are not made on the basis of book values. In these cases the analyst wants a look at the real security offered: (1) what the assets would bring if sold at a forced sale; and (2) the number of claims that would rank ahead of his own in the final settlement. To answer these questions as fully as possible, some supplementary statement must be prepared. One such statement is called a "statement of affairs."

The statement of affairs resembles a balance sheet in that it has on the left side a list of the assets and on the right side a list of the liabilities and the net worth. However, instead of groupings shown on a balance sheet, the assets are grouped under three headings: (1) assets pledged with fully secured creditors; i.e., those assets which will probably bring more than the mortgages on them and will thus provide some cash which may be used for paying the unsecured, general debts; (2) assets pledged with partially secured creditors; i.e., those assets which will bring less than the mortgages or liens against them; (3) free assets; i.e., those assets which are not pledged and which will provide funds to pay unsecured debts. The liability side is divided into comparable sections: (1) liabilities having priority due to legal requirements, such as taxes and wages of employees; (2) fully secured liabilities, where the debt can be fully paid from the sale of the property; (3) partially secured liabilities; i.e., debts owed where the property mortgaged will not bring enough to discharge the debt; (4) unsecured creditors, who have no prior claims on any assets; and (5) the capital stock and surplus.

In spite of its obvious values, the statement of affairs is seldom used except for firms in receivership. For this reason and because the usual form of arrangement makes it fairly difficult to read, it will not be presented here. However, a simplified version, based on the following balance sheet and additional data, will serve to illustrate the value of the statement (see Exhibit 15-9).

BALANCE SHEET

| Assets | | Liabilities and net worth | |
|---|---|---|---|
| Cash........................ | $ 10,000 | Accounts payable.......... | $ 20,000 |
| Accounts receivable (net)(1).... | 60,000 | Accrued taxes and wages... | 10,000 |
| Land and buildings (net)........ | 120,000 | Notes payable (3)......... | 30,000 |
| Machinery (net)............... | 40,000 | Mortgage payable (4)...... | 60,000 |
| Other assets (2)............... | 10,000 | Capital stock............. | 100,000 |
| | | Surplus.................. | 20,000 |
| | $240,000 | | $240,000 |

(1) Accounts receivable will be worth the net amount.
(2) Other assets will sell for $1,000.
(3) Notes payable are secured by mortgage on machinery, which will sell for $25,000.
(4) The mortgage payable is secured by a mortgage on land and buildings, which will sell for $80,000.

In this simplified version of the statement of affairs, all balance sheet amounts are shown in the "Book Value" column. The statement may be read as follows:

1. The machinery has a book value (net) of $40,000. It is mortgaged for $30,000, but will bring only about $25,000 if sold at a forced sale. This will mean a loss of $15,000 to the stockholders and will also mean that the mortgage holders will have an unsecured claim of $5,000. This claim will rank equal to accounts payable and other unsecured creditors.

2. Land and buildings have a book value of $120,000, are mortgaged

EXHIBIT 15-9
Name of Firm—Variation of Statement of Affairs—Date

| Assets and equities | Book value | | Realization and liqui-dation value | Loss or gain | Unse-cured claims | Free assets |
|---|---|---|---|---|---|---|
| | Asset | Equity | | | | |
| 1. Assets fully pledged: | | | | | | |
| Machinery (net)... | $ 40,000 | | $ 25,000 | ($15,000) | | |
| Notes payable se-cured by mtge. on machinery.... | | $ 30,000 | | | $ 5,000 | |
| 2. Assets partially pledged: | | | | | | |
| Land & buildings... | 120,000 | | 80,000 | (40,000) | | |
| Mortgage secured by land and buildings........ | | 60,000 | | | | $20,000 |
| 3. Unpledged (free) assets: | | | | | | |
| Cash............. | 10,000 | | 10,000 | | | 10,000 |
| Accounts receiv-able (net)....... | 60,000 | | 60,000 | | | 60,000 |
| Other assets....... | 10,000 | | 1,000 | (9,000) | | 1,000 |
| Total of all free assets......... | | | | | | $91,000 |
| 4. Liabilities having priority: | | | | | | |
| Accrued wages and taxes........... | | 10,000 | | | | |
| Deduct from free assets........ | | | | | | 10,000 |
| Net free assets... | | | | | | $81,000 |
| 5. Unsecured claims: | | | | | | |
| Accounts payable.. | | 20,000 | | | 20,000 | |
| Total of all unse-cured claims... | | | | | $25,000 | |
| Deduct from free assets........ | | | | | | 25,000 |
| 6. Equity of owners: | | | | | | |
| Capital stock...... | | 100,000 } | | ($64,000) | | $56,000 |
| Surplus.......... | | 20,000 } | | | | |
| | $240,000 | $240,000 | $176,000 | ($64,000) | ...... | $56,000 |

for $60,000, and will probably bring about $80,000. This is enough to pay the mortgage holders and will leave $20,000 for other creditors. The stockholders would suffer a $40,000 loss on the sale, however.

3. Assets not pledged have a book value of $80,000. They are worth $71,000. The stockholders would lose $9,000 on their conversion. The unsecured creditors would have a claim on this $71,000 plus the $20,000 left after paying the loan on the land and building.

4. The law gives certain persons a prior claim on the assets. These amount to $10,000. After these are paid, there will be $81,000 left for unsecured creditors.

5. Open accounts payable (unsecured) amount to $20,000. When this amount is added to the unsatisfied claim from (1), the total unsecured claims amount to $25,000. This leaves free assets of $56,000.

6. The total owner equity of $120,000 minus the estimated losses of $64,000 leaves an owner equity of $56,000—which is equal to the free assets as shown in (5).

The advantages of this statement over a conventional balance sheet are readily seen. While there will be a loss if the firm in the example is forced to dissolve, the losses will not be great enough to impair the equity of the unsecured creditors. But losses from a forced sale would greatly reduce the stockholders' equity. Any person planning a loan, a sale to, or an investment in the stock of this company could quickly adjust the balance sheet figures so that they would reflect the situation following the action planned. He could then see his position and the relative safety of his equity if the firm were forced to discontinue its operations.

## SUMMARY

The first step in the analysis of a balance sheet is the reclassification of all accounts and amounts to agree with sound accounting principles, the analyst's own ideas, or the principles used in establishing the standards with which the amounts are to be compared.

Increase and decrease statements, trend percentages, and common-size balance sheets are the most widely used procedures for evaluating changes in balance sheet amounts. Changes in working capital are best explained by a statement of sources and applications of funds or a statement of changes in working capital. The effect of operating policies on the working capital of a firm is best shown in this type of report.

A statement of affairs is sometimes used to study the security of stockholders and the various creditors of a firm which is in serious financial difficulty. In this type of statement, the realization value of the assets is compared to the claims of the creditors, the "free" assets total is computed and compared with the unsecured creditor claims, and the effect of realization on owner equity is studied to determine the real value of the stockholders' claim.

## QUESTIONS

**1.** Explain why the analyst should begin his study of the balance sheet by reclassifying any accounts which do not appear under what he considers to be proper subheadings.

**2.** Name the six principal subdivisions of assets and describe the type of asset which should be shown under each heading.

**3.** What are the two most common ways of showing prepaid expenses? Which procedure results in the better current ratio?

**4.** Why are temporary investments in government bonds not included under the "Investments" heading?

**5.** All of the following accounts could be considered "intangible" assets. Under what heading is each actually shown?

| | |
|---|---|
| *a.* Accounts Receivable | *f.* Copyrights |
| *b.* Organization Expenses | *g.* Trademarks |
| *c.* Goodwill | *h.* Bond Discount and Expense |
| *d.* Patents | *i.* Interest Receivable |
| *e.* Franchises | *j.* Notes Receivable |

**6.** What is the difference between paid-in surplus and earned surplus?

**7.** What are the most common sources of surplus?

**8.** What are the two principal subdivisions of earned surplus? What is the effect of an entry which debits Earned Surplus and credits the Reserve for Plant Expansion accounts? Does such an entry really reduce the amount which can be paid out as a dividend?

**9.** The following statements are among the most common misconceptions held by beginning students of accounting. Explain why each statement is incorrect.

*a.* Depreciation reserves represent cash which has been set aside to replace fixed assets when they are worn out.

*b.* The Earned Surplus account shows the amount of cash available for dividends.

*c.* Any firm which has a credit balance in its Earned Surplus account can pay dividends.

*d.* If the fixed assets of a firm are destroyed in a fire, the firm can never collect more than their book value (cost less accumulated depreciation).

*e.* The total net worth shown on a balance sheet represents the actual value of the owner equity.

*f.* A firm can never borrow more than about 50 per cent of the book value of the assets which it has to offer as security.

*g.* All assets shown on the balance sheet are worth approximately the amount at which they are carried.

**10.** The Cash balance on the balance sheet of the Ace Company includes the following items. Which are not properly included and what is the correct balance for Cash?

| | |
|---|---:|
| Cash in the bank............................................. | $16,750* |
| Change fund................................................. | 300 |
| Petty cash fund ($60 cash and $40 in receipts for payment)............. | 100 |
| IOUs from employees......................................... | 65 |
| Stamps..................................................... | 26 |
| Cash in pension fund......................................... | 10,000 |
| Total cash as shown......................................... | $27,241 |

\* Cash in Bank A, $17,000; overdraft in Bank B, $250.

**11.** What problems are involved in showing (*a*) notes receivable from officers or directors; (*b*) notes receivable discounted; (*c*) notes or installment accounts receivable, due in 12 to 24 months?

**12.** What weakness is found in each of the following methods of estimating or showing bad debt losses?

  *a.* Bad debts are written off directly. No reserve is used.

  *b.* Estimates of bad debt losses are based on net sales.

  *c.* Bad debt expense is determined by increasing the Reserve for Bad Debts to a desired per cent of the Accounts Receivable balance.

**13.** What is the effect of stolen goods on inventory valuation? What effect does this have on the stated cost of goods sold? What is the effect of an error in taking the inventory, assuming that the error overstates the inventory? Assuming that the error understates the inventory?

**14.** Since no depreciation may be charged on an investment in land, all costs incurred in buying land and buildings must be properly allocated. How much should be in Land and in Buildings after the following entries are recorded?

  *a.* Purchased land on which two old buildings stand, $12,000. The buildings were demolished at a cost of $1,600. Sales of scrap materials brought $400.

  *b.* Legal and other fees incurred in purchase of land above, $60.

  *c.* Paving assessment for street in front of lot, $1,560.

  *d.* Taxes on land held for building site, $60.

  *e.* Architect's fees for new buildings to be erected, $3,000.

  *f.* Cost of digging basement for new building, $460.

  *g.* Cost of constructing new building, $62,000.

  *h.* Cost of drives and loading area, $1,600.

  *i.* Cost of shrubs, fences, lawns, and landscaping, $3,200.

**15.** What three types of accounts are sometimes given names including the words "reserve for"? What titles would you suggest for these accounts?

**16.** Show the per cent of increase or decrease in each of the following cases where a meaningful figure can be computed.

| Account | 1956 | 1957 | % change |
|---|---|---|---|
| Cash (overdraft)............. | ($ 300) | $12,000 | |
| Merchandise inventory........ | 12,600 | 10,800 | |
| Notes receivable............. | | 8,400 | |
| Accounts payable............ | 6,000 | 7,200 | |
| Mortgage payable............ | 15,000 | | |
| Surplus (or deficit).......... | (400) | 12,000 | |

**17.** What amount is used as the base (or 100 per cent) value on a common-size balance sheet? Is the same figure used for both the asset and equity sections?

**18.** How can an ordinary balance sheet be considered a statement of sources and applications of funds? How does a true statement of "sources and applications" differ from a balance sheet?

**19.** Why is depreciation always added to reported net income to find the net working capital provided by operations?

**20.** Indicate whether the following transactions increase, decrease, or have no effect on working capital. (Give amounts used or provided.)

a. Land was purchased at a cost of $12,000.

b. Buildings having a cost of $20,000, and accumulated depreciation of $12,000, were sold for $16,000.

c. 1,000 shares of $100 par, 6 per cent preferred stock were sold at $106 per share.

d. Goodwill of $5,000 was written off against the surplus.

e. Dividends of $6,000 on the preferred and $10,000 on common stock were declared.

f. Operations resulted in a net profit of $26,000 after deducting depreciation of $12,000, bond discount amortized of $600, and a loss on fixed assets junked of $1,200.

**21.** What is the purpose of a statement of affairs? Why has this statement been so little used by our major corporations?

## CHAPTER 16

# THE USE OF RATIOS IN STATEMENT ANALYSIS

There is almost no limit to the number of rates or ratios which could be computed from the figures presented on a firm's income statement and balance sheet. Each individual figure could be compared with every other figure and each grouping of amounts could be compared with every figure or other grouping. This would result in so many possible ratios that only confusion could result from an attempt to use all or even a large number of them. Naturally, then, it is desirable to select only those which are of real significance in answering specific questions which are likely to arise. These rates and ratios are traditionally grouped by the statements from which the basic data may be derived; i.e., whether they are balance sheet ratios, income statement ratios, or ratios requiring data from both statements. This type of classification system has several weaknesses: (1) Business decisions are often based on facts not presented on either statement. (2) Many decisions require the use of a group of ratios, and the grouping of the ratios by questions to be answered is more significant than by source of the data. (3) They have led the student to place more emphasis on the method of computation than upon the importance of understanding and weighing the meaning of the several clues available.

## QUESTIONS WHICH RATES AND RATIOS CAN HELP ANSWER

Rates and ratios obtained from the financial statements are of importance to outside analysts who are attempting to evaluate a firm's current position, the efficiency of the management, and the firm's long-range prospects; but, they are of even more importance in helping the management to evaluate its own operations, to correct its errors, and to avoid conditions which lead to financial instability or business failure. The following paragraphs present a number of specific questions which ratios *help* to answer and explain how these ratios and other data are used. At the end of the chapter the ratios listed under each question are summarized and the computation of each ratio is illustrated.

**Question One.** Will the firm be able to pay its current debts?

If a firm has ten dollars in cash for every dollar which it owes, it should surely be able to pay its current debts. But it would not present a picture of good business management because it would be making poor use of the funds available. On the other hand, if there is no cash on hand, it is quite likely that the firm will have considerable difficulty in meeting its current bills and may become insolvent or even bankrupt. However, since accounts receivable may be collected and marketable securities or inventories or merchandise may be sold, we may not consider cash alone when evaluating the debt-paying ability of a firm.

*The Current Ratio.* The commercial banks of the United States, in their effort to get away from the practice of requiring endorsers and to put the granting of loans on a sound basis, introduced the idea of comparing the amount of assets in cash or to be turned into cash in the near future with the total amount owed to current creditors. This ratio, which was called the "Bankers' Ratio," working capital ratio, or current ratio, is still one of the most widely used of all ratios. It is computed by dividing the total current assets by the total current liabilities and expressing the result as a per cent or as so many dollars of current assets for each dollar of current liabilities. As an example, if the total current assets amount to $240,000 and the total current liabilities amount to $112,000, the current ratio is 240 to 112, or 214 per cent, or 2.14 to 1; which means that the current assets are 214 per cent of current liabilities or that we have $2.14 of current assets for each $1 of current debt.

In the early days, it was said that a ratio of 2 to 1 was considered minimum in a sound business. This rule of thumb has since succumbed to the rule of reason, for there are many factors which throw additional light on the problem and, consequently, may cause a ratio of 2 to 1 to appear poor or a ratio of less than 2 to 1 to be considered good enough.

*The Acid-test Ratio.* One of the most obvious faults of the current ratio is that it includes inventories which have not been sold and therefore do not yet represent fixed dollar obligations to the firm. To reduce the amount to a figure which represents only the most liquid of the current assets, the inventories may be omitted. The cash, trade receivables, and readily marketable securities are totaled and this total is compared with the current debt. As a general rule, the liquid assets listed should at least equal the current liabilities if the business is to be considered in a satisfactory current condition.

Both of the ratios discussed above are quantitative measures; that is, they help to judge whether there are sufficient current assets to pay the current debt. They do not, however, indicate the *quality* of the assets, and this is as important as *quantity* in determining whether the current debts can be paid as they come due. The following two rates are used to estimate the quality of the receivables and inventories.

*Merchandise Inventory Turnover.* A large, slow-moving inventory (relative to industry-wide standards) shows that the inventory cannot be turned into cash as readily as the inventory of a typical firm. This, of course, indicates that a higher current ratio would be necessary for a good rating, since the inventory cannot be depended upon to provide cash within as short a period of time as might be expected for the "average" firm in the industry.

The inventory turnover rate is properly computed by comparing the cost of goods sold to the average inventory for the period; or

$$\frac{\text{Cost of goods sold}}{\text{Average inventory}} = \text{inventory turnover rate}$$

The turnover rate shows the number of times that a typical inventory was sold during the year. The cost of goods sold (or cost of sales) is obtained from the profit and loss statement. The average inventory is ideally found by averaging the monthly inventories. Where inventories are taken only once each year, the beginning and ending inventories must be used. This may sometimes result in an average which is not at all typical of the amount of merchandise normally on hand. For example, if a firm takes inventory only once each year, the ending inventory for one year is the beginning inventory for the following year and all inventory valuations are as of the same date. Since inventories are ideally taken at the end of the natural business year, the two figures used for the average are often both low-point values and the average is far below the typical inventory—which means that the turnover rate will appear to be higher than it actually is.

Since the turnover rate shows the number of times per year that the average inventory is sold, it may be quickly converted into the number of days required to sell the average inventory by simply dividing the rate into 365. Thus if the turnover rate is six times per year, it requires about 61 days ($^{365}\!/_6$) to sell an average inventory.

In addition to giving some indication of the time required to turn the typical inventory, the turnover rate also helps to give some idea of the quality of the goods, since a low turnover of inventory is often the result of including a large amount of obsolete or unsalable merchandise which cannot be disposed of except at drastically reduced prices. Therefore the low turnover rate may suggest the possibility of hidden inventory losses.

*Turnover of Trade Receivables.* The turnover of trade receivables is used to obtain an estimate of the quality of the accounts receivable from customers and to determine the approximate length of time required to collect an average "inventory" of receivables. The rate is computed in a number of ways. Only one way will be discussed at this time; a more complete discussion will be given in connection with the evaluation of credit and collection policies for which the rate is especially valuable.

Since we are interested in the liquidity of the receivables balance, the important question is, approximately how long (how many days) it will take to collect the accounts receivable. First, the annual credit sales are divided by 365 to find the average daily sales on account. The balance in the trade receivables accounts (net) is then divided by the average daily sales to find the number of days' sales on the books. If 60 days' sales are on the books, then 60 days is the approximate time required to collect the receivables.

Attention should be called to the fact that the use of 365 when the store is open only, say, 310 days (365 minus 52 Sundays, New Year's Day, Labor Day, and Christmas) is debatable but seems logical in view of the fact that the final answer is in total days rather than working days. It should also be noted that the receivables balance, if taken shortly after the Christmas rush, could be far larger than normal and far more liquid than indicated by this procedure.

*Other Factors Affecting Current Position.* In addition to the ratios and rates mentioned, the person who would judge a firm's ability to pay its current debts should keep in mind the following points:

1. *Operating costs not on statement.* Neither the balance sheet nor the profit and loss statement show the amount of cash which will be required to meet the weekly or monthly payrolls, to pay the monthly utility bills, the coming month's rent, or the interest on fixed debt except where these amounts were already due and payable at the balance sheet date. A firm which has very little current debt on its balance sheet may be faced with extremely large payrolls, etc., and may be extremely short of ready cash.

2. *The terms of sale and of purchase.* A firm which sells for cash only can have a lower current ratio than one which sells on long credit terms. A firm which buys on long credit terms can have a lower current ratio than one which must pay cash for all purchases.

3. *Bank connections.* A firm which has a good line of credit at its bank can safely have a lower ratio than one which has no bank credit.

4. *Assured sales.* A firm which is selling substantially all its product on an assured market, as on a government contract, can safely have a lower current ratio. However, if the contract is likely to be canceled and the firm must then face a period of reconversion, it would need a much higher current ratio for safety.

5. *Possibility of funding current debt.* If the firm under consideration is in a position to fund its debt; i.e., to issue bonds and use the proceeds to pay its current obligations, then the current ratio is of little significance. This is true for public utilities, for example. When their current debt

becomes too burdensome, they convert it to fixed debt by selling bonds and paying the current creditors.

6. *The effect of seasonal patterns.* Perhaps the most important single consideration in evaluating the current position of a firm is the effect of the seasonal pattern on all the ratios and rates which have been mentioned. Highly seasonal businesses generally use bank funds and current creditor funds to help finance their operations during their peak season. The large inventories, large receivables balances, and large cash requirements for payrolls, etc., are obtained through temporary bank loans and by larger accounts payable balances. For this reason a firm, such as a cannery, will have extremely low current and acid-test ratios at the peak of its season and will appear to be in the best position during its off season. In the same way, it may be shown that a firm which is enjoying a very prosperous year or period of years may actually have a lower current ratio than it had during a period of "recession" a few years before.

The effect of seasonal variations on inventories and receivables balances has already been noted. In each case it may be seen that the firm will make the best showing (highest current ratio, highest liquid ratio, highest turnover rate, and least days' sales on books) if the statements are for the end of the natural business year when inventories and receivables are at their lowest levels and bank loans and accounts payable at a minimum.

7. *Lack of ready cash.* The lack of cash is often indicated by the failure to take purchase discounts, by a "slow-pay" credit record, or by the fact that the firm has resorted to assigning or selling its receivables or has a field warehousing arrangement whereby funds are borrowed on the basis of the inventory as security.

8. *Security for loans.* A firm which can give a bank collateral for a loan, as when stocks and bonds are left for security, may obtain a loan at a lower rate of interest. However, when the bank refuses to make a loan unless security is provided, other prospective creditors may regard this as an indication that the banker has reason to think that the firm in question is not a good credit risk.

**Question Two.** Is the firm reasonably financed? Are the long-term obligations likely to be met?

The "liabilities" and "net worth" sections of a balance sheet show the sources of the funds used to obtain the assets of the firm. If too large a portion of the total is made up of current liabilities, the firm may experience difficulty in paying its debts as they come due. If too large a portion is obtained from long-term creditors, the firm will have a high fixed interest charge which will have to be met even when there are no earnings. (Except for the rather uncommon income bonds where interest is due only if earned.) If all the funds are provided by the stockholders, the company is on very safe grounds but it is not making proper use of the low-cost sources of funds, and it is quite likely that the use of some creditor funds would increase the return on the investment of the owners.

Current creditors should never be considered sources of funds for fixed assets. The fixed asset costs are recovered through depreciation (by making the selling price large enough to pay depreciation and all out-of-pocket costs) too slowly to serve as a source of funds for payment of current debts. Short-term bank loans should not be used to buy fixed assets, and should not even be used to provide the "permanent" working capital. They are used to provide working capital needed at the peak of a season or to carry the business through a temporary shortage of funds. To make certain that it does not provide permanent funds, a bank may require that its borrowers be completely out of debt on bank loans at least once a year.

Long-term debt is infrequently used by small firms, except for mortgages issued when certain fixed properties are purchased. This is true because the costs incurred in floating a bond issue are large, and because most small firms do not have earnings which are sufficiently stable to make a bond issue a desirable means of financing.

To determine the extent to which a company is using the various sources of funds and to help arrive at a decision as to whether the firm is reasonably financed, the following ratios are often used:

1. The ratio of current assets to current liabilities—to be sure that current debt is not being used for noncurrent assets

2. The per cent which current liabilities, long-term liabilities, and owner's equity make of total equities, which is another way of describing the extent to which each major source has been used to provide the total assets

3. The ratio of the owner's equity (net worth) to the total debt, called the "worth to debt" ratio, which is simply another way of comparing the extent of creditor and owner financing

Few small businesses can be considered safely financed if the owners have less than a 50 or 60 per cent interest in the business. For example, if the owner's equity is only 30 per cent, the creditors would then have a 70 per cent equity. If this 70 per cent equity is mostly current debt, the current ratio will be too low. If it is fixed or long-term debt, the fixed interest charge will be too high and the firm will be in danger of being foreclosed if losses are incurred and interest payments cannot be made.

Several factors are of importance in arriving at a decision as to how much of the funds needed can safely be obtained from low-cost, long-term sources. As a good general rule, we may say that the nearer a firm comes to having an assured income, the more it can safely use long-term credit. The following factors help to decide whether a firm's earnings are likely to be sufficiently regular:

1. A firm which sells a necessary item is likely to have much more regular earnings than a firm selling luxury items; e.g., grocery sales are more uniform than jewelry sales; soap sales are more regular than perfume sales.

2. A firm which sells items having a small unit cost will be likely to have more regular earnings than firms selling only large unit-cost items; e.g., shoe sales may be expected to have less fluctuation than sales of locomotives or heavy machinery.

3. Firms which have been in business for a long time and can exhibit steady earnings records and experienced management are more likely to have steady earnings in the future than are relatively new firms, with new products and new and inexperienced management.

4. Firms which are public utilities, public carriers, or whose welfare is so essential to modern life that they cannot be allowed to fail are more likely to have stability than are ordinary manufacturing and merchandising concerns.

*Times Fixed Interest Earned.* One indication of whether the firm is likely to be able to pay its fixed interest charges is obtained from comparing the firm's earnings to its annual fixed interest costs. This is usually done as follows:

$$\frac{\text{Net income plus fixed interest charges}}{\text{Fixed interest charges}} = \frac{\text{times interest}}{\text{charges earned}}$$

Since the fixed interest charges were deducted in obtaining the net income, it is reasonable to add the amount back before dividing by the amount of the fixed interest charges. If the fixed interest charges have already been paid for the current year, the important question is whether or not the interest is likely to be paid in future years. Here the best guide is the economic outlook, the ability of management, and the past record for stability.

*Repayment of Long-term Debt.* The question of the firm's eventual ability to repay its fixed debt is always of importance to management and frequently of importance to creditors. Some analysts have compared the value of the fixed assets pledged as security with the amount of the fixed debt. It is felt that if the debt is relatively small in proportion to the value of the assets, the firm will probably be able to pay off the bonds at their maturity. This conclusion may be entirely unwarranted, however, for at least three good reasons. First, the value shown for fixed assets is usually the original cost minus depreciation to date and may bear little relationship to their actual market value. Second, even if their present market value were known, by the time the bonds mature, which may be 20 or more years in the future, the value of the assets possibly could be so different from their present value as to make the present value of little use. And third, the presence of fixed assets does not necessarily indicate the presence of cash and cash is needed if the bonds are to be repaid. While a high ratio of pledged assets to fixed debt may indicate a strong possibility that the debt will be paid, a good earnings record, a favorable economic outlook, and capable management provide the best assurance of debt-paying ability at a date several years in the future.

The repeated warning against the use of ratios alone sometimes causes the student to feel that the ratios are not of any real value. This is not true. While the presence of satisfactory ratios will not necessarily mean a sound condition, the presence of unsatisfactory ratios almost invariably *does* mean an unsound condition. And ratios help warn the management of a drift toward unsound conditions in time for corrective action to be taken.

**Question Three.** Is the firm earning an adequate or reasonable rate of return?

The financial statements alone cannot answer this question. They can only show what rate of return is being earned. Whether this rate is "reasonable" depends primarily upon two factors which never appear on the statements. First, the adequacy of the return must be judged by alternative uses which could be made of the investment. And second, the earnings for a given year must always be related to the economic conditions and to the success of competitors or comparable firms. Both of the factors are more fully discussed later.

*Net Income as a Per Cent of Sales.* The rate of return which is earned can be computed in a number of ways—the choice of the method often depending upon what the analyst is trying to prove. Perhaps the most easily understood rate is based on sales. It seems reasonable that a firm which has sales of one million dollars per year should expect to make a larger profit than one which has sales of only one hundred thousand dollars per year. The common-size profit and loss statement described in Chapter 13 shows the net income as a per cent of the net sales. If a firm compares this per cent from its own records with industry standards, it can readily determine if the rate is above or below the average and, more specifically, in which quartile its rate is included. Certainly ranking in the lowest fourth is hardly to be considered "good" even though the actual rate earned is fairly high. On the other hand, a firm which is in the top fourth is doing *relatively* well even though profits are small. In evaluating management, we may even conclude that a small loss is not really bad if economic conditions are unfavorable and especially if the firm has, relatively, the smallest loss in the industry.

*Net Income as a Return on the Investment.* If the net income is divided by the total owner's equity, the rate of return on the investment is obtained. Whether this return is adequate depends to a very large extent upon the alternative uses which could be made of the investment. For example, if a bookstore has earned under 2 per cent on the owner's equity in each of the past ten years, it must be obvious that this rate of return is too low. Government bonds would pay this well with far less risk, and most good common stocks would have paid far more.

The question is often asked as to whether the "investment" to be used in computing this rate is the beginning-of-the-year-figure, the end-of-year balance, or the average of these two amounts. No attempt will be made to decide this question since all three may be logically defended and the difference is usually small. A much more significant question should be considered. If we are really interested in alternative uses, we must remember the owner's equity as shown on the statement usually does not represent the "real" or "true" value of the equity, since the inventories are usually not shown at their market value and the fixed assets are almost invariably shown at their original cost less accumulated depreciation and this figure often bears no real resemblance to their present market value or to their replacement value. In addition, the annual depreciation charge is made to recover actual cost rather than replacement cost, and, as a result, profits may be overstated.

The net income figure usually used is the net operating income (after taxes, for corporations) and includes all except extraordinary gains and losses. But, it is always the book income and does not reveal gains or losses due to property appreciation; e.g., a farmer may report a net income of only $4,000 but may, through appreciation of property values, have increased his net worth by far more than this figure. He may have built a barn for $3,000 which is now worth $6,000, cleaned out fence rows, built fences, terraced the fields, stopped erosion, built windbreaks, fertilized the soil, and made other improvements bringing about an over-all increase in market value of many thousands of dollars. This "income" does not appear on the statements and is not subject to taxes until actually sold, when it is subject to a "capital gains" tax on only a fraction of the profit. Nevertheless, it must be considered income in considering alternative investments.

*Net Income as a Per Cent of Assets Used.* The ratio of the net income to the total assets used to produce the income is used to test the reasonableness of the income and to indicate a possible overinvestment in fixed assets. As a measure of overinvestment in fixed assets, however, the ratio of the net sales to the fixed assets used to produce the sales is perhaps a better measure.

**Question Four.** Does the firm provide the owners with a reasonable return on their investment?

This question is essentially the same as the preceding one, but places more emphasis on the point of view of a single stockholder viewing the safety and adequacy of the return on his stockholdings.

*Earnings on Preferred Shares.* The preferred stockholder may be interested in the earnings per share of preferred stock or in the number of times the preferred dividends were earned. These rates are computed as follows:

$$\frac{\text{Net income}}{\text{Preferred dividend requirements}} = \begin{array}{l}\text{number of times preferred} \\ \text{dividends were earned}\end{array}$$

$$\frac{\text{Net income}}{\text{Number of shares of preferred}} = \begin{array}{l}\text{earnings per share of} \\ \text{preferred}\end{array}$$

Unless the preferred stock is "participating," the preferred stockholder is entitled only to the dividend rate specified. The number of times preferred dividends were earned or the earnings per share of preferred simply indicate (1) whether the firm can pay the dividends and (2) the amount of decrease in profits which could take place before preferred dividends are endangered.

*Earnings on Common Stock.* Common stockholders often want to find the earnings per share of common stock or the earnings on the common equity. Since the preferred stockholders have a prior claim on the company's earnings, the preferred dividend requirement is subtracted before considering any of the earnings applicable to common.

$$\frac{\text{Net income} - \text{preferred dividend requirements}}{\text{Number of shares of common}} = \begin{array}{l}\text{earnings per share} \\ \text{of common}\end{array}$$

$$\frac{\text{Net income} - \text{preferred dividend requirements}}{\text{Equity of common stockholders}} = \begin{array}{l}\text{rate earned on common} \\ \text{equity}\end{array}$$

The equity of the common stockholders is sometimes easy to determine and sometimes almost impossible to determine. If the preferred stock is nonparticipating and there are no dividends in arrears, all surplus is included in the common equity. If there are dividends in arrears on cumulative preferred stock, the amount of these dividends must be deducted in determining the common equity. If the preferred stock is partially participating, the preferred stockholders have an equity in the surplus which is really quite difficult to compute. And if the preferred stock is of several classes with features such as being convertible or redeemable and at the same time cumulative and participating, the common equity is even more difficult to compute.

*Market Value to Earnings.* Prospective stockholders often compare the present market price of common stock to the earnings per share of the stock. For example, if the common stock of a company is selling for $120 and the company has earnings after preferred dividend requirements of $12 per share, $120/$12 gives a ratio of 10 to 1, which means that the selling price is 10 times the annual earnings on the share. It is believed that this ratio helps to determine whether the market price is out of line. However, since annual earnings may vary much more violently than the book value of the stock, this ratio cannot be considered more than a doubtful clue. Stocks have been known to sell so far below their real value that, had all the stock been purchased at the price quoted, the firm could have sold its assets, paid all its debts, and had a cash balance remaining of twice the cost of the stock.

**Question Five.** Are the inventories getting out of line?

One of the problems which constantly faces a businessman is keeping his inventories in line. Too large an inventory means added costs for warehousing and handling, more insurance, losses from deterioration, and, where models or styles are important, serious losses from obsolescence. If the inventories are too small, sales are lost and time is lost because of materials shortages. In addition, the cost of financing large inventories and the danger of losses from price fluctuations make the maintenance of proper inventories imperative.

*Inventory Turnover.* The size of the inventory is obviously closely related to the amount of merchandise being sold. This relationship is best pictured by the merchandise inventory turnover, found by dividing the cost of goods sold by the average inventory for the period. It is also often based on a comparison of the net sales to the average inventory (particularly when cost of goods sold cannot be determined).

$$\frac{\text{Cost of goods sold}}{\text{Average inventory}} = \text{inventory turnover rate}$$

$$\frac{\text{Net sales}}{\text{Average inventory}} = \text{acceptable substitute for turnover rate}$$

The ratio of net sales to the average inventory is often used as a substitute for the true turnover rate for two reasons: First, the outside analyst often cannot find the cost of goods sold because it is concealed by including it with other costs on the income statement. Sales and inventories, on the other hand, are always given. Second, even if the cost of sales figure for a particular firm is known, the net sales may be used to make the rate comparable to published rates for the industry— since these published rates are often based on net sales.

Both ratios mentioned give a quick picture of the turnover of the inventory for a given year, but they do not answer the question as to whether the inventory is out of line. To do this we should compare the turnover rate with that of other similar firms or with industry-wide standards. We should also compute our own turnover rate for the past several years to see whether the rate is increasing or decreasing. In general, we should be pleased to see an increase in turnover. However, if the turnover is too rapid, it may indicate a lack of adequate inventories. The analyst should also remember that totals and averages often hide the movement of individual items or amounts. For example, the total inventory for a department store may be decreasing while the inventory of one particular department may be increasing. In the same way, one department may have a much slower turnover and yet, if the other departments have better rates, the total turnover rate may actually be increasing. In no case can the total turnover rate be accepted as an indication of the rate for particular items or departments. Which, of course, means that turnover rates should be computed for each department, and that the movement of each important line of goods should also be watched.

In connection with this problem, we should mention the practice of speculating on inventory price movements. The merchant or manufacturer who stocks up heavily in anticipation of price increases, and cuts his buying sharply if he believes prices will decline, should recognize the fact that he is gambling in a field in which he is quite likely an amateur. The job of the merchant is to buy and sell goods, and speculation in inventories is not an essential part of good merchandising. It is the opinion of the authors that the size of the inventory is a function of the sales potential rather than the anticipated price movement. While fortunes are sometimes made by the firm which guesses right on price rises, the financial graveyards are filled with the bones of firms which guessed wrong. In the long run, the merchant and the small manufacturer will do well to keep their inventories in line with their actual needs and leave speculation to persons with more information and more free time to devote to studying the market.

*Manufacturing Inventory Turnover.* A factory has three inventories of materials and merchandise. Materials which are in the state in which they were purchased are called "raw materials." Those which are partially processed are called "goods in process," and those which are completed and are being held for sale are called "finished goods." The turnover of each type of inventory is computed by comparing the amount leaving each state with the average amount in that state:

$$\frac{\text{Cost of raw materials used}}{\text{Average inventory of raw materials}} = \text{raw materials turnover}$$

$$\frac{\text{Cost of goods manufactured}}{\text{Average inventory of goods in process}} = \text{goods in process turnover}$$

$$\frac{\text{Cost of goods sold}}{\text{Average inventory of finished goods}} = \text{finished goods turnover}$$

All of the figures needed may be obtained from the schedule of the cost of goods manufactured and the profit and loss statement. The turnover rates obtained are a good *general* statement of inventory movements but they do not eliminate the need for watching individual items and departments. They are of most importance as a general indicator when compared with previous years and with other firms operating under similar conditions.

*Other Considerations in Inventory Evaluation.* In all inventory turnover rates used, it is customary to use the *average* inventory rather than the *present* inventory. Since the present inventory may not be the same size as the average, and most likely is not, no ratio based on the average can be a very sound indication of whether present inventories are out of line. They can show whether the typical inventory of the period was in line, if the average is really typical.

It should also be remembered that a large inventory may be due to unsold merchandise carried over from the preceding season, but it may also be due to the firm's having made early purchases for the coming season. These purchases may have been made early to gain price concessions or to take advantage of a seasonally depressed market and may indicate adequate working funds and good business management rather than a slow turnover of inventory. Rates and ratios are valuable aids, but never if they are used blindly.

**Question Six.** Are the credit and collection policies good?

A firm can easily avoid all bad debt losses and can eliminate all credit and collection expense by selling only for cash. Or it can eliminate all bad debt losses by selling only to persons or firms which have top credit ratings. But either of these solutions may, through lost sales, decrease the profits by an amount greater than the total of all costs and losses which might arise from normal sales on account. The best solution is not the one which results in no bad debt losses but rather the one which results in the maximum net profit. This means that the firm must sell to many customers who have less than top credit ratings, on the basis that the great majority will pay. It also means that credit must be refused some potential customers, on the basis that net profits will never be increased by selling to those who probably will not pay. This makes the granting of credit and the evaluation and improvement of credit and collection policies matters of extreme importance.

*Bad Debt Losses.* While some firms use a "direct write-off" method of accounting for bad debt losses, most larger firms attempt to estimate the amount of bad debts which will result from a given volume of credit sales. Until the firm has gained some credit experience, it may use industry standards (usually available in trade association publications) to estimate the probable losses. For example, it may be found that manufacturers in a particular industry lose, on the average, ½ per cent, or 0.5 per cent, of their credit sales. For the first two or three years, the firm may use this figure in setting up its adjustment for estimated bad debts. The entry is a debit to bad debts and a credit to allowance (or reserve) for bad debts for ½ per cent of the credit sales. At the end of each year, the actual losses should be compared with estimated losses. This may be done in several ways, but the easiest way is to observe the balance in the reserve for bad debts account. If the amount actually written off (debits) is equal to the estimate (credit), the account will not increase in size. If the account balance is increasing, the estimate is probably too large; if the account often has a debit balance, the estimate is too small. After a reasonable period, the rate should be adjusted to agree with the firm's own loss experience. By comparing a firm's losses from year to year with figures for the industry, one may arrive at a reasonable evaluation of credit policies. However, the final test of a good credit policy is not how well it conforms to practice, but how it affects net profit.

*Turnover of Receivables.* Similar firms using similar credit terms should be expected to have comparable receivables balances. The number of days' sales on the books can, therefore, be used as a measure of the firm's credit and collection policies.

As explained earlier, the number of days' sales on the books can be found by dividing the average daily sales (credit sales preferably) into the total trade receivables (net) balance. The figure obtained can be converted into a "turnover of receivables" rate by dividing the number 365 by the number of days' sales on the books. Or a receivables turnover can be computed by simply dividing the net sales on account by the balance of trade receivables.

Both of these indicators derive their principal value from comparison with previous years or with industry averages. For example, if the number of days' sales on the books has been 34, 38, 43, 47, and 52 for the past five years, it is readily apparent that our collection policies are growing poorer or that in order to increase sales we are selling to more and more slow-paying accounts. If we compare our figures for the number of days' sales on the books with the industry figures of 32, 34, 33, 32, and 34 for the same periods, we see that the trend is not industry-wide but is due to our own policies. Appropriate action may then be taken. This may mean a change in credit policies, elimination of some slow-paying customers, the credit manager's approval on sales contracts, faster handling of invoices and statements, etc. Or it may not result in any action if it is found that profits have been increased as a result of the increased sales and more liberal credit terms.

In any event, the accounting records have provided the basic data needed and the ratios have focused our attention on the problem. The decision as to what constitutes "appropriate action" must come from management.

**Question Seven.** Is the cost of goods sold (or any other cost or expense amount) getting out of line?

One of the most important groups of ratios is found by comparing each cost and expense item to the net sales produced. These ratios were briefly explained in Chapter 14 under the heading of common-size profit and loss statements.

*Gross Margin on Sales.* Experience has shown that the gross profit (or margin) percentage for a given line of business will vary over a rather narrow range. For example, retail shoe stores use a markup per cent which gives them a gross profit of about 35 per cent of net sales, while retail grocery stores have a gross profit of only about 17 per cent of net sales, or roughly half the amount made by shoe stores. It would be extremely unusual to find a successful shoe store operating on a gross margin of less than 20 per cent or to find a grocery store trying to gain a 35 per cent margin on its sales. Any attempt to increase the margin beyond what is typical for that line of business may result in a loss of sales volume, unless accompanied by an increase in sales effort (which may cost more than the amount obtained from the higher margin). And any attempt to operate on a lower margin, though likely to increase the physical quantities sold, may result in a lower dollar volume, a smaller total gross profit, or a smaller net income. For these reasons, businessmen must watch their gross margins very carefully. A comparison with the rate for previous years will reveal any upward or downward movement and comparisons with the margins earned by successful competitors will show approximately what the margin should be. If the markup* is consciously cut, we may expect a decrease in the gross profit margin percentage, but there can be a decrease in the margin percentage without a change in markup policy. This may be due to an increase in the number of clearance sales held, an increase in the quantities sold during sales, or a shift in sales to low-margin items.

*Costs Compared to Net Sales.* The best way to judge any expense amount is to consider its size in proportion to the net sales for the period and to evaluate the contribution of each cost to the sales program. These per cents should be compared with those of comparable firms in the same line of business and with the firm's own record in preceding years.

---

* The markup may be figured either as a per cent on cost or as a per cent of the selling price. An item which cost $10 and is marked to sell for $15 has a markup of 50 per cent on cost or 33⅓ per cent on sales price. The gross margin is always stated as a per cent of sales.

## COMPUTATION OF RATES AND RATIOS

To summarize the rates and ratios described above and to illustrate how they are actually computed, let us use the balance sheet and combined income and surplus statement of the Polax Company for the year 1957, which are presented in Exhibits 16-1 and 16-2.

1. Will the firm be able to pay its current debts?

   *a.* The current ratio:

$$\frac{\text{Current assets}}{\text{Current liabilities}} = \frac{\$88,300}{\$32,200} = 2.74 \text{ or } 2.74 \text{ to } 1$$

   *b.* The acid-test (or liquid) ratio:

$$\frac{\text{Quick current assets*}}{\text{Current liabilities}} = \frac{\$33,800*}{\$32,200} = 1.05 \text{ or } 1.05 \text{ to } 1$$

   *The figure used here includes cash and all receivables but does not include inventories or prepaid expenses.

   *c.* Merchandise inventory turnover:

$$\frac{\text{Cost of sales}}{\text{Average inventory*}} = \frac{\$346,120}{\$51,340} = 6.74$$

   *(48,380 + 54,300)/2

   *d.* Turnover of trade receivables—number of days' sales on books:

$$\frac{\text{Trade receivables (net)}}{\text{Average daily sales}} = \frac{\$23,140}{\$1,383*} = 16.7$$

   *Average daily sales = \$504,880/365

2. Is the firm reasonably financed? Are the long-term obligations likely to be met?

   *a.* Current ratio
   *b.* Current liabilities to total equities:

$$\frac{\text{Total current liabilities}}{\text{Total liabilities \& net worth}} = \frac{\$32,200}{\$445,800} = 7.2\%$$

   *c.* Long-term debt to total equities:

$$\frac{\text{Long-term debt}}{\text{Total liabilities \& net worth}} = \frac{\$140,600}{\$445,800} = 31.5\%$$

*d.* Total liabilities to total equities:

$$\frac{\text{Total liabilities}}{\text{Total liabilities \& net worth}} = \frac{\$173,660}{\$445,800} = 39.0\%$$

*e.* Owners' equities to total equities:

$$\frac{\text{Total owner equity}}{\text{Total liabilities \& net worth}} = \frac{\$272,140}{\$445,800} = 61.0\%$$

EXHIBIT 16-1
POLAX COMPANY, INC.
Balance Sheet
December, 31, 1957

| *Assets* | | | | *Liabilities* | | | |
|---|---|---|---|---|---|---|---|
| Current assets: | | | | Current liabilities: | | | |
| Cash on hand and in banks | | $ 10,600 | | Accounts payable | | $ 12,600 | |
| Accounts receiv- | | | | Notes payable (trade) | | 3,000 | |
| able | $ 22,800 | | | Wages payable | | 2,600 | |
| Less allow- | | | | Estimated income tax pay- | | | |
| ance for | | | | able | | 14,000 | |
| bad debts | 1,300 | 21,500 | | Total current liabilities | | | $ 32,200 |
| Notes receivable | | 1,640 | | Deferred income: | | | |
| Merchandise inventory | | 54,300 | | Rent collected in advance | | | 860 |
| Prepaid insurance | | 200 | | Long-term debt: | | | |
| Accrued interest receivable | | 60 | | Mortgage payable, 6% | | $ 10,600 | |
| Total current assets | | | $ 88,300 | First mortgage bonds pay- | | | |
| Investments: | | | | able | | 130,000 | |
| Investment in stock of | | | | Total long-term debt | | | 140,600 |
| subsidiary | | $ 84,000 | | Total liabilities | | | $173,660 |
| Ace Corporation bonds | | 25,000 | | | | | |
| Bond sinking fund | | 28,000 | | | | | |
| Cash surrender value of | | | | | | | |
| life insurance | | 14,000 | | | | | |
| Total investments | | | 151,000 | *Net worth* | | | |
| Fixed assets: | | | | | | | |
| Land | | $ 12,000 | | Capital stock: | | | |
| Buildings | $156,000 | | | Preferred stock, 1,000 | | | |
| Allowance for | | | | shares, $100 par, 6% | | | |
| Depr | 16,000 | 140,000 | | cumulative preferred | | $100,000 | |
| Furniture and | | | | Common stock, 14,000 | | | |
| fixtures | $ 18,000 | | | shares, no-par, $10 | | | |
| Allowance for | | | | stated value | | 140,000 | |
| Depr | 8,000 | 10,000 | | Total capital stock | | | $240,000 |
| Total fixed assets | | | 162,000 | Surplus: | | | |
| Intangible assets: | | | | Earnings retained in busi- | | | |
| Patents | | $ 17,000 | | ness | | $ 26,000 | |
| Franchises | | 22,000 | | Capital surplus, excess of | | | |
| Total intangible assets | | | 39,000 | amount paid in over- | | | |
| Deferred charges: | | | | stated value | | 6,140 | |
| Discount on bonds payable | $ 3,000 | | | Total surplus | | | 32,140 |
| Organization expense | 2,500 | | | Total net worth | | | $272,140 |
| Total deferred charges | | | 5,500 | Total liabilities and net worth | | | $445,800 |
| Total assets | | | $445,800 | | | | |

*f.* The worth-to-debt ratio:

$$\frac{\text{Total net worth*}}{\text{Total liabilities}} = \frac{\$272,140}{\$173,660} = 1.57 \text{ to } 1$$

*In many cases the net worth figure used is the net worth as shown on the balance sheet minus intangible assets.

*g.* Times fixed interest earned:

$$\frac{\text{Net income* + fixed interest charges}}{\text{Fixed interest charges}} = \frac{\$74,430 + 8,690}{\$8,690}$$

*The net income figure used is often income after taxes. Fixed interest charges should include interest on fixed or long-term debt.

*h.* Fixed assets to fixed debt:

$$\frac{\text{Fixed assets}}{\text{Fixed debt}} = \frac{\$162,000}{\$140,600} = 1.15 \text{ to } 1$$

Exhibit 16-2
Polax Company, Inc.
Income Statement and Changes in Earned Surplus
for the Year Ended December 31, 1957

Income from sales:
Gross sales...................................................... $522,640
Less returned sales and allowances..................... $ 11,320
Discounts on sales........................................ 6,440    17,760
Net sales....................................................... $504,880
Cost of goods sold:
Merchandise inventory, Jan. 1, 1957...................... $ 48,380
Purchases.................................... $365,470
Returned purchases.................. $13,300
Purchases discounts................. 7,520    20,820
Net purchases............................ $344,650
Transportation in.......................... 7,390    352,040
Cost of merchandise available for sale.................... $400,420
Less merchandise inventory, Dec. 31, 1957................ 54,300
Cost of goods sold.................................... 346,120
Gross profit on sales........................................ $158,760
Operating expenses:
Selling expenses:
Sales salaries................................ $ 24,060
Salesmen's travel expense.................... 1,200
Advertising................................. 13,600
Delivery expense............................ 2,840
Depreciation on store equipment.............. 960
Depreciation on store building................ 3,200
Total selling expense......................... $ 45,860

EXHIBIT 16-2 (*Continued*)

General and administrative expense:

| | | |
|---|---:|---:|
| Office salaries.............................. | $ 6,750 | |
| Officer's salaries........................... | 16,280 | |
| Property taxes.............................. | 3,890 | |
| Insurance................................... | 1,840 | |
| Bad debt losses............................. | 2,300 | |
| Depreciation of office equipment............. | 640 | |
| Depreciation of office building............... | 1,400 | |
| Total general and administrative expense............. | 33,100 | |
| Total operating expense................................ | | 78,960 |
| Net income from operations............................. | | $ 79,800 |

Other income:

| | | |
|---|---:|---:|
| Interest income........................................ | $ 1,240 | |
| Dividend income....................................... | 2,260 | 3,500 |
| Total......................................... | | $ 83,300 |

Other expenses:

| | | |
|---|---:|---:|
| Interest on notes payable.............................. | $ 180 | |
| Mortgage and bond interest expense..................... | 8,690 | 8,870 |
| Net income....................................... | | $ 74,430 |
| Less provision for state and Federal taxes................... | | 32,200 |
| Net income to earned surplus............................... | | $ 42,230 |
| Earned surplus, Jan. 1, 1957.............................. | | 13,770 |
| Total......................................... | | $ 56,000 |

Less dividends paid:

| | | |
|---|---:|---:|
| Preferred stock....................................... | $ 6,000 | |
| Common stock........................................ | 24,000 | 30,000 |
| Earned surplus, Dec. 31, 1957............................. | | $ 26,000 |

3. Is the firm earning an adequate or reasonable rate of return?

a. Net income to net sales:

$$\frac{\text{Net income*}}{\text{Net sales}} = \frac{\$79,800}{\$504,880} = 15.8\%$$

*The net income figure used here is the net income from operations. This is more closely related to sales than the net income ($74,430) or the net income after taxes ($42,230); however, these other "net income" figures are often used.

b. Net income to the owner's equity:

$$\frac{\text{Net income*}}{\text{Net worth}} = \frac{\$42,230}{\$272,140} = 15.5\%$$

*When considering return on the investment, the net income after taxes seems most logical. The Net Worth figure may exclude intangible assets. In no case can it be considered the "true" value of the owner's equity.

*c.* Net income to total assets:

$$\frac{\text{Net income*}}{\text{Total assets}} = \frac{\$74,430}{\$445,800} = 16.7\%$$

\*The net income from operations may be compared with total *operating* assets. Net sales may also be compared to *operating* assets.

4. Does the firm provide the individual owners with a reasonable return on their investment?

*a.* Number of times preferred dividends were earned:

$$\frac{\text{Net income}}{\text{Preferred dividend requirement}} = \frac{\$42,230}{6,000} = 7.04$$

*b.* Earnings per share of preferred stock:

$$\frac{\text{Net income}}{\text{Number of preferred shares}} = \frac{\$42,230}{1,000} = \$42.23$$

*c.* Earnings on common stock:

$$\text{Earnings per share} = \frac{\text{net income} - \text{pref. dividends}}{\text{no. shares of common}}$$
$$= \frac{\$42,230 - \$6,000}{14,000} = \$2.57 \text{ per share}$$
$$\text{Earnings on common equity} = \frac{\text{net income} - \text{pref. dividends}}{\text{equity of common}}$$
$$= \frac{\$42,230 - \$6,000}{\$172,140} = 21.0\%$$
$$\text{Market value to earning} = \frac{\text{market value*}}{\text{earnings per share}}$$
$$= \frac{\$27.50}{2.59} = 10.6 \text{ times}$$

\*Obtained from current market quotations.

*d.* Book value of common stock per share:

$$\frac{(\text{Net assets} - \text{intangibles}) - \text{preferred equity}}{\text{No. of shares of common}} = \text{book value}$$
$$\frac{(\$272,140 - 39,000) - \$100,000*}{14,000} = \$9.51$$

\*Stock owned plus dividends in arrears.

5. Are the inventories getting out of line?

   *a.* The inventory turnover:

$$\frac{\text{Cost of sales}}{\text{Average inventory}} = \frac{\$346,120}{\$51,340} = 6.7 \text{ times}$$

  or

$$\frac{\text{Net sales}}{\text{Average inventory}} = \frac{\$504,880}{\$51,340} = 9.8 \text{ to } 1$$

6. Are the credit and collection policies good?

   *a.* $\dfrac{\text{Bad debt losses}}{\text{Net sales}} = \dfrac{\$2,300}{\$504,880} = 0.0045$ or less than ½ per cent

   *b.* Turnover of receivables:

$$\frac{\text{Net sales}}{\text{Trade receivables (net)}} = \frac{\$504,880}{\$23,140} = 21.8 \text{ times}$$

  or

$$\frac{365}{\text{No. days' sales on books*}} = \frac{365}{16.7} = 21.8$$

$$\text{*No. days' sales on books} = \frac{\text{trade receivables}}{\text{average daily sales}}$$

$$= \frac{\$23,140}{1,383} = 16.7$$

7. Is the cost of goods sold (or any other cost or expense amount) getting out of line?

   *a.* $\dfrac{\text{Cost of sales}}{\text{Net sales}} = \dfrac{\$346,120}{\$504,880} = 68.6\%$

   *b.* $\dfrac{\text{Gross profit on sales}}{\text{Net sales}} = \dfrac{\$158,760}{\$504,880} = 31.4\%$

   *c.* $\dfrac{\text{Operating expenses (individually)}}{\text{Net sales}}$

$$\frac{\text{Selling expenses}}{\text{Net sales}} = \frac{\$45,860}{\$504,880} = 9.1\%$$

$$\frac{\text{Gen. \& adm. expense}}{\text{Net sales}} = \frac{\$33,100}{\$504,800} = 6.6\%$$

## SUMMARY

Ratios and rates computed from balance sheet and income statement data often help to focus attention on business problems which must be solved. (1) The ability of a firm to pay its current debts may be indicated by the current ratio, the acid-test ratio, the inventory turnover rate, and the turnover of receivables. The effect of seasonal patterns, terms of sale and purchase, debts not on statements (such as fixed interest on bonded indebtedness, etc.) cannot be ignored. (2) The ability of a firm to pay its long-term obligations and the soundness of its financial structure may be indicated by the current ratio, the worth-to-debt ratio, and by a component-part balance sheet showing the per cent of total funds from each major source. The number of times fixed interest charges were earned is used to judge the adequacy of current earnings as compared to fixed interest charges. The eventual ability to repay fixed debt is best indicated by a good earnings record, capable management, and a favorable economic outlook rather than by the present book value of fixed assets pledged. (3) Whether a firm is earning a reasonable rate of return can be measured by comparing net income to sales, net income to assets used to produce the income, or by determining the rate of the return on the investment. (4) The return on the individual stockholder's investment may be judged by determining the number of times preferred dividends were earned, the earnings per share of preferred stock, the earnings per share of common stock, the earnings on the common equity, and the ratio of the market value of the stock to the earnings per share. (5) The effectiveness of management policies in inventory control may be judged by inventory turnover rates: raw materials turnover, finished goods turnover, and turnover of goods in process. These rates must be used with caution and factors affecting the size of the inventory must be considered. (6) Credit and collection policies may be judged by bad debt losses and their final effect on net income, and by the turnover of receivables or number of days' sales on the books. (7) Whether the cost of goods sold or any other cost or expense is getting out of line may be judged by comparing the particular cost item to net sales and studying the trend over the past several years. In all cases, industry standards, if based on truly comparable firms, are extremely valuable.

In every case, the accounting records provide the data needed and the ratio helps to focus attention on the problem. The decision as to what constitutes "appropriate action" must come from management.

## QUESTIONS

**1.** What ratios are widely used to focus the attention of the analyst on the ability of a firm to pay its current debts?

**2.** What is the formula for computing each of the following ratios or rates:

*a.* The current ratio?
*b.* The acid-test (or liquid) ratio?
*c.* The merchandise turnover rate?
*d.* The turnover rate for receivables?

**3.** Explain the effect of each of the following conditions on your appraisal of a firm's current position.

*a.* The statements were prepared at the peak of the firm's seasonal pattern.

*b.* Sinking fund contributions and fixed interest charges due in the coming year amount to $150,000.

*c.* The firm has been building war contract items and must soon begin selling consumer goods.

*d.* The firm has a long-term contract to produce parts for a large, nationally known manufacturer.

*e.* The firm is a public utility.

**4.** How do the worth-to-debt ratio and component-part per cents for the equity section of a balance sheet serve the same purpose?

**5.** What are the advantages and disadvantages of each of the following means of financing:

*a.* Obtaining an unusually large part of the working capital from current creditors?

*b.* Obtaining an unusually large part of the firm's total capital from long-term creditors?

*c.* Obtaining an unusually large part of the total funds needed from stockholders?

**6.** Under what conditions may a firm depend upon creditors for a large part of the total investment? What type of firm should have little or no long-term debt?

**7.** What formula is used to determine the number of times fixed interest charges were earned? The ratio of net income to fixed interest charges of the Ace Company was 3 to 1. How many times were the fixed interest charges earned? If sales dropped 25 per cent, do you believe it likely that fixed interest charges would be earned three times?

**8.** The long-term debt of the Ace Company is equal to only 40 per cent of the book value of the assets pledged as security. Does this mean that the 20-year bonds outstanding are likely to be paid at maturity? Why is present book value not a good indication of the firm's ability to retire fixed debt on schedule?

**9.** The Jameson Company reports that its net income was only 3 per cent for 1956. Why is this figure meaningless? On what bases may the per cent earned be figured?

**10.** In what ways can an investor measure the earnings on his investment in a firm's preferred stock? On his investment in the firm's common stock?

**11.** Why is the inventory turnover sometimes judged by the ratio of sales to the inventory rather than the ratio of cost of goods sold to the inventory?

**12.** Would you agree that the firm which has the highest turnover rate is not necessarily doing the best job of inventory control? What are the possible causes for an unusually high turnover rate?

**13.** What are the possible reasons for a low turnover rate? Which of these may indicate good management and which may indicate inventory speculation or poor inventory control?

**14.** Why is the amount of bad debt losses not always a sound basis for evaluating the firm's credit policies?

**15.** How do a firm's credit terms (or terms of sales) affect the number of days' sales which may be expected to remain in accounts receivable? If the terms of sale are 2/10, n/30, approximately how many days' sales should be in accounts receivable? What would be the effect of a clearance sale just before the end of the period on the receivables turnover rate?

## CHAPTER 17

# BUDGETARY PLANNING AND CONTROL

A *budget* is a plan for the future expressed in financial terms. In a business unit budgets represent an operating plan with two primary objectives: (1) to provide a financial forecast of future operations, and (2) to provide standards for the measurement of performance. A company budget is, therefore, both a plan for the future and a means of comparing actual results with the standards established in the budgets. *Budgetary planning* is the work involved in attaining the objectives which a firm hopes to realize through the use of a complete budgetary system. Such planning includes budget conferences with executives and department heads, analysis of past performance, analysis of expected future conditions, study of pricing policies, determination of break-even points, coordination of departmental activities, control of costs by measurement of results, and, of course, the actual forecasting in financial terms.

Accounting is concerned primarily with recording, reporting, and interpreting financial events. It is historical in nature, for its concern is, to a great degree, with the past. Budgeting is concerned primarily with planning for the future; but much of this advance planning is based on historical accounting records, and budgets, to be of full value, must be compared with actual performance as shown by the accounting records. Accounting and budgeting should, therefore, be related in form; that is, the two must be similar in form if comparisons are to be made easily. For that reason, budgets are normally established on the basis of the account classifications employed by a particular firm; but if the account classifications are not sufficiently detailed to provide adequate comparisons, additional accounts should be added.

Various techniques employed in statement analysis serve as valuable tools in the preparation of budgets and the comparisons of budgeted figures with actual results. Trend statements, for instance, provide one basis for estimating growth possibilities; e.g., if trend statements reveal a steady rate of growth in sales, this information, along with other data, may indicate that the same rate of increase can be expected during the next period. Common-size statements and ratios can be employed as an aid in determining the expected or desired proportion of expense items to sales, of assets to total assets, of liability and net worth items to total equities, etc. When actual performance has been reflected by the accounting statements and reports, the various comparative techniques used in analysis can be employed. Actual results can, for example, be compared with budget estimates by preparing comparative statements that include increase-decrease columns for both dollar differences and percentage differences.

## Background for Budgetary Planning

An analysis of prior periods is normally the take-off point in the preparation of a budget, unless radical changes in operations are to be made. Past experience, as reflected by the accounting records and other data, provides valuable information regarding cost-volume-profit relationships, break-even points, growth trends, the flow of cash, etc. Estimating future conditions is always difficult, but estimating without the benefit of such information is even more so. Budgets for a long-established firm should, therefore, be much more accurate than those for a relatively new firm, particularly if the new firm is in an unstable industry.

Past experience, however, can be used *only* as a basis or take-off point. Conditions influencing the past must be compared with conditions expected in the future, and all estimates judged accordingly one by one. The percentage of each expense to sales, for example, cannot be expected to remain the same. Each expense item must be studied individually, with emphasis on both the past and future. The same is true, of course, for all other items.

When possible, budgets should be prepared by, or with the assistance of, the various department heads. There are two distinct advantages in such procedures: first, the department heads are intimately acquainted with their own operations and should be able to supply accurate estimates; second, the department heads feel that the budget is their own and not one that has been imposed upon them by someone who is not familiar with their problems. In many cases their original budgets must be altered in order to meet the over-all objectives of the company, but such alterations can be made acceptable if the department heads are familiar with the objectives and the entire scheme of budgetary planning for their particular firm.

For this and other reasons the officers and department heads should be well informed regarding the over-all plans for budgeting. Many firms accomplish this by holding conferences with all persons who will be concerned with budgetary planning. Those responsible for the final budget explain the procedures involved in the planning, the future conditions that are expected to influence operations, the objectives of the company, and so on. Officers and department heads are encouraged to discuss their problems and expectations and to make any suggestions they feel are pertinent to the preparation of the budget. Officials in charge of budgeting should encourage free discussion and also emphasize the fact that the budget is not to be used as a "club" but rather as a means of providing each of the supervisors with a concrete, detailed guide to assist him in the formation of plans for his own department. Emphasis is also normally placed on the fact that the accounting and budgeting personnel are always available to the supervisors for assistance in the preparation of their department budgets.

### Objectives of Budgetary Planning

The objectives of budgetary planning and the uses for budgets naturally vary from company to company but a number of objectives and uses which are common to most progressive concerns are discussed below.

**Analysis of Operations.** A thorough analysis of operations is necessary to the preparation of an adequate budget. This analysis, and the subsequent attempt to "project" data into the future, bring many factors to light which would otherwise be discovered at a much later date, if at all. As a result, many persons feel that some of the most important benefits of budgeting come from the advance planning that is required. They feel that preplanning without building a comprehensive budget is often haphazard and incomplete.

**Need for Special Studies.** The analysis required for budgetary planning usually indicates changes that can and should be made without further delay and also frequently points to the need for special studies in certain areas. Such analysis, for example, may reveal that the product lines have not changed for many years, despite the fact that customer demand has shifted considerably during this period. Such analysis might also reveal that the total cost of a certain function has grown proportionately larger in the past few years. If the reasons for these changes cannot be readily ascertained, it is likely that there is a need for comprehensive, special studies to discover the causes and possible solutions.

**Integration of Objectives.** There is probably little coordination of objectives if there is no over-all planning such as that required for budgeting. Each department head will have his own objectives, but these may or may not be in harmony with the objectives of top management. In fact, the objectives of top management may be hazy and subject to various interpretations unless they are summarized in the form of comprehensive budget forecasts which make it possible to present plans and objectives in such a fashion that the department heads can understand the aims and goals of the company. Supervisors are then in a position to integrate the objectives of their own departments with the over-all objectives of the entire firm. All concerned will have a better understanding of company objectives and a clearer picture of the plans for the coming period.

**Establishing Standards of Performance.** Among other things, a budget expresses an estimate of the income for the following period. Once this estimate has been established it is possible to forecast what the expenses *should be* for that volume of operations indicated by the expected sales. These expenses are customarily estimated by departments in order to give each supervisor a specific dollars and cents outline of the standard of performance for his own group. Each supervisor then knows what is expected of him and can make detailed plans for the operation of his "responsibility area."

**Budgetary Control and Management by Exception.** Budgetary estimates which are accepted as standards of performance can be employed as a means of measuring management, for each manager should be able to meet his established standards or provide a logical explanation as to why he was unable to do so. The actual results are, of course, compared with budget figures in order to determine if standards have been met. When the comparisons show that there is a significant difference between actual and standard for a given function or department, action can be initiated to discover the causes and determine what should be done. As long as there are no significant differences it is usually assumed that action is not required. Control of costs in this fashion is usually known as "management by exception."

**Profit Planning.** A business must ordinarily maintain a certain profit margin in order to retain or improve its competitive position. To accomplish this under normal circumstances requires advance planning of the type evidenced by budgeting. The budget, in fact, is at the very heart of most profit-planning programs, since only through budgeting can there be detailed forecasting which establishes concrete plans for the earning of a certain income. This often requires the alteration and adjustment of at least the first budget that is drawn. If the original estimates of future income and expense reveal that the budgeted profit would be insufficient, then management can attempt to determine what changes are possible in order to increase the expected profit to a satisfactory point. This procedure requires detailed study and analysis, and the complete understanding and cooperation of the supervisory personnel. They should be informed as to why a certain profit is necessary and as to why it is necessary for some of them to operate on a lower budget than they may have originally expected. Even though they may not wholeheartedly agree with some of the cutbacks—particularly those that affect their own department—they will at least understand that the reductions are being made on the basis of a comprehensive plan and that the changes requested are not made indiscriminately or on a purely personal basis.

## *The Budget Period*

When it is feasible, a summary budget should be prepared for several years in advance. This budget is not intended as a standard for the measurement of performance but is, instead, considered as only a reflection of long-range planning. Most firms, however, prepare only annual budgets, although many also prepare budgets for shorter periods, usually for a month or a quarter. If the latter procedure is employed, it is often necessary to revise the annual budget at the end of each interim period in order to reflect the variances that have developed during the current interim period.

Budgets for a period of one month or one quarter are normally more accurate than budgets for a period of one year or longer, since it is much easier to forecast for the shorter periods.

## *Flexible Budgets*

Many firms have great difficulty in developing reasonably accurate estimates of future sales volume. These firms, in particular, should prepare "flexible" budgets rather than only one budget which is geared to one level of activity. The flexible budgets are simply a series of budgets established on the basis of different levels of sales volume. Actual results are then compared with the budget based on the sales volume which most closely corresponds with the volume actually experienced during the period. The resulting variances are much more meaningful than they would be if the comparisons had been made with a "static" budget which had been based on a level of operations quite different from that actually experienced.

## PREPARATION OF A BUDGET

The explanations and illustrations which follow are based on the assumptions that only one budget is to be prepared, rather than a series of flexible budgets, and that the budget is for a period of one year, without supplementary budgets covering shorter interim periods. The illustrations are based on a process manufacturing concern that produces only one end product, which is composed of two raw materials processed in two departments. If there were more products or more raw materials, the computations shown would simply be repeated for each one; the form of computation would remain basically the same. If the budget were for a nonmanufacturing concern, certain computations (budgets) would obviously not be required. If flexible budgets were to be prepared the same type of computations would be made for each of several different levels of production.

A budget is actually constructed from a series of special budgets, beginning with the one for sales, since this is the budget which determines the level of operations and, consequently, the level of costs that will be incurred.

**Sales Budget.** Sales estimates are normally predicated on past experience, contemplated changes which will affect sales, and forecasts of expected business conditions. Typical of changes which will affect sales are the following: changes in product lines, changes in sales territories, changes in promotional campaigns, and changes in sales prices. Forecasts of expected business conditions are based on such factors as growth trends of the industry and of the particular company, the degree of competition expected, the estimated level of activity for customers, indices of general business conditions, and so on.

The forecast of total sales should be based on estimates prepared by departmental or territorial sales managers. When feasible, the estimates by the sales managers should be compiled from estimates supplied by the salesmen. In this way those who are most familiar with local conditions are made responsible for the estimates that will serve as the standards for the measurement of their performance. This does not mean, of course, that the original estimates are accepted without question. These estimates must be carefully analyzed and revised when necessary, for the estimated total can be no better than its parts.

Illustrated below is the sales budget for the Holmes Manufacturing Company. This is followed in succeeding paragraphs by illustrations of related budgets and, at the end, by a budgeted income statement which is based on the detailed budgets that precede it.

SCHEDULE 1
HOLMES MANUFACTURING COMPANY
Sales Budget for the Year 1958

| Product | Units | Price | Amount |
|---------|---------|-------|-------------|
| X | 410,000 | $10 | $4,100,000 |

**Production Budget.** The quantity to be manufactured (or purchased, if a nonmanufacturing concern) depends on the estimated number of units to be sold and the number of units in the inventories. The number

SCHEDULE 2
HOLMES MANUFACTURING COMPANY
Production Budget for the Year 1958

| | Units of X |
|---|---|
| Sales (Schedule 1)................. | 410,000 |
| Ending inventory................. | 30,000 |
| Total available.................... | 440,000 |
| Deduct beginning inventory......... | 40,000 |
| Required production............... | 400,000 |

of units desired in the ending inventory must be determined and an estimate made of the number that will be in the beginning inventory. The latter figure has to be estimated because the budgets must be prepared some time in advance of the beginning of the budget year.

**Materials Budget.** The amounts of raw materials required for each unit of finished product can usually be determined from bills of materials or similar records, although it may also be necessary to take into account certain allowances for waste and planned alterations in the end product. Standard cost records, if available, would provide most of the necessary data.

SCHEDULE 3
HOLMES MANUFACTURING COMPANY
Materials Budget for the Year 1958

| Product | Materials used | |
| --- | --- | --- |
| | A | B |
| 400,000 units of X (Schedule 2) | 800,000 gal. | 340,000 lb. |

**Purchases Budget.** A purchases budget is an expression of the amount of materials to be ordered and received during the period, not of the amount that is to be consumed. Estimates of the beginning inventories and the desired ending inventories are, therefore, necessary for completion of the computation. Estimates of the purchase prices to be paid are necessary for computing the amount of expected purchases in dollars. (In a nonmanufacturing concern there would be no need for a materials budget and the purchases budget would be computed on the basis of expected sales adjusted for merchandise inventories.)

SCHEDULE 4
HOLMES MANUFACTURING COMPANY
Purchase Budget for the Year 1958

| | A (*gal*) | B (*lb*) |
| --- | --- | --- |
| Materials to be consumed (Schedule 3) | 800,000 | 340,000 |
| Ending inventory | 60,000 | 30,000 |
| Total available | 860,000 | 370,000 |
| Deduct beginning inventory | 80,000 | 20,000 |
| Required purchases | 780,000 | 350,000 |
| Price per unit | $1.10 | $2.40 |
| Purchases in dollars | $858,000 | $840,000 |
| Total purchases | $1,698,000 | |

**Labor Budget.** If standard costs are employed, the basis for unit labor charges will be readily available. If not, estimates can be based on studies of past experience or on time studies. Final estimates will, of course, be influenced by any expected changes in labor rates or efficiency during the budget period.

SCHEDULE 5
HOLMES MANUFACTURING COMPANY
Labor Budget for the Year 1958

| Process | Units produced (Schedule 2) | Hours | | Wage rate | Labor cost |
|---|---|---|---|---|---|
| | | Per unit | Total | | |
| 1 | 400,000 | 1.20 | 480,000 | $1.80 | $ 864,000 |
| 2 | 400,000 | 0.25 | 100,000 | 2.00 | 200,000 |
| | Total labor cost | | | | $1,064,000 |

**Manufacturing Expense Budget.** After the level of production has been budgeted, it is possible to estimate the amount of indirect manufacturing costs that are likely to be incurred. If accurate standard costs are available, the estimation can probably be made without great difficulty. When standard costs are not available, there may be considerable analysis of historical records required. In either case, the estimates must take into account not only the expected volume of production but also any changes in production that are to be made during the budget period and any changes in cost prices that are likely to occur. Fixed expenses, such as straight-line depreciation, taxes, and insurance, normally present few problems in budgeting. Expenses that are truly variable also cause little trouble, but the many expenses that fall into the classification of "semi-variable" are usually difficult to estimate. Some firms also segregate the controllable expenses and budget them by "responsibility areas" in order to show foremen the estimated amounts for those expenses they are able to control. (In the budget below all expenses have been classified as either fixed or variable.)

SCHEDULE 6
HOLMES MANUFACTURING COMPANY
Manufacturing Expense Budget for the Year 1958

Fixed costs:
    Straight-line depreciation.............. $100,000
    Taxes and insurance.................. 60,000 $160,000

Variable costs:
    Indirect labor...................... $110,000
    Supplies........................... 90,000
    Maintenance and repairs............. 95,000
    Utilities........................... 65,000
    Other.............................. 40,000 400,000
Total manufacturing expenses.................. $560,000

**Cost of Goods Manufactured and Sold Budget.** This budget is prepared from data in the preceding budgets, plus estimates of the beginning and ending inventories. Inventory values depend upon the expected number of units, the amounts of materials, labor, and overhead included in the units, and the cost prices of these components. Typical calculations of estimated inventory amounts are illustrated by those shown below for the Holmes Manufacturing Company. Average costs are used for all inventories.

Schedule 7

HOLMES MANUFACTURING COMPANY

Estimated Inventories for 1958

(1)  Materials inventories:

| Item | Quantity (Schedule 4) | Unit cost | Inventory Jan. 1, 1958 | Inventory Dec. 31, 1958 |
|---|---|---|---|---|
| Material A............ | $\begin{cases} 80,000 \\ 60,000 \end{cases}$ | $1.05* 1.10# | $ 84,000 | $ 66,000 |
| Material B............ | $\begin{cases} 20,000 \\ 30,000 \end{cases}$ | 2.30* 2.40# | 46,000 | 72,000 |
| Total............... | | | $130,000 | $138,000 |

   \* Estimated price in beginning inventory.  # Estimated price to be paid, per Schedule 4.

(2)  In process inventories:

| | Units of X | Unit Costs* | Jan. 1, 1958 | Dec. 31, 1958 |
|---|---|---|---|---|
| Materials.............. | 60,000 | $4.055 | $243,300 | |
| Labor................. | 30,000 | 2.60 | 78,000 | |
| Overhead.............. | 30,000 | 1.36 | 40,800 | |
| Unit cost Jan. 1 | | $7.955 | | |
| Materials.............. | 60,000 | $4.24 | | $254,400 |
| Labor................. | 30,000 | 2.66 | | 79,800 |
| Overhead.............. | 30,000 | 1.40 | | 42,000 |
| Unit cost Dec. 31 | | $8.30 | | |
| Inventory totals | | | $362,100 | $376,200 |

   \* $4.055 = ($1.05 × 2) + ($2.30 × .85) Prices per Sch. 7 (1);
     $4.24 = ($1.10 × 2) + ($2.40 × .85) quantities per Sch. 3.
     $2.66 = ($1.80 × 1.2) + ($2.00 × .25) per Sch. 5.
     $1.40 = $560,000 (Sch. 6) ÷ 400,000 (Sch. 2).
     $2.60 and $1.36 = unit costs from prior period.

(3)  Finished goods inventories:

| | | | | |
|---|---|---|---|---|
| Product X............. | 32,935 | $7.955 | $262,000 | |
| Product X............. | 24,651 | 8.30 | | $204,600 |

In this plant a maximum of 60,000 units can be in process at any one time. Management assumes that the maximum amount will be in process at both the beginning and end of the year. Studies show that at any given time the equivalent of one-half the total labor and overhead costs has been introduced into the units in process. In process units at inventory time are, therefore, assumed to be one-half complete for labor and overhead (60,000 × ½ = 30,000 equivalent units). All materials are introduced at the beginning of the first process, so that for material cost purposes the in process inventories are considered complete.

The budget below follows the form of the schedule that will be prepared at the end of the year as a part of the financial statements. Consequently, the two can be compared without difficulty.

SCHEDULE 8

HOLMES MANUFACTURING COMPANY

Cost of Goods Manufactured and Sold Budget for the Year 1958

Cost of materials used:

| | | |
|---|---:|---:|
| Beginning inventory (Schedule 7)......... | $ 130,000 | |
| Cost of purchases (Schedule 4)........... | 1,698,000 | |
| Available............................. | $1,828,000 | |
| Ending inventory (Schedule 7)........... | 138,000 | $1,690,000 |
| Labor cost (Schedule 5)............................... | | 1,064,000 |
| Manufacturing expenses (Schedule 6).................. | | 560,000 |
| Total cost added to in process...................... | | $3,314,000 |
| Beginning in process inventory (Schedule 7)............. | | 362,100 |
| Total cost in process............................. | | $3,676,100 |
| Ending in process inventory (Schedule 7)................ | | 376,200 |
| Cost of goods manufactured......................... | | $3,299,900 |
| Beginning finished goods inventory (Schedule 7)......... | | 262,000 |
| Available for sale................................. | | $3,561,900 |
| Ending finished goods inventory (Schedule 7)............ | | 204,600 |
| Cost of goods sold................................. | | $3,357,300 |

**Budgets for Selling and Administrative Expenses.** These budgets are normally prepared on the basis of the account classifications for the selling and administrative expenses. Each account is analyzed and an estimate made of the amount of expense expected at the budgeted level of production. Such estimates are usually prepared by those persons who will be responsible for the costs incurred, and they should, of course, be determined with the over-all company objectives in mind. The degree of refinement in estimating will depend to a large extent upon the manner of account classification, i.e., whether single accounts are maintained for each type of expense or whether the different types of expense are accumulated by departments or other responsibility areas.

The selling expense budget of the Holmes Manufacturing Company for 1958 shows a total of $176,200; the total of the administrative expense budget for 1958 is $113,000 (these budgets are not illustrated—they would consist of lists of pertinent accounts with estimated balances). Since the company has no "other" income and expenses, all data are now available for the preparation of the budgeted income statement which is shown in Exhibit 17-1.

EXHIBIT 17-1

HOLMES MANUFACTURING COMPANY

Budgeted Statement of Income and Expense for the Year 1958

| | | |
|---|---:|---:|
| Income from sales (Schedule 1)............ | | $4,100,000 |
| Cost of goods sold (Schedule 8)............ | | 3,357,300 |
|    Gross profit......................... | | $ 742,700 |
| Selling expenses................. | $176,200 | |
| Administrative expenses......... | 113,100 | 289,300 |
|    Net profit........................... | | $ 453,400 |

If the budgets for the Holmes Manufacturing Company represented original drafts, management would have to decide whether or not the budgeted profit of $453,400 was satisfactory. Should they feel that the profit is too low, then each item of income and expense would have to be reviewed. If they concluded that the estimate of sales income should not be increased, each expense item would be analyzed and reductions made where it seemed feasible. After any desired changes were made, the budgets would still appear as illustrated, except for certain dollar amounts that would have been changed.

## OTHER BUDGETS

A firm may have numerous budgets in addition to those that have been discussed and illustrated. Three of the more important ones are described in the following paragraphs.

**Cash Budget.** A business normally has to maintain a certain minimum cash balance in order to operate efficiently. Cash shortages can be not only embarrassing and inconvenient, but can also be the prelude to bankruptcy, even for a company whose income statement shows a reasonable profit. It is, therefore, advisable for many firms to prepare monthly budgets of cash receipts, cash disbursements, and the resulting cash balances. Difficulties can then be spotted in advance and plans formulated to alleviate shortages or to make proper use of excesses. Cash budgets prepared on an annual basis are normally not effective in the control of cash balances, since forecasting a satisfactory year-end cash balance does not ensure adequate balances throughout the year.

Much of the information for the cash budget would come from the budgets that have been illustrated: estimated receipts based on the sales budget and estimated disbursements based on the budgets for purchases, labor, manufacturing expenses, selling expenses, and administrative expenses. These estimates would be affected, of course, by the estimated amounts for the various receivables and payables at the beginning and end of the year. Additional estimates would also be made for the following: amounts borrowed, amounts invested by owners, payments on loans, expenditures for capital assets, etc.

**Capital Expenditures Budget.** This is frequently the only budget prepared by many firms, particularly by many of the firms whose properties and equipment constitute a large proportion of their total assets. The starting point in planning such a budget is often the same as for various other budgets; i.e., starting with the department heads, who are requested to submit lists of equipment which they believe should be purchased during the coming period. These lists are carefully reviewed and items approved or disapproved, depending upon the amount of funds available, how much the item is needed, and whether or not the additional cost can be recovered, plus a profit. Data from this budget are used in the preparation of the cash budget and the budgeted balance sheet.

**The Budgeted Balance Sheet.** This budget is customarily prepared by entering estimates of the beginning general ledger balances on a multi-column work sheet (estimates are necessary since the budget is normally prepared before the beginning of the budget period). Summary journal entries which reflect the changes indicated by all other budgets are then prepared and entered on the work sheet, just as adjustments are normally entered. Several examples follow:

|                          |   |   |
|--------------------------|---|---|
| Accounts Receivable      | x |   |
| Sales                    |   | x |
| (From the sales budget)  |   |   |
| Purchases (or Inventory) | x |   |
| Accounts Payable         |   | x |
| (From the purchases budget) |   |   |
| Accounts Payable         | x |   |
| Cash                     |   | x |
| (From the cash budget)   |   |   |

Changes reflected by the journal entries are then added to or deducted from the beginning balances in order to find the estimated ending balances. Ending balances are extended to the appropriate statement columns, net profit from the Income Statement columns is carried to the Earned Surplus columns, and ending earned surplus is carried to the Balance Sheet columns. This procedure provides not only the ending earned surplus balance but also a net profit figure which can be checked with the net profit as already computed on the budgeted statement of income and expense.

When completed, the budgeted balance sheet can be studied by top management, financial officers, and budget officials. If any weaknesses appear or company objectives are not met, steps can be taken to make the necessary changes. When all budgets have been approved as representing the company's operating plan for the coming period, each department head should receive a copy of that part of the budget which affects his section of the company. At the end of each budget period the supervisors should receive statements comparing actual and budgeted figures. Significant variances between actual results and budgetary estimates must be thoroughly investigated and corrective action taken when needed.

## SUMMARY

Budgeting deals primarily with the future, although many budget estimates are based principally on past experience. The sales budget is the first to be prepared, since the volume of sales will determine the volume of operations. This budget is followed in order by budgets for production, materials, purchases, labor, manufacturing expenses, selling expenses, administrative expenses, and one for sundry items of income and expense, if any. The budgeted statement of income and expense can then be prepared from data contained in these supplementary budgets. Budgets for cash and capital expenditures may also be prepared, followed by a budgeted balance sheet.

Budgetary planning is, in itself, a valuable tool of management, for many improvements may be instituted as a result of the advance planning that is required in the preparation of budgets. Budgetary planning also provides for the control of costs by establishing standards that can be employed as a basis for the measurement of performance. It serves, too, as a means of expressing top management objectives in specific terms and thereby providing a basis for the integration and coordination of departmental objectives. Integration and coordination are more easily accomplished when performance is measured by comparison with budgets that have been prepared, or approved, by the department heads themselves.

## QUESTIONS

1. What is a budget? What are the primary objectives of a business budget?
2. How are accounting records used in the preparation of budgets?
3. Why would break-even points be helpful in budget preparation?
4. Why would standard costs be useful in budgetary planning?
5. What techniques employed in the analysis of statements can also be used in the preparation of budgets?
6. Past experience is normally employed as a basis for forecasting the future. Why?
7. What advantages are gained by having department heads prepare their own budgets?
8. Why do many improvements result simply from advance budgetary planning?
9. How are budgets used as a means of measuring performance?
10. What is the meaning of "management by exception"? Of "profit planning"?

**11.** What are "flexible" budgets? What advantages are gained by the use of flexible budgets?

**12.** Why is the sales budget the point of beginning in budgetary planning?

**13.** What is the major difference between a materials budget and a purchases budget?

**14.** Why is it necessary to estimate beginning inventories as well as ending inventories?

**15.** Why is it frequently necessary to revise the original budgets?

**16.** It is possible for a company operating at a profit to be forced into bankruptcy because of a cash shortage. What might be the causes of a cash shortage in such a company?

**17.** Why do many firms that prepare only one budget prepare a capital expenditures budget?

**18.** How is a work sheet employed in the preparation of a budgeted balance sheet?

**19.** What budgets would probably be prepared by a retail or wholesale concern with a complete budgetary system?

# PROBLEMS

## CHAPTER 1

**1-1.** Classification of things acquired for the use or benefit of the business.
A partial list of account titles is shown below:

| | |
|---|---|
| (1) Wages Expense | (6) Cash in Bank |
| (2) Prepaid Insurance | (7) Supplies Used |
| (3) Equipment | (8) Accounts Receivable |
| (4) Rent Expense | (9) Cash on Hand |
| (5) Office Supplies | (10) Investments |

*a.* Identify each of the above as "cash," a "cash substitute," an "unexpired cost," or an "expired cost."
*b.* Increases in things acquired for the intended use or benefit of the business are recorded on which side of the account, left or right?
*c.* Are accounts for cash and costs increased by debits (left-hand side) or credits (right-hand side)? Decreased by debits or credits?
*d.* Which of these accounts represent "costs" which are usually considered as unexpired at time of acquisition, but which are expired as time passes?
*e.* What would be a logical account title for that portion of the prepaid insurance premiums which had expired during the current period?
*f.* Classify each account as either an "asset" or an "expense."

**1-2.** Classification of accounts.
A number of typical general ledger account titles are listed below:

| | |
|---|---|
| (1) Accounts Payable | (8) Accounts Receivable |
| (2) Invested Equity | (9) Wages Expense |
| (3) Cash in Bank | (10) Wages Payable |
| (4) Purchases | (11) Rent Expense |
| (5) Inventory | (12) Sales Income |
| (6) Earned Equity | (13) Depreciation Expense |
| (7) Trucks | (14) Prepaid Rent |

*a.* Classify each of these according to the heading under which it would appear on the statements, i.e., as an asset, liability, owner's equity, income, cost of goods sold, or expense item.
*b.* Which account classifications measure financial condition?
*c.* Which account classifications measure the inward and outward flow of values?

**1-3.** Preparation of simple statements.
Listed below are the account balances for the Service Company as of the end of the company's fiscal year, June 30, 1958:

| Accounts | Dr. balance | Cr. balance |
|---|---|---|
| Cash in bank................ | $ 2,500 | |
| Accounts receivable ........ | 6,000 | |
| Accounts payable............ | | $ 3,800 |
| Wages payable.............. | | 400 |
| Invested equity.............. | | 1,000 |
| Earned equity (July 1, 1957).. | | 4,900 |
| Withdrawals................. | 9,600 | |
| Service income.............. | | 77,500 |
| Wages expense.............. | 64,800 | |
| Other expense............... | 4,700 | |
| | $87,600 | $87,600 |

   *a.* $4,900 is the measure of the owner's equity from earnings retained in the business prior to July 1, 1957. Which of the above accounts measure changes in the Earned Equity during the period from July 1, 1957 to June 30, 1958? Which of these measure the inward and outward flow of values arising from operations?

   *b.* Prepare the following: a statement of income and expense, a statement of changes in earned equity, and a statement of financial condition.

   *c.* Why should the statements be prepared in the order suggested in (*b*) above?

## CHAPTER 2

**2-1.** Inward and outward flow of values.

   A professional man opened his own business on March 1, 1958. On that day he deposited $5,000 in a bank checking account under the business name and rented a completely furnished office. During March he billed two clients for professional services rendered: $300 charged to A and $200 charged to B. A check for $300 was received from A as payment in full; nothing was received from B. During the same period he issued the following checks: $100 for March rent, $40 for supplies that were consumed, $20 for telephone service, and $140 for his personal use (drawings).

   *a.* What was the total value of the assets received by the business during the month? The total value of the assets relinquished during the same period?

   *b.* What was the value of the inward flow of assets received in exchange for services rendered? What was the value of the outward flow of assets relinquished for operating purposes?

   *c.* What was the net increase or decrease in the balance of cash in bank during the month?

   *d.* What was the amount of the net profit or loss for the period?

   *e.* Why was the amount of net profit or loss different from the amount of increase or decrease in the cash balance?

**2-2.** Preparation of original accounting entries.

   Prepare entries in general journal form to record the business transactions described in problem **2-1**. Present the entries in the order in which they have been described (dates have been ignored). Include an explanation as a part of each entry.

**2-3.** Posting transaction data to the general ledger accounts.

B. W. Toms, a young lawyer, opened his own office on July 1, 1958. The general journal entries presented below reflect his business transactions during the first month:

| | | | | |
|---|---|---|---|---|
| 7-1 | Cash in Bank | | 600 | |
| |     Invested Equity | | | 600 |
| | (Opened checking account for the business) | | | |
| 7-1 | Rent Expense | | 80 | |
| |     Cash in Bank | | | 80 |
| | (Paid rent for July) | | | |
| 7-10 | Supplies Used | | 30 | |
| |     Cash in Bank | | | 30 |
| | (Paid cash for supplies that will be used this month) | | | |
| 7-16 | Cash in Bank | | 50 | |
| |     Fee Income | | | 50 |
| | (Cash received in exchange for services performed) | | | |
| 7-31 | Cash in Bank | | 280 | |
| |     Notes Payable | | | 280 |
| | (Borrowed from bank; principal and interest due in 90 days) | | | |
| 7-31 | Account Receivable—A. B. Don | 300 | | |
| |     Fee Income | | | 300 |
| | (Billed client for work completed this month) | | | |
| 7-31 | Withdrawals | | 190 | |
| |     Cash in Bank | | | 190 |
| | (Funds withdrawn by owner for his personal use) | | | |

*a.* Transfer (post) data from the original entries shown above to the appropriate general ledger accounts. Use accounts in the form of the example below. The following account titles should be employed: Cash in Bank, Account Receivable—A. B. Don, Notes Payable, Invested Equity, Earned Equity, Withdrawals, Fee Income, Rent Expense, and Supplies Used.

*b.* Compute and record month-end balances for each of the accounts. Include "dr." or "cr." after each balance.

*c.* Prepare a trial balance of the general ledger account balances.

Example of the account form to be used in the above problem:

Account Title

| Date | Explanation | Debit | Credit | Balance |
|------|-------------|-------|--------|---------|
| | | | | |
| | | | | |
| | | | | |

**2-4.** Preparation of statements.

    *a.* Prepare financial statements from the trial balance obtained in problem **2-3***c* above. The statements should be prepared in the following order: statement of income and expense, statement of changes in earned equity, statement of financial condition.

    *b.* Why are statements usually prepared in the order suggested above?

    *c.* What does each of the statements describe and measure?

**2-5.** Preparation of general journal entries.

    Prepare entries in general journal form to record the following business transactions:

1958

June  1—A professional man opened his own business by depositing $2,000 in a bank checking account in the name of the business. He then issued a check for $120 to pay the rent on his office space for the month of June.

    1—He issued a $30 check as payment for supplies that would be consumed during June.

  10—A check for $250 was received from a client as payment in full for services rendered.

  30—He issued a check for $240 to his secretary for work performed in June. Her gross pay is $260 per month; $20 is withheld for Federal income taxes (credit Federal Income Taxes Withheld).

  30—An invoice for $300 was mailed to a client for services rendered to date.

**2-6.** The accounting cycle.

    Use the transaction data below to illustrate the accounting procedures in the accounting cycle. Complete the steps in the following order:

    *a.* Prepare entries in general journal form for the regular operating transactions.

    *b.* Post to the general ledger accounts and compute account balances.

    *c.* Journalize and post the necessary adjusting entries and prepare a trial balance.

    *d.* Prepare a statement of income and expense.

    *e.* Prepare a statement of financial condition.

    *f.* Journalize and post the closing entry.

    Tom Smith began operating a transfer business on January 1, 1958. During the month, the following transactions occurred:

Jan.  1—Tom Smith invested $6,000 cash in The Smith Transfer Co.

    1—Rented warehouse: paid one year's rent in advance, $600.

    1—Bought truck (debit Equipment): paid $600 cash and gave a $1,600 note for the balance; the note bears 6 per cent interest and is due in 60 days.

    1—Paid insurance premium of $240 for one year's protection on warehouse contents.

  15—Transfer income, $900 cash.

  15—Paid driver's wages: gross $200, income tax withheld, $10.

  20—Paid for gas and oil to date, $50.

  30—Transfer income: $700 on account, ABC Co.; $400 cash sale; $600 on account, XYZ Co.

  31—Paid: driver's wages, gross $200, income tax withheld $10; miscellaneous expense, $80; gas and oil, $40.

Adjustments:
(1) Adjust Prepaid Rent to show expired portion as expense.
(2) Adjust Prepaid Insurance to show expired portion as expense.
(3) Record depreciation on the truck, assuming a service life of 5 years and a trade-in value of $400.
(4) Record interest expense (and interest payable) on note for truck.

**2-7.** Computation of profit under the cash basis and under the accrual basis.

A service-type enterprise had the following transactions during 1958:

(1) Collected the $20,000 balance on accounts which were receivable as of December 31, 1957; collected $80,000 on receivables arising from services performed in 1958. Accounts receivable as of December 31, 1958 amounted to $10,000.
(2) Wages paid during 1958 amounted to $50,000—this included $4,000 that was due and payable as of December 31, 1957. Employees' earnings of $5,000 were unpaid as of December 31, 1958.
(3) The total of "other expenses" incurred during 1958 was $7,000. Of this amount $6,000 had been paid and a liability existed for the balance of $1,000.

*a.* Compute the net profit for 1958, assuming that the cash basis of accounting is employed.
*b.* Compute the net profit for 1958, assuming that the accrual basis of accounting is employed.
*c.* If you were planning to buy or invest in this business, what method of reporting would you prefer for the preparation of the statements that would be analyzed by you? Why?

# CHAPTER 3

**3-1.** Journal entries to record cash and costs and their sources.

Things obtained for the intended use or benefit of the business are recorded on the left; "sources" are recorded on the right. Descriptions of business transactions which include increments in cash, costs, and sources will be found below:

1958
Sept. 1—The owner of a small business invested a building valued at $30,000.
10—He borrowed $4,000 from the bank for business use and gave the bank a promissory note in exchange.
14—A note for $2,500 was issued as payment in full for equipment acquired to use in the business.
16—Merchandise for resale to customers was purchased from ABC Co. on credit; cost $1,400.
20—A cash sale for $300 was completed.
27—The Mon Company was billed for a credit sale of $600.
30—The warehouse rent of $300 for September was unpaid at the end of the month.

*a.* Prepare general journal entries to record the transactions described above.

*b.* Describe each of the things obtained for the intended use or benefit of the business as one of the following: cash, cash substitute, unexpired cost, or expired cost.

*c.* Identify the source in each of the entries as one of the following: the owner, a creditor, or a customer.

**3-2.** Accounting entries based on business papers.

Prepare the necessary entries, in general journal form, to reflect the financial changes indicated by the following business papers. Use *a, b,* etc., to key the entries.

*a.* A check in the amount of $26 was received for a cash sale.

*b.* The buyer for Department A forwarded a purchase requisition to the purchasing department. This requisition requested that 100 men's hats at a cost of three dollars each be purchased from Apex Co.

*c.* Checks to cover gross payroll of $560 were issued ($360 for sales salaries and $200 for office salaries). Income tax withheld was $60.

*d.* The purchasing department mailed a purchase order for 300 pairs of socks at 40 cents per pair; the purchase order was addressed to Socks, Inc.

*e.* A credit sales invoice for $340 was mailed to the George Company. This invoice covered merchandise that had been shipped to the purchaser on the previous day.

*f.* A receiving report covering 600 men's hats at a cost of four dollars each was forwarded to the accounting department.

*g.* An invoice from Enter Corp. for the 600 men's hats was received a day later. One of the bookkeepers attached the appropriate purchase requisition, purchase order, and receiving report to the invoice. Payment is to be made on the tenth of the next month.

*h.* A check for $86 was issued in payment of the light bill for the current month.

**3-3.** Entries in the general journal.

Prepare general journal entries to record the following transactions and adjustments:

*a.* Cash sales for the day were $712.

*b.* A credit of $84 was allowed (on the Bing Co.'s Account Receivable) for merchandise returned as defective.

*c.* Merchandise and the covering invoice for $406 were received from the N.Y. Suppliers. Payment is to be made by the tenth of the following month.

*d.* A portion of the merchandise received from N.Y. Suppliers was defective. A credit of $42 was requested and granted.

*e.* As of the last day of the period, the following financial data had not been recorded:

(1) Wage expense incurred but not paid:

$$\begin{array}{ll} \text{Gross}\dots\dots\dots\dots\dots & \$600 \\ \text{Income tax}\dots\dots\dots\dots & 70 \\ \text{Net}\dots\dots\dots\dots\dots\dots & \$530 \end{array}$$

(2) Depreciation on the equipment is computed at 10 per cent of the original cost of $14,000, or $1,400 for the period.

(3) Merchandise, cost $76, had been returned to Penn Co. for credit (assume the credit will be allowed).

(4) All supplies had been charged to the asset account, Supplies on Hand, at the time of purchase. Supplies valued at $280 had been used during the period.

(5) A purchase invoice for merchandise with a cost of $584 was received from the FOG Co. after the journals had been totaled and posted. The merchandise had been received on the last day of the period.

(6) Rental income of $260 had been earned but payment had not yet been received.

(7) Interest expense on a $10,000 loan had not been recorded. The loan had been outstanding for three months as of the last day of the period; the interest rate is 4 per cent a year.

**3-4.** Computation of cost of goods sold.

The inventory of Valley Retailers as of January 1, 1958, was valued at $4,000. During 1958 purchases of merchandise for resale to customers amounted to $76,000. Unsold merchandise with a cost of $2,000 was still on hand at the year end.

*a.* Compute the cost of goods sold for the year.

*b.* How is the total of purchases for the year accumulated?

*c.* How are the inventory values probably established?

**3-5.** Preparation of a general ledger trial balance.

A company that reports on a calendar-year basis has the following unadjusted account balances as of December 31, 1958. Assume that all accounts have a normal balance; i.e., Cash in Bank has a debit balance, Wages Payable has a credit balance, etc.

| Sales Income | $60,000 | Earned Equity Jan. 1, 1958 | $ 4,000 |
|---|---|---|---|
| Rent Expense | 6,000 | Purchases | 20,000 |
| Cash in Bank | 5,000 | Accounts Receivable | 14,000 |
| Invested Equity | 5,000 | Accounts Payable | 3,000 |
| Prepaid Insurance | 500 | Wages Payable | 1,500 |
| Other Expense | 4,000 | Wages Expense | 15,000 |
| Inventory Jan. 1, 1958 | 9,000 | | |

*a.* Prepare a general ledger trial balance with the accounts presented in their usual order, i.e., assets, liabilities, owner's equity, income, and expenses.

*b.* What account measures the value of the inward flow of assets received in exchange for merchandise sold? Which two assets are usually received in exchange for the merchandise sold?

*c.* What is a "sale"? When is a sales transaction completed?

*d.* What accounts in the trial balance represent expired costs?

**3-6.** Preparation of adjusting entries.

Prepare entries in general journal form to record the *adjustments* necessary as of the end of a firm's fiscal year (December 31, 1958), assuming the following data as of that date. No adjustments had been made during 1958.

(1) A note payable for $10,000 had been issued on October 1, 1958. Principal and 6 per cent interest are due in six months from that date. (Debit Interest Expense and credit Interest Payable.)

(2) A one-year loan for $3,000 had been negotiated with a local bank as of November 1, 1958. The loan had been discounted at 4 per cent for one year, so the firm actually received only $2,880 from the bank on that date. (Debit Interest Expense and credit Prepaid Interest.)

(3) Rent due the landlord as of the end of the period amounted to $160.

(4) A portion of the office space is rented to another party; this party had not yet paid the $40 due for December rent.

(5) Gross wages of $400 had not been paid as of December 31, 1958; the withholding for Federal income taxes amounts to $60.

(6) Equipment that had cost $46,000 is expected to have an average useful life of ten years, with an estimated scrap value of $4,000 at the end of that time. The Accumulated Depreciation account had a credit balance of $21,000 as of January 1, 1958. All of the equipment had been purchased before 1958.

(7) Accounts receivable at December 31, 1958, amount to $15,000; the Allowance for Doubtful Accounts has a zero balance. The credit manager estimates that 1 per cent of the accounts will not be collected.

(8) Prepaid Insurance has a balance of $620 at the end of the year; $510 of this amount represents the cost of expired insurance.

**3-7.** Preparation of a working trial balance.

    *a.* Enter the following unadjusted trial balance for XYZ Co. on a working trial balance:

| *Accounts* | *Balances as of Dec. 31, 1958* | |
|---|---:|---:|
| Cash in bank..................... | $ 4,600 | |
| Accounts receivable............... | 12,000 | |
| Merchandise inventory............. | 17,500 | |
| Supplies on hand.................. | 1,400 | |
| Equipment........................ | 42,600 | |
| Accumulated depreciation.......... | | $ 6,500 |
| Accounts payable................. | | 8,900 |
| Invested equity.................. | | 21,000 |
| Earned equity.................... | | 36,600 |
| Withdrawals...................... | 6,000 | |
| Sales income..................... | | 94,000 |
| Purchases........................ | 50,000 | |
| Wages expense.................... | 26,000 | |
| Utilities expense................ | 1,800 | |
| Rent expense..................... | 4,800 | |
| Other expense.................... | 300 | |
| Totals........................ | $167,000 | $167,000 |

    *b.* Enter the following adjusting data on the working trial balance:
1. Depreciation for 1958—$1,800.
2. Estimated bad debts for 1958—$200.
3. Supply inventory as of December 31, 1958—$300.
   (Additional accounts needed may be added below totals.)

    *c.* Complete the working papers (the merchandise inventory as of December 31, 1958, is valued at $20,000).

    *d.* Prepare the closing entry.

**3-8.** Preparation of financial statements from a working trial balance.

    Prepare the following statements from the working trial balance of problem **3-7.**

    *a.* Statement of income and expenses.

    *b.* Statement of changes in earned equity.

    *c.* Statement of financial condition.

## CHAPTER 4

**4-1.** Comparison of general journal and a combined columnar journal.

The business transactions of the ABC Company for the month of April, 1958, are shown below. The company has controlling accounts for Accounts Receivable and Accounts Payable.

1958

Apr. 2—Cash purchase of $360.
4—Credit purchase of $690 from Doe Co.
5—Cash sale of $410.
6—Credit sale of $570 to Volks Corp.
9—Check issued as payment of account payable due Lord Co.: amount due $400; 2 per cent discount was taken.
10—Check received as payment of account receivable from Clark Corp.: amount receivable $600; 1 per cent discount was taken.
12—Credit purchase of $480 from Kern Co.
18—Cash sale of $210.
21—Credit sale of $530 to Burr Corp.
24—Cash purchase of $170.
30—Check issued to pay wages: gross of $400; $50 withheld for income taxes.

a. Record the above transactions in a general journal in the usual way.
b. Record the same data in a combined columnar journal and foot (total) each column after all the data have been entered.
c. Prepare a "preposting proof" of the columnar totals.
d. Why should the sum of all the debit totals equal the sum of all the credit totals?
e. Why is posting from *special* columns faster than posting data from general journal entries?
f. Why should there be fewer posting errors when a columnar journal is used rather than only a general journal?

**4-2.** Posting from a combined columnar journal.
a. Assume that as of April 1, 1958, the ledger accounts of the ABC Co. (problem **4-1**) showed: Cash, $1,000 dr.; Invested Equity, $1,000 cr. Enter these amounts in the ledger accounts and post the entries made in **4-1b** to appropriate general ledger accounts.
b. Prepare a trial balance of the general ledger accounts after the posting has been completed.

**4-3.** Entries in special journals.
Assume that the ABC Co. in problem **4-1** used the following journals: a cash receipts journal, a cash disbursements journal, a sales journal, a purchases journal, and a general journal.
a. Enter the transaction data from problem **4-1** in the appropriate special journals.
b. Total all columns and prepare a "preposting proof" for each of the cash journals.
c. Assume that as of April 1, 1958, the ledger accounts of the ABC Co. showed: Cash $1,800 dr.; Invested Equity, $1,200 cr.; and Earned Equity, $600 cr. Enter these amounts in the ledger and then post from the special journals prepared in **4-3a** and b.

    *d.* Take a trial balance.

    *e.* What are the advantages of special journals?

**4-4.** Entries in a cash receipts journal.

    From the transactions below select those that represent increases in cash and make appropriate entries in a cash receipts journal:

**1958**

    Sept.  1—Cash sales for the day were $616.

            4—Rent of $200 was paid.

            7—A purchase order for merchandise costing $347 was issued.

         10—A check for $576 was received from ABC Co. as payment on a merchandise account (no discount).

         12—Payment of $60 was made on the gas bill.

         13—Cash sales for the day were $569.

         19—A check for $46 was received from X. Y. Jones in payment of rent for the current period.

         24—$32 was received from C. D. Johnson as payment on a note receivable.

         27—Payment in full on an account receivable from NOG Co. for $300 was received. A 3 per cent cash discount had been deducted.

**4-5.** Entries in a cash disbursements journal.

    From the transactions below select those that represent decreases in cash and make appropriate entries in a cash disbursements journal. (Assume that all payments are by check and that the checks are issued in numerical sequence.)

**1958**

    May  1—Cash sales for the day were $489.

          3—Check number 911 for $300 was issued to W. W. Smith to pay the rent for the current period.

         6—Merchandise and a covering invoice in the amount of $280 were received from Mountain Wholesalers. Payment is to be made in fifteen days.

        10—A check for $130 was delivered to a local jobber, ABC Corp., in exchange for merchandise.

        18—Payment was made in full on an account payable of $400 that was due the Empire Co. Two per cent was deducted, since the payment was made within the discount period.

        21—An invoice addressed to Brown, Inc. was prepared for merchandise sold on credit—amount $193.

        26—A check was issued to Wm. J. Zane, sales clerk, for salary for the current period:

                    Gross pay.................. $380

                    Income tax withheld..........   40

                    Net paid................... $340

**4-6.** Journalizing transactions in special and general journals.

    Enter the following transactions in the proper journals. The company uses special journals for cash receipts, cash disbursements, and credit sales, but has no purchases journal. Assume discounts are taken when available. Prepare preposting proofs.

1958

May 1—Check No. 246 was issued for a three-year insurance policy—amount $360 (charge Prepaid Insurance).

5—Cash sales for the day were $4,000.

10—Sold merchandise to ABC Co., $300; terms 1/15, n/60.

13—Issued a $200 check, No. 247, for merchandise.

20—A sale in the amount of $600 was made to the XYZ Co.; terms 1/15, n/30.

26—Cash sales for the day, $2,000.

27—The next check in the series was issued for merchandise invoiced at $800 by Vendor Co. on May 20 at 2/10, n/30. (This purchase had not been recorded previously.)

31—A check for $594 was received from the XYZ Co. in payment of the sale made May 20.

31—Payment of $500 was made to Jones Co. for an invoice that had been recorded as an account payable at the end of April—no discount.

31—There are two unpaid and unrecorded invoices for merchandise on hand on this date:

Tom Company........... $ 700
Brown Company......... 1,200

31—Paid wages to date—$1,000 gross (withholding tax $140).

31—Adjust Prepaid Insurance for the portion of the premium expired this month.

**4-7.** Posting to a general ledger account from special journal.

Use a general ledger account for Purchases and post the following data to this account. The balance in the account on September 30, 1958, was $3,400; show the ending account balance as of October 31, 1958.

*a.* Total of the Purchases column in the cash disbursements journal for the month of October, 1958, was $620.

*b.* The October, 1958, total in the purchases journal was $1,030.

*c.* The following entry was recorded in the general journal:

| 10-16-58 | Purchases | 400 | |
| | Notes Payable | | 400 |
| | (Gave a 60-day note for merchandise) | | |

**4-8.** Postings to subsidiary accounts receivable and the controlling account.

Below you will find a sales journal, a cash receipts journal, and two general journal entries. Prepare the subsidiary accounts for credit customers and the general ledger controlling account.

*a.* Post the appropriate data from the journals to the accounts.

*b.* As of the end of the month, prepare a schedule of the balances in the subsidiary accounts and compare the total of this schedule with the balance in the controlling account.

(1) Balances in the customers' accounts as of November 1, 1958, were as follows (enter these opening balances in the subsidiary accounts):

| Customer | Dr. Balances |
|----------|--------------|
| A | $100 |
| B | 240 |
| F | 70 |
| H | 180 |
| P | 390 |
| W | 160 |

(2) Balance of the general ledger control account as of November 1, 1958, was $1,140.

(3) The sales journal for November, 1958, appeared as follows:

Sales Journal

| Date | Customer | Amount |
|------|----------|--------|
| 11-6 | F | $ 210 |
| 11-9 | W | 80 |
| 11-14 | B | 340 |
| 11-20 | D | 130 |
| 11-29 | P | 500 |
| | | $1,260 |

(4) The cash receipts journal for November, 1958, appeared as follows:

Cash Receipts Journal

| Date | Name | Dr. Cash | Cr. Sales | Cr. Accts. Rec. |
|------|------|----------|-----------|-----------------|
| 11-4 | A | $ 100 | | $ 100 |
| 11-12 | F | 280 | | 280 |
| 11-14 | | 400 | $ 400 | |
| 11-20 | B | 340 | | 340 |
| 11-21 | H | 180 | | 180 |
| 11-23 | | 600 | 600 | |
| 11-25 | D | 70 | | 70 |
| 11-27 | W | 200 | | 200 |
| | | $2,170 | $1,000 | $1,170 |

(5) The following entries had been recorded in the general journal during November, 1958:

| | | | |
|---|---|---|---|
| 11-20 | Sales Returns and Allowances | 40 | |
| | Accounts Receivable (W) | | 40 |
| | (Credit allowed for defective merchandise) | | |
| 11-24 | Sales Returns and Allowances | 20 | |
| | Accounts Receivable (H) | | 20 |
| | (Credit allowed for returned merchandise) | | |

**4-9.** Entries in special and general journals.

Enter the following transactions in the proper journals. The company has a general journal and special journals for cash receipts, cash disbursements, credit sales, and credit purchases. Foot the journal columns and be certain that total debits equal total credits in the cash journals.

1958

Jan. 1—Jones began operating a local grocery store as a sole proprietor. His original investment consisted of cash $20,000, building $60,000, equipment $10,000.

2—Made cash purchases: gross $2,000; 2 per cent cash discount taken; check number 101.

4—Received invoices from ABC Co. for $4,000 for merchandise already received.

9—Issued check number 102 for cash purchase of equipment; cost, $3,000.

10—Cash sales: $5,000 gross; allowed $50 cash discount.

10—Paid ABC Co. in full. Took 3 per cent discount for prompt payment. Check number 103.

14—Credit sales: Smith, $60; Jobe, $140.

21—Received payment in full from Smith and Jobe. Allowed them 5 per cent cash discount.

24—Issued check number 104 to sales clerk: gross wages $100; withheld $10 for income taxes.

25—Received invoice for $1,500 from Auto Co. for purchase of delivery truck.

29—Invoice of $1,000 received with shipment of stock from XYZ Co. Terms 2/10, n/30.

31—Bad debts for the month were estimated at $100. Depreciation for the month was $40.

**4-10.** Accounting cycle problem with special journals and subsidiary ledgers.

Assume that the Machinery Wholesalers has a fiscal year which ends on October 31; interim statements are prepared monthly; and subsidiary ledgers are maintained for both accounts receivable and accounts payable. Data for November, 1958, are shown on page 402:

MACHINERY WHOLESALERS
General Ledger Trial Balance as of November 1, 1958

| Accounts | Dr. | Cr. |
|---|---|---|
| Cash in bank | $ 5,000 | |
| Accounts receivable | 10,000 | |
| Inventory | 15,000 | |
| Equipment | 30,000 | |
| Accumulated depreciation | | $ 4,000 |
| Accounts payable | | 8,000 |
| Invested equity | | 46,000 |
| Earned equity | | 2,000 |
| Totals | $60,000 | $60,000 |

Schedule of Accounts Receivable as of November 1, 1958

| | |
|---|---|
| A Company | $ 6,000 |
| H Company | 1,000 |
| K Company | 3,000 |
| | $10,000 |

Schedule of Accounts Payable as of November 1, 1958

| | |
|---|---|
| X Company | $ 3,000 |
| W Company | 5,000 |
| | $ 8,000 |

This company buys and sells *machinery*. For the month of November, 1958, the transactions are as follows (assume that discounts are taken if available):

1958

Nov. 1—Purchased machinery costing $2,000 from X Company. Terms: 3/15, n/30.

4—Bought a delivery truck for company use, cost $3,000 (debit the Equipment account). Issued a promissory note for the full amount.

8—Machinery costing $5,000 was purchased from Z Company on terms of 2/20, n/60.

10—Sold machinery, sales price $6,000, to H Company. Terms: 2/15, n/30.

16—Paid $1,000 for machinery.

20—Cash sales for the day were $4,000.

21—Cash paid for supplies $1,000 (debit Supplies on Hand).

22—Received payment in full from H Company. Old balance was past due.

22—Paid X Company in full. No discount.

23—Paid Z Company in full.

25—Received $100 cash from X Company as an allowance for defective machinery purchased.

26—Charge sale for $2,000 made to K Company. Terms 2/15, n/30.

30—Credit of $1,000 allowed K Company for return of defective machine.

30—Paid utility bills, $100, and bills for miscellaneous expenses, $200.

(Ending inventory as of November 30, 1958, is $16,000.)

a. Enter the beginning balances as of November 1, 1958, in both the general ledger and subsidiary ledger accounts. The following general ledger accounts will be needed, in addition to those on the trial balance: Supplies on Hand, Rent Payable, Sales, Sales Returns and Allowances, Purchases, Purchase

Returns and Allowances, Rent Expense, Depreciation Expense, Utilities Expense, Supplies Expense, Miscellaneous Expense, Sales Discounts Allowed, and Purchases Discounts Earned.

b. Enter the November transactions in the following journals: cash receipts, cash disbursements, sales, purchases, and general.

c. Post to the accounts and bring down a balance in each account.

d. Enter the unadjusted general ledger trial balance on a working trial balance.

e. Enter adjustments for the following on the working papers:

(1) Depreciation on the equipment is $200 for the period.
(2) Supplies with a cost of $400 are on hand at the end of the period.
(3) November rent of $400 has not been paid.

f. Complete the working trial balance.

g. From the working trial balance prepare a statement of income and expense and a statement of financial condition.

h. Schedule the subsidiary receivable and payable balances and compare the totals with the controlling account balances.

i. Why is it unnecessary to prepare closing entries at the end of an interim period?

## CHAPTER 5

**5-1.** Bases for estimating bad debt.

Compute the proper amounts and prepare the necessary adjusting entries for:

a. Company A: Net sales for the month are $10,000. It is estimated that ¼ per cent of the net sales will not be collected.

b. Company B: Credit sales for the month are $20,000, cash sales $15,000. Company experience shows that 1 per cent of the credit sales are usually uncollectible.

c. Company C: At the end of the year the accounts receivable total $60,000. There is no balance in the Allowance for Doubtful Accounts. The credit manager estimates that 2 per cent of the receivables will not be collected.

d. Company D: Assume the same conditions as in (c) above, except that the Allowance for Doubtful Accounts has a credit balance of $200 as of the year end.

**5-2.** Straight-line depreciation and its effect on earned equity.

The ABC Co. began business on January 1, 1957. On that same day equipment with a cost of $40,000 was purchased. The equipment had an estimated life of twenty years; it was also estimated that this equipment would not have any salvage or trade-in value at the end of the twenty years. Net profit for 1957 was $20,000; for 1958, $10,000. (Depreciation had been deducted in both years.)

a. On a straight-line basis, what would be the adjusting entry for the depreciation on this equipment at the end of 1957? At the end of 1958? (Assume that the company books are closed only once a year.)

b. What is the balance of Earned Equity at the end of 1957? At the end of 1958?

c. What would be the net book value for equipment as shown on the balance sheet at the end of 1957? At the end of 1958?

d. If depreciation had not been recorded in 1957 and 1958, what would have been the balance of Earned Equity at the end of each year?

    *e.* If depreciation had not been recorded, by what amount would Earned Equity be overstated at the end of 1958? By what amount would Equipment be overstated at the end of 1958?

**5-3.** Adjustments of recorded balances.

Prepare general journal entries to record the following adjustments for a company that closes its books and prepares statements only at the end of each calendar year:

    *a.* The Vehicles account had a debit balance of $60,000 at the beginning of the year. A truck costing $10,000 was purchased on July 1 of the current year. All vehicles are estimated as having a five-year life, with a trade-in value equal to 10 per cent of the original cost at the end of that time.

    *b.* It is estimated that ¾ per cent of the accounts receivable will not be collected. Balances at the end of the year are: Accounts Receivable, $80,000; Allowance for Doubtful Accounts, $150.

    *c.* All supplies had been charged to the Supplies Used Expense account (total, $720), but at the end of the year there were supplies with a cost of $90 still on hand.

    *d.* The Unearned Subscriptions Income account had a $9,200 credit balance at the end of the year, but $5,000 of this amount actually represented subscriptions income that had been earned by this time.

    *e.* Both fire and liability insurance had been renewed as of the first day of the year: the five-year premium for fire insurance had cost $600; the two-year premium for liability insurance had cost $180.

    *f.* On July 1 of the current year the company had borrowed $20,000 for one year, discounted at 7 per cent; that is, the interest had been "taken out" or, in effect, paid in advance. (Prepaid Interest was debited.)

**5-4.** Accruals of unrecorded data.

Prepare general journal entries to record the following data for a company that closes its books and prepares statements only at the end of each calendar year:

    *a.* Unpaid wages at the end of the year were: gross, $4,000; Federal income tax withholding, $600; FOASI withholding, $90.

    *b.* Rent of $200 was receivable as of the last day of the year.

    *c.* The company had borrowed $30,000 at 5 per cent on October 1 of the current year. Interest is due and payable the following October 1.

    *d.* Property taxes of $360 should be accrued as of the year end.

    *e.* The plant manager had borrowed $5,000 from the company on September 1. Principal and 4 per cent interest are due May 1 of the following year.

    *f.* A $400 credit sale to Jones Corp. on December 31 of the current year has not been recorded.

**5-5.** Preparation of adjusting entries.

In each of the following examples assume that the company is closing its books for the *year* 1958. Prepare the necessary adjusting entries.

    *a.* The year-end balance of Supplies on Hand is $1,600. An inventory as of December 31, 1958, shows that only $200 of supplies are actually still on hand.

    *b.* A three-year premium of $720 for fire insurance had been charged to the Prepaid Insurance account on January 1, 1958; a one-year premium of $240 had been charged to the account on July 1, 1958.

    *c.* A $10,000 loan at 6 per cent for 90 days had been obtained from the bank on December 1, 1958. Interest is payable at maturity.

    *d.* Rent of $600 for the month of December, 1958, had not yet been paid to the landlord.

*e.* December rent of $100 on space subleased to an insurance man had not yet been received at the year end.

*f.* The Unearned Commissions Income account had a credit balance of $3,000 as of December 31, 1958. Two-thirds of these commissions had been earned by the company before the year ended.

*g.* The following bills, dated in December, 1958, were unpaid and unrecorded at the end of the year:

| | |
|---|---:|
| Telephone bill............... | $ 60 |
| Light bill.................... | 94 |
| Merchandise invoice, Tela Co. | 216 |

**5-6.** Cash and accrual statements from cash records.

The only records maintained for a lawyer's office were cash journals, a general journal, and a list of balances due from clients. At the end of the month of January the cash receipts journal showed that $2,000 had been collected from clients during the month: $1,600 represented payment for services rendered in January; $400 was for prior services. The cash disbursements journal showed that $1,800 had been expended: $800 of this was for December wages, the balance for current expenses.

At the end of the month $500 was receivable from clients for January services; wages of $200 were due employees for January work; and there was an unpaid bill of $100 on hand for supplies consumed during the month.

What would be the net profit for January if the income statement were prepared: (a) on the cash basis? (b) on the accrual basis? Show your computations. (Assume that there is no depreciation expense.)

**5-7.** Preparation of closing entries for a service enterprise.

Prepare all closing entries as of the end of the firm's fiscal year, assuming the following account balances (use a P & L Summary account.)

| | *Dr.* | *Cr.* |
|---|---:|---:|
| Withdrawals | 4,500 | |
| Fee Income | | 47,600 |
| Salaries Expense | 30,000 | |
| Rent Expense | 3,600 | |
| Utilities Expense | 1,300 | |
| Supplies Expense | 470 | |
| Other Expense | 180 | |

**5-8.** Preparation of closing entries for a trading enterprise.

*a.* Prepare closing entries (using a P & L account) for the temporary accounts and inventory accounts listed below. All accounts have normal balances:

| | |
|---|---:|
| Inventory (beginning) | $ 9,700 |
| Withdrawals | 8,400 |
| Sales | 106,200 |
| Purchases | 73,100 |
| Rent Expense | 6,000 |
| Depreciation Expense | 7,400 |
| Supplies Expense | 1,460 |
| Other Expense | 630 |
| Inventory (ending) | 5,800 |

*b.* Prepare a closing entry using the "direct" method. Close the withdrawals in a separate entry.

## CHAPTER 6

**6-1.** Statements for a service enterprise.

The adjusted trial balance of the Swanson Company at the end of January, 1957, showed the following balances:

SWANSON COMPANY
Adjusted Trial Balance
January 31, 1957

| Accounts | Dr. | Cr. |
|---|---:|---:|
| Cash in bank........................................... | 360 | |
| Accounts receivable.................................. | 800 | |
| Supplies.............................................. | 216 | |
| Prepaid insurance.................................... | 165 | |
| Rental equipment..................................... | 16,000 | |
| Allowance for depreciation, rental equipment............... | | $ 7,600 |
| Tools................................................ | 3,200 | |
| Office equipment..................................... | 2,400 | |
| Allowance for depreciation, office equipment................ | | 800 |
| Accounts payable..................................... | | 180 |
| Notes payable........................................ | | 600 |
| J. A. Swanson, capital (Jan. 1, 1957)..................... | | 11,166 |
| J. A. Swanson, drawings............................... | 500 | |
| Income from rentals of equipment........................ | | 2,608 |
| Income from saw filing................................ | | 680 |
| Income from mower repairs.............................. | | 1,240 |
| Rent expense......................................... | 160 | |
| Insurance expense.................................... | 15 | |
| Wages............................................... | 300 | |
| Depreciation of rental equipment......................... | 400 | |
| Tools expense........................................ | 240 | |
| Depreciation of office equipment......................... | 40 | |
| Utilities expense..................................... | 52 | |
| Miscellaneous expenses................................ | 26 | |
| Totals........................................... | $24,874 | $24,874 |

Use these data to prepare an income statement and a classified balance sheet.

**6-2.** Statements for a merchandising enterprise.

    The adjusted trial balance of the Adair Company at the end of their fiscal year is given below. Use these data to prepare a multiple-step income statement and a classified balance sheet.

ADAIR COMPANY
Adjusted Trial Balance
June 30, 1957

| Accounts | Dr. | Cr. |
|---|---:|---:|
| Cash in bank............................................. | $ 8,600 | |
| Accounts receivable.................................... | 37,450 | |
| Allowance for bad debts............................... | | $ 680 |
| Notes receivable....................................... | 2,400 | |
| Merchandise inventory, July 1, 1956.................... | 28,600 | |
| Land................................................... | 4,900 | |
| Buildings.............................................. | 32,000 | |
| Allowance for depreciation, buildings.................. | | 6,400 |
| Furniture and fixtures, store.......................... | 8,600 | |
| Allowance for depreciation, furniture and fixtures.......... | | 1,200 |
| Office equipment....................................... | 3,450 | |
| Allowance for depreciation, office equipment............... | | 690 |
| Store supplies......................................... | 650 | |
| Office supplies........................................ | 280 | |
| Prepaid insurance...................................... | 145 | |
| Accounts payable....................................... | | 3,520 |
| Notes payable, trade................................... | | 1,450 |
| Mortgage payable....................................... | | 12,500 |
| J. C. Adair, capital (invested and earned equity)........... | | 67,931 |
| J. C. Adair, drawings.................................. | 5,600 | |
| Sales.................................................. | | 362,000 |
| Sales returns and allowances........................... | 3,450 | |
| Purchases.............................................. | 248,500 | |
| Purchases returns and allowances....................... | | 1,600 |
| Freight on purchases................................... | 12,620 | |
| Advertising expense.................................... | 4,800 | |
| Sales salaries......................................... | 36,450 | |
| Depreciation expense—furniture and fixtures............. | 600 | |
| Miscellaneous selling expense.......................... | 4,780 | |
| Bad debt expense....................................... | 320 | |
| Depreciation expense—buildings ........................ | 800 | |
| Depreciation expense—office equipment ................. | 300 | |
| Store supplies used.................................... | 3,120 | |
| Office salaries........................................ | 8,600 | |
| Expired insurance...................................... | 145 | |
| Office supplies used................................... | 2,560 | |
| Miscellaneous office expense........................... | 1,780 | |
| Utilities expense...................................... | 1,256 | |
| Discount on purchases.................................. | | 4,320 |
| Interest expense....................................... | 435 | |
| Totals................................................ | $462,291 | $462,291 |

    The merchandise inventory as of June 30, 1957, was $31,465.

**6-3.** Preparation of the Statement of Earned Surplus.

From the following list, select the data which are needed for a statement of earned surplus and prepare the statement for the Saling Corporation for Dec. 31, 1957:

| | |
|---|---:|
| Dividends declared, 1957* | $ 32,000 |
| Earned surplus (Dec. 31, 1956) | 156,000 |
| Capital stock, common | 400,000 |
| Capital stock, preferred | 150,000 |
| Net income (1957 after taxes) | 54,000 |
| Dividends payable | 16,000 |
| Estimated income tax payable | 56,000 |
| Paid-in surplus | 16,800 |

*Of the $32,000 dividends declared in 1957, $16,000 has been paid and $16,000 will be paid on January 5 of the following year.

**6-4.** Statements of a manufacturing concern.

The Bowen Manufacturing Company prepares a Profit and Loss statement and supporting schedules similar to those of the Apex Company showing (A) cost of goods manufactured and (B) raw materials used. They also prepare a classified balance sheet with subheadings as recommended in Regulation S-X of the SEC. Indicate on which statement or supporting schedule the following accounts would appear, and show the section of the statement if the account appears on the balance sheet or the profit and loss statement. Prepare your answer in the following manner:

| *Account* | *Statement* | *Section* |
|---|---|---|
| Cash | Balance sheet | Current asset |
| Sales Returns | P & L statement | Income from sales |
| Interest Expense | P & L statement | Other expense |
| Depr. on Machinery | Schedule of cost of goods manufactured | |

(1) Accounts Payable
(2) Accounts Receivable
(3) Accrued Interest Receivable
(4) Bad Debt Expense
(5) Depr. on Delivery Equipment
(6) Freight Out
(7) Sales Salaries
(8) Raw Materials Inventory, Jan. 1
(9) Officers' Salaries
(10) Notes Payable
(11) Mortgage Payable
(12) Capital Stock, Common
(13) Earned Surplus
(14) Premium on Preferred Stock
(15) Discount on Sales
(16) Goodwill
(17) Estimated Income Tax Payable
(18) Investment in Subsidiary
(19) Rent Collected in Advance
(20) Dividends Payable
(21) Factory Supplies Used
(22) Office Supplies Used
(23) Store Supplies Used
(24) Prepaid Insurance
(25) Allowance for Bad Debts
(26) Land
(27) Machinery and Equipment
(28) Heat, Lights, and Power
(29) Depreciation on Store Bldg.
(30) Goods in Process, Jan. 1
(31) Finished Goods, Dec. 31
(32) Manufacturing Expense, Misc.
(33) Stationery and Supplies
(34) Interest Income

## CHAPTER 7

**7-1.** Use of an imprest petty cash fund.

Prepare entries in general journal form to record the following information:

   *a.* A check for $100 is cashed in order to establish an imprest petty cash fund. The currency and coin are left with one of the clerks in the front office.

   *b.* One month later a check is drawn to reimburse the fund. At that time the contents of the fund were as follows:

| | |
|---|---:|
| Currency | $ 3.00 |
| Coin | 1.60 |
| Receipts for postage | 47.10 |
| Bills for stationery | 48.00 |

   *c.* A check for $20 is drawn and cashed in order to increase the imprest petty cash fund to $120.

**7-2.** Bank reconciliation.

The general ledger account, Cash in Bank, has a balance of $3,510 as of the end of the month. The bank statement for the month shows a final balance of $3,800. A deposit of $300, recorded on the company books as of the last day of the month, was not included on the bank statement. Three checks recorded in the cash disbursements journal have not yet been returned by the bank: check number 213 for $87, 234 for $193, and 235 for $316. A service charge of $6 had been deducted by the bank but had not yet been recorded in the accounting records.

Prepare a bank reconciliation based on the above data.

**7-3.** The effects of depreciation on profits and earned equity.

The XYZ Co. failed to record depreciation during its first two years of operation. Net income for 1957 was reported as $6,000; for 1958, as $14,000. Buildings with a cost of $200,000 and an expected life of 50 years had been owned by the firm during the entire two-year period. Equipment purchased January 1, 1957, at a cost of $30,000 had an expected useful life of ten years.

   *a.* What was the valuation reported for fixed assets at the end of each year? The valuation of earned equity at the end of each year?

   *b.* If depreciation had been properly recorded, what would have been the net income reported for 1957 and 1958? What amount of earned equity would have been reported at the end of each year? What valuation would have been shown for fixed assets at the end of each year?

   *c.* What are the differences between the original fixed asset valuations at the end of each year and the amounts that would be shown if depreciation were properly entered? What are the differences between the original earned equity balances and the correct earned equity balances? Are these differences the same? Why?

**7-4.** Computation of depreciation under the composite method.

The ABC Company charges the cost of furniture and fixtures to one general ledger account and assumes that all such assets will have an expected useful life of ten years. Any additions during the year are depreciated from the first day of the month following the date of purchase. Depreciation is computed to the last day of the month in which any asset is sold. Below you will find the asset account as it appeared for 1957:

### Furniture and Fixtures

| | | | | | |
|---|---|---|---|---|---|
| 1-1-57 | Balance | $16,000 | 2-28-57 | Files sold | $2,000 |
| 3-18-57 | Desks | 1,800 | | | |
| 6-29-57 | Files | 900 | | | |
| 9-10-57 | Fixtures | 1,200 | | | |

*a.* Compute the 1957 depreciation charge for furniture and fixtures.

*b.* Original cost of the files sold February 28, 1957, was $2,000; accumulated depreciation on these files was $1,600. The files were sold for $200 cash. Prepare a general journal entry to reflect the sale.

**7-5.** Computation of depreciation on productive machinery under three different methods.

The York Manufacturing Co. purchased a metal lathe on March 1, 1957. Invoice cost of the lathe was $2,000, freight in was $100, in-transit insurance $50, and installation cost $250. The lathe was estimated as having a useful life of six years and no salvage value. During the six years it was estimated that the machine would operate 6,000 hours and produce 24,000 parts.

By the end of 1957 the machine had operated 700 hours and produced 3,000 parts. What would the 1957 depreciation expense be if computed: (a) by the straight-line method? (b) by the working-hours method? (c) by the units-of-product method?

**7-6.** FIFO and LIFO methods applied to cost of goods sold and inventory for a non-manufacturing concern.

The Denver Wholesale Co. had an opening inventory valued at $4,000 and purchases for 1957 with a cost of $80,000. Freight in for the year amounted to $1,200; purchase returns and allowances were $2,800. A physical inventory taken on December 31, 1957, was valued, on the basis of latest invoice prices, at $5,400.

*a.* Compute the cost of goods sold under the FIFO method.

*b.* If opening inventory had been valued at $3,800 and the ending inventory valued at $4,100 (on the basis of earlier—not latest—costs) what would the cost of goods sold be when computed by the LIFO method?

**7-7.** FIFO, LIFO, and average costs applied to one item of raw material in a manufacturing business.

The Eldorado Manufacturing Co. maintains perpetual inventory cards for each item in its raw materials inventory. Prepare inventory cards with three major headings (received, issued, on hand) and enter the following data for rough castings, first using the FIFO method, second the LIFO method, and third the average cost method:

| Castings Received | | | Castings Issued | |
|---|---|---|---|---|
| Date | Quantity | Unit Price | Date | Quantity |
| 1-28 | 200 | $2.00 | 6-7 | 300 |
| 5-14 | 400 | 2.10 | 11-18 | 400 |
| 10-2 | 300 | 2.20 | | |

Which method yields the highest cost of goods sold and the lowest gross profit? Why?

**7-8.** Journal entries for amortization.

Prepare entries in general journal form to record the following data:

*a.* The company's lease on its office building expires June 30, 1967. During June, 1957, the company had new openings cut in various walls of this building and new doors and windows installed. The cost of the work, which was completed June 30, was $4,800. (A check was issued on this date as payment in full.)

*b.* Amortize a portion of the above cost as of December 31, 1957, the end of the firm's fiscal year.

*c.* An oil company had estimated underground reserves of 500,000 barrels (cost $2,000,000) as of the beginning of their fiscal year, November 1, 1957. During the following year 100,000 barrels were pumped and sold. Prepare an amortization entry as of October 31, 1958.

*d.* A mining company had an estimated ore reserve of 300,000 tons (cost $900,000) at the beginning of their fiscal year. By the end of the year 80,000 tons had been mined and 70,000 tons had been sold. Prepare the necessary entry as of August 31, 1958, the end of the current fiscal year.

**7-9.** Use of imputed costs.

Harry Trueblood has an opportunity to sell his business for $80,000. At the same time he is offered a position as manager of a similar enterprise, with an annual salary of $10,000. Working hours and conditions would be about the same as those he has experienced with his own business. Harry feels sure that he can average a 5 per cent return on any funds that he invests in securities at this time.

Harry's business has earned an average net profit of $11,000 over the past five years and he expects the average for the next five years to be about $12,000 per year.

*a.* What is the imputed profit or loss for the business?

*b.* What factors should Harry evaluate before he makes his final decision?

## CHAPTER 8

**8-1.** Partnership formation.

John Cotton and Joe Mathers have agreed to form a partnership and combine their talents to operate a cash register repair and sales company. Cotton has been a salesman for a large cash register company and Mathers has operated his own repair shop for several years. Cotton agrees to invest $20,000 in cash. Mathers is to invest $5,000 in cash and the following assets of his present firm: Tools, which cost $4,600 and have an estimated value of $3,000 at the present time; land, which cost $5,000 and which could be sold for $8,000 (expenses of selling would be approximately $550); a building which cost $23,000 ten years ago, has an estimated total life of 40 years, and would cost $36,000 to build at this time; accounts receivable of $8,600 on which Mathers has set up an allowance for bad debts of $600—(they now estimate that $860 will not be collectible); second-hand cash registers which Mathers has rebuilt and which are expected to sell for $4,800 (a margin of 35 per cent of sales is believed typical); and supplies which cost $840. The firm is to assume Mathers' liabilities, which are: trade payables, $1,040; accrued taxes, $180; miscellaneous accrued payables (utilities, etc.), $60. Make the journal entries required to record the investment of each partner, using amounts which you think are most equitable.

**8-2.** Admission of a new partner.

Assume that A, B, and C are partners in a retail drug store. They have capital balances of $15,000, $10,000, and $25,000, respectively, and share profits in the ratio of 5, 3, and 2. D wishes to join the firm. What entry should be made under each of the following assumptions:

*a.* He invests $25,000 and receives a one-third interest in the firm.

*b.* He invests $25,000 for a one-fourth interest in the firm and goodwill is allowed the old partners.

*c.* He invests $30,000 for a one-fourth interest in the firm and the old partners are given a bonus.

*d.* He invests $10,000 for a one-fourth interest and the total capital will be $60,000.

*e.* He invests $15,000 for a one-fourth interest and the total capital is to be $80,000.

**8-3.** Distribution of partnership profits.

Jones, Ford, and Dale are partners having the following capital balances: Jones, $30,000; Ford, $45,000; Dale, $25,000. The firm has a net profit of $30,000 for the year. Give the journal entry to transfer the profits to the partners' capital accounts, assuming each of the following profit-sharing agreements:

*a.* Profits are distributed equally.

*b.* Profits are distributed in the ratio of partners' investments.

*c.* Profits are distributed in the ratio of 5, 3, and 2, respectively.

*d.* Each partner is allowed 6 per cent on his investment and the balance is distributed equally.

*e.* The partners are allowed salaries of $4,000, $6,000, and $5,000, respectively, and the balance is distributed equally.

*f.* The partners are allowed 6 per cent on their investments, salaries of $4,000, $6,000, and $5,000, and the balance is divided equally.

*g.* What entry would you have made for (*f*) if the amount to be distributed had been only $15,000.

**8-4.** Dissolution and liquidation of a partnership.

The firm of Baker, Crane, and Dale has been unsuccessful and is to be liquidated. Profits and losses are shared in the ratio of 4, 3, and 3, respectively. On Jan. 21, 1958, the firm's balance sheet showed the following facts:

| | | | |
|---|---:|---|---:|
| Cash | $20,000 | Accounts payable | $12,000 |
| Noncash assets | 60,000 | Baker, loan | 8,000 |
| | | Baker, capital | 4,000 |
| | | Crane, capital | 20,000 |
| | | Dale, capital | 36,000 |
| | $80,000 | | $80,000 |

*a.* What journal entries would be required in each of the following cases?

Feb. 2. The noncash assets were sold for $50,000.
    3. The accounts payable were paid.
    4. The partners were paid for their loan and capital balances.

*b.* What journal entries would be required in each of the following cases?

Feb. 2. The noncash assets were sold for $40,000.
    3. The accounts payable were paid.
    4. The partners were paid for their loan and capital balances.

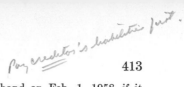

*Pay creditor's in liabilities first.*

c. How would you distribute the $20,000 cash on hand on Feb. 1, 1958, if it appears that it will be several months before the noncash assets can be sold, and the partners want to withdraw the cash available to them now?

*Bye $8,000*

*Distrib of assets is accord to balances in accts.*

## CHAPTER 9

**9-1.** Journal entries for changes in net worth.

Prepare entries in general journal form to record the following changes (stock is issued in exchange for cash unless otherwise noted):

*a.* 20,000 shares of $10 par value common stock are issued at par for cash.

*b.* 5,000 shares of no-par value common stock are issued at $17 per share; $12 per share is to be the recognized stated value.

*c.* 4,000 shares of $50 par common are issued at $54 per share.

*d.* 3,000 shares of $40 par preferred stock are issued at $42 per share.

*e.* 6,000 shares of $60 par common stock are issued at $66 per share.

*f.* Cash dividends of $8,000 are declared on common stock.

*g.* Common dividends mentioned in (*f*) above are paid.

*h.* A corporation has $100,000 (par) of 5 per cent noncumulative preferred issued and outstanding, and common outstanding with a total par of $300,000. The directors *declare*, December 31, 1957, that cash of $12,000 is available for 1957 dividends—to be distributed in the required manner. (There should be separate accounts for each type of dividend and payable.)

*i.* Assume that the preferred in (*h*) above was cumulative and that dividends had not been paid on this stock for 1956 and 1957. Make the entries necessary as of December 31, 1957.

*j.* 1,000 shares of nominal-par common stock ($1 per share) are issued at $6 per share.

*k.* A building with an appraisal value of $340,000 is received in exchange for preferred stock with a total par value of $300,000. Debit $340,000 to the Building account.

**9-2.** Purchase, sale, and presentation of treasury stock.

A corporation has earned surplus of $80,000 and 200,000 shares of $1 par common outstanding. The company purchases 20,000 shares of its own $1 par common at 95 cents a share. A few weeks later 10,000 of these 20,000 shares are sold at $1.05 per share (credit the gain to Paid-in Surplus).

*a.* Prepare journal entries to record the purchase and sale of the stock.

*b.* Prepare the stockholders' equity section after the above transactions (assume that 300,000 shares of the common stock have been authorized).

**9-3.** Derivation of earned surplus.

In a period of 100 years the Olds Corporation has had a total inward flow of assets arising from operations valued at $100,000,000. In the same period of time assets valued at $90,000,000 have been relinquished as a result of operations. The owners have invested $20,000,000 of assets in the firm and $5,000,000 in assets have been distributed in the form of dividends.

*a.* What is the firm's net profit for the period?

*b.* How would you define net profit?

*c.* What is the amount of earned surplus at the end of the period?

*d.* What is earned surplus?

**9-4.** Presentation of appropriated earned surplus.

Before any adjustment at the year end, the net worth section of a corporation appears as outlined below:

| | | |
|---|---:|---:|
| Preferred stock.............. | $100,000 | |
| Common stock.............. | 300,000 | |
| Total capital stock................. | | $  400,000 |
| Paid-in surplus.............. | $ 20,000 | |
| Earned surplus.............. | 580,000 | |
| Total surplus..................... | | 600,000 |
| Net worth....................... | | $1,000,000 |

As of the last day of the year the directors resolve to appropriate $200,000 o earned surplus for plant expansion and $100,000 for possible losses.

  *a.* Outline the net worth section as it should be presented in order to reflect these changes.

  *b.* What is the theoretical dollar limit on the amount of assets that can now be distributed in the form of dividends?

  *c.* What would actually determine the limit on dividends in most instances?

**9-5.** Book value per share.

The stockholders' equity section of a corporate balance sheet appears as follows:

| | | |
|---|---:|---:|
| Capital stock: | | |
| Preferred, 6% cumulative; $40 par; | | |
|     2,000 shares authorized and issued | $ 80,000 | |
| Common, $15 par; 10,000 shares | | |
|     authorized and issued.......... | 150,000 | $230,000 |
| Surplus: | | |
| Premium on common stock........ | $ 20,000 | |
| Earned surplus.................. | 180,000 | 200,000 |
| Net worth............................ | | $430,000 |

  *a.* What is the book value per share of the preferred, assuming there are no dividends due the preferred stockholders? If dividends on preferred for the three preceding years and the current year are unpaid, what is the book value per share of the preferred stock?

  *b.* What is the book value per share of the common under each of the assumptions made in (*a*) above?

**9-6.** Closing entries, earned surplus statement, and stockholders' equity.

Shown below is an annual trial balance for the Dallas Corp. as of December 31, 1958. Prepare:

  *a.* A statement of earned surplus.

  *b.* The stockholders' equity section of the balance sheet.

  *c.* Journal entries to close the firm's books.

| | | |
|---|---:|---:|
| Cash............................ | $ 1,000 | |
| Equipment....................... | 120,000 | |
| Accumulated depreciation........... | | $ 20,000 |
| Dividends payable—preferred........ | | 2,000 |
| Common stock.................... | | 60,000 |
| Preferred stock................... | | 30,000 |
| Earned surplus.................... | | 10,000 |
| Dividends—common............... | 3,000 | |
| Dividends—preferred.............. | 2,000 | |
| Sales (income earned).............. | | 210,000 |
| Wages........................... | 160,000 | |
| Rent............................ | 40,000 | |
| Depreciation..................... | 4,000 | |
| Other expense.................... | 2,000 | |
| Totals...................... | $332,000 | $332,000 |

**9-7.** Capital stock subscribed.

Present general journal entries to record the following information for the Eastern Company:

a. On July 1, 1958, 10,000 shares of the company's $100 par common stock are subscribed for at $104 per share. Shares are to be issued as subscriber's accounts are paid in full.

b. During July the firm receives $40,000 as part payment on subscriptions.

c. In August, payments of $80,000 are received. After these payments are posted to the accounts in the subscribers' ledger, we find that subscriptions receivable for shares with a par value of $10,000 have been paid in full.

**9-8.** Make-up of earned surplus.

From the following account balances compute the total earned surplus. The dividends account has already been closed to Earned Surplus, Unappropriated.

| | |
|---|---:|
| Premium on preferred stock............. | $11,000 |
| Earned surplus, unappropriated......... | 81,000 |
| Dividends payable.................... | 10,000 |
| Appropriated for plant expansion........ | 30,000 |
| Reserve for bad debts................. | 7,000 |
| Surplus from donations................ | 15,000 |
| Cash................................ | 33,000 |
| Appraisal surplus..................... | 5,000 |
| Appropriated for contingencies.......... | 20,000 |

**9-9.** Declaration and payment of dividends.

Prepare general journal entries for the following transactions:

a. The directors declare a cash dividend of $6,000 as of December 20, 1957.

b. January 8, 1958, is the date of record for the above dividends.

c. Above dividends are paid on January 26, 1958.

d. The directors declare a property dividend as of July 1, 1958. Securities of other companies are to be distributed to the stockholders. These securities are recorded in the Investments account at a value of $8,000.

e. The securities mentioned in (d) are mailed on July 3, 1958, to all shareholders of record as of July 1, 1958.

*f.* The net worth section of a corporate balance sheet on November 30, 1957, is as follows:

Common stock, $10 par; 6,000 shares
    authorized; 1,000 shares issued...... $10,000
Earned surplus..................... 80,000
    Total net worth.................. $90,000

The board of directors of this corporation declares on December 14, 1957, a stock dividend of 5,000 shares of the common stock already authorized. All stockholders of record on January 6, 1958, are to receive additional shares.

*g.* The common stock dividend shares are distributed to the owners on January 18, 1958.

*h.* XYZ Corp. has 2,000 shares of $180 par common authorized, issued, and outstanding. These shares as of March 1, 1958, are retired and replaced by 6,000 shares of common with a par of $60.

*i.* What is the term that describes the procedure employed in (*h*) above? What is the advantage of having stock with a lower par value?

**9-10.** Various classifications of surplus.

Prepare general journal entries to record the transactions described below:

*a.* 1,000 shares of $40 par common were issued at $46. Cash payment in full was received immediately.

*b.* A building with a current market value of $30,000 was donated to the corporation by a principal stockholder.

*c.* 2,000 shares of no-par common stock with a stated value of $20 were sold for cash at $28 per share.

*d.* Land with a book value of $14,000 is appraised at $84,000. The appraisal increment is to be recorded in the books and is to appear on the statements.

**9-11.** Earned surplus statement.

From the data below prepare a statement of earned surplus for the Garbo Corp.:

Net profit for 1958............................... $30,000
Common dividends declared and paid............... 20,000
Common dividends declared but not yet paid........ 20,000
Earned surplus, Jan. 1, 1958...................... 90,000
Preferred dividends declared but not yet paid........ 5,000

**9-12.** Net worth on the balance sheet.

Prepare a net worth section from the information itemized below:

Premium on preferred stock.............. $ 6,000
Earned surplus, free balance............. 70,000
Paid-in surplus on no-par common........ 80,000
Appropriated for plant expansion.......... 40,500
Preferred stock: 10,000 shares authorized;
    6,000 shares issued, par $10
Common stock: 40,000 shares authorized
    and issued; no-par value; stated value $6;
    sales price $8

**9-13.** Dividends on cumulative preferred.

Carriers, Inc. has outstanding 5,000 shares of $100 par cumulative preferred stock which carries a 5 per cent dividend rate. The company also has 50,000 shares of $60 par common stock outstanding. How much should the preferred and common shareholders receive as dividends for 1958 under each of the three assumptions outlined below?

*a.* At the end of 1958 the directors declare $20,000 available for dividends.

*b.* At the end of 1958 the directors declare $125,000 available for dividends. Dividends on the cumulative preferred have been paid through 1957.

*c.* At the end of 1958 the directors declare $125,000 available for dividends. Dividends on the cumulative have not been paid for 1956, 1957 and the current year, 1958.

**9-14.** Journal entries for long-term debt financing.

Present journal entries to reflect the events outlined below:

*a.* The corporation borrowed $6,700 from a local bank on the basis of an unsecured note.

*b.* An $80,000 loan was negotiated with a national insurance company. A mortgage on the office building serves as collateral for the loan.

*c.* One thousand $500 bonds were issued to the public in exchange for $500,000 cash. The bonds carry a 4 per cent interest rate and are due in ten years.

*d.* Semiannual interest on the above bonds is paid.


## CHAPTER 10

**10-1.** Recording sales on account.

The Dorn Paint Company uses cash journals, a sales journal, and a general journal. Chain discounts of 20 per cent and 10 per cent are allowed all retail paint stores and 10 and 10 per cent discounts are allowed department stores handling their paint. Some customers pick up their paint at the factory but a majority have the paint shipped to them. All terms are 2/10, n/30. The company occasionally prepays the freight and adds it to the customer's account.

*a.* Set up a three-column sales journal such as they might use (columns should be Accounts Receivable, Dr.; Freight Out, Cr.; and Sales, Cr.) and record the following sales on account:

> July 1. Sold to Miller Paint Store, $1,200; less 20 and 10%, f.o.b. destination.
> 2. Sold to Nelson Dept. Store, $800; less 10 and 10%, f.o.b. destination.
> 5. Sold to Jonas Paint Shop, $2,600; less 20 and 10%; f.o.b. shipping point; prepaid freight charged to Jonas, $56.
> (The freight payment has already been entered in the cash payments journal; all freight on sales is charged to Freight Out when paid.)
> 6. Sold to Green Paint Co., $960; less 20 and 10%; f.o.b. destination.
> 7. Sold to House Paint Co., $1,250; less 20 and 10%; f.o.b. shipping point, freight prepaid, $32.

*b.* What one discount is equivalent to a chain discount of 20 and 10%? Of 10 and 10%?

*c.* Assume that the total freight paid on sales was $1,600. Of this amount $980 was paid on f.o.b. destination orders and $620 paid on f.o.b. shipping point orders.

Set up a T account for Freight Out, showing the debit amount and the journal from which it came and the credit amount and the journal from which it came. What is the balance in the account? Does this agree with the f.o.b. destination freight charges?

**10-2.** Departmental profit and loss statements.

The Apex Stores, Inc., has three departments. Net operating profits are determined by departments and the profit and loss statement is made to reveal departmental and total figures.

*a.* Use the data given below to show how their operating statement should be prepared:

| | Department | | | Total |
|---|---|---|---|---|
| | A | B | C | |
| Sales | 82,000 | 52,000 | 66,000 | |
| Returned Sales and Allowances | 1,600 | 2,300 | 3,200 | |
| Merchandise Inventory, Jan. 1 | 40,000 | 36,000 | 39,000 | |
| Purchases | 46,000 | 38,000 | 53,000 | |
| Freight On Purchases | 1,750 | 1,620 | 2,450 | |
| Returned Purchases and Allowances | 400 | 650 | 850 | |
| Sales Salaries | 5,100 | 3,050 | 6,200 | |
| Other Selling Expenses | | | | 15,500 |
| Officers' Salaries | | | | 3,200 |
| Occupancy Costs | | | | 6,400 |
| Misc. General and Adm. Expense | | | | 3,600 |

All items for which departmental amounts are shown were obtained from the departmentalized ledger accounts. Items for which only the totals are shown could not be departmentalized but are to be allocated as follows:

| Item | Basis of Allocation |
|---|---|
| Other Selling Expense | Gross Sales |
| Officers' Salaries | Gross Sales |
| Occupancy Costs | Floor space: A, 20%; B, 30%; C, 50%. |
| Misc. Gen. & Adm. Expense | Ratio of 30%, 30%, and 40% based on volume of paper work |

Final inventories, obtained from a count of goods on hand, were: A, $41,000; B, $38,000; C, $42,500.

*b.* Did the firm operate at a profit? Did each of the departments operate at a profit?

*c.* What should be done about Department C?

*d.* Is there any reason to question the basis used for allocating occupancy costs? Officers' salaries? Miscellaneous general and administrative expense?

**10-3.** Retail method of estimating inventory.

Use the following data to estimate the inventory of the Caroline Company on January 31, 1958:

Inventory, January 1, 1958—Cost, $73,000; Selling Price, $96,000.
Purchases for January—Cost, $24,000; Selling Price, $32,500.
Freight on Purchases, $975.
Markups (in addition to original markup), $370.
Markdowns, $950.
Sales, $38,600.

Arrange your answer in a form similar to the one illustrated in the text.

**10-4.** Basic entries for installment sales.

The Lake City Appliance Co. began the year 1956 with the following account balances:

| | | |
|---|---:|---:|
| Cash | $ 23,000 | |
| Installment Accounts Receivable | 60,000 | |
| Inventory | 97,000 | |
| Deferred Gross Profit, 1955 | | $ 18,000 |
| Accounts Payable | | 28,000 |
| J. A. Dalton, Capital | | 134,000 |
| | $180,000 | $180,000 |

Record these balances in T accounts and show how installment sales are recorded by entering the following summarized transactions in these and other accounts affected. Use letters to identify transactions.

*a.* Total purchases for the year, on account, $200,000.

*b.* Total operating expenses paid, $28,000.

*c.* Total installment sales, $270,000—cost of installment sales, $180,000.

*d.* Total collections on installment sales, $283,000.

*e.* Total paid on accounts payable, $196,000.

*f.* Close Installment Sales and Cost of Installment Sales and set up Deferred Gross Profit—1956.

*g.* Take up realized gross profit. An analysis of installment accounts receivable shows $2,000 due on 1955 sales and $45,000 due on 1956 sales.

*h.* Close realized gross profit accounts to Profit and Loss summary.

*i.* Close operating expense to Profit and Loss summary.

*j.* Close net income to owner's Capital account.

Use these T accounts: Cash, Installment Accounts Receivable, Inventory, Deferred Gross Profit—1955, Deferred Gross Profit—1956, Accounts Payable, Installment Sales, Cost of Installment Sales, Operating Expenses, Realized Gross Profit, Profit and Loss Summary, J. A. Dalton, Capital.

**10-5.** Basic entries for home office and branch accounting.

The Yeaston Brothers Feed and Implement Company has its store in Portland. To increase its sales, the company has decided to open branch stores in several nearby towns. Assume that you have been made manager of one of these branch stores. Although you are not the bookkeeper, you want to know the effect of various transactions on the books of your branch. Set up T accounts needed and enter the following transactions:

*a.* The home office arranges to lease a building from the Doan Realty Co. The rent is to be paid monthly on the first of each month.

*b.* Cash of $5,000 is received from the home office.

*c.* Rent for January is paid, $250.

*d.* Merchandise worth $23,350 is received from the home office; also received, office equipment for use but to be carried on home office books.

*e.* Purchases of merchandise from local suppliers on account, $6,500.

*f.* Sales of merchandise on account, $16,250.

*g.* Payments on account, $6,300.

*h.* Received from customers on account, $12,500.

*i.* Paid operating expenses: Salaries, $850; Utilities, $36; Insurance, $20.

*j.* Depreciation on office equipment, $25. Equipment and Allowance for Depreciation accounts carried by home office.

*k.* Closed cost and revenue accounts and set up final inventory of $16,780.

*l.* Closed Profit and Loss summary.

*m.* Sent home office a check for $5,000.

Give the journal entries which the home office would make, lettering your entries to correspond with the letters assigned the transactions.

(Suggested T accounts for Branch: Cash, Accounts Receivable, Merchandise Inventory, Accounts Payable, Home Office, Shipments from Home Office, Purchases, Sales, Rent Expenses, Salaries, Depreciation of Office Equipment, Miscellaneous Operating Expenses, and Profit and Loss Summary.)

**10-6.** Basic entries for consignment sales.

Assume that you are operating a small farm supply store. A manufacturer of power mowers wants you to handle his machines on a consignment basis. You agree to sell his machines under the following conditions: you are to be repaid for any freight or other charges in getting the machines to your store; all advertising will be handled by the manufacturer; you pay for demonstrating and selling and any local advertising; you receive a commission of 30 per cent on the selling price of machines sold; you are to sell for cash (or handle your own accounts receivable); you are to make a report and a remittance at the end of each month. During the month the following transactions occur:

*a.* The Ace Corporation sends you 12 machines, carried on their books at cost of $80 each, $960.

*b.* You receive the machines and pay $16.80 shipping charges.

*c.* During the month you sell seven of the machines at $140 each, $980. (Five of these sales were for cash and two were on account.) Your commission on these sales is $294.

*d.* You send the Ace Corporation a sales account for the month and a check for $669.20.

Set up T accounts to show how the foregoing transactions will affect your accounts, and answer the following questions:

1. Will the five machines which you have left be counted in your inventory?
2. How much did the Ace Corporation make on this consignment?
3. What will be the value of the five machines which you have on the Ace Corporation's inventory?

## CHAPTER 11

**11-1.** Preparation of an income statement and supporting schedules.

From the data below prepare the following for the Kay Manufacturing Co.:

*a.* Schedule of materials used
*b.* Schedule of manufacturing expenses
*c.* Schedule of cost of goods manufactured
*d.* An income statement

The data, unless otherwise indicated, represent account balances as of the last day of the fiscal year, June 30, 1958:

| | |
|---|---:|
| Materials Inventory | $ 72,000 |
| In Process Inventory | 61,500 |
| Finished Goods Inventory | 92,600 |
| Sales | 560,000 |
| Sales Returns and Allowances | 10,000 |
| Purchases—material | 200,000 |
| Freight In | 5,400 |
| Sales Salaries | 19,200 |
| Office Salaries | 16,300 |
| Direct Labor | 167,000 |
| Indirect Labor | 29,400 |
| Sales Commissions | 5,100 |
| Advertising | 9,300 |
| Freight Out | 2,700 |
| Depreciation—furniture and fixtures | 1,600 |
| Depreciation—factory | 8,400 |
| Heat, Light, and Power—factory | 14,300 |
| Utilities—offices | 2,100 |
| Taxes and Insurance—factory | 7,600 |
| Taxes and Insurance—office | 1,100 |
| Inventories, July 1, 1957: | |
|     Materials inventory | $ 74,600 |
|     In process inventory | 73,900 |
|     Finished goods inventory | 98,700 |

**11-2.** Entries on a stock ledger card.

Use the average cost method and enter the following data on a perpetual inventory stock ledger card. Show quantity, unit cost, and amount for items received, issued, and on hand.

| | Received | | | Issued |
|---|---|---|---|---|
| Date | Quantity | Unit cost | Date | Quantity |
| 1–2 | 200 | $2.04 | 1–10 | 160 |
| 1–14 | 100 | 2.06 | 1–17 | 110 |
| 1–25 | 300 | 2.10 | 1–29 | 280 |

**11-3.** FIFO and LIFO costs.

    *a.* What was the total cost of materials charged to goods in process in problem **11-2** above?

    *b.* What would the cost have been if FIFO costing had been used?

    *c.* If LIFO costing had been used?

**11-4.** Computation of predetermined overhead rates.

A manufacturing concern with a job order cost accounting system must customarily estimate future manufacturing expenses and develop a rate for the application of estimated overhead amounts to specific job lots.

For the coming year a manufacturing concern is expected to have $600,000 of manufacturing expenses while operating at an estimated level of 400,000 direct labor hours. The average hourly rate for direct labor during this period is expected to be $1.94.

   *a.* What would be the predetermined rate if total direct labor hours are the basis?

   *b.* What would be the predetermined rate if total direct labor cost is the basis?

   *c.* How much overhead would be charged to a job lot with 200 direct labor hours and $400 of direct labor cost if the rate in (*a*) were applied? If the rate in (*b*) were applied?

**11-5.** Use of fixed and variable rates in the analysis of manufacturing expense balances.

   The total of manufacturing expenses for the year was estimated as $260,000 ($150,000 fixed expenses; $110,000 variable expense); however, manufacturing expenses actually total $270,000 at the end of the year ($150,000 fixed expenses; $120,000 variable expense). The expected level of production was estimated as 50,000 direct labor hours, but the actual total for the year was 52,000.

   *a.* What was the predetermined rate for the year? What portion represents fixed expenses? Variable expense?

   *b.* What was the difference between the actual costs incurred and the amount of costs applied? Were costs underapplied or overapplied?

   *c.* Analyze the difference in (*b*) above; i.e., compute capacity gain or loss and budget variation gain or loss.

**11-6.** Entries for the transfer of costs in a job order cost accounting system.

   The Dant Manufacturing Co. uses a job order cost accounting system. Materials purchased are charged to a Materials Inventory account, productive labor is charged to a Direct Labor account, and all other production costs incurred are charged to a Manufacturing Expense account. The system includes monthly summaries of material requisitions and job time tickets, a predetermined overhead rate, and job order sheets for each job put into process.

   Prepare journal entries based on the information presented below:

   *a.* Total of materials requisitioned for the month, $4,750 (per the summary of material requisitions).

   *b.* Total of direct labor costs for the month, $3,860 (per the summary of job time tickets).

   *c.* The predetermined rate for manufacturing expenses is 80 per cent of direct labor cost.

   *d.* Total cost of jobs completed during the month, $9,100 (per the summary of job lots completed).

   *e.* Total cost of finished units sold during the month, $8,900 (per the summary of cost of goods sold).

   *f.* Post the above entries to appropriate T accounts.

   *g.* The total of what summary should agree with the month-end balance of the Goods in Process account?

**11-7.** Preparation of a job cost sheet.

   Two hundred units of product X were put into process by the ABC Co. on June 6, 1958, and were completed by June 15, 1958. Enter the following data for these units on job cost sheet number 189:

   (1) The summary of materials requisitioned shows that $506 is to be charged to job 189.

   (2) The summary of job time tickets indicates that $620 of direct labor cost is to be charged to job 189 (there were 330 hours of direct labor charged against the job).

   (3) The predetermined rate for the application of manufacturing expenses is $1.40 per direct labor hour.

**11-8.** Entries for the transfer of costs in a process cost accounting system.

The Chemical Processing Corp. manufactures one end product. There are two processes within the plant; one is identified as Department 1, the other as Department 2. No distinction is made between direct and indirect materials or labor. Materials are added in both departments. Labor and manufacturing expense accounts are maintained for each department.

Prepare journal entries based on the information presented below:

a. Total of materials requisitioned for the month—$8,400 to Dept. 1 and $3,100 to Dept. 2 (per the summary of material requisitions).

b. Labor costs for the month—$4,200 for Dept. 1 and $3,900 for Dept. 2 (as recorded in the payroll records).

c. The predetermined rates for manufacturing expenses are: 50 per cent of labor cost for Dept. 1 and 70 per cent of labor cost for Dept. 2.

d. Cost of product transferred from Dept. 1 to Dept. 2—$12,800 (per the production report for Dept. 1).

e. Total cost of jobs completed and transferred from Dept. 2 to the finished goods warehouse—$21,300 (per the production report for Dept. 2).

f. Total cost of finished units sold during the month—$19,700 (per the summary of cost of goods sold).

g. Post the above entries to appropriate T accounts.

**11-9.** Computation of equivalent units.

All materials are added at the beginning of Process 1. As of the beginning of the month there were 4,000 gallons in process; 36,000 gallons were added during the month; and there were 6,000 gallons in process at the end of the month. It is estimated that only one-fourth of the labor and overhead costs had been added to the units in process at the beginning and two-thirds to the units in process at the end.

a. What is the number of units to be accounted for and how are they accounted for?

b. What is the number of equivalent units for labor and expense (assuming that both are added to production at the same rate)?

c. What is the average unit processing cost? Assume the following:

|  | Costs in process at the beginning | Costs added during the period |
|---|---|---|
| Material........ | $8,000 | $72,000 |
| Labor.......... | 3,600 | 33,400 |
| Expense......... | 1,800 | 16,700 |

d. Account for the total costs involved.

**11-10.** Preparation of a process production report.

In the first of three process departments there were 8,000 units in process at the beginning of May, 6,000 units in process at the end of May, and 40,000 units added during the month of May. The ending inventory included all materials but only one-half of the labor and overhead costs. The opening inventory also included all materials but only three-fourths of the required labor and overhead.

Costs in process at the beginning of the month were as follows: materials $4,000, labor $2,000, and manufacturing overhead $1,000. Costs added during the month were: materials $21,000, labor $12,000, manufacturing overhead $6,200.

Prepare a complete production report for Process 1 for the month of May. Carry unit costs to four decimal places.

**11-11.** Journal entries for standard costs.

A "job order" firm employs standard costs as the basis for developing unit product costs. Differences between actual costs and standard costs are charged or credited to appropriate variance accounts.

Prepare journal entries to record the following data for this firm:

*a.* Material with a standard cost of $1,800 is purchased for $1,840 (credit Vouchers Payable).

*b.* Material requisitions show that materials with a cost of $10,200 have been charged to jobs with standard material costs of $10,050 in total.

*c.* Labor time tickets for the period total $14,060, but the standard labor cost for the period amounts to $14,000. The cost of hours worked in excess of standard was equal to $100. Men working at labor rates lower than standard "saved" the company $40. (Assume that the cost of productive labor had been charged originally to a Direct Labor account.)

**11-12.** Analysis of a burden balance when standard costs are employed.

Analyze the balance in the following account:

Manufacturing Expenses

| Actually incurred | 60,000 | Charged to in process | 50,000 |
|---|---|---|---|

Normal activity for the company is expressed as 30,000 direct labor hours for the period. For the current period, standard hours are 25,000 and hours actually worked are 28,000. Fixed expense for each period is estimated at $45,000. Variable expense at the normal activity level of 30,000 hours is expected to be $15,000.

## CHAPTER 12

**12-1.** Preparation of payroll entries.

The ABC Co., a partnership, employs twelve persons. They are paid on the fifth of each month for the preceding month. Payroll data as of the end of the current month are as follows:

(1) Gross pay for the current month is $5,000.

(2) Federal income tax of $600 should be withheld from the gross of $5,000.

(3) The FOASI rate is 2.25% for both the employer and employees.

(4) The employer has an SUI merit rate of 2.2 per cent.

(5) The FUI rate is 0.3 per cent.

(6) The highest cumulative pay to date for any one employee is $2,600.

*a.* Prepare the accrual entry for payroll as of the end of the month.

*b.* Prepare the accrual entry for the employer's payroll tax expense for the current month.

*c.* Payroll checks are issued to the employees on the 5th day of the following month. Prepare a general journal entry to record the transaction.

**12-2.** Computation of ordinary income for tax purposes.

Shown below in summary form is an income statement for a sole proprietorship. The statement has been prepared according to generally accepted accounting principles and includes only income and expenses which are considered business items.

Income:

| | |
|---|---|
| Sales......................................... | $58,000 |
| Interest from municipal bonds....................... | 500 |
| Dividends from qualifying corporations............... | 1,000 |
| | $59,500 |

Expenses:

| | | |
|---|---|---|
| Wages and salaries......................... | $18,200 | |
| Depreciation............................... | 6,400 | |
| Maintenance and repairs.................... | 7,000 | |
| Taxes and insurance....................... | 5,100 | |
| Political contributions....................... | 200 | |
| Charitable contributions..................... | 800 | |
| Miscellaneous............................. | 3,800 | 41,500 |
| Net profit......................................... | | $18,000 |

a. Compute "ordinary income" for Federal income tax purposes by preparing a statement of income and deductions.

b. Which items excluded from the computation in (a) would be included on the individual return of the proprietor (Form 1040)? Assume that the owner will itemize his personal deductions.

**12-3.** Methods of reporting income.

Jayson Jewelry Store sold a diamond ring for $1,200 during 1957. The customer pays $300 in 1957, $500 in 1958, and $400 in 1959. The ring was purchased at a cost of $600.

a. In 1957 what amount would be reported as income for tax purposes under each of the following methods of reporting income?

(1) Accrual basis
(2) Installment basis

b. Which of the above methods provides a more accurate statement of earnings for the period?

c. Could the cash basis be used? Why?

d. Why is the installment method sometimes preferred as a method of reporting for tax purposes?

**12-4.** Reporting capital gains and losses.

T. J. Sparker was the sole owner of a small retail concern, a partner in a wholesale firm, and a stockholder in a manufacturing enterprise. As an individual he bought and sold various securities. The following transactions took place during 1957:

(1) Sparker's retail concern sold for $2,000 a delivery truck (book value $1,400) that had been owned and used for five months.

(2) The wholesale firm in which he was a partner sold for $6,000 a machine with a book value of $4,000. The machine was used in the business and had been acquired two years before the date of sale. Sparker's share of all gains and losses is 50 per cent.

(3) The corporation in which Sparker is a principal stockholder sold operating equipment for $8,000 (book value $4,000). This equipment was three years old.

(4) Sparker sold XYZ common stock for $3,000. It had been purchased 16 months before the date of sale at a cost of $1,400.

(5) He sold ABC preferred stock for $1,800. It had been purchased four months before the date of sale at a cost of $2,200.

*a.* What gain would be included as ordinary income on the statement of income and deductions for one of the firms?

*b.* What capital gain transaction would be included in the computation of business profit for tax purposes and would not be included on the individual income tax return of T. J. Sparker?

*c.* Outline the capital gains and losses that would be reported on Sparker's personal income tax return for 1957; compute and identify the final net balance.

*d.* What portion of the final net balance computed in (*c*) would be included in Sparker's taxable income for 1957?

**12-5.** Capital loss carry-over.

During 1957 a calendar-year taxpayer sells common stock at a gain of $1,600 and bonds at a loss of $3,800. In 1958 the taxpayer sells preferred stock that he has held for seven months (sales price $600, cost basis $500). His ordinary income exceeded $1,000 in both 1957 and 1958.

*a.* What is the capital loss for 1957?

*b.* What portion of the capital loss can be deducted from ordinary income in 1957?

*c.* What is the amount of the capital loss carry-over to 1958?

*d.* What portion of the carry-over can be used as a deduction in 1958?

*e.* What is the amount of the capital loss carry-over to 1959?

**12-6.** Alternative capital gains tax.

A husband and wife have taxable income of $40,000; consequently, the upper brackets of their income are taxed at a rate in excess of 50 per cent. Included in their taxable income is $2,000 which represents one-half of a net long-term capital gain of $4,000. What is the maximum amount of income tax that they should pay on the net long-term capital gain of $4,000?

**12-7.** Accelerated depreciation methods.

A taxpayer purchases a new truck as of the first day of his taxable year. The truck cost $3,000, has an estimated useful life of four years, and an estimated salvage value of $600.

Prepare depreciation schedules for the asset described above, using each of the methods noted below. The schedules should contain columnar headings for the following: Year, Book Value at Beginning of Year, Rate or Fraction, Annual Depreciation.

*a.* Straight-line method.

*b.* Sum-of-the-years digits method.

*c.* Declining balance method (at maximum rate).

*d.* Mileage method (expected mileage during useful life—100,000 miles: first year—20,000; second year—30,000; third year—25,000; fourth year—25,000).

*e.* Which method results in depreciation charges that most clearly reflect usage?

*f.* If the taxpayer purchased the truck on the basis of a 24-month contract, which method would defer as much income tax as possible to the years after the contract was fully paid?

*g.* Some persons believe the total of maintenance and depreciation charges should be as nearly the same each year as possible. Which of the above methods should be employed if this is the objective?

**12-8.** Net operating loss carry-backs and carry-overs.

Tom Brown is the sole owner of a small retail store. The net profit or loss reported for tax purposes for each year from 1955 through 1961 is as follows:

| | |
|---|---|
| 1955—$ 5,000 profit | 1959—$ 6,000 profit |
| 1956— 3,000 profit | 1950— 7,000 profit |
| 1957— 14,000 loss | 1961— 10,000 profit |
| 1958— 4,000 profit | |

Brown has no other source of income. He takes a standard deduction, since his personal deductions, when itemized, do not exceed 10 per cent of his adjusted gross income. He is entitled to one exemption for himself.

*a.* What is the amount of operating loss carry-back from 1957 to 1955? To 1956? (Assuming no adjustments are required.)

*b.* What is the amount of operating loss carry-over to 1958?

*c.* The $4,000 profit for 1958 consisted of $3,000 of ordinary income plus one-half of a $2,000 net long-term capital gain, or $1,000. What is the amount of carry-over to 1959? To 1960? To 1961? (Assuming no further adjustments are required.)

*d.* Can Brown obtain tax refunds for the years 1955 and 1956? How?

**12-9.** Exclusions from income reported for tax purposes.

*a.* Which of the items below would be entirely excluded from reported income on the income tax return of an individual?

*b.* Which of the items below would be partially excluded from taxable income on the income tax return of an individual?

  (1) Wages.

  (2) Benefits from unemployment insurance.

  (3) Interest from a savings account.

  (4) Reimbursements to an employee for expenses incurred by him on behalf of the employer.

  (5) Excess of net long-term capital gains over net short-term losses.

  (6) Commissions.

  (7) Interest from municipal bonds.

  (8) Dividends from "qualifying" corporations.

  (9) Federal old-age benefits.

 (10) Contest prizes.

**12-10.** Computation of adjusted gross income.

The W-2 form of a taxpayer shows that his salary for the year was $10,000 and that he had been reimbursed $260 for out-of-town travel costs. During the year he had actually expended funds for the following: $300 for out-of-town travel, $80 for local business transportation, and $146 for entertaining customers. All of these costs were incurred for the benefit of his employer.

*a.* Compute the taxpayer's adjusted gross income for tax purposes.

*b.* How is adjusted gross income used as the basis for determining whether a taxpayer should itemize his deductions or take a standard deduction?

**12-11.** Computation of taxable income.

A taxpayer and his wife have total income from salaries of $8,000. They have no dependents and no other source of income. Compute taxable income to their best advantage, taking into account their personal deductions for the year, as itemized on the following page:

(1) Drugs and medicines, $100.
(2) Medical and dental, $400.
(3) Boy Scouts, $30.
(4) Church, $150.
(5) Property taxes, $290.
(6) Interest on car contract, $130.

**12-12.** Allowable exemptions.

A man and wife with adjusted gross income of $6,000 have allowable personal deductions of $840. What is the amount of their net taxable income if they furnish more than half the support for their two children, both under nineteen years of age, and for an aunt who is seventy-two?

**12-13.** Capital gains and losses.

A taxpayer has the following transactions during 1957:

| Item | Purchased | Sold | Cost | Sales Price |
|------|-----------|------|------|-------------|
| Stock | 6-5-54 | 9-1-57 | $2,400 | $ 3,600 |
| Bonds | 1-4-57 | 7-3-57 | 1,000 | 800 |
| Lot | 7-10-56 | 3-9-57 | 4,000 | 4,400 |
| Home | 8-15-39 | 4-20-57 | 6,500 | 13,200 |

The taxpayer purchased another home on May 1, 1957, for $16,000. He wants to pay as little income tax as possible for 1957.

*a.* What amount of capital gain or loss should be reported for 1957?

*b.* What amount should be included in taxable income?

**12-14.** Computation of tax due with the return.

Bill Smith, age sixty-six, and his wife Mary, age fifty, furnish over one-half the support both for Mary's mother, age seventy-nine, whose income for the year was $430, and for their son, age twenty-five, who is a college student with income for the year of $704 (income tax of $58.40 was withheld from his earnings).

Bill's salary for the year was $7,600 (income tax of $800 was withheld). He also received $106 as interest on savings in the company's credit union, and $210 as dividends on his stock in "qualifying" corporations. His share of ordinary income from a partnership amounted to $3,100.

Bill's and Mary's personal deductions for the year total $1,480. They paid $400 on their declaration of estimated tax for the current year.

Compute the amount of tax due:

*a.* On a joint return for Bill and Mary.

*b.* On an individual return for their son.

Use the tax rates provided in Chapter 12 of the text. Show all computations.

## CHAPTER 13—NO PROBLEMS

## CHAPTER 14

**14-1.** Comparative profit and loss statements.

Comparative profit and loss statements for the Bronson Company for the years 1954 through 1957 are presented below:

| | 1954 | 1955 | 1956 | 1957 |
|---|---|---|---|---|
| Gross sales................... | $263,450 | $286,560 | $311,420 | $346,570 |
| Less returned sales and allowances.................. | 7,450 | 8,640 | 7,400 | 16,370 |
| Net sales................ | $256,000 | $277,920 | $304,020 | $330,200 |
| Cost of goods sold: | | | | |
| Inventory, beginning of year.. | $ 26,300 | $ 32,320 | $ 36,450 | $ 39,220 |
| Purchases (net).............. | 186,450 | 193,750 | 206,740 | 229,360 |
| Transportation in........... | 4,350 | 5,450 | 6,280 | 7,200 |
| Total.................... | $217,100 | $231,520 | $249,470 | $275,780 |
| Less inventory, end of year.... | 32,320 | 36,450 | 39,220 | 41,360 |
| Cost of goods sold......... | $184,780 | $195,070 | $210,250 | $234,420 |
| Gross profit on sales........... | $ 71,220 | $ 82,850 | $ 93,770 | $ 95,780 |
| Operating expenses: | | | | |
| Selling expenses.............. | $ 42,450 | $ 48,270 | $ 56,350 | $ 62,390 |
| Administrative expenses....... | 27,630 | 28,400 | 29,570 | 28,780 |
| Total expenses............. | $ 70,080 | $ 76,670 | $ 85,920 | $ 91,170 |
| Net operating income.......... | $ 1,140 | $ 6,180 | $ 7,850 | $ 4,610 |
| Other income................. | 970 | 1,140 | 2,640 | 3,200 |
| | $ 2,110 | $ 7,320 | $ 10,490 | $ 7,810 |
| Other expenses................ | 1,350 | 1,560 | 2,110 | 2,420 |
| Net income for year........... | $ 760 | $ 5,760 | $ 8,380 | $ 5,390 |

a. Use the data presented above to prepare comparative profit and loss statements for 1956 and 1957, showing the amount of increase or decrease and the per cent of change.

b. Using 1954 as a base year, prepare trend percentages for all items shown for the four-year period.

c. Point out any significant changes observed in parts (a) and (b).

**14-2.** Common-size income statement.

Assume that a trade publication provides the following common-size data for firms operating under conditions comparable to the Bronson Company:

COMMON-SIZE INCOME STATEMENT

|  | Industry Standard, per cent | Bronson Company—1957, per cent |
|---|---|---|
| Gross sales | 102.3 | |
| Less returned sales and allowances | 2.3 | |
| Net sales | 100.0 | 100.0 |
| Cost of goods sold: | | |
| Inventory, beginning | 9.3 | |
| Purchases (net) | 72.4 | |
| Transportation in | 2.0 | |
| Total | 83.7 | |
| Less inventory, ending | 9.5 | |
| Cost of goods sold | 74.2 | |
| Gross profit on sales | 25.8 | |
| Operating expenses: | | |
| Selling expenses | 13.4 | |
| Administrative expense | 9.3 | |
| Total expense | 22.7 | |
| Net operating income | 3.1 | |
| Other income | 1.4 | |
|  | 4.5 | |
| Other expense | 1.7 | |
| Net income before taxes | 2.8 | |

*a.* Prepare a report similar to the one above. Fill in the amounts for the Bronson Company (see problem **14-1**).

*b.* Write a paragraph pointing out any significant difference between the "standard" and the common-size figures of the Bronson Company.

**14-3.** Analysis of variation in gross profit.

Assume that the accountant for the Bronson Company prepares the following summary of variation in gross profit for 1956 and 1957:

|  | *1956* | *1957* | *Change* |
|---|---|---|---|
| Net sales | $304,020 | $330,200 | $26,180 |
| Cost of goods sold | 210,250 | 234,420 | 24,170 |
| Gross profit on sales | $ 93,770 | $ 95,780 | $ 2,010 |

An index of prices charged using 1954 as a base year shows the following trend in sales prices: 1954—100.0; 1955—102.6; 1956—104.0; 1957—109.2. While the index rose 5.2 points from 1956 to 1957, the 1957 prices charged are only 5.0% higher [(109.2 − 104.0)/104.0 = 5.0] than 1956 prices.

Using these data, analyze the variations in gross profit for the Bronson Company.

a. Prepare an analysis similar to the one illustrated in the text.

b. What has been the per cent of increase in sales volume (quantity of goods sold)?

c. What has been the per cent of increase in the prices paid for goods?

**14-4.** Analysis of the break-even point.

An analysis of the costs and expenses of Department X of the Wilson Manufacturing Company reveals the following facts:

| | |
|---|---|
| Fixed costs and expenses.................. | $125,000 |
| Variable costs (55% of net sales)............ | 220,000 |
| Total costs and expenses................. | $345,000 |
| Estimated sales at practical capacity........ | $400,000 |

a. Prepare a break-even chart which will graphically portray the probable earnings at 20, 40, 60, 80, and 100 per cent of practical capacity.

b. Compute the break-even point for the department using the formula:

(Variable costs at break-even point) + (Fixed Costs) = Break-even point.

NOTE: If variable costs are 55 per cent of sales at the break-even point, fixed costs must be 45 per cent of sales. If X equals sales at the break-even point, X = 125,000 + .55X.

c. The firm is planning to install new machinery which would increase annual fixed costs to $140,000 but would reduce the variable costs to 45 per cent of sales. What would be the break-even point if the proposed changes are made? What profits would result if the plant is operated at 90 per cent of capacity—before changes? After changes?

# CHAPTER 15

**15-1.** Classification of balance sheet accounts.

The accounts listed below are found on the adjusted trial balance of the Woodbury Manufacturing Company on December 31, 1957. Set up an answer sheet with one line for each of the following classifications and write the number of each account which should be classified under that heading on the line following the classification.

Account classifications:

A. Current Assets    G. Current Liabilities    M. Capital Surplus

B. Investments    H. Long-term Debt    N. Accounts not on the bal-

C. Fixed Assets    I. Deferred Credits      ance sheet

D. Intangible Assets    J. Capital Stock

E. Deferred Charges    K. Earned Surplus (Free)

F. Other Assets    L. Appropriated Earned Surplus

Accounts to be classified:

(1) Accounts Receivable (Trade)
(2) Accounts Payable (Trade)
(3) Allowance for Bad Debts
(4) Accumulated Depr.—Building
(5) Advances to Salesmen
(6) Appraisal Surplus
(7) Bad Debts
(8) Cash on Hand
(9) Advertising Supplies
(10) Notes Receivable
(11) Notes Payable
(12) Accrued Interest Receivable
(13) Accrued Rent Payable
(14) Accrued Wages Payable
(15) Buildings
(16) Land
(17) Investment in United States Bonds
(18) Surplus from Stock Donations
(19) Office Supplies
(20) Tools
(21) Factory Supplies
(22) Patents
(23) Copyrights
(24) Depreciation—Buildings
(25) Premium on Common Stock
(26) Earned Surplus
(27) Reserve for Bond Sinking Fund
(28) 5% First Mortgage Bonds
(29) Employee Pension Fund
(30) Raw Materials Inventory (Ending)

(31) Finished Goods (Beginning)
(32) Machinery and Equipment
(33) Federal Income Tax Withheld
(34) FICA Payable
(35) Rent Collected in Advance
(36) Investment in Subsidiary
(37) Goods in Process (Ending)
(38) Accrued Int. on Bonds Payable
(39) Accrued Property Taxes
(40) Bond Sinking Fund
(41) Discount on Bonds Payable
(42) Subscriptions Rec. (Common)
(43) Investment in Land
(44) Treasury Stock
(45) Organization Expense
(46) Loss on Sale of Fixed Assets
(47) Notes Receivable from Officers
(48) Sales Tax Payable
(49) Unexpired Insurance
(50) Fuel on Hand
(51) Notes Receivable Discounted
(52) Accrued Advertising Expense
(53) Common Stock Subscribed
(54) Common Stock Authorized
(55) Unissued Common Stock
(56) Estimated Income Tax Payable
(57) Dividends Payable
(58) Dividends Paid
(59) Stock Dividend Payable
(60) Unearned Interest on Notes Receivable

**15-2.** Preparation of increase—decrease balance sheets.

Use the data provided below to prepare comparative balance sheets as of December 31, 1955 and 1956; include dollar totals, dollar changes, and per cent changes.

The comparative balance sheets shown below will also be used as the basis for problems **15-2, 3, 4,** and **5.**

DENCE COMPANY
Comparative Balance Sheets
as of December 31, 1954, 1955, 1956

| *Assets* | *1954* | *1955* | *1956* |
|---|---|---|---|
| Cash.................................... | $ 8,000 | $ 6,000 | $ 10,000 |
| Accounts receivable....................... | 40,000 | 44,000 | 50,000 |
| Inventory................................ | 36,000 | 40,000 | 48,000 |
| Total current assets..................... | $ 84,000 | $ 90,000 | $108,000 |
| Land.................................... | $ 10,000 | $ 10,000 | $ 14,000 |
| Building (net)........................... | 80,000 | 88,000 | 88,000 |
| Machinery (net).......................... | 60,000 | 70,000 | 80,000 |
| Furniture and fixtures (net)................ | 6,000 | 9,000 | 9,000 |
| Total fixed assets........................ | $156,000 | $177,000 | $191,000 |
| Patents.................................. | | $ 15,000 | $ 14,000 |
| Total assets............................ | $240,000 | $282,000 | $313,000 |

*Equities*

| | | | |
|---|---|---|---|
| Accounts payable......................... | $ 50,000 | $ 40,000 | $ 44,000 |
| Notes payable............................ | 30,000 | 20,000 | 10,000 |
| Total current liabilities................... | $ 80,000 | $ 60,000 | $ 54,000 |
| 5% preferred stock........................ | $ 30,000 | $ 30,000 | $ 40,000 |
| Common stock............................ | 170,000 | 170,000 | 170,000 |
| Earned surplus........................... | (40,000) | 22,000 | 49,000 |
| Total net worth.......................... | $160,000 | $222,000 | $259,000 |
| Total equities........................... | $240,000 | $282,000 | $313,000 |

**15-3.** Preparation of trend percentage statement.

Prepare trend percentage balance sheets for the Dence Company (use all three years).

**15-4.** Preparation of common-size balance sheets.

Prepare a common-size statement for the Dence Company, based on the data presented above. Include both dollar amounts and percentages for all three years.

**15-5.** Interpretation of comparative statements.

On the basis of statements prepared in problems **15-2, 3,** and **4** above, express your opinion as to the financial standing of the Dence Company at the present time (December 31, 1956) and express your "guess" as to the company's future standing. Provide specific examples to support your opinions. (Assume that the management is experienced, honest, and progressive and that the company's primary competition consists of several large, old companies that are not concentrating on the area served by the Dence Company.)

**15-6.** Preparation of statement of sources and applications of funds.

On the basis of the balance sheet data for Waysafe Co., shown below, prepare a statement of sources and applications of funds for the year 1956.

| *Assets* | *12-31-55* | *12-31-56* |
| --- | --- | --- |
| Cash.................................. | $ 90,000 | $ 60,000 |
| Accounts receivable...................... | 110,000 | 150,000 |
| Inventories............................ | 200,000 | 290,000 |
| Land................................. | 40,000 | 40,000 |
| Building (less accumulated depr.)........... | | 300,000 |
| Equipment (less accumulated depr.)........ | | 140,000 |
| Total.............................. | $440,000 | $980,000 |

| *Equities* | | |
| --- | --- | --- |
| Accounts payable........................ | $160,000 | $170,000 |
| Notes payable*......................... | 20,000 | 50,000 |
| Bonds payable.......................... | | 200,000 |
| Common stock.......................... | 240,000 | 500,000 |
| Earned surplus......................... | 20,000 | 60,000 |
| Total.............................. | $440,000 | $980,000 |

\* Due within one year of balance sheet date.

Assume that bonds were sold at par, capital stock was sold at a premium of $16,000 (credited to Earned Surplus), dividends paid amounted to $20,000, and there were no extraordinary gains or losses. Depreciation charges amounted to $40,000—Buildings, $25,000; Equipment, $15,000.

**15-7.** Comparative balance sheets with increase and decrease per cents.

Use the data in the balance sheet of the Richards Company to prepare comparative balance sheets for 1955 and 1956 showing increase and decrease amounts and per cents.

Data for problems **15-7 8, 9,** and **10:**

RICHARDS COMPANY
Comparative Balance Sheets
December 31, 1954, 1955, 1956

| *Assets* | *1954* | *1955* | *1956* |
|---|---|---|---|
| Current assets: | | | |
| Cash on hand and in bank.................... | $ 23,500 | $ 16,800 | $ 27,400 |
| Notes receivable............................ | 3,500 | 8,600 | 9,200 |
| Accounts receivable......................... | 46,600 | 52,500 | 58,600 |
| Allowance for bad debts.................... | (960) | (1,400) | (1,650) |
| Merchandise inventory...................... | 64,400 | 56,400 | 68,800 |
| Accrued receivables......................... | 1,400 | 2,600 | 2,400 |
| Supplies inventory.......................... | 1,960 | 2,340 | 1,560 |
| Total current assets...................... | $140,400 | $137,840 | $166,310 |
| Investments: | | | |
| Investment in subsidiary company stock (cost).. | $ 32,000 | $ 32,000 | $ 36,000 |
| Bond sinking fund.......................... | 5,000 | 10,000 | 15,000 |
| Total investment........................ | $ 37,000 | $ 42,000 | $ 51,000 |
| Fixed assets: | | | |
| Furniture and fixtures....................... | $ 23,500 | $ 23,500 | $ 26,240 |
| Allowance for depreciation................. | (2,300) | (4,650) | (7,050) |
| Buildings.................................. | 82,000 | 82,000 | 82,000 |
| Allowance for depreciation................. | (2,050) | (4,100) | (6,150) |
| Land...................................... | 16,000 | 16,000 | 18,000 |
| Total fixed assets....................... | $117,150 | $112,750 | $113,040 |
| Deferred charges: | | | |
| Discount on bonds......................... | $ 2,000 | $ 1,900 | $ 1,800 |
| Organization expense....................... | 3,800 | 3,800 | 3,800 |
| Total deferred charges................... | $ 5,800 | $ 5,700 | $ 5,600 |
| Total assets................................. | $300,350 | $298,290 | $335,950 |
| *Liabilities and net worth* | | | |
| Current liabilities: | | | |
| Accounts payable........................... | $ 16,500 | $ 26,200 | $ 25,400 |
| Notes payable.............................. | 8,200 | 1,600 | 2,200 |
| Accrued payables........................... | 2,400 | 2,560 | 2,650 |
| Total current liabilities................... | $ 27,100 | $ 30,360 | $ 30,250 |
| Fixed liabilities: | | | |
| 5% first mortgage bonds..................... | $100,000 | $100,000 | $100,000 |
| Total liabilities............................. | $127,100 | $130,360 | $130,250 |
| Capital stock and surplus: | | | |
| 6% preferred stock.......................... | 50,000 | 50,000 | 50,000 |
| Common stock............................. | 100,000 | 100,000 | 120,000 |
| Earned surplus............................. | 18,250 | 7,930 | 20,700 |
| Appropriated earned surplus................. | 5,000 | 10,000 | 15,000 |
| Total owner's equity........................ | $173,250 | $167,930 | $205,700 |
| Total equities............................... | $300,350 | $298,290 | $335,950 |

**15-8.** Comparative balance sheet, trend percentages.

Use the data of the Richards Company to prepare trend percentages for 1954, 1955, and 1956, using 1954 as the base year.

**15-9.** Common-size balance sheets.

Use the balance sheet of the Richards Company for 1956 to prepare a common-size (100 per cent) statement to be used to compare the Richards Company with industry standards.

**15-10.** Statement of changes in net working capital.

Use the comparative balance sheets of the Richards Company for 1955 and 1956 and the additional data provided below to show the sources and uses of working capital for the year:

*a.* Net profits reported for the year, $28,570.

*b.* Common stock having a par value of $20,000 was sold for $20,200.

*c.* Dividends paid on preferred stock, $3,000.

*d.* Dividends paid on common stock, $8,000.

*e.* Earned surplus appropriated in accordance with bond indenture, $5,000.

*f.* Total depreciation shown on income statement, $4,850.

*g.* Fixtures having a book value of $200 were junked. Original cost was $600; accumulated depreciation, $400.

*h.* New fixtures which cost $3,340 were purchased.

*i.* All extraordinary gains and losses were shown on the income statement.


CHAPTER 16


**16-1.** Computation of rates and ratios.

Use the balance sheet and the profit and loss statement of the Apex Company, on the following pages, to illustrate the computation of each of the rates and ratios listed:

*a.* The current ratio

*b.* The acid-test ratio

*c.* The inventory turnover rate

*d.* Ratio of sales to inventory

*e.* Number of days required to turn average inventory

*f.* Number of days' sales in accounts receivable

*g.* Current liabilities to total equities

*h.* Per cent of total funds which were provided by long-term creditors

*i.* Per cent of total funds provided by creditors

*j.* Equity of owners as a per cent of total equities

*k.* Worth-to-debt ratio

*l.* Number of times fixed interest charges were earned

*m.* Ratio of fixed assets to fixed debt

*n.* Net operating income to net sales

*o.* Final net income to owner's tangible net worth

*p.* Net income to total assets

*q.* Net sales to net operating assets

*r.* Number of times preferred dividends were earned

*s.* Earnings per share of preferred stock outstanding

*t.* Earnings per share of common

*u.* Earnings on the common equity

*v.* Market price to earnings per share of common, assuming a market price of $46

w. Book value per share of common stock
x. Cost of sales as a percentage of sales
y. Gross margin per cent
z. Depreciation as a per cent of depreciable fixed assets

APEX COMPANY
Statement of Profit and Loss
for the Year Ending December 31, 1958

Income from sales:
| | | | |
|---|---|---|---|
| Gross sales............................................ | | | $462,000 |
| Less returned sales and allowances....................... | $ | 4,060 | |
| Discount on sales.................................... | | 6,140 | 10,200 |
| Net sales............................................ | | | $451,800 |

Cost of goods sold:
| | | | |
|---|---|---|---|
| Merchandise inventory, Jan. 1, 1958...................... | | $ 68,500 | |
| Purchases..................................... | $332,800 | | |
| Returned purchases................... | $2,600 | | |
| Purchases discount................... | 5,800 | 8,400 | |
| Net purchases............................... | $324,400 | | |
| Transportation in........................... | 6,200 | 330,600 | |
| Cost of merchandise available for sale.. .................. | | $399,100 | |
| Less merchandise inventory, Dec. 31, 1958................ | | 72,300 | 326,800 |

| | | | |
|---|---|---|---|
| Gross profit on sales....................................... | | | $125,000 |

Operating expenses:
Selling expenses:
| | | | |
|---|---|---|---|
| Sales salaries................................ | $ 40,000 | | |
| Salesmen's travel expense...................... | 3,000 | | |
| Advertising................................... | 6,000 | | |
| Delivery expense............................. | 4,500 | | |
| Depreciation on delivery equipment............ | 1,200 | | |
| Store rent................................... | 9,000 | | |
| Total selling expense................................. | | $ 63,700 | |

General and administrative expenses:
| | | | |
|---|---|---|---|
| Office salaries............................... | $ 6,000 | | |
| Officers' salaries............................ | 18,000 | | |
| Taxes (property)............................. | 800 | | |
| Insurance................................... | 760 | | |
| Depreciation of office equipment.............. | 340 | | |
| Rent (office building)........................ | 1,200 | | |
| Total general and administration expense.............. | | 27,100 | |
| Total operating expense.................................. | | | 90,800 |

| | | | |
|---|---|---|---|
| Net income from operations............................... | | | $ 34,200 |

Other income:
| | | | |
|---|---|---|---|
| Interest income............................... | $ 3,200 | | |
| Income from rental of delivery equipment......... | 600 | $ 3,800 | |

Other expenses:
| | | | |
|---|---|---|---|
| Interest expense........................................ | | 2,200 | |
| Net other income and expense............................ | | | 1,600 |

| | | | |
|---|---|---|---|
| Net income before provision for income tax.................... | | | $ 35,800 |
| Provision for estimated income taxes........................ | | | 14,000 |
| Net income for 1958....................................... . | | | $ 21,800 |

Apex Company
Balance Sheet for December 31, 1958
*Assets*

Current assets:

| | | | |
|---|---|---|---|
| Cash........................................ | | $16,240 | |
| Accounts receivable............................ | $46,360 | | |
| Trade notes receivable.......................... | 3,140 | | |
| | $49,500 | | |
| Less allowance for bad debts.................... | 1,670 | 47,830 | |
| Merchandise inventory......................... | | 72,300 | |
| Marketable securities.......................... | | 4,950 | |
| Accrued receivables........................... | | 420 | |
| Prepaid insurance............................. | | 80 | |
|    Total current assets................... | | | $141,820 |

Fixed assets:

| | | | |
|---|---|---|---|
| Delivery equipment............................ | $ 7,200 | | |
| Less allowance for depreciation................. | 2,400 | $ 4,800 | |
| Office equipment.............................. | $ 3,400 | | |
| Less allowance for depreciation................. | 680 | 2,720 | |
|    Total fixed assets..................... | | 7,520 | |

Other assets:

| | | | |
|---|---|---|---|
| Land (held as future building site)............... | $20,000 | | |
| Goodwill..................................... | 12,000 | | |
| Investment in stock of Ace Company (at cost)............... | 6,000 | | |
|    Total other assets.................... | | 38,000 | |
| Total assets.................................. | | $187,340 | |

*Liabilities*

Current liabilities:

| | | | |
|---|---|---|---|
| Accounts payable.............................. | $26,400 | | |
| Notes payable (to bank)........................ | 10,000 | | |
| Accrued taxes................................ | 800 | | |
| Provision for income taxes...................... | 14,000 | | |
|    Total current liabilities.............. | | $ 51,200 | |

Long-term debt:

| | | |
|---|---|---|
| Purchase money mortgage (for land), 6%.................. | 16,000 | |
| Total liabilities............................... | $ 67,200 | |

*Net worth*

Capital stock:

| | | |
|---|---|---|
| Preferred stock, 6% cumulative, $100 par; 1,000 shares author-ized; 300 shares issued.............................. | $30,000 | |
| Common stock, no-par value; stated value $10 per share; 10,000 shares authorized; 5,000 shares issued and outstanding...... | 50,000 | |
| Premium on common stock............................ | 10,000 | |
|    Total invested equity.................. | $ 90,000 | |

Earned surplus:

| | | |
|---|---|---|
| Unappropriated earned surplus............................ | 8,960 | |
| Reserve for building and expansion*...................... | 21,180 | |
|    Total owner equity.................... | $120,140 | |
| Total liabilities and owner equity........................ | 187,340 | |

* Surplus is being appropriated to provide for a building which is to be erected in 1960.

**16-2.** Evaluation of financial condition.

The condensed balance sheet of the Franklin Company on December 31, 1956, was as follows:

FRANKLIN COMPANY
Condensed Balance Sheet
December 31, 1956

| *Assets* | | | | *Liabilities* | | | |
|---|---|---|---|---|---|---|---|
| Cash................... | $ | 52,000 | | Accounts payable. | $ 84,000 | | |
| Accounts receivable (net).. | | 98,000 | | Accrued payables. | 4,000 | | |
| Inventories............... | | 216,000 | | Total................. | | $ | 88,000 |
| U.S. government bonds..... | | 980,000 | | Capital stock, pre- | | | |
| Plant and equipment: | | | | ferred......... | $ 20,000 | | |
| Cost........ $850,000 | | | | Common stock... | 850,000 | | |
| Accumulated | | | | Total....... | $870,000 | | |
| depreciation. 800,000 | | 50,000 | | Earned surplus... | 452,000 | $1,322,000 | |
| Other assets.............. | | 14,000 | | Total liabilities and net | | | |
| Total assets............ | | $1,410,000 | | worth................ | | $1,410,000 | |

The company produces electrical equipment. It was founded in 1906 and has been owned by the Franklin family since it was first organized. The plant and equipment are quite old and have not been remodeled since 1927. As a consequence, the firm is encountering more and more serious price competition and has had a net loss from operations in four of the past five years. The earnings on the government bonds, which have been held since World War II, amounted to $22,050 in 1956. This was enough to offset the operating loss of $20,400 and caused a final income of $1,650. No dividends have been paid for the past four years.

Using the balance sheet data and the brief summary provided, compute any ratios which you think significant and evaluate the company from the point of view of:

a. A short-term creditor

b. A management consultant

c. A young man interested in the company as a place to begin work as an electrical engineer

**16-3.** Evaluation of financial condition.

The following condensed balance sheets show the financial position of the Newman Company and the Oldman Company on Dec. 31, 1955 and 1956:

COMPARATIVE BALANCE SHEETS

| Assets | Newman Company 1955 | Newman Company 1956 | Oldman Company 1955 | Oldman Company 1956 |
|---|---|---|---|---|
| Cash................................. | $ 16,000 | $ 8,000 | $ 14,000 | $ 8,000 |
| Accounts receivable (net)............. | 24,000 | 42,000 | 53,000 | 51,000 |
| Inventories......................... | 52,000 | 84,000 | 72,000 | 76,000 |
| Other current assets................. | 4,000 | 6,000 | 5,000 | 5,000 |
| Total current assets.............. | $ 96,000 | $140,000 | $144,000 | $140,000 |
| Plant and equipment: | | | | |
| Cost........................... | $112,000 | $223,000 | $340,000 | $340,000 |
| Accumulated depreciation.......... | (3,000) | (10,000) | (102,000) | (120,000) |
| Land.............................. | 8,000 | 24,000 | 14,000 | 14,000 |
| Bond discount and expense........... | | | 600 | 400 |
| Other assets....................... | 800 | 1,500 | 2,300 | 2,400 |
| Total assets................... | $213,800 | $378,500 | $398,900 | $376,800 |

| Liabilities | | | | |
|---|---|---|---|---|
| Accounts payable.................... | $ 30,000 | $ 52,000 | $ 50,000 | $ 54,000 |
| Notes payable (trade)................ | 5,000 | 14,000 | | 10,000 |
| Notes payable (bank loan)............ | 10,000 | 20,000 | 30,000 | 30,000 |
| Estimated income tax payable........ | 2,000 | 16,000 | | |
| Total current liabilities........... | $ 47,000 | $102,000 | $ 80,000 | $ 94,000 |
| 6% bonds payable (due 1958)........ | | | $100,000 | $100,000 |
| Mortgage payable, 6%.............. | $ 20,000 | $ 80,000 | | |
| Total liabilities................. | $ 67,000 | $182,000 | $180,000 | $194,000 |

| Capital | | | | |
|---|---|---|---|---|
| Preferred stock $100 par, 6%......... | | | $ 50,000 | $ 50,000 |
| Common stock...................... | $100,000 | $150,000 | 100,000 | 100,000 |
| Surplus | | | | |
| Earned surplus (free).............. | 36,300 | 30,000 | 68,900 | 32,800 |
| Paid-in surplus.................... | 10,500 | 16,500 | | |
| Total owner equity............. | $146,800 | $196,500 | $218,900 | $182,800 |
| Total liabilities and net worth........ | $213,800 | $378,500 | $398,900 | $376,800 |

*a.* Compute the following ratios for the two companies for 1956:

   (1) Current ratio

   (2) Liquid (acid-test) ratio

   (3) Worth-to-debt ratio

   (4) Per cent of total funds obtained from:

      Current creditors

      Long-term creditors

      Total, all creditors

      Owners

Compare the financial position of the two companies on the basis of these rates and ratios for 1956.

*b.* Use the data for 1955 to find the same rates and ratios as were computed for 1956. What additional conclusion can now be drawn about the financial position of the two firms?

*Additional data:*

### Condensed Income Statements—1956

| | Newman Company | Oldman Company |
|---|---|---|
| Net sales.................................... | $493,500 | $343,700 |
| Cost of sales................................ | 326,000 | 265,000 |
| Gross profit on sales......................... | $167,500 | $ 78,700 |
| Operating expense............................ | 120,000 | 103,600 |
| Net operating income (loss)................... | $ 47,500 | ($ 24,900) |
| Other income and expenses (net)*............. | (5,200) | ( 8,200) |
| Net income (loss)............................ | $ 42,300 | ($ 33,100) |
| Provision for Federal tax..................... | 16,000 | |
| To surplus................................... | $ 26,300 | ($ 33,100) |

\* Including bond discount amortizations.

*Newman Company:* The company was started in 1955 and has been growing rapidly. During the year 1956 the company sold 300 shares of $100 par common stock at $120 and gave a $60,000 mortgage to help finance fixed asset acquisitions. It is still leasing a large part of its plant, however. New equipment which cost $12,600 and had not yet been insured was destroyed by a fire on December 12. The loss was written off directly to Earned Surplus. No cash dividends have been paid, but a $20,000 stock dividend was declared on December 20, 1956. The owners realize that they are obtaining a large part of their capital from creditors but feel that, since they cannot afford additional investment in stock, there is no other practical way to finance the expansion program which they desire. Mortgage payments of $5,000 annually begin December 31, 1957.

*Oldman Company:* The company was founded in 1940. Large profits were earned during the war years and operations have been profitable since then except for 1950, 1955, and 1956. Dividends have been paid on the preferred stock but no other dividends were paid during 1956. The bonds payable will be due December 31, 1958.

*c.* Prepare statements of changes in working capital for the two firms, using the information provided in the balance sheet and the additional data, above.

*d.* Using the ratios which you have computed, the statements of changes in working capital, and any other ratios or rates you may think of value, evaluate the two companies from the point of view of:

(1) A short-term creditor

(2) A long-term creditor

(3) A young man interested in going to work for this type of firm

**16-4.** Evaluation of financial condition.

The condensed balance sheets and income statements of the Joseph Hadley Company for 1951 and 1956 are presented below. At the time of the 1951 report the company was working on war contracts in addition to its regular line of products. In 1956 they were no longer manufacturing war goods and their business had returned to its normal, peacetime level.

### JOSEPH HADLEY COMPANY
### Balance Sheet

| Assets | 1951 | 1956 |
|---|---|---|
| Cash........................................................... | $ 16,000 | $ 32,000 |
| Accounts receivable (net)............................... | 42,000 | 34,000 |
| Raw materials........................................ | 52,000 | 23,000 |
| Goods in process...................................... | 13,000 | 5,600 |
| Finished goods........................................ | 21,300 | 14,500 |
| Other current assets.................................. | 8,300 | 5,200 |
| Total current assets.................................. | $152,600 | $114,300 |
| Plant and equipment................................... | 586,000 | 590,000 |
| Accumulated depreciation........................... | (140,000) | (208,000) |
| Land................................................. | 18,000 | 18,000 |
| Other assets.......................................... | 24,000 | 16,000 |
| Total assets......................................... | $640,600 | $530,300 |

| Liabilities and net worth | | |
|---|---|---|
| Accounts payable...................................... | $ 51,300 | $ 33,400 |
| Notes payable......................................... | 100,000 | |
| Total current liabilities............................. | $151,300 | $ 33,400 |
| Capital stock, preferred.............................. | 100,000 | 100,000 |
| Capital stock, common................................. | 300,000 | 300,000 |
| Earned surplus........................................ | 76,700 | 84,300 |
| Paid-in surplus....................................... | 12,600 | 12,600 |
| Total liabilities and net worth...................... | $640,600 | $530,300 |

### Income Statement

| | 1951 | 1956 |
|---|---|---|
| Net sales............................................. | $586,000 | $350,000 |
| Cost of goods manufactured and sold................... | 432,000 | 276,000 |
| Gross profit on sales................................. | $154,000 | $ 74,000 |
| Less selling and administrative expense............... | 68,400 | 62,300 |
| Net income........................................... | $ 85,600 | $ 11,700 |

The Company has earned a net profit each year since it was started in 1941. In 1951 the inventories were large because of the war orders. Receivables, however, were only slightly above average because collections were quickly made. The cash balance in 1951 was sometimes too low to meet the larger payrolls and accounts payable. A temporary bank loan was arranged in the summer of 1951 to help finance the larger current asset balances. By 1954 this loan had been retired.

Use these data to compute the following ratios for each year:

a. Current ratio.

b. Liquid ratio.

c. Receivables turnover.

d. Inventories as a per cent of sales.

e. Per cent of total funds from creditors.

f. Per cent of total funds from owners.

In which year does the firm appear in the best financial condition? In which year is the firm most profitable? Is it unusual for a firm to appear to be in precarious condition when it is trying to handle too much business?

## CHAPTER 17

**17-1.** Preparation of budgets for a wholesale firm.

Olympic Wholesalers, Inc., sell foreign sports cars which they import from Europe. During the coming calendar year, 1959, the sales managers estimate that they will sell 10,000 Wolks at $1,400 each and 6,000 Vagans at $1,500 each. The purchasing department expects to pay an average of $1,000 for each Wolks and an average of $1,200 for each Vagan. Shipping charges from Europe to the United States are estimated at $1,440,000 for 1959. It is estimated that the inventory as of January 1, 1959 will consist of 400 Wolks at $980 each and 300 Vagans at $1,100 each. The year-end inventory is expected to be 500 Wolks and 200 Vagans. Cost of goods sold is computed on the basis of FIFO.

After a careful study of expense items, the head sales manager forecasts total selling expenses of $2,400,000. The treasurer and controller estimates the total of general and administrative expenses as $1,038,000 for the year.

From the information above prepare the following:

*a.* Sales budget.

*b.* Purchases budget.

*c.* Cost of goods sold budget.

*d.* Budgeted statement of income and expense.

**17-2.** Preparation of budgets for a retail store.

The Valley Clothing Company estimates that net sales for the company for the coming year (1959) will be $400,000; that the inventory on Jan. 1, 1959, will be valued at $60,000; that total selling expenses for 1959 will be 15 per cent of net sales; that general and administrative expenses will be 20 per cent of net sales; and that gross profit will be equal to 40 per cent of net sales. The company desires an inventory of $80,000 as of December 31, 1959.

Prepare the following budgets:

*a.* Purchases budget.

*b.* Budgeted income statement.

(Since the company sells many different items, the estimates and budgets are in dollars only.)

**17-3.** Budgets for a process manufacturing concern.

The Midwest Corporation manufactures, in one process, a product identified as Formula 920. All materials are added at the beginning of the process. For the next fiscal year, 1959, management estimates: (1) an in process inventory at the beginning of 10,000 gallons (cost value $24,000), (2) an in process inventory at the end of 20,000 gallons (cost value $53,000), (3) no finished goods inventories, and (4) sales during the year of 220,000 gallons at $4.00 per gallon. To manufacture one gallon of Formula 920 requires one-half gallon of $X$ and four pounds of $Z$. Estimates pertaining to these two items of raw material are as follows:

| | $X$ (gal.) | $Z$ (lb.) |
|---|---|---|
| Inventory as of Jan. 1, 1959 | 20,000 | 60,000 |
| Inventory as of Dec. 31, 1959 | 30,000 | 80,000 |
| Unit prices in Jan. 1 inventory | $ .90 | $ .20 |
| Unit purchase prices during 1959 | $1.00 | $ .20 |

Twenty-four minutes of productive labor are required to produce one gallon of Formula 920. The average wage cost for productive labor is expected to be $2.40 per hour  Other estimates for 1959 are as follows: manufacturing expenses,

$180,000; selling expenses, $120,000; general and administrative expenses, $70,000. The company employs the FIFO method of costing.

Prepare budgets for:

*a.* Sales.

*b.* Production.

*c.* Materials.

*d.* Purchases.

*e.* Labor.

*f.* Cost of goods manufactured.

*g.* Statement of income and expense.

Use (*a*), (*b*), etc., to indicate cross references from one budget to another. All budgets are to be for the year 1959.

# INDEX